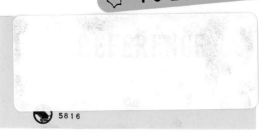
675665 ✓

Santa Clara County Free Library

California

Alum Rock

Campbell

Cupertino

Gilroy

Los Altos { Main Woodland

Milpitas { Calaveras Community Center Sunnyhills

Morgan Hill

Saratoga { Quito Village

Stanford-Escondido

Reference Center—Cupertino

For Bookmobile Service, request schedule

...e Region Series

THE PACIFIC COASTAL WILDLIFE REGION

REVISED EDITION

By Charles Yocom, Ph. D.
Professor of Game Management

and

Raymond Dasmann, Ph. D.
Chairman, Division of Natural Resources
of Humboldt State College, Arcata, California

TABLE OF CONTENTS

Introduction 3
Key to Plant Parts 6
Common Plants 7
    Coastal Strand 7
    Coastal Marshes 14
    Coastal Brushfields 17
    Coniferous Forests 24
    Coastal Hardwood Forest 45
    Woodland-Prairie 50
Common Animals 55
    Mammals 55
    Birds 76
    Reptiles and Amphibians 103
    Fishes 115
Suggested References. 117
Index 117

Published by Naturegraph Co., Healdsburg, California

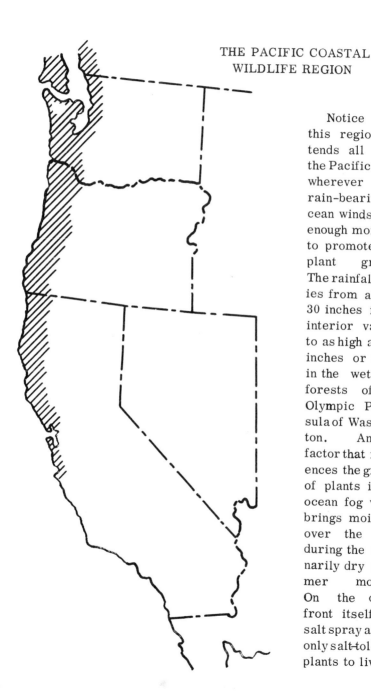

THE PACIFIC COASTAL
WILDLIFE REGION

Notice that this region extends all along the Pacific Coast wherever the rain-bearing ocean winds bring enough moisture to promote lush plant growth. The rainfall varies from around 30 inches in the interior valleys to as high as 120 inches or more in the wet rain forests of the Olympic Peninsula of Washington. Another factor that influences the growth of plants is the ocean fog which brings moisture over the land during the ordinarily dry summer months. On the ocean front itself the salt spray allows only salt-tolerant plants to live.

INTRODUCTION

This book is the third of a series on the wildlife regions of America. Wildlife regions, such as the Pacific Coastal Wildlife Region, are distinctive natural geographic areas of similar climate and topography, which tend to have characteristic animals and vegetation within their boundaries. Overlapping between regions makes it impossible to draw a rigid line separating them. Some species of plants and animals appear in several regions.

The Pacific Coastal Wildlife Region, as defined in this book, extends from Monterey County, California, north to the southern part of British Columbia. Farther north, in coastal Canada and and Alaska, similar plant and animal life may occur, but, in addition, various northern species are found which are not included in this book. The famous California redwoods are the dominant trees of the southern part of the region. Farther north Sitka spruce, cedar and hemlock join with Douglas fir to form magnificent forests renowned for their fine lumber. Living in this region are a variety of interesting and unique animals, ranging from the majestic Roosevelt Elk to the tiny Red Tree Mouse.

The purpose of this book is to acquaint you with the characteristic plants and animals of the region. Since the book has been kept small to make its selling price reasonable, only basic information is given about the plants and animals most likely to be encountered. For more details, the reader should seek the larger and more complete books listed in the bibliography.

In the first section of this book the plants are grouped in the vegetation communities in which they most commonly occur. In the coniferous forest, which occupies the greatest area in the region, certain species are typical. Other species are more typical of other habitats, such as the coastal strand, or the woodland prairie. Photographs of these plant communities or habitats are shown at the beginning of each habitat section. Following the descriptions of the plants of each habitat is a list of the common mammals, birds, reptiles and amphibians most likely to be encountered in that vegetation type. Learning to recognize the plant communities, vegetation types, or habitats is the first step in learning to recognize the animals that live there.

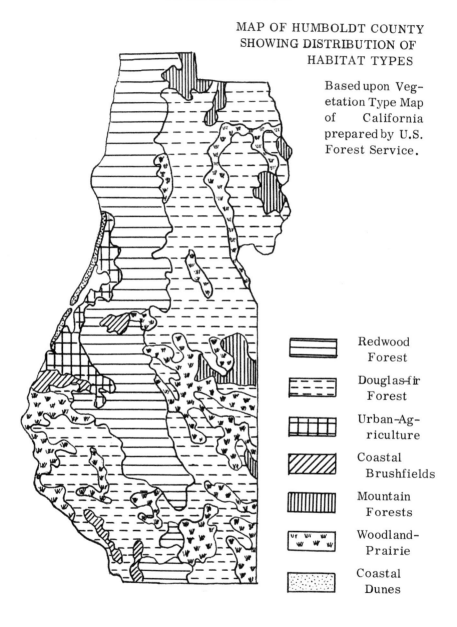

MAP OF HUMBOLDT COUNTY
SHOWING DISTRIBUTION OF
HABITAT TYPES

Based upon Veg-
etation Type Map
of California
prepared by U.S.
Forest Service.

Redwood
Forest

Douglas-fir
Forest

Urban-Ag-
riculture

Coastal
Brushfields

Mountain
Forests

Woodland-
Prairie

Coastal
Dunes

The "mountain forests" shown on this map are dominated by
ponderosa (or yellow) pine and actually belong to a different wildlife region, the Sierra Nevadan Wildlife Region (see volume 2).

In later sections of the book the mammals, birds, reptiles, amphibians and fish most likely to be encountered within the region are illustrated and described. The reader who finds an animal species listed for a particular vegetation type, should then turn to the appropriate section of the book to find the illustration and description for that species.

PACIFIC COASTAL REGION WILDLIFE HABITATS

If you were to travel inland from the seacoast in the vicinity of Eureka, California, to the higher mountain ranges of the interior, you would pass through a series of vegetation types, such as are shown in the map on page 4 and illustrated in the habitat sections: coastal strand, coastal marshes, coastal brushfields (or northern coastal scrub), coniferous forests (including both redwood forests and spruce and fir forests), hardwoods, and finally, farther inland, the woodland-prairie area, with its groves of oaks interspersed with grasslands. All of these habitats may not be encountered in any one section through the coastal region, or their arrangement may vary from one location to another.

Another type of habitat, important in most wildlife regions, is the streamside woodland. But in this relatively well-watered coastal region, the streamsides are usually not characterized by distinctive vegetation, and are therefore included, for the most part, with other vegetation types. Man-created habitats, found around cities, towns and in agricultural areas, also are not described separately, but are, nevertheless, important areas where wildlife is found. The diversification of vegetation that occurs near human habitations often favors the presence of larger numbers of animals, particularly birds, than will be found in the adjoining, less disturbed areas. So forest birds will move into the parks and wooded gardens, while prairie or grassland birds and mammals will visit vacant lots, fields and the more open gardens.

To aid in understanding identification and distribution, names of habitats are marked on the margin of each description as follows: Strand = coastal strand, Marsh = coastal marsh, Brush = coastal brushfields, Conif. = coniferous forests, Hardw. = hardwood forests, and Wd. Pr. = woodland-prairie. Besides these main habitats (all pictured in the book) some other habitats mentioned include: Meadow = forest meadow, Water = fresh and salt water, Str. Wd. = streamside woods, Rocks = rocks, Oak = oaks.

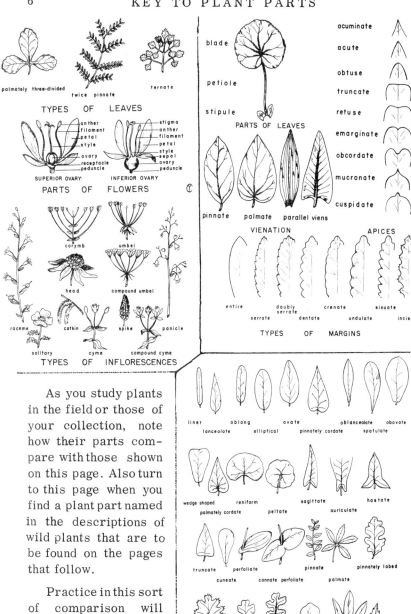

palmately three-divided   twice pinnate   ternate

TYPES OF LEAVES

anther
filament
petal
style
ovary
receptacle
peduncle

stigma
anther
filament
petal
style
sepal
ovary
peduncle

SUPERIOR OVARY   INFERIOR OVARY

PARTS OF FLOWERS

blade
petiole
stipule

PARTS OF LEAVES

acuminate
acute
obtuse
truncate
retuse
emarginate
obcordate
mucronate
cuspidate

pinnate   palmate   parallel viens

VIENATION   APICES

corymb   umbel

head   compound umbel

raceme   catkin   spike   panicle

solitary   cyme   compound cyme

TYPES OF INFLORESCENCES

entire   doubly serrate   crenate   sinuate

serrate   dentate   undulate   incised

TYPES OF MARGINS

As you study plants in the field or those of your collection, note how their parts compare with those shown on this page. Also turn to this page when you find a plant part named in the descriptions of wild plants that are to be found on the pages that follow.

Practice in this sort of comparison will greatly help you in correctly identifying the common plants you find.

liner   oblong   ovate   oblanceolate   obovate
lanceolate   elliptical   pinnately cordate   spatulate

wedge shaped   reniform   sagittate   hastate
palmately cordate   peltate   auriculate

truncate   perfoliate   pinnate   pinnately lobed
cuneate   connate perfoliate   palmate

pinnately cleft   pinnately divided   palmately three-cleft
pinnately parted   palmately three-lobed   palmately three-parted

TYPES OF LEAVES

COMMON PLANTS AND
WILDLIFE HABITATS

In the following pages only the more common and most frequently encountered species are described, the few exceptions being those plants that are of special interest. A complete listing of the plant species alone would take a book many times this size. In order to identify the plants, illustrations and brief descriptions are given. It will aid you in understanding the descriptions if you study the illustrations on page 6 and learn to recognize the shapes and kinds of plant parts.

Ocean shore, Humboldt Co. Photo reproduced by permission of the Redwood Empire Association.

PLANTS OF THE COASTAL STRAND AND BLUFFS

Sand dune areas and nearby bluffs are everywhere characterized by distinctive vegetation. Because sand has a low capacity for holding water, many of the plants found along the coast will be closely related to species found in arid habitats, such as dry high mountain or desert regions, farther inland. Coastal strand vegetation varies from low growing succulents along the high tide line, through grasslands, brush areas (dominated by bush lupine

and other shrubs), to well-developed forests in which the beach
and Monterey pines are characteristic. The great variety of
vegetation is very favorable to birds of many kinds.

BEACH PINE (Pinus con-
torta). This scrub pine,
which seldom grows over 35'
high, has comparatively
thick branches, forming a
Strand round-topped, compact and
symmetrical, or an open,
picturesque head. The ovoid
to sub-cylindric cones are
usually 1-2" long and remain
on the tree from 4 to 5 years
or more. This attractive
seacoast tree, which has little commercial value, ranges
from Mendocino Co. north
along the coast to Alaska.

Strand

← MONTEREY PINE
(Pinus radiata). A 25 to
75' or higher tree, usu-
ally well-shaped, but
sometimes with a flat-
tened or broken top when
old. The bark is dark,
rough, hard and often
deeply fissured; the dark
green needles appear in
3's, rarely in 2's, and
are 3-6" long; the cones
are light or reddish-
brown in color and 2 1/2
to 4" long. It is found in
a few scattered colonies
from Santa Cruz Co. S.

Strand BISHOP PINE (P. muricata) is found from Humboldt Co. south,
and has very long (4-6") needles in 2's; cones often with spurs.

BISHOP PINE (Pinus muricata). A small tree usually not over 60' tall. The bark is dark, purplish brown, deeply furrowed and scaly. The needles are 3'' to 5'' long, yellow green, in dense clusters at the branch ends. Both the male and female flowers are clustered at the ends of the branches. The mature cones are 2'' to 3 1/2'' long, unsymmetric with large black seeds. The tree is too small for commercial use, though it is widely used for fuel.

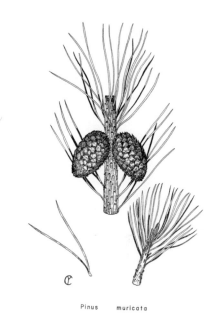

Pinus muricata

MONTEREY CYPRESS (Cupressus macrocarpa). A 15 to 80' tree, with tiny, scale-like and overlapping, grayish-green leaves; the small cones with brown seeds; bark dark brown. These unusual trees grow in dense stands only in restricted localities on the headlands around the mouth of the Carmel River in Monterey Co., California. A very similar-looking tree (though sometimes a low shrub), is the MENDOCINO CYPRESS (Cupressus pygmaea) of the Mendocino coast, which has black instead of brown seeds. There is also the GOWEN CYPRESS of the Monterey coast, which grows only from 1 to 5' high and has a smooth, compact crown.

Strand

Stand of Monterey Cypress on cliffs at Cypress Point, California. Photo courtesy of Southern Pacific Company.

WAX MYRTLE (see p. 18).

TREE LUPINE (<u>Lupinus</u> <u>arboreus</u>). From Humboldt Co. S. to Santa Barbara Co. this bushy lupine makes the beaches beautiful during the late spring and early summer when the <u>bright yellow flowers</u> are in bloom. The seeds, born in a typical bean-like pod, furnish food for quail and other seed-eating birds and mammals. The bushy plants are often 3-4' tall and spread out over several square feet of area. Several other species of lupines, usually with blue flowers, are found along the coast. Two lupines common on the Oregon and Washington coasts are the BICOLORED LUPINE (<u>L. bicolor</u>), with broad petals, one of them purple and white (this species is also in California); and the SEASHORE LUPINE (<u>L. litoralis</u>), which lies flat on the sands.

Strand

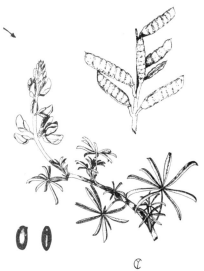

← BEARBERRY (Arcto-staphylos uva-ursi). A trailing, prostrate plant, with shiny, glabrous, oval or obovate, 1" long leaves. Common among the dunes from Mendocino Co. N. to Alaska. In some areas it is common under the beach pines. It has white or pinkish flowers, and brilliant red or pink berries, often eaten by animals and Indians. The smooth, dark red bark is distinctive.

SAND STRAWBERRY (Frageria chilensis). This plant is an important sand-binder in the coastal dunes and extends numerous prostrate stems or runners. The relatively large white flowers are carried in cymes. The small strawberries are edible and are eaten by many birds and mammals. The upper surface of the leaf is dark green & shiny smooth; the under surface is densely hairy, as are other parts of the plant. This plant is found along the sand dunes, beaches and cliffs from San Luis Obispo Co., California, north to Alaska.

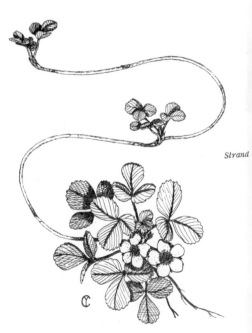

SAND VERBENA (Abronia latifolia). This is a common seaside plant in the sandy soil and among the dunes, which it helps to hold in place with its long roots. It has showy, yellow flowers that are borne at the end of stalks in a *Strand* many-flowered head. The stout stems of this prostrate, creeping plant are from 1' to 2' long. The herbage is very juicy and glandular; the leaves are opposite. This species is found along the coast from Santa Barbara, California, N. to British Colum.

LIZARD-TAIL (on page 22).

SEASIDE PAINTED CUP (see page 22).

COAST GOLDENROD (Solidago spathulata). In the *Strand* fall, from Coos Co., Oregon, south, this plant's yellow flowers, borne in a spike-like panicle, brightens the sand dunes and hills all along the sea. The usually smooth-surfaced leaves are spatulate to obovate and toothed beyond the middle. Several 15-18" high stems rise from a creeping base. The flower heads usually have 5-10 quite small ray flowers. Indians ate the young leaves in salad.

SEASIDE DAISY (page 22).

COMMON ANIMALS OF THE COASTAL STRAND

Mammals
Bobcat, 59
Raccoon, 61
Long-tailed weasel, 63
Short-tailed weasel, 63
Striped skunk, 64
Black-tailed jackrabbit, 65
Brush rabbit, 65
Pocket gopher, 67
White-footed mouse, 71
Meadow vole, 71
Harvest mouse, 71
Bats, 75

Reptiles & Amphibians
Western fence lizard, 104
Western skink, 104
Foothill alligator lizard, 104
Gopher snake, 107
Common garter snake, 107
Western toad, 114

Birds
Turkey vulture, 81
Duck hawk, 82
Sparrow hawk, 82
California quail, 84
Killdeer, 84
Long-billed curlew, 85
Willet, 85
Dowitcher, 86
Gulls, 86
Swallows, 92
Raven, 93
Wren-tit, 94
Pygmy nuthatch, 94
Bewick wren, 94
Myrtle warbler, 98
White-crowned sparrow, 101
Golden-crowned sparrow, 101
Song sparrow, 102

14

COASTAL MARSHES

Two types of marshes are encountered along the coast. (1) The salt-water marsh is characterized by extensive tidal flats. Below the average low tide mark are found fields of EELGRASS (Zostera marina). These are easily recognized by being largely submerged maritime herbs with very narrow, grass-like leaves, 1-4" long and sheathed at their bases. The flowers have no petals, but appear as simple, single stamens or pistils on flattened, fleshy spikes. Eelgrass is an important food for the black brant.

Marsh

Higher parts of the salt water marsh are characterized by PICKLE-WEED (Salicornia), a low, very juicy-stemmed herb with jointed stems and scale-like leaves; and SALT GRASS (Distichlis spicata), with rigid, erect stems, surrounded usually by two rows or ranks of stiff leaves, and topped by short, dense, few-flowered panicles. These marshes usually then give way to grasslands or to other upland vegetation.

Photo shows fresh water marsh with partly- submerged ARROWHEAD PLANTS (Saggitaria), with 4-15" arrow-head shaped leaf and small, white, 3-petaled flowers. Indians

Water Marsh

Photo by J. A. Munro, courtesy Canadian Wildlife Service.

boiled or baked the roots like potatoes, hence "Indian potato" is a name sometimes given to this plant.

(2) The <u>fresh</u> <u>water</u> <u>marsh</u> is characterized by submerged aquatic plants, such as pondweeds and arrowheads, a few floating plants, such as the water lily, and, toward the shore line, emergent plants, such as the cattail and bulrush. The marshes form an important habitat for many birds and mammals.

COMMON CAT-TAIL (<u>Typha</u> <u>latifolia</u>). Not illustrated. This common marsh plant, which often grows from 3-6' tall in the coastal area from California to Alaska, is well-known to most people. The attractive cat-tails, or thick brown flower spikes, are often used in decorating homes in the fall. The leaves were used in basket-making by the Indians. These leaves arise long, stiff and grass-like from the shallow water. The plant is an important food for muskrats and other aquatic mammals and birds.

Marsh

SKUNK CABBAGE (<u>Lysichitum</u> <u>americanum</u>). This is a showy, perennial, glabrous (hairless) herb with large leaves, and each spike of flowers of a single sex (unisexual). The flowers are crowded onto a spadix (thick spike) surrounded by a yellow spathe (clasping leaf). The basal leaves are from 1-4' long and usually about 1' wide, rising from a stout rootstock. Skunk cabbages are common in fresh water marshes from the Santa Cruz Mts. of California north to Alaska. Indians sometimes used this plant for food.

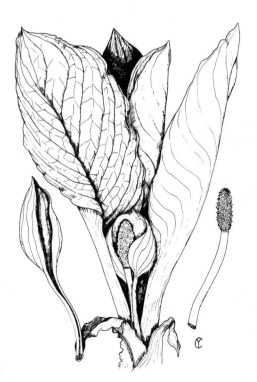

*Conif.
Marsh*

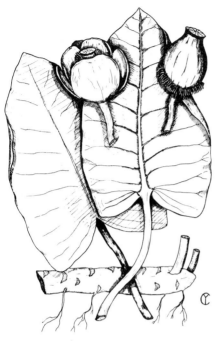

YELLOW WATER LILY (Nuphar polysepalum). The large, heart-shaped leaves of this plant, 6 to 12" broad and 6 to 14" long, are very distinctive. They are attached to a creeping rootstock by means of a long stem or scape. This is a common plant in many of the lowland marshes and lakes along the coast from Santa Cruz Co., California, to British Columbia. It is also found in lakes at higher elevations. Indians used this plant for food, and it is also eaten by muskrats and waterfowl.

COMMON ANIMALS OF THE COASTAL MARSHES

Mammals
Raccoon, 61
Mink, 62
Otter, 63
Beaver, 68
Muskrat, 69
Meadow vole, 71
W. jumping mouse, 71
Shrew-mole, 73
Vagrant shrew, 73
Most bats, 74

Reptiles & Amphibians
Pacific pond turtle, 108
Common garter snake, 109
Western garter snake, 107
Tiger salamander, 110
Frogs (except yellow-legged), 114
Western toad, 114

Birds
Grebes, 77
Great blue heron, 78
American egret, 78
Black-crowned night heron, 78
Marsh hawk, 82
Duck hawk, 82
Canada goose, 79
Ducks, 79-80
Virginia & sora rails, 84
American coot, 84
Shore birds (except willet), 84-86
Yellowthroat, 97
Red-winged blackbird, 98
Brewer blackbird, 98
Song sparrow, 102

Photo of coastal brushfields between Eureka & Crescent City, California, taken by Gabriel Moulin Studios of San Francisco.

On mountain slopes facing the ocean, where climate does not permit forests to develop, dense brushfields are frequently encountered. Similar habitats develop farther inland where soil or rock conditions do not favor forest development. Logged or burned areas of forest also spring up temporarily into stands of dense brush which are only slowly replaced by forest trees. In these burnt over areas, however, and especially in the mountains, trees, shrubs and plants of the hardwood forests (see page 45) may temporarily take the place of the coniferous forests.

These brush fields often superficially resemble the chaparral of interior regions, but typically consist of different species and are more luxuriant and often more difficult for men to break through. They give safe hiding places for many animal species.

COW PARSNIP (Heracleum lanatum). Illustrated p. 18. 4-5' high herb, with leaves sheathing the stems and divided into 3 large, toothed and lobed leaflets, each 3-6" broad; white flowers are in large compound umbels, usually appearing flat-topped. Coastal.

NORTHWEST CRIMSON COLUMBINE(see page 41)

Heracleum lanatum

WAX MYRTLE (<u>Myrica californica</u>). One of the typical
plants of the coastal brushfields is this evergreen shrub or tree
that grows from 8-30' high. The nutlet fruit is one of the major
foods for band-tailed pigeons at certain times of the year. The thickish, dark green, glossy, oblong or oblanceolate leaves remain on the branches during the winter and make this plant one of the most attractive species found along the coast. Wax myrtles extend from Santa Monica Mts. N. to Wash.

CANYON GOOSEBERRY (see forest section, p. 32).

← **CALIFORNIA BLACK-BERRY (<u>Rubus vitifolius</u>).** This is a common evergreen bush that trails over the ground or climbs over other vegetation in the coastal brushfields and the forest edges. It has slender, straight thorns; doubly serrate leaves that are usually pinnately 3-5 foliolate (3-5 leaflets); that are about 1" across; flowers and oblong berries that are black when ripe. The fruit makes fine jam and jelly, and is an important food for fruit-eating birds and some mammals. It is common from California to British Columbia.

SALMON-BERRY (Rubus spectabilis). This is an erect plant that grows from 6-9' high. The bark is reddish-brown and is sparingly thorned except the sterile shoots, which are very well thorned. The deciduous leaves are formed into three leaflets, which have doubly serrate margins. The flowers are from one to three in a cluster; petals red; berries scarlet to yellow; often eaten by Indians when mixed with other foods; popular with birds.

Brush Conif.

← HIMALAYA BERRY (Rubus thrysanthus). This is an introduced evergreen vine that is common along the coast. It is a robust plant with large, recurved thorns that make it almost impossible for a person to get through thickets formed by this species. The leaves are formed in five leaflets in most cases; the white flowers are relatively large; the berries are dark blackish and used as food by many birds and mammals, especially bears.

Brush

*Brush
Wd.Pr.
Hardw.*

**TOYON or CHRIST-
MAS BERRY (**<u>Hetero-
meles arbutifolia</u>**)**
A large shrub or
small tree with fuzzy
young branchlets;
leaves 2-4" long, dark
green and shining
above, but pale be-
neath, and toothed;
numerous small
white flowers in ter-
minal corymb-like
panicles; fruit be-
comes bright red.
California coast.

**VARICOLORED LU-
PINE (**<u>Lupinus</u> variicol-

*Brush
Strand*

<u>or</u>). The 2-3' long stems usually lie along the ground; the flow-
ers are similar to those of the lupine on page 10, but with flowers
colored variously whitish, yellow, pinkish, purple or bluish.

BLUE-BLOSSOM (<u>Cea-
nothus</u> <u>thyrsiflorus</u>**).** In
the spring months along
the roadsides in the red-
wood region and north to
Coos Bay, Oregon, many
brushfields take on a bluish
color from the blossoms of
this 3-25' tall shrub or
small tree. It is an important deer food, sometimes
called blue myrtle or lilac.

Brush

Several other kinds of
ceanothus are found in this
region, of which probably
the most important is deer
or buck brush (page 31).

SALAL (see page 34).

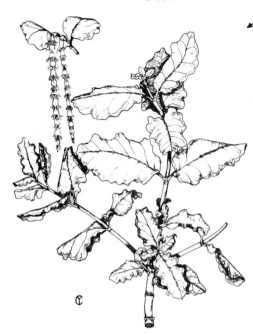

SILK TASSEL (<u>Gar-rya</u> elliptica). This 5-9' or, more rarely, 20' high shrub or tree has simple, opposite leaves with noticeable undulating margins. It has dioecious flowers (with stamens & pistils on different flowers on different plants),which are borne along a pen-dulous, catkin-like structure. This plant is common in the coast-al ranges on the sea-ward side from Mon-terey Co., Calif. to Lane Co., Oregon.

Brush

BEAR BRUSH (<u>Gar-rya</u> <u>Fremontii</u>). 3-10' high bush with slender branches, smooth bark (the above has rough bark), dark leaves, purplish berries.

Brush

BLACK TWINBERRY (<u>Lonicera</u> <u>involucrata</u>). An erect shrub, 3-10' high, with simple, entire leaves that occur in pairs, as do also the at-tractive yellow flowers, and the black berries. Below the flowers are large and conspicuously broad bracts, which be-come reddish as the fruit develops. Most of region.

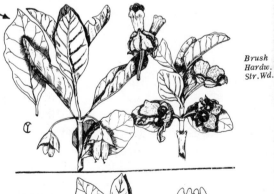

*Brush
Hardw.
Str.Wd.*

WEDDED HONEY-SUCKLE (<u>Lonicera</u> <u>con-jugialis</u>). This is a close relative of the twinberry, with blackish-purple flowers, and red berries

*Brush
Str.Wd.*

(at maturity) which are 2/3
joined (as shown). Hum-
boldt Co. & North.

BUSH MONKEY FLOWER
(Mimulus aurantiacus).
3-5' bush with large,
brownish-yellow, funnel-
shaped, narrow-throated
flowers. It is easily told
by its sticky foliage and
dark green leaves. From
Curry Co., Oregon, south
along the coast.

Mimulus aurantiacus

SEASIDE PAINTED CUP
(Castilleia latifolia). 1/2
to 1 1/2' herb with sticky,
hairy foliage; the greenish-yellow flowers surrounded by yellow
bracts; leaves usually 3-lobed. Sea cliffs.

CASCARA SAGRADA (Rhamnus purshiana). See page 30.

HAIRY MANZANITA (Arctostaphylos columbiana). Page 33.

Sunflower Fam. (tiny flowers concentrated into heads)

LIZARD TAIL (Eriophyllum staechadifolium).   A diffusely-
Brush spreading, 1 1/2 to 3' high bush with narrow leaves, narrowest at
Strand base, and with a dense, felt-like, whitish fuzz underneath, green
glabrous above. Flower heads are yellow. From Coos Co. S.

PEARLY EVERLASTING FLOWER (see page 43).

Brush   SEASIDE DAISY (Erigeron glaucus). This beautiful little daisy
Strand rises 2-14" high from stems spreading over the ground. It has
leaves; flowers that are in solitary, terminal heads or loose
corymbs; and large ray flowers, lilac or violet in color. Ore.
coast & south.

Brush

COYOTE BRUSH (<u>Bac-</u>
<u>charis</u> <u>pilularis</u>). This is a
common shrub from 2-5'
high that occurs along the
coast of Calif. and north to
Tillamook Co., Ore. It has
small white flower heads &
these are either alone or in
clusters on the many leafy
branchlets. The leaves are
obovate or cuneate, entire
or few-toothed. The young
branchlets are scaly & sticky.

COMMON ANIMALS OF THE COASTAL BRUSHFIELDS

Mammals
Black-tailed deer, 57
Mountain lion, 58
Bobcat, 58
Gray fox, 60
Raccoon, 61
Ring-tailed cat, 61
Long-tailed weasel, 63
Short-tailed weasel, 63
Spotted skunk, 64
Striped skunk, 64
Townsend chipmunk, 67
Mountain beaver, 68
Woodrats, 69
White-footed mouse, 71

Birds
Quail, 83-84
Hummingbirds, 89
Bush-tit, 93

Birds (continued)
Wren-tit, 94
Winter wren, 95
Bewick wren, 94
Pileolated warbler, 97
Scrub jay, 92
American goldfinch, 100
Towhees, 100
Oregon junco, 101
Fox sparrow, 102
Song sparrow, 102

Reptiles & Amphibians
Gopher snake, 109
W. garter snake, 107
W. ring-necked snake, 107
Alligator lizards, 104
Western skink, 104
Western fence lizard, 104
Calif. slender salamander, 113
Eschscholtz's salamander, 113

CONIFEROUS FORESTS

The Pacific coastal coniferous forest is the most characteristic habitat type of this region. It is, in mature form, a dense forest of tall trees (often over 300 feet), of great diameter. The crowns of the trees commonly touch to form an overhead screen which shades out most light from the forest floor. Only the most shade-tolerant plants can survive there. The dominant trees are conifers (cone-bearing trees, with needle-like or flattened, linear leaves, which are evergreen). These trees give a continuous shade to the ground below throughout the year. Where a dominant conifer has died and fallen a variety of shrubs and smaller trees usually spring up in the clearing, to be gradually replaced as a new tall conifer grows up and overshadows them.

The nature of the forest varies within the region, dependent largely upon the amount of rainfall and moisture available. Near the coast, in the more moist sites, the sitka spruce and lowland fir are dominant (particularly in Washington and northern Oregon). Farther inland, in drier sites, giant cedar and western hemlock prevail. On the driest coastal forest sites the Douglas fir dominates the scene. In the southern part of the region, in California, redwoods take the place of the spruce-fir and cedar-hemlock types.

Rain forest, sitka spruce type; courtesy Olympic Nat. Park.

Redwood Grove in Del Norte County, with sword ferns and small herbs dominating undergrowth. Photo reproduced by courtesy of Redwood Empire Association.

Douglas fir forest along Eel River in northwestern California.
Photo reproduced by courtesy of Redwood Empire Association.

Interior forest of Washington Coast on Soleduck River, featuring giant cedar and western hemlock. Photo reproduced by permission of National Park Service at Olympic National Park.

The trees described as characteristic of the coastal hardwood forest habitat (see page 45) also occur as understory or second-growth trees in the coniferous forest. Similarly the shrubs of the coastal brushfields (see page 17) often occur as undergrowth or in clearings in the coniferous forests along with other, more shade-tolerant shrubs.

*   *

REDWOOD (Sequoia sempervirens). This is a characteristic tree of the belt from southern Oregon to Monterey Co., California. Seldom does this species occur inland for more than 20 miles. The sharp-pointed, dark green leaves are usually 2-ranked on most of the branches. This tall, massive tree reaches its greatest development in Humboldt Co., California, where the tallest known tree (367 feet) occurs. Redwoods are important recreation and lumber trees.

Conif.

DOUGLAS FIR (Pseudotsuga menziesii). This widely distributed tree of the western states and Canada is one of the most important lumber trees of the Pacific Northwest, including northern California. The inch-long needles are flattened and usually in 2 ranks on each side of the rib. The 3-forked cone bracts (shown) are different from those of any other conifer, which makes identification easy. Height to 250'.

Conif.

Conif. SITKA SPRUCE (Picea sitchensis). This large forest tree often grows nearly 200 feet tall in the moist, often swampy situations along the coast. The wood is light brown, with thick, whitish sapwood, light and relatively weak. In the past the wood has been used for shipbuilding and for aero-

planes. It is easily identified by its very stiff, pungent-smelling leaves, which are whitish above and with a ridge in the middle and rounded strongly outward below. Alaska to Mendocino coast.

Conif.

LOWLAND FIR (Abies grandis). The leaves of this attractive tree of the low moist valleys along the coast are 2-ranked and form flat sprays. The upper surface is dark green, the lower silvery-white. The cones are 2.5 to 4" long and stand upright on the branches. The branches are grayish in color. Sonoma Co. N.

Conif. WESTERN HEMLOCK (Tsuga heterophylla). The light, hard, tough, pale yellow-brown wood of this attractive western tree is important for building purposes, and the bark is used in tanning hides. The weeping-willow-like top is distinctive, as are the grooved and ridged leaves. From the Mendocino coast of California, it is found north along the coast mainly on drier, higher ground than spruce or redwood.

GIANT CEDAR (Thuja plicata). This attractive tree is found in moist bottom land or occasionally on dry ridges from sea level to approximately 6,000' altitude, and from the Mendocino coast north to Alaska. Minute, scalelike leaves thickly cover the branches, which form into flat sprays. The short cones are held on short lateral branchlets. The bark is cinnamon-red and the tree may grow 180' or more high. Formerly Indians burnt out the trunks to make canoes.

Conif.

RED ALDER (Alnus rubra). This fast-growing tree, with light, soft wood that is used for furniture and for smoking salmon in the Pacific Northwest, is abundant along the coast from Santa Barbara Co., California, to Alaska. It grows from 20-90' high and forms groves in the bottom-lands and along creeks. The leaf edges are all double-toothed (serrate) and the bark is pale gray or whitish-mottled.

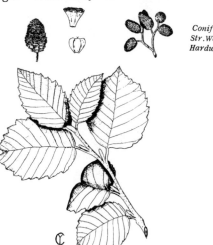

Conif.
Str.Wd.
Hardw.

Quercus chrysolepis

CANYON or MAUL OAK (Quercus chrysolepis). 30-65' high tree; young twigs covered with whitish fuzz; has smooth, ashy-gray bark; dark green leaves thick and leathery; thick walls to acorn cups covered with rusty fuzz. Canyons from S. Ore. south.

*Conif.
Str.Wd.*

← WESTERN AZALEA (Rhododendron occidentale). This is one of the most attractive shrubs along the coastal areas in California north into Oregon, with its large, whitish flowers tinged with yellow and pink shades. The blooms appear in May and continue for several weeks; in the fall the deciduous leaves turn bright colors.

*Conif.
Hardw.
Brush*

CALIFORNIA RHODODENDRON or ROSE BAY (Rhododendron macrophylum). This is usually an erect shrub from 4-8' high, but in the redwood belt in California it often occurs as a small tree up to 30' high. ℂ The large, rose-purple flowers, borne in a cluster, make this one of the primary attractions of the coniferous forests along the west coast in the spring months. The thick, entire-margined, evergreen leaves make this plant attractive also during the winter months. Rhododendrons are found along the California coast and north to Washington and British Columbia.

CASCARA (Rhamnus purshiana). A small tree or shrub from 8-20' high, with thin, deciduous leaves, 3-8" long. The flowers are greenish and the berries black. The bark possesses cathartic properties peculiar to the genus and is collected and sold as

*Conif.
Hardw.
Brush*

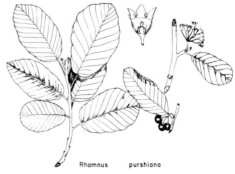

Rhamnus   purshiana

Cascara Sagrada. It occurs from central Calif. N. to Wash.

DEER BRUSH (Cea-
nothus integerrimus). A
variety of ceanothus or
wild lilac are found in
California and southern
Oregon. This widely-

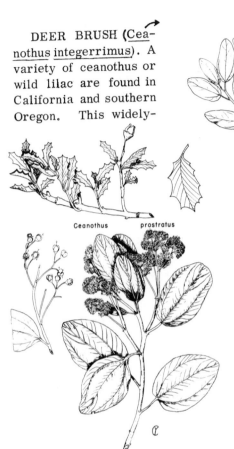

Ceanothus   prostratus

Ceanothus   velutinus

branched shrub is from 4-
12' high and occurs along
the coast or near it as far
north as southern Douglas
Co., Oregon. The showy
white or blue flowers have
a fragrant smell and are
borne in clusters along a
main branch. The leaves
are thin, deciduous (falling
off in winter) and entire
margined. This is an im-
portant deer food.

*Conif.
Hardw.
Brush*

SQUAW MAT (Ceanothus
prostratus). This plant
often groups together to
form flat patches with the
stems stretching over the

Conif.

ground. It is usually found in the pine area of the interior, but
does occur along the coast too. The toothed, evergreen leaves
are distinctive because of their resemblance to holly.

SNOW BUSH or TOBACCO BUSH (Ceanothus velutinus). This
shrub grows up to 12' high; has evergreen, varnished, eliptical
leaves; and large, compound panicles of white flowers. The
leaves are also prominently 3-nerved. It is a plant of the inland mountains, but occurs also along the coast from Humboldt
Co., California, north to British Columbia.

*Conif.
Brush
Hardw*

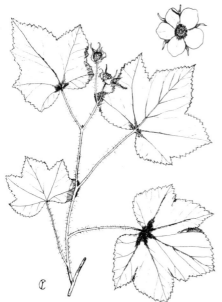

← THIMBLE-BERRY (Ru-bus parviflorus). This common shrub is from 3-6' high with shreddy bark. It has deciduous, simple and palmately-lobed leaves from 3-7" wide, and it is common in the coastal coniferous forests north to Alaska. Its flowers are scarlet, mild in taste and edible.

CANYON GOOSEBERRY (Ri-bes menziesii). One of the common gooseberries found along

the coast is this well-thorned, 4-8' high shrub. It has white-petaled flowers with red or purple sepals; the berry is a dark purple, about 1/4" in diameter, and covered with stiff, spine-like, gland-tipped bristles. The berries were mixed into other food by the Indians for flavoring.

RED-FLOWERING CUR-RANT (Ribes sanguineum).
This is one of the first shrubs of the coast to flower. It has blood-red to pinkish flowers, depending on the variety. The un-armed stems are slender, erect or spreading, and are from 3-10' high. Varieties of this species occur from San Luis Obispo Co., California, north to British Columbia. The bluish-black berries are slightly edible.

*Conif.
Hardw.
Brush*

PRICKLY CURRANT (R. lacustre). (Not illustrated.) The 3-7' stems usually lie along or near to the ground, with 1-3 spines at each joint; leaves heart-shaped; flowers purple.

*Conif.
Str.Wd.*

HAIRY MANZANITA (Arctostaphylos columbiana). Many manzanitas are found in California, but this common evergreen shrub, covered with hairs and with white flowers borne in clusters, is one of the few that occurs north into Oregon and Washington along the coast. Like all manzanitas, it has a dark, smooth, red bark, and is very leafy, growing from 4-8' high in the immediate coastal area. The berries were ground up

*Conif.
Rocks
Brush*

and mixed with other food as flavoring by the Indians.

Conif.
Hardw.
Str.Wd.

BLACK HUCKLEBERRY (Vaccinium ovatum). This attractive evergreen shrub that grows from 4-8' high is one of the dominant cover plants in the redwood region in California. It has shiny, stiff and leathery leaves; and small, pinkish, urn-shaped flowers borne in racemes. The blackish fruits are eaten by many wild animals in the fall; they also make excellent jams and jellies. This species is found along the coast from Santa Barbara County, in California, to British Columbia. Why not try a wild huckleberry pie?

Conif
Hardw.

RED HUCKLEBERRY (Vaccinium parvifolium). This shrub grows from 3 to nearly 20' high. The leaves are thin, oval, and deciduous (falling off in winter). The branches and branchlets are greenish and sharply angled; the fruit is bright red and very pleasant to eat; the flower is globular and greenish or pinkish in color. Many birds and animals eat the berries in the fall. This shrub is found from the Santa Cruz Mts., California, north to Alaska.

Conif.
Hardw.
Brush

SALAL (Gaultheria shallon). (Illustration on top of next page.) This is one of the most common cover shrubs in the redwood region, growing from 1-6' high and often covering the forest floor. The evergreen leaves are shiny above and from 3-6' long. The white to pinkish flowers are urn-shaped and are borne in racemes. This species is found in the woods from California north to British Columbia. The berries make fine jelly and are eaten by Indians, and by many birds and mammals, especially bears.

OREGON GRAPE (Mahonia nervosa). 2-16' high, evergreen shrub, with pinnately-compound leaves, yellow flowers borne in racemes, dark blue berries and yellow wood. It is found all along the coast. ↓

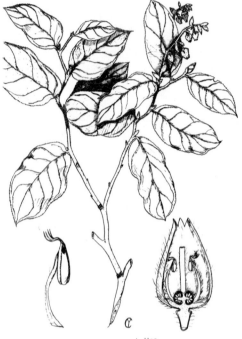

Conif.
Hardw.
Ds.Brush

Gaultheria   shallon

Montia   sibirica

INDIAN   LETTUCE
(Montia sibirica). This 9-18" high herb blooms among the earliest flowers in

Conif.
Hardw.
Meadow

Mahonia   nervosa

moist places in the coastal woods from Calif. N. to Alaska. The flowers are white with pink veins or pink with reddish veins. Edible leaves.

Conif.   REDWOOD SORREL (Oxalis oregana). The obcordate (reversed, heart-shaped) leaves of this small plant that grows in the deep coastal woods are all basal. The single flowers on each scape (flower stem) are pink, white or rose-colored. This sorrel is very common in the redwood forests of the California coast, but less common on north to Washington. It often completely carpets the forest floor.

(The following 12 species belong to the Lily Family, and all have parallel-veined leaves.)

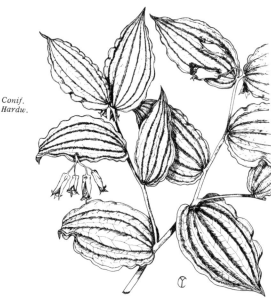

Conif.
Hardw.

FAIRY LANTERN or FAIRY BELL (Disporum smithii). This herb grows about 3' high and is found in the deep woods or along stream banks in the coastal mountains from Santa Cruz Co., California, north to British Columbia. The leaves are sessile and cordate (heart-shaped) at the base. The flowers are creamy-white or greenish, hanging in bell-shaped clusters underneath the leaves so as to be often invisible from above. The fruit is a yellow or reddish berry, which is not edible.

Oaks
Brush   COMMON TRILLIUM (Trillium sessile). Not illustrated. It
Conif. looks like T. ovatum on next page, except the flower petals are
Hardw. sessile, rising directly from the 3 large leaves. 4-12" high.

WESTERN WAKE-ROB-
IN or TRILLIUM (Trillium
ovatum). This is a glabrous,
erect, unbranched herb that
grows from 6-10" high.
There are three bright green
leaves in a whorl at the sum-
mit of the stem. Extending
beyond these leaves is a
white, lily-like flower that
turns to a pinkish-rose col-
or a few days after it has
opened. This plant is common in the woods along the
coast from the Santa Cruz
Mts. of Calif. N. to Br. Col.

BROOK TRILLIUM (T.
rivale). Similar to above
flower, but leaves have separate stems; flowers white.

*Conif
Hardw.*

*Conif
Hardw.
Str. Wd.*

Trillium   ovatum

Lilium   columbianum

OREGON LILY (Lilium co-
lumbianum). This reddish-
orange lily, with many dark
purple spots, blooms in the
redwood country along the
coast during June and July.
It grows from 2-4' tall and
usually, but not always, has
the leaves in whorls of 3's at
the nodes. It extends from
Humboldt Co., California,
north to British Columbia.

*Str. Wd.
Hardw.
Conif.*

WASHINGTON LILY (L.
Washingtonianum). Has 4-6'
tall stems and 3-3 1/2" long,
white flowers with fine purple
dots, the whole turning purplish with age; leaves 1 1/2 to

*Hardw.
Conif.*

5" long, and usually in several whorls. Found in open woods at
middle altitudes from northern Humboldt Co. to N. Oregon.

See illustration on next page.

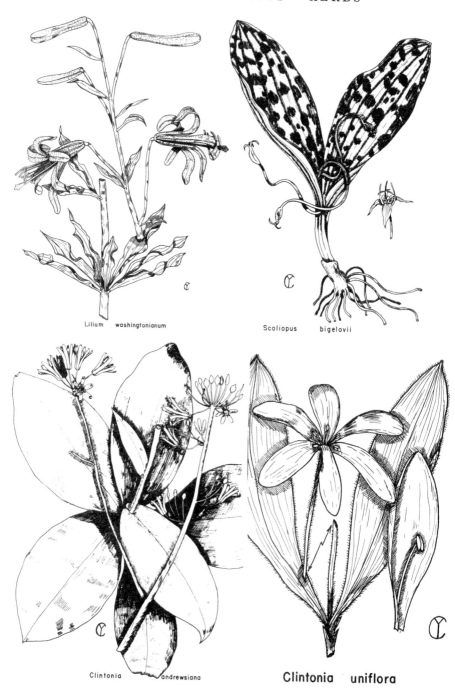

Lilium   washingtonianum

Scoliopus   bigelovii

Clintonia   andrewsiana

Clintonia   uniflora

CALIFORNIA FETID ADDER'S TONGUE or SLINK-POD (Scoliopus bigelovii). This very short, largely subterranean plant produces two large mottled leaves (4-9" long), and an umbel of flowers which are mottled with green and purple. The flowers occur in January through March and the plants appear in deep, cool, shaded areas in the redwood forest from Santa Cruz County north to the southwestern part of Oregon.

RED CLINTONIA (Clintonia andrewsiana). This is a glabrous herb that has large elliptical leaves that are from 7-13" long; the red, lily-like flowers are borne at the top of a long, bare, 15-20" stem. The berries are dark blue. This plant is common in the redwood forests and is found from southwestern Curry County, Oregon, to Monterey County, California.

ONE-FLOWERED CLINTONIA (C. uniflora). Has solitary white flowers on comparatively short stems, and only 2-3 leaves instead of 4-5 (for the above flower). Middle altitudes, Humboldt County north to British Columbia.

OREGON COLTSFOOT or TWO-LEAVED SOLOMON'S SEAL (Maianthemum dilatatum). This glabrous (smooth) herb that grows on moist shaded banks in the coastal woods from Marin County, California, north along the coast to Alaska, usually has two large, cordate (heart-shaped) leaves. Above these it bears a terminal raceme of small white flowers. The stem is simple and erect and grows from a few inches to 14" high. A bright red berry.

*Conif.
Hardw.*

FALSE SOLOMON'S SEAL

(<u>Smilacina</u> <u>racemosa</u>). A 1-4' high herb with two flat rows of oblong to oblong-lanceolate leaves; usually sessile and with tiny hairs beneath; hairy stems topped by a dense panicle of tiny white flowers, which turn into round, red-mottled berries. From Monterey C. north to Br. Col.

Conif.
Hardw.
Oaks

Smilacina   racemosa

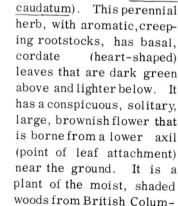

WILD GINGER (<u>Asarum</u> <u>caudatum</u>).

This perennial herb, with aromatic, creeping rootstocks, has basal, cordate (heart-shaped) leaves that are dark green above and lighter below. It has a conspicuous, solitary, large, brownish flower that is borne from a lower axil (point of leaf attachment) near the ground. It is a plant of the moist, shaded woods from British Columbia S. to Sta. Cruz Mts., Cal.

Conif.

Asarum   hartwegi

Conif. GER (<u>Asarum Hartwegi</u>). Very similar, but leaves are marbled.

MARBLED WILD GIN-

NORTHWEST CRIM-SON COLUMBINE (Aqui-legia formosa). This plant has red spurs and sepals and yellow petals. It is found mainly inland in open woods, but does occur in the coastal mountains and along the coast from southern California north to British Columbia.

Conif.
Hardw.
Brush
Rocks

VAN HOUTTE'S COL-UMBINE (A. eximia). Similar to the above, but sticky, hairy all over. Mendocino Co. to San Mateo Co., California.

Rocks
Conif.
Hardw.
Brush

INSIDE-OUT FLOWER (Van-couveria hexandra). This low, creeping, perennial herb grows from slender, creeping root-stocks. The white, nodding flow-ers are reflexed (which means the petals and sepals point in an op-posite direction from the stamens) and this gives the plant its name. They are borne on an open pani-cle at the top of an 8-21" high stem. This species is found in the open woods from Mendocino Co., California N. to Washington.

Conif.
Hardw.
Oak

SMALL-FLOWERED VANCOU-VERIA (V. planipetala). Flowers more numerous than in above, and covered with sticky hairs (where-as V. hexandra is smooth). Red-wood forests & N. to Curry Co., Or.

Conif.
Oak
Hardw.

DEER-FOOT (Achlys tri- phylla). This perennial herb, which is about 1' high, spreads by slender root- stocks. The leaves consist of three sessile (without stems) leaflets about 2-6" across, while the flowers have no se- pals or petals and are borne on a short, dense spike. The fruits are dry, moon-shaped seeds. Deer-foot is common in the coastal woods from Mendocino County, Califor- nia, north through Oregon and Washington to British Columbia.

← PACIFIC BLEEDING HEART (Dicentra formosa). The beautiful rose-purple flowers of this plant top an 8-18" stem that is surroun- ded by basal leaves, each leaf being on a long stem and finely-divided into separate parts. It blooms in the spring from the San Fran- cisco Bay Region north to British Columbia.

ONE-FLOWERED DI- CENTRA (D. uniflora). The small, white or pinkish flow- er (sometimes there are 2) tops a 1-3" stem, surround-

Dicentra formosa

ed by a few much-divided leaves. The outer petals are more strongly recurved than in formosa. Humboldt Co. N. to Wash.

(See illustration on next page).

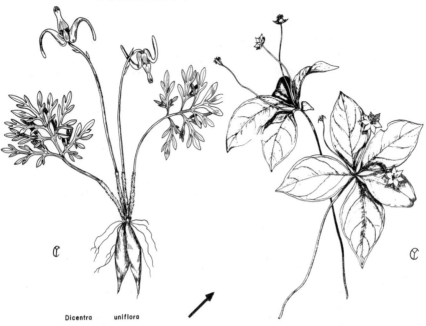

Dicentra   uniflora

STAR FLOWER (<u>Trientalis europaea</u>). This 2-6" high, glabrous plant is common in the woods along the coast from Monterey County, California, north to Alaska. The star-like white to pinkish flowers grow on thin stalks that spring from a whorl of 3 to 6 leaves that are usually from 1-2" long.

Conif. Oak Hardw.

PEARLY EVERLASTING (<u>Anaphalis margaritacea</u>). This 1-2' high composite (with flowers combined into dense heads) blooms in the fall and is often used for winter bouquets. The yellow flowers are surrounded by pearly-white bracts and the heads are arranged in compound corymbs. The bracts form overlapping series, which are persistent long after the flowers have dried up. From Monterey County north to Alaska.

Conif. Brush Hardw.

Anaphalis   margaritacea

Hardw.
Conif.
Str.Wd.

LOWLAND CUDWEED.

(Gnaphalium palustre). 3-9" high herb, branching at the base, the stems and leaves covered with long, loose wool (often falling off the leaves), in which the flowers are imbedded. Low places.

COMMON ANIMALS OF THE CONIFEROUS FORESTS

Mammals

Roosevelt elk, 56
Black-tailed deer, 57
Black bear, 58
Bobcat, 59
Ring-tailed cat, 61
Marten, 62
Fisher, 62
Weasels, 63
Skunks, 64
Snowshoe hare, 65
Chickaree or red
  squirrel, 66
Flying squirrel, 66
Townsend chipmunk 67
Mountain beaver 68
Wood rat, 69
White-footed mouse, 71
Red tree mouse, 71
Calif. red-backed vole, 71
Townsend mole 73
Shrew-mole 73
Pacific water shrew, 73
Trowbridge shrew, 73
Pacific shrew 73
Dusky shrew, 73
Bats, 74

Birds

Sharp-shinned hawk, 81
Blue grouse, 83
Horned owl, 88
Screech owl, 87
Spotted owl, 88
Pacific nighthawk, 88
Vaux swift, 89
Allen hummingbird, 89
Yellow-bellied sapsucker, 90
Red-shafted flicker, 90
Pileated woodpecker, 90
Hairy woodpecker, 90
Downy woodpecker, 90
Olive-sided flycatcher, 91

Birds (continued)

Western wood peewee, 91
Western flycatcher, 91
Violet-green swallow, 92
Tree swallow, 92
Purple martin, 92
Canada jay, 92
Steller jay, 93
American crow, 93
Chestnut-backed chicka-
  dee, 93
Red-breasted nuthatch, 94
Pygmy nuthatch, 94
Brown creeper, 94
Robin, 95
Varied thrush, 96
Russet-backed thrush, 96
Hermit thrush, 96
Mexican or Western
  bluebird, 95
Winter wren, 95
House wren, 95
Golden-crowned kinglet, 96
Ruby-crowned kinglet, 96
Cedar waxwing, 97
Hutton vireo, 97
Townsend warbler, 98
Orange-crowned warbler, 97
Audubon warbler, 98
Black-throated gray
  warbler, 98
Pileolated warbler, 97
Myrtle warbler, 98
Western tanager, 99
Black-headed grosbeak, 99
Evening grosbeak, 99
Purple finch, 99
Pine siskin, 100
Red crossbill, 100
Spotted towhee, 100
Oregon junco, 101
Fox sparrow, 102
Chipping sparrow, 101

Reptiles

Western fence lizard, 104
Western skink, 104
No. alligator lizard, 104
Rubber snake, 108
Western ring-necked
  snake, 107
Sharp-tailed snake, 107
Gopher snake, 109
Northwestern garter
  snake, 107
Western garter snake, 107
Common garter snake, 109

Amphibians

Olympic salamander, 110
Pacific giant salamander, 114
Northwestern salamander,
  109
Long-toed salamander, 109
Rough-skinned newt, 114
Western red-bellied
  newt, 110
Dunn's salamander, 110
Del Norte salamander, 110
Western red-backed
  salamander, 113
Van Dyke's salamander, 113
Eschscholts's salamander,
  113
California slender
  salamander, 113
Clouded salamander, 113
Black salamander, 113
Western toad, 114
Tailed frog, 113
Pacific tree-frog, 114
Yellow-legged frog, 114
Red-legged frog, 114

COASTAL HARDWOOD FOREST

Hardwood forests as such are nowhere widespread within this region. However, they are frequently interspersed among the coniferous forests, as hardwood stands occupy sites that, for one reason or another, are not suited to the taller, coniferous trees. Hardwood stands also frequently replace the coniferous forests following fire, logging, or other disturbance. Once established, they may maintain themselves for many years before finally being replaced by conifers.

Most of the hardwood forests of this region are made up of evergreen, broad-leaved trees. The madrone and tan oak are the two most characteristic species. In addition to these broad-leaved evergreen species, such deciduous, broad-leaved trees as the big-leaf maple and the red alder (see page 29) often form groves particularly in the more moist sites.

The understory vegetation of the hardwood forests differs little from that of the coniferous forests, although the hardwood trees themselves provide a source of food for species of animals that are not so well adapted to the coniferous groves.

Mixed hardwood growing near Maple Creek, Humboldt County. with madrone, bay, alder & oak. Photo by William McKittrick.

Hardw.
Conif.

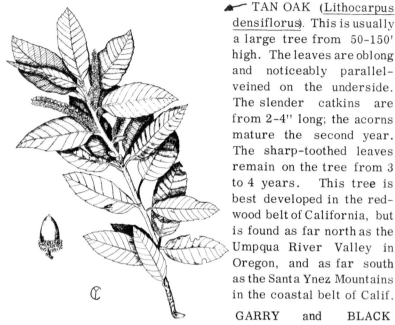

TAN OAK (<u>Lithocarpus densiflorus</u>). This is usually a large tree from 50-150' high. The leaves are oblong and noticeably parallel-veined on the underside. The slender catkins are from 2-4" long; the acorns mature the second year. The sharp-toothed leaves remain on the tree from 3 to 4 years. This tree is best developed in the red-wood belt of California, but is found as far north as the Umpqua River Valley in Oregon, and as far south as the Santa Ynez Mountains in the coastal belt of Calif.

GARRY and BLACK OAKS (page 51).

CANYON OAK (See page 29)

Hardw.
Conif.

MADRONE (<u>Arbutus menziesii</u>). This is an evergreen tree with glossy, leathery leaves that have finely serrate margins. It grows from 20 to over 100' tall, and has smooth, orange-red colored bark when it is new, dark brown and fissured into small scales when it is old. Flowers are white; fruits are red or orange berries. It is common from Monterey Co., Calif. north to British Columbia.

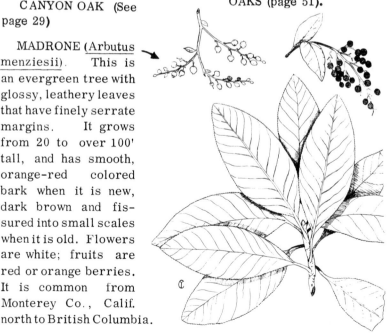

Hardw.
Str.Wd.

CALIFORNIA LAUREL or OREGON MYRTLE (Umbellularia californica). This is a dense-crowned, evergreen tree that grows from 20-60' high. It is usually found close to water, and is especially common in the alluvial flood plains along the rivers in northwestern California and southwestern Oregon, but is also found on shady hillsides and canyons. The fine wood is used in cabinet making and souvenirs. It is found as far south as San Diego Co. in California.

BIG-LEAF MAPLE (Acer macrophyllum). This broad-crowned tree grows from 30-100' tall, and has large five-lobed leaves that are from 4-10" broad. The small, greenish-yellow, bell-shaped flowers occur in corymbs or dense, cylindrical racemes. The winged fruits are hairy. This species occurs west of the crest of the Sierra Nevada throughout California and north along the west coast to Alaska.

Hardw
Str.Wc

*Hardw.
Conif.
Brush*

Castanopsis sempervirens

*Hardw.
Brush*

←— BUSH CHINQUAPIN (<u>Castanopsis sempervirens</u>). This evergreen, spreading shrub is from 2-8' high and has smooth brownish bark. The obtuse leaves are usually lanceolate-oblong and entire. The catkins are usually branched and the nutlets are borne in chestnut-like burs. This species is found in the coastal mountains of California and southern Oregon, but it is not found near the sea.

CHINQUAPIN (C. chrysophylla). A tree, 40–90' high with rusty, scaly branchlets and thick bark; leaves sharp-pointed. Sometimes a 3-15' shrub with clustered branches. Washington to Calif.

*Hardw.
Brush*

FIRE-WEED (<u>Epilobium angustifolium</u>) This perennial herb grows from 2-6' high; the leaves are entire, narrow and 4-6" long. The flowers are lilac-purple and often appear flame-like among the greenery. Fireweed is common in the moist, burnt-over areas in the north Coast Range of Calif. north to Alaska.

*Hardw.
Brush
Str.Wd.*

NORTHERN WILLOW-HERB (<u>E. adenocaulon</u>). 1-3 1/2' tall; flowers & flower stems sticky-hairy; petals white.

*Hardw.
Brush*

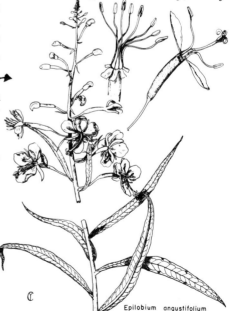

Epilobium angustifolium

COMMON ASTER (Aster chilensis). A common fall-blooming, white, bluish-red or bluish aster of the hills along the coast of N. Calif., growing 4-16" high; leaves usually hairy and the margins scaly.

Hardw.
Meadow
Brush
Wd.Pr.

YARROW (Achillea millefolium). This is a perennial herb with leaves pinnately divided into many fine segments. The flowers are borne in heads in a terminal corymb; the ray flowers are white and the disk flowers are yellow. Calif. coast north to Wash.

Hardw.
Brush

COMMON ANIMALS OF THE COASTAL HARDWOOD FOREST

Mammals

Most of the species found in the coniferous forests (page 44) also occur in this habitat, but particularly the following:

Chickaree, 66
Wood rat, 69
White-footed mouse, 71

Birds

Many coniferous forest species (page 44) are found here, but particularly the following:

Sharp-shinned hawk, 81
Blue grouse, 83

Birds (continued)

Ruffed grouse, 83
Band-tailed pigeon, 87
Belted kingfisher, 89
(along streams)
Downy woodpecker, 90
Yellow-bellied
sapsucker, 90
Flycatchers, 91
Bush-tit, 93
Dipper (by streams), 95
Varied thrush, 96
Hermit thrush, 96
Russet-backed thrush, 96
Kinglets, 96
Cedar waxwing, 97
Hutton vireo, 97
Warblers, 97-98

Evening grosbeak, 99
Oregon junco, 101
Fox sparrow, 102

Reptiles

Western fence lizard, 104
Western skink, 104
No. alligator lizard, 108
Foothill alligator lizard, 104
Rubber snake, 108
W. ring-necked snake, 107
Sharp-tailed snake, 107
Gopher snake, 109
Garter snakes, 107, 109

Amphibians

Most amphibians are found in this habitat, pages 109-115, except bull and spotted frogs.

WOODLAND-PRAIRIE

Throughout the coastal forest region grasslands occur. Some of these are natural, reflecting a difference in soils. Others are man-caused, the result of burning tree and shrub cover, and seeding the burned-over lands to grasses. In either case, the grasslands, known locally as prairies, support a different group of plants and a characteristic animal population.

Woodland-Prairie. Photo from files of U. S. Forest Service.

In the interior of the region, in the coastal mountains, are many areas in which the vegetation represents an intermixture of woodland and prairie. The woodland usually consists of stands of Garry Oak, sometimes with Black Oak in combination, and a variety of understory plants similar to those described in this book under Hardwood Forest (page 45) and Coastal Brushfields (p. 17). The oak stands vary from dense, close-canopy forests to an open savanna with scattered trees in a predominantly grassland area. The trees are all deciduous hardwoods, shedding their leaves in winter. They produce an abundance of acorns to provide food for a variety of animals. The grasses are of numerous kinds, of which three very common ones are described here.

Wd.Pr.
Oak

GARRY or OREGON WHITE OAK (Quercus garryana). This is a typical, round-topped oak tree that grows from 25-60' tall. The lobed leaves are from 3-6" long; the acorns are smooth and shiny and are important deer food in the fall of the year, while the Indians ground them up for acorn mush and bread. This oak is found all along the coast and inland to the base of the Cascades from British Columbia south to the Santa Cruz Mts. in California.

CALIFORNIA BLACK OAK (Q. kelloggii). This broad, round-topped tree grows from 30-80' high. The leaves are 3-lobed on each side and have from one to three bristle-tipped teeth. The acorns are deep-set in the cup. This oak occurs in the Coast Ranges as far north as southwestern Oregon, but does not occur near the sea. The acorns were ground into meal and leached of their poisonous tannin by pouring boiling water over the meal in a sand pit when the Indians prepared them for eating.

Wd.Pr.
Oak

Aesculus   californica

CALIFORNIA BUCKEYE
(<u>Aesculus</u> <u>californica</u>).

A shrubby tree, seldom over 30' high with a short smooth trunk and a flat open topped crown. The bark is light grey. Dark green leaflets 3-7" long are palmately arranged in groups of five on a petiole 4-5" in length. The flowers are pinkish white and grow in erect panicles. The fruit is pear shaped containing one seed that is about 2" in diameter.

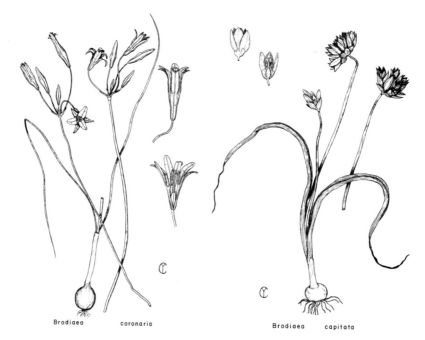

Brodiaea   coronaria

Brodiaea   capitata

WESTERN WILD OAT-GRASS (Danthonia californica).   2-3'
high, tufted perennial with spreading branches and usually purplish bracts surrounding the flowers.   North to British Columbia. *Wd.Pr.*

PACIFIC REED GRASS (Calamagrostis nutkaensis). 2 1/2 to
5' high, with very long stiff leaves, and a narrow panicle of pale
green or purplish spikelets.   From California to Alaska. *Wd.Pr.*

VELVET GRASS (Holcus lanatus). 1-2' high grass with very
distinctive covering of tiny, velvety hairs; narrow panicles of
purple-tinged spikelets.   Coast Ranges north to Washington. *Wd.Pr.*

← FIRE-CRACKER   PLANT
(Brodiaea ida-maia). The red *Wd.Pr.*
flowers tipped with yellow are
borne on a stalk that grows from
1-3' high. This attractive plant
grows near Oregon Caves, Oregon, and south through the Trin-
ity Mountains to Marin and Con-
tra Costa counties, California.
It is a plant of the hillsides in
open areas and is not found along
the ocean coast.

HARVEST BRODIAEA (B. *Wd.Pr.*
coronaria). Violet-purple flowers with long, droopy petals.

COMMON BRODIAEA (B. capitata).   Flower stem twisting, higher than leaves, and topped by dense
head of deep, violet purple (or rarely) reddish-purple flowers. All the
stamens have yellow anthers on top.

Wd.Pr.

COMMON MONKEY FLOWER
(Mimulus guttatus). 1-3' high herb,
found in moist areas from California N. to Alaska.   The flowers are

*Wd.Pr.
Meadow
Str.Wd.*

yellow with brown or purple dots in the flower throat, and are usually found in terminal racemes.

COMMON ANIMALS OF THE WOODLAND-PRAIRIE

Mammals
Black-tailed deer, 57
Black bear, 58
Mountain lion, 58
Bobcat, 59
Coyote, 59
Ring-tailed cat, 61
Badger, 64
Striped skunk, 64
Black-tailed jackrabbit, 65
Gray squirrel, 66
Chickaree, 66
Ground squirrel, 67
Pocket gopher, 67
Meadow vole, 71
White-footed mouse, 71
Moles, 73
Bats, 75

Birds
Turkey vulture, 81
Hawks, 81-82
Blue grouse, 83
Ruffed grouse, 83
Mountain quail, 83
California quail, 84
Band-tailed pigeon, 87
Mourning dove, 87
Most owls, 87-88
Pacific nighthawk, 88
Downy woodpecker, 90
Yellow-bellied sapsucker, 90
Red-shafted flicker, 90

Birds (continued)
Western wood pewee, 91
Raven, 93
Crow, 93
Bush-tit, 93
Mexican bluebird, 95
Kinglets, 96
Warblers, 98
Western tanager, 99
Black-headed grosbeak, 99
Purple finch, 99
Goldfinches, 100
Oregon junco, 101
Chipping sparrow, 101
Fox sparrow, 102

Reptiles
Western fence lizard, 104
Western skink, 104
Foothill alligator lizard, 104
Racer, 107
Western ring-necked snake, 107
Common king snake, 107
Gopher snake, 109
Western garter snake, 107
Common garter snake, 109
Western rattlesnake, 104

Amphibians
Rough-skinned newt, 114
Western red-bellied newt, 110
Eschscholtz's salamander, 113
Calif. slender salamander, 113
Western toad, 114

COMMON ANIMALS
MAMMALS

Mammals are those animals which have hair and give milk to their young. Most people call mammals simply "animals", but scientists apply this name to all living things except plants and viruses. Mammals are among the most complex of living things. The study of mammals is a profitable field for the amateur and systematic observation, combined with careful note-taking, can reveal new and important facts about many species.

Most mammals are not seen by most people, even when they live in large numbers near the edges of towns. This is partly because of their inconspicuous ways, their camouflaging coloring, and their nocturnal habits. The times when most mammals will be seen are early morning and late evening. Motorists will sometimes encounter them on roads at night, picked up briefly by the headlights of the cars.

The larger mammals are easy to identify, the smaller ones much more difficult. As a guide to identification we have compared them in the following pages to the size of four common and well-known mammals: House Mouse (3-4")

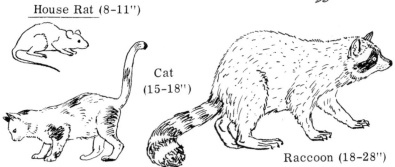

House Rat (8-11")

Cat
(15-18")

Raccoon (18-28")

In the mammal descriptions mouse + means slightly larger than a house mouse rat - means slightly smaller than a house rat, and so forth. Only the length of head and body, not the tail, is stated and compared.

By comparing sizes, looking at the pictures, reading the descriptions, and noting the type of habitat in which the mammal usually occurs, you will be able to name most of the species which you will encounter.

HOOFED MAMMALS
(All of Deer Family or Cervidae)

Meadow
Conif.
Hardw.
ROOSEVELT ELK (<u>Cervus</u> <u>canadensis</u>). Height 4 1/2 to 5'. This is one of the largest deer, with individuals weighing between 500 and 900 pounds. Antlers are massive, with a single main beam from which the tines (or points) branch forward, and are carried only by males. The antlers are shed in winter and re-grown again in the spring. During the growth period they are covered with velvety skin which is shed before the fall rutting season.

Elk were originally found throughout the region, but are now common only in coastal Oregon and Washington. In California a few herds remain at Prairie Creek and Maple Creek in Humboldt County and in the high mountains of Del Norte County. The Prairie Creek herd is usually near Highway 101 and may be seen by the auto traveller.

Elk are at their best in the fall rutting season, at which time the bulls form harems of cows and sometimes fight spectacular battles with rival males. Their principal habitat is dense forest and brush-fields particularly where interspersed with meadows or prairies.

COLUMBIAN BLACK-TAILED DEER (<u>Odocoileus</u> <u>hemionus</u>). *Meadow Wd.Pr. Brush Hardw. Conif.*
Height 3 to 3 1/2'. Tail black or deep brown on top, white underneath. The antlers of the adult males are usually forked, and, in older males, each tine often forks so that four or more points may occur. This is the only common small deer in the region.

This deer is common throughout the region and is often seen feeding in open glades or low brushfields, or in the woodland-prairie region. It is rare in dense forests. The breeding season in this species takes place in the fall and early winter, at which time the bucks lose much of their normal caution and may often be seen in prominent, open places. The small, spotted fawns are born in spring and early summer. Where food is abundant most does will have twin fawns. Sometimes as many as 80 to 100 of these deer have been recorded per square mile.

Formerly the WHITE-TAILED DEER (<u>O</u>. <u>virginianus</u>) was a common animal in central Oregon and Washington, but is now restricted to remnant herds near Roseburg, Oregon, and the mouth of the Columbia River in Washington. This deer is easily distinguished by its long, light brown tail, and by the antlers of the males, in which the tines are directed backward from a single main beam.

ORDER OF CARNIVORES (CARNIVORA)

Brush Wd.Pr. Hardw. Conif.

THE BEAR FAM. (Ursidae).

BLACK BEAR (Ursus americanus). Height 2-3'. With the extinction of the grizzly bear, the only remaining member of the bear family in the coast region is the black bear. This bear ranges in size from 200-500 pounds. The color varies from cinnamon brown to black, with most being black. Although sometimes dangerously friendly in the national parks, the bear is generally a wary animal, rarely seen, while common from Sonoma Co. N.

CAT FAM. (Felidae)

Brush Wd.Pr. Rocks

MOUNTAIN LION (Felis concolor). Length 3 1/2 to 4 1/2'. Otherwise known as the cougar or puma, this is the largest member of the cat family in our region, and the only one with a long tail. The color ranges from tawny to grayish, with the tip of the tail dark brown. Although widely distributed in the region, it is extremely shy and is rarely seen. It feeds mainly on deer and is a healthful preventer of overpopulation.

Bobcat

BOBCAT (Lynx rufus). See illustration on page 54. Raccoon
size.   The bobcat or wildcat is a common animal in the region, *Strand*
but its wary disposition prevents it from being often seen.   It *Wd.Pr.*
is nevertheless more likely to be abroad in the daytime than any
other large carnivore.   Twice the size of a large house cat, it
has a short, bobbed tail and tufted ears. It is often found stalk-
ing softly after such small mammals as the brush rabbit and
woodrat, or quietly lying in wait for them along a trail, but a
large bobcat can attack and kill a deer.   Like other carnivores,
the bobcat is an important natural check on numbers of smaller
mammals and should be protected except in areas where it is
actually known to be doing damage.

THE DOG   FAMILY (Canidae)

COYOTE (Can- *Most*
is latrans). Rac- *habitats*
coon + size. The
coyote somewhat
resembles   a
small   German
Shepherd   dog.
The gray fox is
much shorter in
the legs, also is
longer-bodied &
more   bushy-
tailed and with
more   striking
color markings.

The coyote is occasionally seen in the wild as it trots across
openings, or hunts mice in meadows. It is more often heard than
seen. A series of high-pitched yaps, howls and barks constitute
the coyote "song", heard most often at dusk or in early morning. It is a relative newcomer to this area, however, having become common only since the opening up of the country by the
fires and logging activities of the white men. Where livestock do
not occur the coyote is a colorful and useful member of the native fauna and should be protected. Usually, when a coyote runs,
the tail is held between the legs, whereas a dog generally car-
ries its tail higher when running.

Most habitats   GRAY FOX (Urocyon cinerioargenteus). Raccoon size. This fox is much less dog-like than the coyote and, in many of its postures and actions, resembles a cat.   It is a dainty, neat-looking animal with conspicuous, contrasting gray, black and reddish-brown markings. The long, bushy tail, held straight out when the animal is running, is distinctive.   Although both coyote and fox usually avoid heavy timber, the fox is found more commonly in brushy areas than is the coyote, and may be seen along road or trail sides or hunting mice in grassy fields.   The fox is much less noisy than the coyote, and its call usually consists of one or a few subdued barks or yaps. It is found as far north as southern Oregon.   The RED FOX (Vulpes fulva) occurs in the coastal region of northern Oregon and Washington. It may readily be distinguished by its usually yellowish to orange-red color, and very large and bushy tail. It is more typical of the high mountains.

THE RACCOON FAMILY (Procyonidae)

RACCOON (<u>Procyon</u> <u>lotor</u>). See illustration on page 56. The
black, robber mask and bushy, ringed tail serve to distinguish
the raccoon from most other mammals.   While the ring-tailed
cat has similar tail-markings, it is a much more slender animal, lacks the face mask, and has a much longer tail than the
raccoon.   Where the raccoon gives the appearance of a short,
bulky, relatively slow-moving animal, the ring-tailed cat is lithe,
slender and much more rapid and graceful in movement.   The
raccoon is frequently seen crossing or travelling down roads or
highways at night, and is a common highway casualty throughout
the region. It likes wooded areas near water, and its baby-like,
flat-heeled tracks are common in mud and sand.

Str.Wd.
Strand
Wd.Pr.
Hardw.

CACOMISTLE FAMILY (<u>Bassariscidae</u>)

RING-TAILED CAT (<u>Bassariscus</u> <u>astutus</u>).   House cat size
with long, ringed tail, large ears and eyes. It is primarily an
animal of warmer, drier regions to the south and west, but is
fairly numerous in our region in northern California and southern Oregon.   It is almost entirely nocturnal and is rarely seen,
even in areas where it is relatively common. It is a quiet hun-
ter of small rodents, which it stalks in the narrow, brushy trails.

Brush

Conif.

THE WEASEL FAMILY
(Mustelidae)

MARTEN (Martes americana). House cat -. This slender, graceful animal has a bushy, somewhat squirrel-like tail, cat-like ears and fur that is golden-brown in color. Probably Olympic National Park in Washington has the greatest number of martens of any place in the region. Normally it is an animal of the higher mountains, but it is also present in the densely-forested country along the coast. It hunts squirrels in the trees.

Conif.

FISHER (Martes pennanti). House cat +. Even more rare and less likely to be seen than the marten is the fisher. Like the marten it probably reaches greatest abundance in the Olympic Peninsula, but is found occasionally in the wilder areas. The fisher is larger than the marten, and is darker in color, ranging from brownish-gray to almost black. Like the marten it feeds mainly on squirrels.

*Water
Marsh
Conif.
Hardw.
Strand*

MINK (Mustela vison). House cat -. The mink is about the size of the marten, but has much smaller ears and is dark-brown in color. Unlike the marten and fisher, the mink is fairly common in the coastal region. It is largely confined to the vicinity of streams, lake and ocean margins. It is an expert swimmer.

RIVER OTTER (Lutra canadensis). Raccoon size. The otter somewhat resembles a small seal, but with legs and long tail. The tail, thick at the base and tapering to a point, is used as a rudder in swimming. The fur is short and soft; the ears short and inconspicuous; and the feet webbed. All of these help in swimming and the catching of fish, at which it is

Water Marsh Str.Wd.

expert. Otters are playful animals and often make clay slides on the banks for splashing into the water. Found throughout region.

LONG-TAILED WEASEL (Mustela frenata). Rat size. This is the most common of the weasel-like animals, and is larger than the short-tailed weasel, as well as lacking the white line which runs down the inside of the hind leg in the latter species. It is generally brown in color, but with whitish on forehead and belly,

Brush Wd.-Pr. Hardw. Rocks

though the whole body may change to white in winter if there is heavy snowfall. It does not do so in most of the coastal region. It is not rat-like in appearance, and has a 5-6" long tail. When moving it has an undulating, almost snake-like appearance. It often stands with back arched. It twists and turns very swiftly as it follows down a mouse or rabbit.

SHORT-TAILED WEASEL (Mustela erminea). Rat -. Much smaller and shorter-tailed that the long-tailed weasel and with a white line on the inside of the hind leg. It is also known as the ermine and becomes white in snowy areas in winter; usually brown with white belly.

Most habitats

BADGER (<u>Taxidea</u> <u>taxus</u>). Raccoon size. The short legs, heavy, wide body, and distinctive black and white markings on the face make the badger difficult to mistake for any other animal. Its strongly-developed, digging claws and feet, which make efficient shovels, help it dig rapidly into the ground after burrowing animals, such as ground squirrels, on which it feeds. It occurs as far north as Eureka on the coast.

SPOTTED SKUNK (<u>Spilogale putorius</u>). Rat size. The broken, white lines and the white-tipped tail easily distinguish this skunk from the larger striped skunk. It feeds on insects, small animals & plants.

STRIPED SKUNK (<u>Mephitis</u> <u>mephitis</u>). Cat size. The two broad white stripes down the back are distinctive. Both skunks stamp their feet and spread their tail hairs stiffly when alarmed, and throw a very strong-smelling and irritating scent when attacked. This species also eats omnivorously. It is more commonly seen on roads at night and in more open country.

HARE AND PIKA ORDER (LAGOMORPHA)

HARE FAM. (Leporidae)

BLACK-TAILED JACK-RABBIT (Lepus californicus). Cat + size. This is an animal of the open country which enters the coastal area only where natural or man-made clearings are found. It extends northward into Oregon, but is found there only in inland valleys. It does not use burrows.

Wd.Pr.
Strand
Op.Brush
Meadow

SNOWSHOE HARE (Lepus americanus). Cat size. The smaller size, shorter legs and ears and more compact body distinguish this animal from the black-tailed jack-rabbit. Its larger size, and darker, more rusty brown color serve to distinguish it from the brush rabbit. From south Oregon north. It usually turns white if much snow.

Brush
Hardw.
Conif.

BRUSH RABBIT (Sylvilagus bachmani). Rat + size. Unlike the two hares, the brush rabbit is primarily an animal of the coastal forest and brush. It differs from the cottontail of inland regions by its darker color, less white on the tail, and its shorter ears. It does not extend north of the Columbia River, and is always found close to dense cover.

Brush

Oak
Hardw.
Conif.

SQUIRREL FAM (Sciuridae)

WESTERN GRAY SQUIR-
REL (Sciurus griseus). A
rat + size, all gray squirrel,
with a long, bushy tail and
conspicuous white under-
parts. The Calif. ground
squirrel lacks the bushy tail
and has dark shoulders. The
chickaree is darker and is
more reddish. The gray
squirrel lives mostly inland.

Conif
Hardw.
Oak

CHICKAREE (Tamiascurus
douglasii). Rat size. The
chickaree or Douglas Squirrel
is a small, reddish, highly active and noisy tree dweller,
feeding on the seeds of douglas
fir and other conifers. Its
presence may be detected by
finding piles of remnant fir
cones dropped below feeding
stations. It is found all through
the region. Feeds on nuts.

Conif.

NORTHERN FLYING SQUIR-
REL (Glaucomys sabrinus). It
is rat - The conspicuous
flap of skin that connects the
wrist and ankle of this animal,
and serves as a gliding wing,
distinguishes it from any other.
The large eyes are proof of its
nocturnal nature, for it is rarely active except at night. It is
chestnut-brown in color. It can
glide 50 yards or more from a
branch or trunk to a lower one.
Feeds on eggs, insects & nuts.

TOWNSEND CHIPMUNK (Eutamias townsendi). Rat -. This characteristic animal of the coastal forest is larger and darker in color than most other chipmunks. Its stripes on the head distinguish it from the somewhat similar Golden-mantled Ground Squirrel (Citellus lateralis), which may enter the region in the drier, interior mt. areas. The similar-appearing SONOMA CHIPMUNK (Eutamias sonomae) occurs from Del Norte Co. south to the San Francisco Bay. It is smaller and tends to inhabit drier areas. Both chipmunks do little tree climbing, living mainly on ground.

Conif. Brush Hardw. Rocks

Op.Brush Rocks

CALIFORNIA GROUND SQUIRREL (Citellus beecheyi). Rat size. Otherwise known as Douglas ground squirrel or Beechey, this animal is familiar in the drier grasslands of California and Oregon, and is, therefore, not typical of our region. It is occasionally seen climbing oak trees, but quickly runs down when frightened and not up, as does the gray squirrel. It also has a chunkier body and a browner coat, with dark shoulder colors, and a shorter, less bushy tail. Most often it is seen sitting bolt upright at the entrance to is burrow, which stays open, unlike the gopher's. It is common in colonies whose members call back and forth.

Grass Oak Wd.Pr. Rocks

POCKET GOPHER (Thomomys bottae and other species). There are several species of pocket gopher within the coastal forest region. Rat - . The two principal ones are the Valley Pocket Gopher (T. bottae) & the Northern Pocket Gopher (T. talpoides), the first being found in California and the

Grass Brush Wd.-Pr.

second in Oregon and Washington. The pocket gopher is rarely seen above ground, and usually shows its presence by a circular pile of freshly-dug earth pushed out from the underground tunnel. Moles do this too, but mole burrows usually show narrow ridges of earth extending for several feet or more. The usually brown-colored gopher has visible slits which mark the openings into its external cheek pouches, short ears, and a naked, short, blunt tail.

Conifer
Brush
Meadow

APLODONTIA FAM.
(Aplodontidae)

MOUNTAIN BEAVER (Aplodontia rufa). Cat size. Few animals are as badly misnamed as this, which is not a beaver, and does not necessarily dwell in mountains. It looks like a large, dark-brown, tail-less gopher, and digs gopher-like holes below the surface of the ground, but leaves no dirt-piles at the entrance-ways. Feeds on plants and has colonies.

BEAVER FAMILY (Castoridae)

BEAVER (Castor canadensis). Raccoon size. This rodent is almost entirely aquatic and is a powerful swimmer, but slow and clumsy on land. Its large size and broad, flat tail are distinctive. It cuts down willows, alders and cottonwoods for food, and builds dams in the smaller streams, but the coastal form rarely builds the big lodges that the beavers in the mountains construct.

Water
Marsh
Hardw.

Instead it lives in burrows dug in the banks, and in the larger rivers dams are not constructed.   The chisel-like teeth of the beaver leave characteristic marks on the felled hardwood trees along the stream banks and show the presence of the animals. Branches and sections of the trunks are often stored underwater.

NATIVE RATS AND MICE FAMILY (Cricetidae)

MUSKRAT (Ondatra zibeth- ica). Rat +.   The tail of the muskrat is its most distinctive feature, being long, hairless and strongly flattened from side to side.   The tail of the beaver is flattened from top to bottom. The fur is brown. Large, cone-shaped lodges, made of piles of rushes, cat- tails and other aquatic vegeta- tion, are sure signs of musk- rats, but, in some areas, they in- habit holes in banks. Found from Coos Co., Ore., N. into Wash.

Marsh Water

WOOD RAT (Neotoma cinerea and N. fuscipes). In Washington the bushy- tailed woodrat (N. ciner- ea), and in California, the dusky-footed wood rat (N. fuscipes) are the most common species. Both occur in Oregon.

Conif. Brush Oak Hardw.

The bushy-tailed wood rat has a squirrel-like tail and whitish hind feet, while the dusky-footed wood rat has a short-haired tail and dark feet.   Both wood rats, otherwise known as pack rats, are attractive rodents, with large eyes and ears, and none of the repulsive features of the house rat.   Wood rat lodges are com- monly cone-shaped piles of short sticks which cover and conceal the nests, feeding chambers, and runways.   The rats frequently signal to each other by rattling their tails against dry leaves, but, on the whole, are comparatively solitary animals.   They feed mainly on fruits and nuts, and like to collect bright objects.

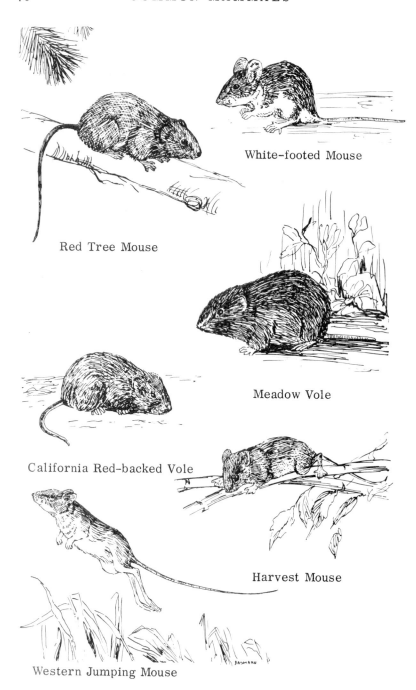

White-footed Mouse

Red Tree Mouse

Meadow Vole

California Red-backed Vole

Harvest Mouse

Western Jumping Mouse

WHITE-FOOTED MOUSE (Peromyscus maniculatus). Mouse size.   A large-eared, large-eyed mouse with a long tail, but shorter than head and body combined.   The contrasting gray or brownish upperparts, and the clear white underparts are distinctive. It is secretive, coming out mainly at night, and sometimes enters houses. It is more attractive than the brown house mouse.

Most habitats

RED TREE MOUSE (Phenacomys longicaudus). Mouse size. This is a small, vole-like mouse with short ears, but it differs from the true voles by its longer tail, and by living mainly in the tops of coniferous trees, mainly Douglas and lowland firs, where it builds a large nest, a foot or more in diameter,   among   the branches. It is more reddish in color than the red-backed vole and has a contrasting blackish tail. It is confined to the coastal strip from north-central Oregon to central California.

Conif.

MEADOW VOLE (Microtus californicus and related species). Mouse +.   There are four or more related   species in our region, too closely alike to be separated save by an expert. All are short-tailed,   short-eared   mice that dwell in tall, dense grasslands where their runway systems form an intricate   network both above and below ground. Color brownish-gray.

Wd.Pr. Marsh

CALIFORNIA RED-BACKED VOLE (Clethrionomys californicus). Mouse size. Dark chestnut-brown in color, with a relatively short tail and ears. The reddish back distinguishes it from the meadow vole, as does its forest floor habitat.

Conif.

HARVEST MOUSE (Reithrodontomys megalotis).   Mouse -. This species resembles a small, white-footed mouse, but the front incisor teeth have distinct, vertical grooves, which the white-footed mouse does not have. It is also more characteristic of grassy areas than is the white-footed mouse.

Wd.-Pr. Strand

JUMPING MOUSE FAMILY (Zapodidae)

WESTERN JUMPING MOUSE (Zapus princeps). Mouse size. The extremely long tail and large hind feet distinguish this mouse from other species in the region. The ears are smaller than the white-footed mouse. It is essentially a tri-colored mouse with a yellow side stripe separating the brown back from the whitish belly area.   It is often seen at night, jumping kangaroo-like in the moonlight across roads or through damp meadows.   These mice usually hibernate during the winter.

Meadow Marsh

Pacific Water Shrew

Trowbridge Shrew

Shrew Mole

Townsend Mole

ORDER OF INSECTIVORES (INSECTIVORA)

THE SHREW FAMILY (Soricidae)

PACIFIC WATER SHREW (Sorex bendirei). Mouse size. All shrews are mouse-like animals, from which they differ external- *Water* ly in their smaller size, long-pointed nose, ear-less appearance *Marsh* and small, bead-like eyes. They usually hide themselves secretively when they sense the footsteps of a larger animal or a man and come out mainly at night. The water shrew differs from others in this region in having a row of stiff, bristle-like swimming hairs on the sides of the hind feet. The Northern Water Shrew(S. palustris) occurs in this region only in northern Washington. The northern species prefers cold mountain streams whereas the Pacific Water Shrew is more at home in slow streams, but both are expert swimmers and hunters of water insects and larvae.

TROWBRIDGE SHREW (S. trowbridgei). Mouse -. Other than water shrews there are 5 species of shrews in our region. Of the *Marsh* group the Trowbridge and Vagrant Shrews (S. vagrans) are the *Conif.* more abundant, with the former common among the coniferous *Hardw.* forests and the latter preferring marshes, bogs and meadows (as *Str.Wd.* does the Masked Shrew of northern Washington, S. cinereus). Two other species, the Pacific Shrew (S. pacificus) and the small Dusky Shrew (S. obscurus) occur mainly among the conifers. All these animals are brown in color & hunt insects, worms & mice by nose.

THE MOLE FAMILY (Talpidae)

SHREW-MOLE (Neurotrichus gibbsi). Mouse size. This animal does not burrow like the true moles, but forms an intricate network of runways deep in the forest litter. It resembles a *Conif.* large shrew, but differs in having a thick and heavy tail with stiff *Marsh* black hairs, unlike the mouse-like tail of a shrew. It differs *Str.Wd.* from the mole in having long, narrow, walking feet.

TOWNSEND MOLE (Scapanus townsendi). Rat -. Moles are rarely seen, dwelling as they do in either deep or close-to-the-surface burrows. The surface burrows appear as conspicuous *Wd.Pr.* ridges of dirt, often many yards long. Moles have broad, strong- *Hardw.* clawed, digging feet, little suited for above-ground walks. Their *Meadow* eyes are very tiny and they lack external ears. The fur is velvety soft and dark brown or black in color. The California Mole (S. latimanus) and the Pacific Mole (S. orarius) are similar.

ORDER OF BATS (CHIROPTERA)

PLAIN-NOSED BAT FAMILY (Vespertilionidae)

Water
Marsh
Wd.Pr.
Brush

LITTLE BROWN BAT (Myotis lucifugus). Wingspread 8-10". The little brown bat is a typical example of the Myotis or mouse-eared group of bats, of which 7 species occur in this region, all difficult to recognize separately save by an expert. But all are among the smallest bats in the region and have mouse-like snouts, tail membranes that are not furred on the top side, and are generally brown in color. Like most bats, they roost by day in caves, buildings or hollow trees, hanging head downward. In the evening they appear usually later than some of the larger bats, flying low and erratically, while they chase insects, often over water.

Hardw.
Conif.
Meadow

BIG BROWN BAT (Eptesicus fuscus). Wingspread 13". This looks like a large, plain-snouted Myotis, but it lacks fur on the tail membrane and has relatively small ears. It is usually the first bat out in the evening, and is a rapid flier, without erratic or jerky flight. Usually only 1 or 2 are present hunting together.

Hardw.
Conif.
Meadow

SILVER-HAIRED BAT (Lasionycteris noctivagans). Wingspread 12". This bat is dark brown in color with silvery hair in the middle of the back. It is the darkest colored bat in the region, and the tail membrane is furred only on the basal half. The ears are relatively short. It is an early evening flier along with the Big Brown Bat, but usually flies higher and more erratically, and more often in larger numbers.

Hardw.
Conif.
Meadow

HOARY BAT (Lasiurus cinereus). Wingspread 16". This is the largest bat in the region, and a large, short-eared bat appearing late in the evening will usually be this species. White-tipped hairs over the body give a silvery color. Tail membrane furred all over.

Most
habitats

WESTERN BIG-EARED BAT (Corynorhinus rafinesque) and PALLID BAT (Antrozous pallidus). Wingspreads 12" and 14". These bats may be distinguished from others by their large ears, which are usually over 1" in length. The big-eared bat has the ears joined together over the forehead (as illustrated), while the pallid bat has its ears separated, and is much paler in color. The big-eared bat has two large lumps on its nose; the pallid bat does not have these. The big-eared bat is the more common in this region, while the pallid bat enters the southern part of the region but does not occur in coastal Washington. Both are cave-dwellers.

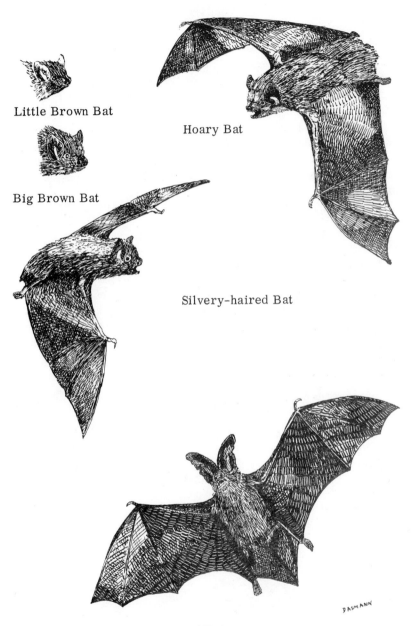

Little Brown Bat

Hoary Bat

Big Brown Bat

Silvery-haired Bat

Western Big-eared Bat

BIRDS

The following pages will help to familiarize the reader with the common birds of this region. It would be difficult in a book of this size to describe even half of the several hundred species which occur in the coastal forest belt. From each major family or order of birds a few of the species most common in, or most characteristic of, the coastal region have been selected. These are the ones that are most likely to be observed. If the characteristics of these species are learned, it will aid in the identification of the other members of the families to which they belong. In many instances only the male bird is illustrated or described. The female will often be seen in the same vicinity as the male, and in most instances will be similar in shape and size, but somewhat less strikingly colored.

Many of the species illustrated are seasonal visitors, abundant at one season, but absent at others, while other birds are permanent residents. As you read the descriptions, you will be helped greatly in identifying the birds by carefully noting the season of the year and the habitats in which each species is commonly found. However, it should be remembered that habitat and seasonal preferences are not always strictly observed and that exceptions sometimes occur to prove the rule.

Size descriptions are given by comparison with the following commonly known birds:

Warbler (4-5")

Sparrow (5-6 1/2")

Robin (8-10")

Dove (11-13")

Crow (18-24")

Mallard (20-28")

ORDER GAVIIFORMES - LOONS

Loons are capable divers, remaining submerged for long periods. They are stream-lined, swimming low in water, duck-size or larger, & with a stout, pointed bill. The similar-looking cormorants are blacker with a longer neck and tail, and more rapid flight.

PACIFIC LOON (Gavia arctica). Mallard size. Common to abundant winter visitor. Straight bill and dark color distinguish it *Water* from the Red-throated Loon (G. stellata), which has a slightly upturned bill. Smaller size and thinner bill distinguish it from the Common Loon (G. immer). Feeds on fish, usually in salt water.

ORDER COLYMBIFORMES - GREBES

Grebes are usually seen swimming or diving in ponds, lagoons and lakes. They are smaller than ducks, with a slender neck, pointed bill and small head. Their feet are lobed rather than webbed as in ducks.

HORNED GREBE (Colymbus auritus). Dove size. The dark

back and top of head contrast *Water* sharply with the white underparts. The slender neck, small head, and sharp-pointed bill are distinctive. Salt water.

PIED-BILLED GREBE (Podilymbus podiceps). Dove size. *Water* The brownish color and chickken-like, marked bill are distinctive. Resident in ponds.

ORDER CICONIIFORMES - HERONS

Long-legged, long-necked wading birds, most frequently seen standing along edges of marshes or ponds; commonly, but incorrectly, called "cranes". Fly with head pulled back and neck in S-shape (cranes straight).

Marsh
Water
Strand
Meadow

GREAT BLUE HERON (Ardea herodias). About 4' high. Common resident throughout region. The long legs, long neck, blue-gray color, and long, sharp-pointed bill are distinctive.

Marsh
Water

AMERICAN EGRET (Casmerodius albus). Slightly smaller than blue heron. A common resident, and a large, all white bird with long neck and long legs. Differs from Snowy Egret (C. thula), which is rare in this region, by larger size and yellow bill. Snowy has black bill. Calif. & S. Ore.

Water
Marsh

BLACK-CROWNED NIGHT HERON (Nycticorax nycticorax). Crow size plus. A medium-sized heron with black back and whitish under parts. The contrasting black and white on head is distinctive. Commonly seen with neck retracted, giving a large-headed, short-legged, neckless appearance.

Marsh

The immature birds resemble the plain brownish-streaky American Bittern (Botaurus lentiginosus), which is rare in the region, but they differ in gray general color & lack of black wing tips. Resident in Calif., summering to north. Often in salt water.

ORDER ANSERIFORMES - DUCKS, GEESE, AND SWANS

BLACK BRANT (Branta berni-cla). Mallard size and +. Medium-sized goose with black head, neck and breast. Small white patch on neck. The related Canada Goose (B. canadensis) has a white patch on the cheek & light-colored breast. The brant largely depends on eelgrass for food in winter. Winter visitor, bay shore.

Marsh Water

MALLARD (Anas platyrhynchos). The males are distinctively green-headed with white neck ring. Both sexes have yellowish bills and wing patches bordered with white. Female mottled brown. A common resident.

Marsh Water

E.D.

CANVAS-BACK (Aythya valisineria). Mallard size. Common in winter. Males appear white with reddish head and neck. Has flat profile with forehead sloping strongly back from bill, which distinguishes it from similar red-head duck.

Marsh Water

SPOONBILL or SHOVELLER (Spatula clypeata). Mallard -. A winter visitor. The males appear largely black and white with large pale blue wing patch & large, flattened spoonlike bill. Reddish belly & sides.

Marsh Water

Marsh Water

LESSER SCAUP (<u>Aythya</u> <u>affinis</u>). Mallard -. The high forehead is distinctive; appears blackish on head, breast and tail; white to gray on wings and underbelly. Females less brightly marked and with white area at base of bill. Abundant winter visitor on bays, estuaries and adjoining marshes.

Marsh Water

AMERICAN MERGANSER (<u>Mergus</u> <u>merganser</u>). Mallard size. Mergansers differ from other ducks in having slender bills with toothed edges. They feed on fish. Males of this species are largely white, with black head and back, and an orange bill; females have crested red-brown heads & red bills. Resident.

Marsh Water

RUDDY DUCK (<u>Oxyura</u> <u>jamaicensis</u>). Mallard -. One of the smaller ducks. White cheeks, dark crown, and <u>up-turned, spiny tail</u> feathers are distinctive. It dives almost as readily and frequently as do loons and grebes. Resident, on ponds, lakes and coastal bays.

Marsh Water

BALDPATE (<u>Mareca</u> <u>americana</u>). Not illustrated. The male is quite distinctive, with a gray head topped by a white crown, a glossy-green patch on the side of the head being sometimes visible in good light; the body appears mainly brownish. The female is more reddish-brown, with gray neck and head. In flight both sexes can be recognized by the large white patch that shows clearly on the front edge of the wing. Mainly winter visitor.

Marsh Water

PINTAIL (<u>Dafila</u> <u>acuta</u>). A long slender neck, a long pointed tail, a white line on neck, and white belly mark the male. Res.

ORDER FALCONIFORMES
HAWK-LIKE BIRDS

TURKEY VUL-TURE (Cathartes aura**).** Crow size and +. 6' wing spread. Common in summer; most often seen soaring with wings lifted at an angle above horizontal, while eagles hold wings *Strand Wd.Pr. Rocks Brush* horizontal from body. The black color combined with the naked, reddish head and narrow tail are distinctive. Feeds on carrion.

SHARP-SHINNED HAWK (Accipiter striatus**).** Dove size. The Accipiter hawks have short, rounded wings, and a long tail. This is the smallest & commonest of 3 species in the region, and has a *Conif. Hardw. Wd.Pr. Brush* square-ended tail. The Cooper Hawk (A. cooperi) is larger than the sharp-shin, but is best distinguished by the rounded end to the tail. The Goshawk (Astur atricapillus) is nearly twice the size of the Cooper & lighter gray. All eat birds.

RED-TAILED HAWK (Buteo jamaicensis**).** Crow size and +. The Buteo hawks have short tails, usually spread fanlike in flight, and long, blunt-ended wings. Red-topped tail distinctive. Resident. *Strand Wd.-Pr. Meadow*

MARSH HAWK (<u>Circus</u> <u>cyaneus</u>).

Marsh
Meadow
Wd.Pr.

Crow size. Long, rounded wings combined with a long, square-ended tail and <u>a conspicuous white rump patch</u> serve to distinguish this species. The old males are pale grey, almost white; the females brownish.

Low flight. Common in summer in north; resident in California.

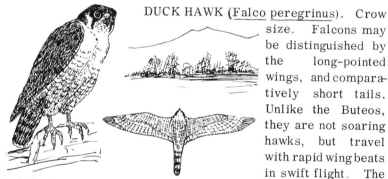

DUCK HAWK (<u>Falco</u> peregrinus). Crow

Rocks
Marsh
Water
Strand

size. Falcons may be distinguished by the long-pointed wings, and comparatively short tails. Unlike the Buteos, they are not soaring hawks, but travel with rapid wing beats in swift flight. The duck hawk, or Peregrine Falcon, is the largest falcon in the region, and is distinguished by its dark, nearly black color above, and the <u>dark, moustache pattern on its face</u>. Resident; hunts mainly the large birds, such as ducks; very fast flight.

SPARROW HAWK (<u>Falco</u> sparverius). Robin +. The spar-

Strand
Meadow
Wd.Pr.

row hawk or kestrel is the smallest American falcon. It is distinguished by the <u>bright, reddish-brown color of the tail</u>, and by its tendency to hover with rapid wing beats, while hunting mice & grasshoppers. Call a rapid "killy-killy-killy!" Often lights on telephone wires.

E.D.

ORDER GALLIFORMES - CHICKEN-LIKE BIRDS

BLUE GROUSE (<u>Dendragapus</u> <u>obscurus</u>). Crow size and ÷. A large, dark, blue-gray, chicken-like bird, with a <u>light band at the tip of its tail</u>. Often seen on the ground, or high in coniferous trees. The dull, muffled, hooting call of the blue grouse is often heard in the spring. Resident.

Conif.
Hardw.
Wd.Pr.

RUFFED GROUSE (<u>Bonasa umbellus</u>). Crow size & +. The uncommon ruffed grouse is distinguished from the above species by its red-brown color, and the <u>black band near the tip of the tail</u>. The drumming call of the male is distinctive. From Mendocino Co. north into British Columbia; most common in burnt-over land.

Brush
Hardw
Conif.

MOUNTAIN QUAIL (<u>Oreortyx picta</u>). Dove size & +. Resident and locally common. Distinguished by bright chestnut and blue-gray color, white barring on flanks, and <u>long, straight plume on the head</u>. Usually found in small flocks, called coveys, and characteristic of more mountainous areas. Gives a loud, mellow "wook" or "t-wook" cry.

Brush
Wd.Pr
Hardw
Conif.

Brush
Wd.-Pr.

CALIFORNIA QUAIL (Lo-phortyx californica). Dove size. Smaller than mountain quail, less brightly colored, & with short, forward-curving head plume. Common resident from southern Oregon south; found in large or small coveys. Gives "quer-ca-go!" cry; female calls young with "pt-pt-pt!"

ORDER GRUIFORMES - CRANES, RAILS, ETC.

Water
Marsh
Meadow

AMERICAN COOT (Ful-ica americana). Mallard -. This duck-like bird with a whitish, chicken-like bill is slate gray to black   color all over.   It is commonly seen swimming with head moving back and forth; a slow, clumsy flier. Per-manent resident, abundant, often in large flocks.

ORDER CHARADRIIFORMES - SHORE BIRDS & GULLS

The shore birds include the sandpipers, plovers, gulls, terns and their relatives. They are characteristically birds of the sandy beaches, mud flats, or rocky ocean shores. At least 45 species occur within this region, including many forms difficult for the beginner to distinguish. Of these we have illustrated only six representative species.

Strand
Marsh
Water
Meadow

KILLDEER (Charadrius vo-ciferus). Robin size. This plover is a common resident of the region. The even, dark-brown colored upper-parts, and the two dark breast bands are distinctive, as is the loud, sharp "ki-deer" or "ki-dee" call. Often nests on river bars.

WILSON'S SNIPE (Capella gallinago). Robin +. The long slender bill, color pattern and size distinguish the "Jack snipe". When alarmed, it flies off in a sharp and zig-zagging flight. It probes in mud for insect larvae, etc. Resident.

Water Marsh Meadow

LONG-BILLED CURLEW (Numenius americanus). Crow +. Bill is 5-7" long. Curlews are known by their long, slender, strongly downcurved bills. Two species occur in this region, of which this is the larger. Migrant and winter visitor.

Water Marsh Strand

WILLET (Catoptrophorus semipalmatus). Dove +. The relatively large size, long straight bill, and even brownish-gray color are distinctive when the bird is on the ground. In flight, a striking black and white wing pattern is displayed. The legs are blue-gray in color. Common migrant and wintering bird on the beaches. Gives a loud "Kay-ti!" call in winter.

Water Strand

DOWITCHER (Limno-
dromus griseus).   Dove
size.   A squat, long-
billed sandpiper, with
legs much shorter than
the willet. Much heavier
in build than the Wilson's
snipe.   The lower back
and tail are white. Com-
mon migrant in fall and
winter.   Call, a thin
"kleeek", often repeated.

Marsh
Water
Strand

Water
Strand
Bldg.

WESTERN   GULL
(Larus occidentalis). Size
of crow and +.   Of the
10 species of gulls which
occur in fair numbers
within this region, the
Western may be recog-
nized as one of the larger,
with a dark, almost black
back, a white head, and
white underparts. Other
E.D. gulls of similar size are
light gray above. This is the only common resident gull over all
the region, found mainly on or near salt water.

GLAUCOUS-WINGED GULL (Larus glaucescens).   Crow +.
Equal in size to the western Gull, but lacking in black coloring.

Water
Strand
Bldg.

Pale gray above, white
below, with   wing-tips
marked with gray rather
than black.   Feet pink.
All gulls are confusing
when   immature, being
variously marked with
gray or brown. The white
underparts and head may
not appear until the third
year. Breeds along Wash.
coast; winters all region.

ORDER COLUMBIFORMES - PIGEON-LIKE BIRDS

BAND-TAILED PIGEON (Columba fasciata). Dove +. *Oak Hardw. Conif.* Similar in size to the domestic pigeon. Tail fan-like, and with broad pale band near tip. White crescent on nape of neck. General color is blue-gray. Travels in flocks of varying size, and gives owl-like "whoo-ooo-ooo" cry. Summer resident.

MOURNING DOVE (Zenaidura macroura). Smaller than the pigeon, more slim in build, and with a long, pointed tail. Often solitary, or in pairs, but gathering in larger aggregations during migration. The tail feathers flash white in flight and the wings whistle. A mournful "coo-coo-coo" cry is heard.

Wd.Pr. Hardw. Str.Wd.

ORDER STRIGIFORMES - OWLS

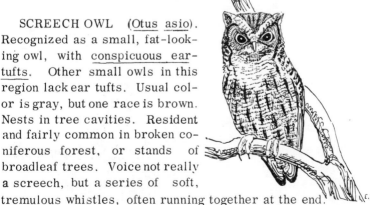

SCREECH OWL (Otus asio). Recognized as a small, fat-looking owl, with conspicuous ear-tufts. Other small owls in this region lack ear tufts. Usual color is gray, but one race is brown. Nests in tree cavities. Resident and fairly common in broken coniferous forest, or stands of broadleaf trees. Voice not really a screech, but a series of soft, tremulous whistles, often running together at the end.

Conif. Brush Hardw. Wd.Pr.

Wd.Pr.
Hardw.
Brush
Conif.

GREAT HORNED OWL (Bubo virginianus). Crow +. A large owl with conspicuous horn-like ear tufts. In flight
all owls differ from hawks by large-headed
neckless appearance, and soft, noiseless
wing beats. The horned owl is larger
and more heavily bodied than the red-
tailed hawk, and is likely to be seen only
at dusk or early morning. A fairly common resident; an active killer of harmful
rodents and rabbits. Large, grayish pel-
lets at the base of a tree, each made up
of hair and bones, tell of the owl's presence and the food it eats. A deep "hoo hoo!"

SPOTTED
OWL (Strix occidentalis). Crow size.
A large, earless owl with heavily spotted
and barred underparts. Instead of the
deep hoot of the horned owl, this bird
has a high-pitched "hoo-whoowhoo-ooo"
that may sound like a dog barking. Resident and fairly common in the region.

Conif.
Hardw.

ORDER CAPRIMULGIFORMES
NIGHTHAWKS & RELATIVES

PACIFIC NIGHTHAWK (Chordeiles minor). Robin size. Most
often seen flying at dusk over open areas. Flight erratic, as it

Wd.Pr.

darts after insects. Wings narrow, pointed, marked with conspicuous white spot near the tip.
Throat white, underparts and
tail barred. Nighthawks have
weak legs, and rest on ground
or broad limbs when in flight.
A loud "peent" call advertises
its presence. Roosts in open
coniferous forest; flies over open
country catching insects, generally in the evening. A summer
resident.

ORDER APODIFORMES - SWIFTS & HUMMINGBIRDS

VAUX SWIFT (Chaetura vauxi). Warbler size. This is a small, cigar-shaped bird with long, slightly curved, stiff wings. Wings more stiff and slender than those of swallows. General color dark; tail inconspicuous. A summer visitor, flying high in the air to catch insects, roosting at night in high trees.

Conif.
Hardw.
Meadow

RUFOUS HUMMINGBIRD (Selasphorus rufus). Warbler -. Hummingbirds are the smallest of birds, marked with irridescent colors, and characterized by a wing beat so rapid that the wings are almost invisible. Often seen hovering in front of flowers and probing them with a long, tube-like bill. 2 species occur commonly in this region. The rufous is the only one with a bright, red-brown back; the Allen Hummingbird (S. alleni) has a green back and is found from Humboldt Co. S. Males of both have bright, reddish-orange throats. The Anna (Calypte anna) of S.F. Bay has red throat.

Brush
Cultiv.

Conif.
Brush
Oak

ORDER CORACIIFORMES
KINGFISHERS, ETC.

BELTED KINGFISHER (Megaceryle alcyon). Robin +. The blue-gray color, large head, stout bill, and uneven crest serve to distinguish this bird. Gives a rattling call in flight; feeds on small fish.

Water
Str.Wd.
Cultiv.

ORDER PICIFORMES - WOODPECKERS

Hardw.
Oak
Str.Wd.
Conif.

DOWNY WOODPECKER (<u>Dendrocopus</u> <u>pubescens</u>). Sparrow +. The smallest woodpecker in the region. The white back, spot of red on black and white head, and small, weak bill distinguish it from others. The similar <u>Hairy Woodpecker</u> (<u>D</u>. <u>villosus</u>) is larger and has a stronger bill. The downy often clings to branches and works around them, often upside down, seeking insects.

Hardw.
Oak
Conif.

YELLOW-BEL-LIED SAPSUCKER (<u>Sphyrapicus</u> <u>varius</u>). Robin -. Red crown and throat, black and white wings and back, and yellow belly are distinctive. Females have white throat; however the broad expanse of red on the head is characteristic. Resident. Has a nasal, churring cry.

Wd.-Pr.
Hardw.
Conif.

RED-SHAFTED FLICKER (<u>Colaptes</u> <u>cafer</u>). Dove size. The only woodpecker regularly seen on the ground where it feeds on ants, etc. Brown back, <u>red under wings and tail</u>, white rump, and black crescent below throat are distinctive.

Conif.

PILEATED WOODPECKER (<u>Dryocopus</u> <u>pileatus</u>). Crow size. This is the largest and most striking woodpecker in the region, with large head and conspicuous <u>red crest</u>; a black and white pattern shows in flight. Resident.

ORDER PASSERIFORMES - PERCHING BIRDS

Flycatcher Family, Tyrannidae

OLIVE-SIDED FLYCATCH-
ER (Nuttallornis borealis).
Sparrow +. Flycatchers are
distinguished by their habit of
seeking high or exposed perches
from which they dart out into the
air, capture insects on the wing,
and return to their perch. The
olive-sided flycatcher is the
largest of the family in the region, and is more commonly
heard than seen, with a distinctive three-note call, with middle note highest. Distinguished
also by large head and bill, white

*Conif.
Hardw.
Meadou*

throat and dark side patches separated by white belly. Summer.

WESTERN WOOD PEWEE (Contopus richardsonii). Sparrow size. A
gray-brown flycatcher. Two white
wing bars, and absence of white eye-
ring separate it from olive-sided flycatcher, which lacks wing bars, and
the smaller western flycatcher, which
has a conspicuous eye ring. Cry, a
nasal "pee-eee". Summer visitor to
forest edges and open forest.

*Conif.
Hardw.
Oak*

WESTERN FLYCATCHER (Em-
pidonax difficilis). Sparrow -
This is a small flycatcher with a
conspicuous eye ring, two white
wing bars, and yellowish underparts. Call, a sharp "see-seet" or
"ps-seet", rising on second note.
Common in summer, particularly
near streams or forest edges.

*Conif.
Hardw.
Str.Wd.*

Swallow Family (Hirundinidae)

Wd.Pr.
Meadow
Rocks
Bldg.
Strand

E.D.

VIOLET GREEN SWAL-LOW (Tachycineta thalassina). Sparrow size. Swallows are most often seen in flight. The long, slender wings, and gliding, easy flight are distinctive. The green and purple upperparts, clear white underparts, white patches to side and above the tail, and the white extending partly around the eye are distinctive in this species. Summer resident, nesting on cliffs, buildings; hunting insects in open. Similar Tree Swallow (Iridoprocne bicolor) lacks white patches.

Meadow
Conif.
Hardw.

PURPLE MARTIN (Progne subis). Robin -. This is the largest of the swallows, and only one dark blue-black all over in male; brown in female, with pale collar and whitish belly. Summer resident; nests in tree holes in open forest.

Conif.
Meadow
Hardw.

Crow & Jay Fam. (Corvidae)

Conif.

CANADA JAY (Perisoreus canadensis). Robin +. A large gray bird with a black bill and white head; underparts whitish. Has many harsh & soft cries, including a soft whistled "whee-ahh". Young are dark gray. A resident from Mendocino Co. N.

Wd.-Pr.
Oak

SCRUB JAY (Aphelocoma californica). Robin +. Blue head, wings & tail; no crest.

E.D.

STELLER JAY (Cyanocittà stelleri). Robin +. This is a large bird, black in front, blue toward rear, with prominent black crest. Common resident. Call a hoarse "tchay-tchay-tchay!, also many other calls, including copy of redtail hawk scream. Resident.

Conif.
Oak
Hardw.

RAVEN (Corvus corax). Crow +. This huge, all black bird, is nearly twice as big as a crow. Unlike the Crow (C. brachyrhynchos), it soars with wings held horizontal from body (not angled). Croaking call different from "caw" of crow. Resident.

Wd.-Pr
Strand
Rocks

Str.Wd
Strand
Wd.Pr.
Hardw.

Titmouse Family (Paridae)

CHESTNUT-BACKED CHICKADEE (Parus rufescens). Warbler size. The black and white face mask and small size are distinctive; also the reddish-brown back.

Hardw.
Conif.

BUSH-TIT (Psaltriparus minimus). Warbler -. A small, gray bird, traveling in flocks, except at nesting time. Lacks distinguishing marks other than small size, uniform color, rather fat body, and long tail. Common resident.

Hardw.
Oak
Brush

Nuthatch Family (Sittidae)

RED-BREASTED NUTHATCH
(Sitta canadensis). Warbler size.
Nuthatches are small, short-tailed
birds that are often seen walking up
and down vertical tree trunks, or
clinging upside down from large
branches. This species is distin-

guished by reddish underparts and a black line through the eye.
It is blue-gray above, light-colored below, black capped. The
Pygmy Nuthatch (S. pygmaea), has gray-brown cap. Mendocino S.

Creeper Family (Certhiidae)

BROWN CREEPER (Certhia
familiaris). Warbler size. Has
striped brown back, a stiff, short
tail, and a curved bill. It creeps
spirally up vertical tree trunks
then flies to bottom of next tree.
It never climbs down a trunk as
does a nuthatch. Has a whispering "seeee" note. Resident.

Wren-tit Family (Chamaeidae)

WREN-TIT (Chamaea fasciata). Sparrow size. A brownish bird, dark above,
with a short, slightly curved bill, and a
long tail, usually held upright. N. to Ore.

Wren Family (Troglodytidae)

BEWICK WREN (Thryomanes
bewicki). Warbler size. A wren
with a white eye line, and white
edge to end of tail; the tail rather
long. Resident in most of region.

WINTER WREN (Troglodytes troglodytes). Warbler size. Wrens are characterized by narrow, stiff tails, which are
usually held upright, and a relatively long,
down-curved bill. This species is dark
brown, with a heavily-barred flank & belly.
Has a light, but not white, line above eye; a
very short tail. Resident. The House Wren
(T. aedon) has longer tail, unbarred flanks, no eye marks. Res.

Brush
Hardw.
Conif.

Oak
Str.Wd.
Brush
Hardw.

Dipper Fam. (Cinclidae)

DIPPER (Cinclus mex-
icanus). Robin -. A
short-tailed, heavy-bod-
ied, slate-gray bird.
Dips up and down while
standing on rocks by swift
water; runs and flies un-
der water hunting water
insects. Resident in mts.
Nests of moss often hid-
den under waterfalls.

Water
Str.Wd.
Rocks

Thrush Fam. (Turdidae)

ROBIN (Turdus migra-
torius). A familiar bird of
the city lawn and shade tree.
Breast is orange-red, body
is brown. Males are black-
headed; females more
brownish or paler on the
head.

Cultiv.
Meadow
Wd.-Pr.
Conif.

MEXICAN BLUEBIRD (Sialia mexi-
icana). Sparrow +. Mostly blue, with
reddish breast and back; sometimes
back also is blue; the female is dull
brownish above and is otherwise paler
than the male. Voice, a sharp "tew!"
or "mew!"; also has loud chatter.

Wd.Pr.
Hardw.
Meadow
Conif.

Conif.

VARIED THRUSH (Ixoreus naevius). Robin size. This is a robin-like bird with an orange stripe above the eye and a black band across the breast; the female has a gray breast band, while young birds have a broken breast band. Has a long, whistled note that quavers eerily. Resid.

Conif.

HERMIT THRUSH (Hylocichla guttata). Robin -. Grayish-brown above, with spotted breast and reddish tail. Runs on ground, or often stands still while watching for insect prey, slowly bobbing tail. Has a lovely, clear and flute-like song. Resident. The Russet-backed Thrush (H. ustulata) looks the same but has no

Str.Wd.
Hardw.

reddish tail; a summer visitor, with lovely song that spirals down.

Conif
Hardw.
Oak
Brusn

Kinglet Family (Sylvidae)

GOLDEN-CROWNED KINGLET (Regulus satrapa). Warbler -. This is a very small gray bird with a short tail, and black and gold stripes on crown. Resident.

Conif.
Hardw.
Oak
Brush

RUBY-CROWNED KINGLET (Regulus calendula). Warbler -. A short-tailed grey bird with white eye ring, and two white wing bars; the bright red crown patch is usually unseen.

Waxwing Fam., Bombycillidae

CEDAR WAXWING (Bombycilla cedrorum). Sparrow +. Waxwings are crested birds with black masks and yellow bands at the ends of their tails. The cedar waxwing is brownish in color; the rarer Bohemian Waxwing (B. garrula) is larger, grayer, and has white patches on the wings, visible as the wings are folded. Resident, feeding on berries; breeds by streams, & winters in brushy areas or woodland.

Brush Hardw. Str.Wd. Wd.Pr.

Vireo Family (Vireonidae)

HUTTON VIREO (Vireo huttoni). Warbler size. Somewhat like a kinglet, but larger, more olive in color, and slower and more deliberate in movements. Two white wing bars, light spot in front of eye, darker area on top of eye, and incomplete white eye ring are distinctive. Resident.

Oak

Warbler Family (Parulidae)

YELLOW THROAT (Geothlypas trichas). Males are yellow birds, brownish backed, with black eye masks. Females and young without mask. Song, a very sharp "whitchity-t-whichity-t-whichity- etc." Resident.

Marsh Hardw. Str.Wd.

PILEOLATED WARBLER (Wilsonia pusilla). Male is yellow, with black cap on top of its head; black eyes contrasting with bright yellow face. Song a wheezy "chee-chee-che-chit, etc.", becoming faster and louder. Summer resident.

Brush Str.Wd. Hardw.

ORANGE-CROWNED WARBLER (Vermivora celata). A dull-colored

Brush Oak Str.Wd. Hardw.

warbler, with weak, trilling song.

Conif.
Hardw.
Oak

TOWNSEND WARBLER (Dendroica townsendi). A black, white & yellow warbler, with distinctive black & gold pattern on head and bright yellow breast. Winters in Calif., summer to the north. The

Oak
Hardw.
Conif.

Black-throated Gray Warbler (D. nigrescens) has same   pattern, but colors all black, white & gray.

Conif.
Hardw.
Op.Brush
Meadow

MYRTLE WARBLER (Dendroica coronata). This and the similar Audubon Warbler (D. auduboni) are black and white warblers with yellow crown & rump patch. The myrtle has a white throat; Audubon a yellow throat. Myrtle is often seen on ground. Summer in forest; win. in open.

<u>Blackbird Fam. (Icteridae)</u>

Marsh

RED-WINGED   BLACKBIRD (Agelaius phoeniceus).   Robin size.   The male is a shiny black bird with a red shoulder patch, the female is streaked and brownish. Call, a loud "keck!" or "tear". Song, a gurgle-like   "kunk-el-o-ree" or "ok-la-er-ree!"   Often builds nests among cattails in fresh-water marshes.

Marsh
Grass
Cultiv.

BREWER BLACKBIRD (Euphagus cyanocephalus). Robin size.   The male is all black with a purple or greenish iridescent sheen, and white eyes. The female is dull brownish. Resident in marshes in summer; in grassland in winter. Call, a harsh "keck!"

Tanager Family (Thraupidae)

Conif.
Hardw.

WESTERN TANAGER (Piranga ludoviciana). Sparrow ÷. The black-winged, yellow-bodied, red-headed male is unmistakable. The female is yellow below and greenish above. Both have heavy, almost finch-like bills. Summer.

Finch Family (Fringillidae)

All finches have short, thick bills, adapted for seed-cracking.

BLACK-HEADED GROSBEAK (Pheucticus melanocephalus). Sparrow ÷. A large finch with thick, heavy bill and reddish-brown breast. The male has black and white wings and black head. Summer resident.

Conif.
Hardw.

EVENING GROSBEAK (Hesperiphona vespertina). Robin size. A large-billed bird with black and white wings. Body uniformly yellowish in color. Song is a short, wobbling warble. Resident, breeding in dense forest, wintering where berry trees and bushes occur. A camp scavenger in summertime.

Conif.
Hardw.
Brush

PURPLE FINCH (Carpodacus purpureus). Sparrow size. Male has a reddish head, breast and rump on an overall brownish body. The male House Finch or Linnet (C. mexicanus) is similar, but has dark streaks on the belly and does not have the deeply-notched tail of the purple finch. The females of both species are plain-looking, streaked brown birds. The house finch is found in more open country in summer and its song is much looser and less compact. Residents.

Conif.
Brush
Oak

Brush
Wd.-Pr
Meadow
Cultiv.
Bldg.

Conif.
Hardw.
Vd.Pr.

PINE SISKIN (Spinus spinus). Warbler +. A goldfinch-like bird, but with yellow only in wing and tail. The general appearance is of a small, brownish, streaked finch. Three calls, a loud, clear "chee-eep", a soft "ti-ti-teet", and a very buzzing "shzzzreeee!" Resident, nesting in conifers; winter feeder in more open country, such as woods' edges.

Hardw.
tr.Wd.
Brush
Vd.Pr.

AMERICAN GOLDFINCH (Spinus tristis). Warbler +. Male in summer recognizable as a yellow bird with a black forehead, wings, and tail. Female, and male in winter, are greenish-yellow with black wings. It is resident, usually nesting along the streams; forages in brush, etc.

Conif.

RED CROSSBILL (Loxia curvirostra). Sparrow size. The male has a red head and body, with darker brownish wings and tail. Bill slender for a finch, with mandibles crossed near tip. Summers to north and in higher mountains, winters southward. The call is a harsh "pip-ip-ip". Feeds on seeds and nuts.

Brush
Oak
Hardw.
Conif.

SPOTTED TOWHEE (Pipilo maculatus). Robin -. Male with black head; neck and back marked with white spots. Sides are red-brown, underparts white. Females similar in pattern, but with brown replacing black. Gives a long, buzzing "chzzzeee!" and also a meow-like call. Common resident. The Brown Towhee (P. fuscus) is found as far north as S.W. Oregon, and is all brown save for rufous under tail.

Brush
Oak
Hardw.

OREGON JUNCO (Junco oreganus). Sparrow size. Juncos are characterized by a blackish head, neck and upper breast and by the white-edged tail. This species has a reddish-brown back and sides, and a white belly. Has a soft clicking call; also soft twittering. Summers in conifers; winters in open.

Conif.
Brush
Hardw.
Wd.Pr.

CHIPPING SPARROW (Spizella passerina). A small sparrow with an unmarked grayish breast, a red-brown crown, a white line over the eye, and a black line through the eye. The song is a wheezy, rattling trill, all at one level; call, a dry "cht". Summer.

Hardw.
Oak
Conif.
Wd.Pr.

WHITE-CROWNED SPARROW (Zonotrichia leucophrys). This is a medium-sized sparrow with an unmarked grey breast and alternating black and white stripes on the crown. Song starts with 3 or 4 bright, plaintive whistles, followed by a sneeze-like trill. The first note is often long and quite high, and the rest go down in scale. However, the song varies greatly in the south.

Wd.Pr.
Brush
Strand
Grass

GOLDEN-CROWNED SPARROW (Zonotrichia atracapilla). It is similar to white-crowned sparrow, but with broad yellow stripe on center of head and without a light line over the eye. The three-note song, sounding like the tune of "Three Blind Mice", is very distinctive. This and the above species of sparrow go in small to large flocks. Winter visitor.

Brush
Hardw.
Strand

Conif.
Brush
Hardwd

FOX SPARROW (Passerella iliaca). A large sparrow with a heavily-spotted breast, and an evenly-brownish colored back and wings. Usually seen scratching vigorously in leaf litter. It is chiefly a winter visitor in the more open forests or brush.

Brush
Wd.-Pr.
Hardw.
Marsh
Strand

SONG SPARROW (Melospiza melodia). This is a sparrow with a heavily-streaked breast with a dark central spot, and with dark chin streaks on each side of bill. The back and wings are brownish. The beautiful song usually starts with "sweet-sweet-sweet cheer" and continues with a variety of both musical and buzzy notes. It is an abundant resident in open shrubby areas near marshes and streams, and is common also in urban and agricultural areas. The Lincoln Sparrow (M. lincolni), which lives mainly along streams and in marshy spots, has finer streakings on the breast, not so obvious a central spot, and buff-colored band on the upper breast. Song has swift, upward pitch, and gurgles sweetly. Resident in north; winter in south.

Wd.-Pr.

Wd.Pr.

SAVANNAH SPARROW (Passerculus sandwichensis). Not illustrated. Similar to song sparrow, with yellow over eye, and a notched tail, but with a shorter tail, a whitish stripe through the crown, and light pinkish legs. Song, soft and whispering "tsee tseeeeee". Resident in open country.

REPTILES AND AMPHIBIANS

Only a few representatives of the reptiles and amphibians are illustrated in this book, because of space limitations. However, we have inserted two charts, one for reptiles and the other for amphibians, which show most of the species found in this region in relation to the habitats in which they live. Since the living habits of these animals in this region are often very specialized, this information will help you identify almost any species of reptile or amphibian you encounter, if you carefully note the type of habitat in which it is found. The interested reader will find further information about these two groups in the references listed on page 109. Compared to the numbers of species of birds and of mammals, there are few kinds of reptiles and amphibians in this region. But they are easier to catch and keep in captivity.

Reptiles may be distinguished from other vertebrates by their dry, scale-covered skin, which lacks hair or feathers. Their many other distinctive characteristics are not always apparent to casual observation. If it is remembered that snakes, lizards, crocodiles, and turtles are reptiles, there will be little difficulty in distinguishing this group.

Amphibians, like reptiles, represent a distinct class of vertebrate animals, equal in rank to the mammals or birds. As the name indicates, they are creatures which have not completely adapted themselves to life on dry land, but require water or moist places in which to lay their eggs, or in which to spend the early "tadpole" stage of their existence. A characteristic of amphibians is the ability to breath through the skin. In some species this is a secondary method of respiration, but in other groups lungs may be entirely absent.

In the pages that follow we have placed first the chart of the reptiles, then descriptions of outstanding reptile species, next the chart of the amphibians, followed by descriptions of the most common amphibians. As you find reptiles or amphibians in the wild, note their habitats and appearances and compare with the information in the charts plus the pictures of representative species in order to identify them. Most of these creatures may be easily raised in captivity if sufficient care is given to them to make their quarters homelike and their food representative.

CHART OF REPTILE HABITATS AND CHARACTERISTICS

Name	Appearance	Habitats	Range
PACIFIC POND TURTLE (Clemmys marmorata). Illus. on page 102	5-7" long; dark brown, olive to blackish in color above, yellowish below.	Prefers quiet water of small lakes, ponds, slow streams, rivers and marshes.	From N. Ore. S., but avoids Calif. coast from Del Norte to Mendocino.
PAINTED TURTLE (Chrysemys picta).	4-9" long; general brown color, lined and bordered with yellow; red marks on head.	Quiet, shallow waters of rivers, marshes, ponds, ditches, small lakes, etc.	Along Columbia and lower Willamette Rivers
COAST HORNED LIZARD (Phrynosoma coronatum).	3-4" less tail; 2 rows of spines at sides of body; 2 long horns at back of head.	Grass, brush, and edges of hardwood and coniferous forests.	From Sonoma Co. to Monterey Co., Calif. & S.
WESTERN FENCE LIZARD (Sceloporus occidentalis).	2 to 3 1/2" body and head length; tail a little long; scales above eyes separated from central head scales by row of small scales.	Likes wooded, rocky areas, especially in canyons or along a stream; also talus slopes, old buildings, fences, wood piles, burrows of rodents, brush.	From Seattle south, avoiding the coast of Washington and northwest Oregon.
WESTERN SKINK (Eumeces skiltonianus).	2 1/2 to 3 1/2" body and head length; tail around 1 1/2 X as long. Brownish color with light and dark stripes down sides; the scales very smooth. Young have blue tails.	Found under rocks, logs, surface litter, inside rotten wood; in hardwoods, woodland-prairie, brush, conifers. Prefers some shrubs nearby.	From central and S.W. Ore. south to Monterey Co., Calif. & south.
NORTHERN ALLIGATOR LIZARD (Gerrhonotus coeruleus). See illus. on p. 102	3-5" body and head length; described and pictured on page 102. Has dark lines on edges of belly scales.	In or near coniferous forests; also in nearby meadows, hardwoods and brush; often under damp debris or leaves.	In all of region except major part of Willamette Valley in Oregon.
FOOTHILL ALLIGATOR LIZARD (Gerrhonotus multicarinatus).	4 to 6 1/2" body and head length. Like above lizard, but lighter colored, and with dark lines in middle of whitish belly scales.	Usually found in oak wood or brush, but also in grass; usually under debris, logs, leaves, etc.	From interior valleys of Ore. south and then along California coast.
RUBBER SNAKE (Charina bottae). See illustration on page 102.	About 1-2' long; pale brown to dark brown color; tail so blunt it looks like head; no apparent neck.	Usually found in damp localities, in or near coniferous forests; often found under rocks or debris or burrowing.	Found in most of region except far W. Washington and N.W. Oregon.
WESTERN RATTLESNAKE (Crotalus viridis)	1 1/2 to 5' long; easily told by rattles, long fangs, & arrowhead-shaped head.	Brush, woodland-prairie; especially near or in rocks.	From Douglas Co., Ore. and Humboldt Co. S.

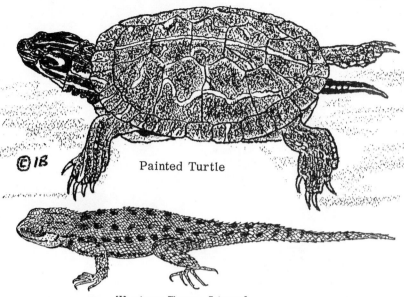

Painted Turtle

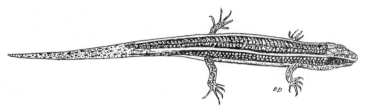

Western Fence Lizard

Western Skink

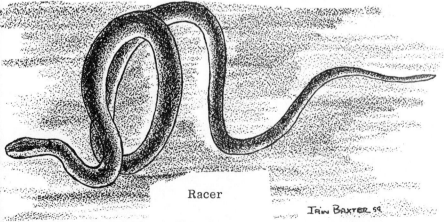

Racer

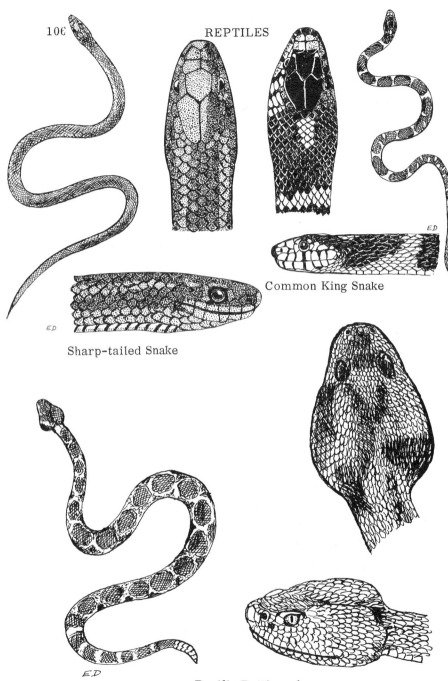

Sharp-tailed Snake

Common King Snake

Pacific Rattlesnake

CHART OF REPTILE HABITATS (continued)

Name	Appearance	Habitats	Range
RACER (Coluber constrictor).	2 to 4 1/2" long; uniformly brownish or dark color above, white below. Very active and fast. Young are saddle-marked.	Woodland-prairie, meadows, edges of forests, in thin brush; sometimes climbs in bushes.	Tacoma, Wash. area; interior valleys of Ore.; S. along coast from Curry Co.
SHARP-TAILED SNAKE (Contia tenuis).	10-16" long; rather stout body, with sharp scale at end of tail; belly appears with black and white cross bars; brown to yellowish-gray on upper body.	Usually in moist places, under bark, boards, etc., near a stream; also in oaks, brush, hardwood forest.	From Medford, Ore., and Del Norte Co., California, south.
WESTERN RING-NECKED SNAKE (Diadophis amabilis).	10-22" long; uniformly blackish-gray, or blue-gray, etc. above; with distinct neck ring of yellow, red or orange, and belly of same light color.	Found in coniferous forest, oaks, woodland prairie, hardwood forest; usually under debris, boards, leaves, etc.; rare in marsh.	Found from Portland, Ore. south, avoiding northwest Ore. coast district.
CALIFORNIA MOUNTAIN KING SNAKE (Lampropeltis zonata).	1 1/2 to 2 1/2' long; has alternating black and white rings, the black rings usually being split by red rings.	Found in coniferous forest, hardwoods, oak and brush; usually secretive in habit, so rarely seen.	Found in interior mountains from Douglas Co., Oregon, south.
COMMON KING SNAKE (Lampropeltis getulus).	2 1/2 to 3 1/2'; has creamy or light-colored rings against a brown to black ground color.	Found in most habitats, except water, but prefers forest edges, open brush and oak woods.	From Douglas Co., Ore. south and from Mendocino Co., Calif. S. on coast.
GOPHER SNAKE (Pituophis catenifer). See illus. p. 103.	2 1/2 to 7' long; a brown and yellowish blotched snake; see full description on page 103.	Found in almost every habitat, but prefers woodland-prairie and brush.	Reported from Olympia area in Wash. From Portland south.
COMMON GARTER SNAKE (Thamnophis sirtalis).	2-4' long. See full description and picture on page 103. Very easily angered.	Common in meadows, marshes, and in forests along streams, and in streams, ponds.	Found in all of region except driest areas.
NORTHWESTERN GARTER SNAKE (Thamnophis ordinoides).	1-2' long; has 3 longitudinal light-colored stripes against dark ground color; belly often red-marked; not easily angered; slow moving.	Common in meadows, forest clearings and along streams in damp localities. Secretive in habit and very docile.	Found in most of region except drier areas.
WESTERN GARTER SNAKE (Thamnophis elegans).	1-3' long. Has a bewildering variety of forms, either striped or spotted; aquatic type has more pointed nose scales. Rarely has red marks.	Terrestrial types prefer meadows, clearings, and brush; aquatic type prefers water and banks of streams.	All of region except extreme W. coast Wash. & central & NW. coast of Ore.

Water
Str.Wd.

PACIFIC POND TUR-
TLE (Clemmys mar-
morata). 5-7". This
is the only common tur-
tle in the coastal region,
and it is not likely to
be confused with any-
thing else. It is found
throughout the region in
fresh water.

Conif.
Hardw.

NORTHERN ALLIGATOR
LIZARD (Gerrhonotus coerule-
us). 3-5" body and head length.
Alligator lizards are distin--
guished by a fold of skin along the side of the body separating the
dorsal from the ventral scales. The color above is greenish to
bluish with transverse black markings; the ventral color is whitish, with dark lines along the edges of the belly scales.

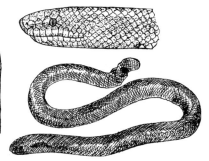

Conif.
Hardw.

RUBBER SNAKE
(Charina bottae). 1-
2' long. A small rel-
ative of the tropical
boas. The blunt tail,
which looks like the
head, and the uni-
formly brownish up-
perparts are distinc-
tive. It is a secre-
tive snake, usually found underneath boards or logs or hidden in
leaf mold in damp, forested areas. It sometimes actually moves
the tail as if it were a head, so as to confuse an enemy. It hunts
mainly for worms and insect larvae in the leaf mold, but occasionally may catch a mouse. It is one of the most unique and interesting creatures of all the region and should not be harmed in
any way. Like most snakes, save the rattlesnake, it is harmless.

COMMON GARTER SNAKE (Thamnophis sirtalis). 2-4' long. This is a snake with yellowish stripes running the length of the body, set off against grayish or brownish background color. Reddish marks or stripes are often present on the sides. The belly is pale-colored and often bluish. This snake often strikes savagely when attacked or handled and, as with most garter snakes, gives off a bad odor and slimy secretion. Scales keeled. A good swimmer in ponds and streams. Common all over.

GOPHER SNAKE (Pituophis catenifer). 2 1/2 to 8' long. A large, heavy-bodied snake with head not wider than the body. Has light or brownish ground color with large, square to oval dark blotches on the dorsal surface; the scales are keeled. This is a harmless snake with a very loud hiss. It does a lot of good by eating harmful rodents and rabbits and should, therefore, be protected. Sometimes rattles tail in dry leaves.

Most habitat

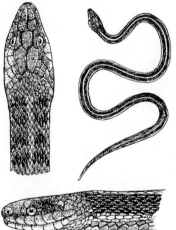

Meadow Str. Wd Water Strand Conif. Hardw.

CHART OF AMPHIBIAN HABITATS

Name	Description	Habitats	Range
LONG-TOED SALAMANDER (Ambystoma macrodactylum)	2-6' long head and body; head broad and somewhat flattened; a broad greenish-yellow to tan stripe (or blotches) down brown back.	Found under loose rocks or logs or debris near lakes or ponds; also found in rotting wood or bark.	From Del Norte Co., California, north to Alaska.
NORTHWESTERN SALAMANDER (A. gracile)	2-6" head and body; large glands present on back of head; dark brown body color.	Found on land beneath driftwood, rocks, etc. near streams; in water.	From Sonoma Co., California N. to Alaska.

CHART OF AMPHIBIAN HABITATS (continued)

Name	Description	Habitats	Range
TIGER SALA-MANDER (Ambystoma tigrinum)	2-6" long body and head. Black on back, with numerous spots or bars of yellow; eyes small; head broad and flat.	In dry weather adults live in crevices, rotten logs, animal holes, etc. in open country. In wet weather, found in water or nearby debris.	Santa Cruz, Santa Clara & Monterey Cos., California, in our region.
PACIFIC GIANT SALAMANDER (Dicamptodon ensatus). See illus. p. 106	4-7" body and head. See description and illustration on page 106. The large, thick, spotted body is very distinctive.	In dry coniferous and hardwood forests, in the water or under logs, rocks, bark, etc. near a cool stream.	From Santa Cruz Co., California, north to British Columbia
OLYMPIC SALA-MANDER (Rhyacotriton olympicus).	1 1/2 to 2 1/2" long head and body. A small, slim animal with very short legs and toes; yellow belly; dark mottled above (Ore. and Calif.) or brown with light flecks (Wash.).	Found in or very near swift, cold, shallow water, well-shaded; or under rocks in moss-covered seepages and springs.	Found from Mendocino Co., California, north to Washington.
WESTERN RED-BELLIED NEWT (Taricha rivularis).	2 1/2 to 3 3/4" long head and body. Eyes rather large and protuberant; color usually black to dark brown above, sharply distinct from bright red undersides; eyes dark.	Found in or near to streams in redwood forest; usually found under logs, rocks, boards, debris, etc. Crawls over ground in wet weather.	Found from Sonoma Co., California, north to Humboldt Co. in same state.
ROUGH-SKINNED NEWT (Taricha granulosa). See illustration on page 106.	2 to 3 1/2" head and body length. Light color on head does not reach lower eyelid; brown or black above, orange on the undersides.	Found in humid coniferous and hardwood forests; also in meadows; always near to streams, ponds & lakes; under objects in dry time.	Found from Santa Cruz Co., California, north to British Columbia.
CALIFORNIA NEWT (Taricha torosa).	2 1/2 to 3 1/2" head and body length. Light color on head reaches up to lower eyelid; color reddish-brown or tan above, pale yellowish-orange below.	Found in or near canyon streams, usually associated with oak trees; travels clumsily overland in wet weather. Both adults and young are good swimmers.	From Monterey Co. to Sonoma Co. in California
DEL NORTE SALAMANDER (Plethodon elongatus).	2 3/8 to 3" head and body length. There are 17-19 grooves on the side between the legs. Color usually black or with reddish-brown stripe; belly slate-gray.	Found in or very near old rock slides or piles of rock that are usually damp and covered with moss; generally near to streams or seepages.	Found from Humboldt Co., California, to just north of the Rogue River in Oregon.
DUNN'S SALA-MANDER (Plethodon dunni).	2 1/2 to 3" head and body length. Side grooves 14-16; back stripe yellowish-tan or green.	Found in moss-covered rock piles in shaded seepages near permanent streams.	Found from southwestern Oregon to S.W. Washington

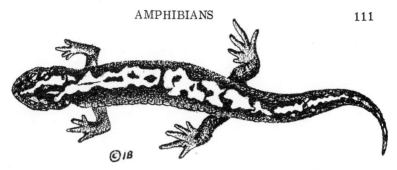

Long-toed Salamander

Iain Baxter

California Slender Salamander

Arboreal Salamander

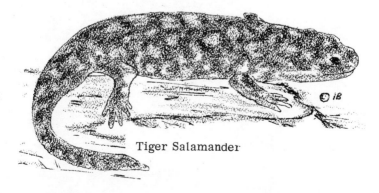

Tiger Salamander

Tailed Frog

Spotted Frog

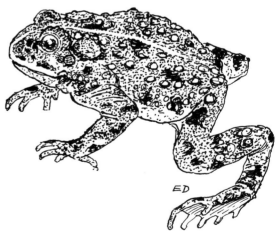

Western Toad

CHART OF AMPHIBIAN HABITATS (continued)

Name	Description	Habitats	Range
WESTERN RED-BACKED SALAMANDER (Plethodon vehiculum).	2 to 2 1/3" head and body length; side grooves 16 or 15; light-colored back stripe reaches to tip of tail, but a few animals all black or all yellowish-orange; belly bluish-gray mottled.	Found in damp coniferous forests or hardwoods, usually under rocks, bark, rotting wood, logs, moss, crevices, etc. and with moist soil.	From Coos Co., Oregon, north to British Columbia.
VAN DYKE'S SALAMANDER (Plethodon vandykei).	2 to 2 1/2" head and body length. A swollen area back of head; side grooves 13 or 14; tan to yellowish back stripe; body brown or black; belly dark with tiny white flecks or spots.	Found under wet or damp rocks near streams; also in mossy rock seepages and under damp bark or surface litter; usually with douglas fir or maples near.	Found in Olympic Peninsula and southwestern Washington.
ESCHSCHOLTZ'S SALAMANDER (Ensatina eschscholtzii).	1 1/2 to 3" head and body length. The only salamander with the tail very narrow at the base. Variable color patterns.	Found in Douglas fir-maple forest; also in redwoods, oaks & brush. In dry periods lives in holes; wet, on surface.	Found in all of region.
CALIFORNIA SLENDER SALAMANDER (Batrachoseps attenuatus).	1 1/4 to 2" head and body length. This and the following are the only salamanders in our region with extremely long, slender bodies and tiny legs.	Found in same habitats as above salamander, but more often under bark and forest debris or leaf mold.	Found from Curry Co., Oregon south through California.
OREGON SLENDER SALAMANDER (Batrachoseps wrighti).	1 1/2 to 1 3/4" long head and body length; very slender & with tiny legs. Conspicuous white spots.	Found associated with red cedar, Douglas fir and maple; usually under rotting wood & bark.	Found only in Oregon Cascades and foothills.
CLOUDED SALAMANDER (Aneides fereus).	2 1/4 to 2 3/4" long head and body. Tips of toes square-tipped and broad for tree climbing; color dark brown, mottled with yellow, gray or whitish.	Found under bark of fir, cedar, redwood, etc. or in leaf litter of tree crotches or hollow stumps; likes recently cleared areas.	Found on Vancouver Island, Willamette Valley, & from Lane Co., Ore. to Mendocino.
ARBOREAL SALAMANDER (Aneides lugubris).	2 1/2 to 3 3/4" head and body length; jaw muscles bulge outward; body is brown, spotted with pale yellow; belly is whitish.	Found under bark, logs, rocks, leaf litter, etc.; also in tree cavities or rotten logs, usually in oak woods.	From southern Humboldt Co., California, south along the coast.
BLACK SALAMANDER (Aneides flavipunctatus).	2 1/2 to 3" long head and body. Toes rounded; belly very dark gray or black; dark above, light speckled.	Found commonly under damp rocks, less commonly under logs or bark, usually on forest edges.	From Santa Cruz and Santa Clara Cos., N. to Humboldt Co.
TAILED FROG (Ascaphus truei)	1-2" long, not including "tail". Outer toe of hind foot broad; pupil vertical.	Lives in or near cold, swift streams under redwood, fir & spruce.	From Mendocino Co. north to Brit. Colum.

Name	Description	Habitats	Range
PACIFIC TREE FROG (Hyla regilla). Illus. on page 107.	2" long or less; the only small frog of region with suction-tip toes. See also page 107.	Found in brush along streams, rock fissures, rodent holes, building crevices; near water.	Found in all of region.
RED-LEGGED FROG (Rana aurora). See illus. on page 107.	About 5" long; almost always with red under legs; a blackish eye-mask reaches from the nose to angle of jaw.	Found mainly in quiet or slow-moving water, but sometimes in nearby ferns and other damp vegetation.	Found all over region near or in water.
YELLOW-LEGGED FROG (Rana boylei).	2 to 3 1/2" long; always colored whitish or cream on belly, changing to yellow on underside of legs.	Found close to water, preferring creeks with rocky bottoms and with moving (not swift) water.	From upper Willamette Valley & Coos Co. in Oregon south into Calif.
SPOTTED FROG (Rana pretiosa).	3-4" long; very similar to red-legged frog, but smaller and has up-turned eyes.	Found in quiet water; not a strong jumper and can be captured easily.	Found in Willamette Valley & S. to Medford area, Oregon.
BULLFROG (Rana catesbiana).	Around 8" or more long; eardrums unusually large. Very large size is distinctive.	Found mainly in quiet water, but sometimes in mountain streams.	Scattered localities from Santa Clara Co., Calif. N. to B.C.
WESTERN TOAD (Bufo boreas).	2 1/2 to 5" long. Body covered with warts.	Found in most habitats except dry brush.	Found in all of region.

PACIFIC GIANT SALA-MANDER (Dicamptodon ensatus). 4-7" long. One of the largest of western salamanders. The black blotches on a brown or gray skin are distinctive. Skin not folded on side of body; has strange, barking call. Eats insects, mice.

ROUGH-SKINNED NEWT (Taricha granulosa). 2 to 2 1/2" long head and body. The newt, mud puppy, or water dog, is one of the most commonly observed salamanders. The bright orange-colored under-parts, contrasting with the brown or blackish upper surface, are distinctive. This species usually is found near streams, but, in wet weather, may travel a considerable distance from permanent water.

PACIFIC TREE TOAD (Hyla regilla). 1-2" long. This small frog is often found well away from water, and not uncommonly is seen or heard in bushes or small trees. The black eye stripe in a frog of this size is distinctive. The color is variable and tends to resemble its habitat, which is most generally bright green. Has toe disks, and a two-syllable, high-pitched call note, surprisingly loud.

Water Str.Wd. Marsh Hardw. Conif. Brush

RED-LEGGED FROG (Rana aurora). Approximately 5" in length. Usually found near permanent streams, ponds, or lakes, avoiding swift-running water, where the related yellow-legged frog (page 106) will often be found. Color brown to greenish above, with black spots. Legs with black bars or blotches and with reddish coloring on the under-side of the hind legs. It has a low-pitched, gutteral call note.

Water Marsh Str.Wd.

*   *   *   *   *   *

FISHES

If oceans and bays are excluded, there are relatively few species of fish in this region. But the streams of the coast are noted for their sports fishing. Most anglers seek the salmon and steelhead, which abound in the larger rivers, but others prefer to seek the cutthroat trout in the smaller coastal streams. Large numbers of salmon and steelhead return each year to the coastal rivers. Here the salmon spawn and die, if they are not caught by fishermen. The steelhead spawn and return downstream.

Distinguishing features between salmon and trout:

Salmon: anal fin rays 12 - 19; mouth lining black.
Trout: anal fin rays 9 - 12; mouth lining white.

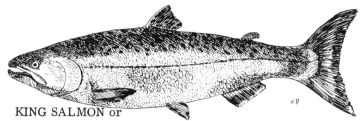

KING SALMON or
CHINOOK (<u>Onchorhynchos</u> <u>tschawytscha</u>). An important sports
fish. The first year of life the young fish move downstream to the
ocean. In the fifth year the adults move up the rivers to spawn.

SILVER SALMON or COHO (<u>Onchorhynchos</u> <u>kisutch</u>). Distinguished from chinook   by black spotting being confined to back
& upper lobes of tail.   Has needle-like teeth.

STEELHEAD and   RAINBOW TROUT (<u>Salmo</u> <u>gairdnerii</u>).
The steelhead, a famous sporting fish, is simply a sea-running
rainbow trout.   Both lack the red throat mark of the cutthroat.
Dark spots on back large.

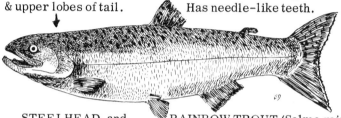

CUTTHROAT TROUT (<u>Salmo</u> <u>clarkii</u>). Like the steelhead the
cutthroat is spawned in fresh water, but spends most of its growing period in salt water. Adults enter streams in autumn or winter. The red streak on each side of lower jaw is a distinguishing
feature; also the long head.   A prized sport fish.

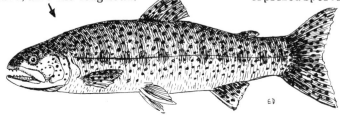

SUGGESTED REFERENCES

Abrams, Leroy, ILLUSTRATED FLORA OF THE PACIFIC STATES. 4 volumes. 1940–1960. Stanford University Press

Bailey, Vernon. 1936. THE MAMMALS AND LIFE ZONES OF OREGON. North American Fauna No. 55. U.S. Department of Agriculture.

Brown, Vinson and Henry G. Weston, Jr. 1961. HANDBOOK OF CALIFORNIA BIRDS. Naturegraph Publishers.

Burt, William H. 1952. A FIELD GUIDE TO THE MAMMALS. Houghton Mifflin Co.

Dalquest, Walter W. 1948. MAMMALS OF WASHINGTON. University of Kansas Publications, Museum of Natural History, Vol. 2.

Gabrielson, Ira N. and S. G. Jewett. 1940. BIRDS OF OREGON. Oregon State College Monographs, Studies in Zoology, No. 2.

Grinnell, Joseph; J. S. Dixon; and J. M. Linsdale. 1937. FUR-BEARING MAMMALS OF CALIFORNIA, their natural history, systematic status, and relations to man. University of California Press (2 volumes).

Hoffman, Ralph. 1955. BIRDS OF THE PACIFIC STATES. Houghton Mifflin, Boston.

Ingles, Lloyd Glenn. 1956. MAMMALS OF CALIFORNIA AND ITS COASTAL WATERS. Stanford University Press.

Jepson, W. L. 1957. A MANUAL OF THE FLOWERING PLANTS OF CALIFORNIA. University of California Press.

Jewett, S.G.; W. P. Taylor; W. T. Shaw; and J. W. Aldrich. 1953 BIRDS OF WASHINGTON STATE. University of Washington Press.

McMinn, Howard E. 1939. AN ILLUSTRATED MANUAL OF CALIFORNIA SHRUBS. J. W. Stacey, San Francisco.

Miller, Alden H. 1951. AN ANALYSIS OF THE DISTRIBUTION OF THE BIRDS OF CALIFORNIA. Univ. of Calif. Publ. Zool., vol. 50, number 6.

Stebbins, Robert C. 1954. AMPHIBIANS AND REPTILES OF WESTERN NORTH AMERICA. McGraw-Hill, New York.

Yocom, Charles F. 1951. WATERFOWL AND THEIR FOOD PLANTS IN WASHINGTON. University of Washington Press.

INDEX

(NOTE: In this index individual species are listed by name only if there is just one of the kind in the book or if the plant or animal belongs to a group, such as the oaks, which covers more than two pages. For other species, look under group names such as "bats", or generic names, such as Quercus or Plethodon, which appear underlined.)

Abies grandis, 28
Abronia latifolia, 12
Accipiter striatus, 81
Acer macrophyllum, 47
Achillea millefolium, 49
Achlys triphylla, 42
Adder's tongue, 39
Agelaius phoeniceus, 98
Alder, red, 29
Alnus rubra, 29
Ambystoma, 110
Amphibians, 109–115
Anaphalis, 43
Anas platyrhynchos, 79
Aneides, 113
Anseriformes, 79
Antrozous pallidus, 74

Aphelocoma californica, 92
Aplodontia family, 68
Aplodontia rufa, 68
Apodiformes, 89
Aquilegia, 41
Arbutus menziesii, 46
Arctostaphylos, 33
Ardea herodias, 78
Arrowhead, 14
Asarum, 40
Ascaphus truei, 113
Aster chilensis, 49
Aster, common, 49
Astur atricapillus, 81
Aythya, 79–80
Azalea, western, 30

Baccharis pilularis, 23
Badger, 64
Bassariscidae, 61
Bassariscus astutus, 61
Batrachoseps, 113
Bats, 74–75
Bear, black, 58
Bear brush, 21
Beaver, 68
Beaver, mountain, 68
Bittern, 78
Blackberry, California, 18
Blackbird, 98
Bluebird, Mexican, 95
Blue-blossom, 20
Bleeding-heart, Pacific, 42
Bobcat, 59

Bombycilla, 97
Bombycillidae, 97
Bonasa umbellus, 83
Botaurus lentiginosus, 78
Brant, black 79
Branta, 79
Brodiaea, 52-53
Brodeaeas, 52-53
Bubo virginianus, 88
Bufo boreas, 114
Bulrush, 15
Bush-tit, 93
Buteo jamaicensis, 81

Cacomistle family, 61
Calamagrostis nutkaensis,53
Calypte anna, 89
Canis latrans, 59
Capella gallinago, 85
Caprimulgiformes, 88
Carnivores, 58
Carpodacus, 99
Cascara, 30
Casmerodius, 78
Castanopsis, 48
Castilleia latifolia, 22
Castor canadensis, 68
Castoridae, 68
Cat family, 58
Cat, ring-tailed, 61
Cat-tail, 15
Cathartes aura, 81
Catoptrophorus semipal-
    matus, 85
Cedar, giant, 29
Ceanothus, 20, 31
Certhia familiaris, 94
Cervus canadensis, 56
Chaetura vauxi, 89
Chamaea fasciata, 94
Charadriiformes, 84
Charadrius vociferous, 84
Charina bottae, 104, 108
Chickadee, chestnut-backed,
    93
Chickaree, 66
Chinook, 116
Chinquapin, 48
Chipmunk, 67
Chiroptera, 74
Chordeiles minor, 88
Chrysemys picta, 104
Ciconiiformes, 78
Cinclus mexicanus, 95
Circus cyaneus, 82
Citellus, 67
Clemmys marmorata, 104,
    108
Clethrionomys californicus,
    71

Clintonia, 39
Clintonias, 39
Coho, 116
Colaptes cafer, 90
Coltsfoot, 39
Coluber constrictor, 107
Columba fasciata, 87
Columbiformes, 87
Colybiformes, 77
Columbines, 41
Colymbus auritus, 77
Contia tenuis, 107
Contopus richardsonii, 91
Coot, 84
Coraciiformes, 89
Corvus, 93
Corynorhinus rafinesque, 74
Coyote, 59
Coyote brush, 23
Cranes, 84
Creeper, 94
Creeper family, 94
Crossbill, red, 100
Crotalus viridis, 104-105
Crow, 76, 93
Crow family, 92
Cudweed, lowland, 44
Cupressus macrocarpa, 9
Curlew, long-billed, 85
Currants, 33
Cyanocitta stelleri, 93
Cypress, 9

Dafila acuta, 7
Daisy, seaside, 22
Danthonia californica, 53
Deer, 56-57
Deer family, 56-57
Deer brush, 31
Deer-foot, 42
Dendragapus obscurus, 83
Dendrocopus, 90
Dendroica, 98
Diadophis amabilis, 106, 107
Dicamptodon ensatus, 110,
    114
Dicentra, 42
Dicentras, 42
Dipper, 95
Disporum smithii, 36
Distichlis spicata, 14
Dog family, 59
Dove, mourning, 76, 87
Dowitcher, 86
Dryocopus pileatus, 90
Ducks, 79-80

Eelgrass, 14

Egrets, 78
Elk, Roosevelt, 56
Empidonax difficilis, 91
Ensatina eschscholtzii, 113
Epilobium, 48
Eptesicus fuscus, 74
Erigeron glaucus, 22
Eriophyllum staechadifolium,22
Eumeces skiltonianus, 104
Euphagus cyanocephalus, 98
Eutamias, 67

Fairy lantern (or bell), 36
Falconiformes, 81
Falcon, peregrine, 82
Falco, 82
Felis concolor, 58
Fern, sword, 25
Finch family, 99
Finches, 99
Firs, 24, 27, 28
Fire-cracker plant, 53
Fire-weed, 48
Fisher, 62
Flicker, red-shafted, 90
Flycatcher family, 91
Flycatchers, 91
Foxes, 60
Fragaria chilensis, 11
Frogs, 113, 114, 115
Fulica americana, 84

Galliformes, 83
Garrya, 21
Gaultheria shallon, 34
Gavia, 77
Gaviiformes, 77
Geese, 79
Geothlypis trichas, 97
Gerrhonotus, 104, 108
Ginger, wild, 40
Glaucomys sabrinus, 66
Gnaphalium, 44
Goldenrod, coast, 12
Goldfinch, American, 100
Gooseberry canyon, 32
Gophers, 67
Goshawk, 81
Grape, Oregon, 35
Grasses, 53
Grebes, 77
Grosbeaks, 99
Grouse, 83
Gruiformes, 84
Gulls, 86

Habitats, types, 5
Hare, snowshoe, 65
Hare family, 65
Hawks, 81-82

Hemlock, western, 26, 28
Heracleum lanatum, 17, 18
Herons, 78
Hesperiphona vespertina, 99
Himalaya berry, 19
Hirundinidae, 92
Holcus lanatus, 53
Honeysuckle, wedded, 21
Huckleberries, 34
Hummingbirds, 89
Hyla regilla, 114, 115
Hylocichla, 96

Icteridae, 98
Indian lettuce, 35
Insectivores, 73
Inside-out flower, 41
Ixoreus naevius, 96

Jackrabbit, black-tailed, 65
Jays, 92, 93
Junco, Oregon, 101
Junco oreganus, 101

Killdeer, 84
Kingfishers, 89
Kinglets, 96

Lagomorpha (order), 65
Lampropeltis, 106, 107
Larus, 86
Lasionycteris noctivagans, 74
Lasiurus cinereus, 74
Laurel, California, 47
Leporidae, 65
Lepus, 65
Lilium, 37
Lilies, 37
Limnodromus griseus, 86
Linnet, 99
Lion, Mountain, 58
Lithocarpus densiflorus, 47
Lizards, 104, 105, 108
Lizard tail, 22
Lonicera, 21
Loons, 77
Lophortyx californica, 84
Loxia curvirostra, 100
Lupines, 10
Lupinus, 10
Lutra canadensis, 63
Lynx rufus, 59
Lysichiton americanum, 15

Madrone, 46
Mahonia nervosa, 35
Maianthemum dilatatum, 39
Mallard, 76, 79

Manzanita, hairy, 33
Maple, big-leaf, 47
Mareca americana, 80
Marten, 62
Martes, 62
Martin, purple, 92
Megaceryle alcyon, 89
Melospiza, 102
Mephitis mephitis, 64
Merganser, American, 76
Mergus merganser, 76
Mice family, native, 65
Microtus californicus, 67
Mimulus, 22, 53
Mink, 62
Mole family, 73
Moles, 73
Monkey flower, bush, 22
   common, 53
Montia sibirica, 35
Mountain beaver, 68
Mouse, harvest, 70, 71
   house, 55
   jumping, 70, 71
   meadow, 70, 71
   red-backed, 70, 71
   red tree, 70, 71
   white-footed, 70, 71
Muskrat, 69
Mustelidae, 63, 64
Mustela, 63
Myotis lucifugus, 74
Myrica californica, 18
Myrtle, Oregon, 47
   wax, 18

Neotoma, 69
Neurotrichus gibbsi, 73
Newts, 110, 114
Nighthawk, Pacific, 88
Nuphar polysepalum, 16
Numenius americanus, 85
Nuthatch family, 94
Nuthatches, 94
Nuttallornis borealis, 91
Nycticorax nycticorax, 78

Oak, black, 51
   canyon, 29
   Garry, 51
   Oregon white, 51
   tan, 46
Odocoileus, 57
Onchorhynchus, 116
Ondatra zibethica, 69
Oreortyx picta, 83
Otter, river, 64
Otus asio, 87
Owls, 87, 88
Oxalis oregana, 36
Oxyura jamaicensis, 80

Painted cup, seaside, 22
Paridae, 93
Parsnip, cow, 17, 18
Parulidae, 97
Parus rufescens, 93
Passerculus sandwichensis, 102
Passerella iliaca, 102
Passeriformes, 91
Pearly everlasting, 43
Perisoreus canadensis, 92
Peromyscus maniculatus, 71
Pewee, western wood, 91
Phenacomys longicaudus, 81
Pheucticus melanocephalus, 99
Phrynosoma coronatum, 104, 105
Picea sitchensis, 28
Piciformes, 90
Pickle-weed, 14
Pigeon, band-tailed, 87
Pines, 8
Pine siskin, 100
Pinus, 8
Pipilo, 100
Piranga ludoviciana, 99
Pituophis catenifer, 107, 109
Plant parts, 6
Plethodon, 110, 113
Podilymbus podiceps, 77
Procyonidae, 60
Procyon lotor, 61
Progne subis, 92
Psaltriparus minimus, 93
Pseudotsuga menziesii, 27

Quail, 83, 84
Quercus, 29, 51

Rabbit, brush, 65
Raccoon, 55, 61
Raccoon family, 60
Rana, 114, 115
Rat, wood, 69
Raven, 93
Redwood, 27
Regulus, 96
Reithrodontomys megalotis, 71
Rhamnus purshiana, 30
Rhododendron, California, 30
Rhododendron, 30
Rhyacotriton olympicus, 110
Ribes, 32, 33
Robin, 95
Rodents, 66
Rose bay, 30
Rubus parviflorus, 32
   spectabilis, 19
   thrysanthus, 19
   vitifolius, 18

Saggitaria, 14

Salal, 34
Salamander, arboreal, 113
    black, 113
    clouded, 113
    Del Norte, 110
    Dunn's, 110
    Eschscholtz's, 113
    long-toed, 109
    northwestern, 109
    Olympic, 110
    Pacific giant, 110, 116
    slender, 113
    tiger, 110
    Van Dyke's, 113
    Western red-backed, 113
Salicornia, 14
Salmo, 116
Salmon-berry, 19
Salmon, 116
Salt grass, 14
Sapsucker, yellow-bellied, 90
Scapanus, 73
Sceloporus occidentalis, 104
Sciuridae, 66
Sciurus griseus, 66
Scoliopus, 39
Selasphorus, 89
Sequoia sempervirens, 27
Shrew family, 73
Shrews, 72, 73
Shrew-mole, 72, 73
Sialia mexicana, 95
Silk tassel, 21
Sitta, 94
Sittidae, 94
Skink, western, 104, 105
Skunks, 64
Skunk cabbage, 15
Slinkpod, 38, 39
Smilacina racemosa, 40
Snake, garter, 107, 109
    gopher, 107, 109
    king, 106, 107
    racer, 106, 107
    rattle, 104, 105
    ring-necked, 106, 107
    rubber, 104, 108
    sharp-tailed, 107
Snow bush, 31
Snipe, Wilson's, 85
Solidago spathulata, 12

Solomon's seal, 39, 40
Sorex, 73
Soricidae, 73
Sorrel, redwood, 36
Sparrows, 101, 102
Spatula clypeata, 79
Sphyrapicus varius, 90
Spilogale putorius, 64
Spinus, 100
Spizella passerina, 101
Spruce, Sitka, 24, 28
Squaw mat, 31
Squirrel family, 66-67
Squirrels, 66-67
Star flower, 44
Steelhead, 116
Strawberry, sand, 11
Strigiformes, 87
Strix occidentalis, 88
Swallow family, 92
Swallows, 92
Swans, 79
Swift, Vaux, 89
Sylvidae, 96
Sylvilagus bachmani, 65

Tachycineta thalassina, 92
Talpidae, 73
Tamiasciurus douglassi, 66
Tanager, western 99
Tanager family, 99
Taricha, 110, 114
Taxidea taxus, 64
Thamnophis, 105, 107
Thimbleberry, 34
Thomomys, 67
Thraupidae, 99
Thrush family, 95
Thrushes, 95, 96
Thryomanes bewicki, 94
Thuja plicata, 29
Titmouse family, 93
Toad, western, 114
Tobacco bush, 31
Towhees, 100
Trientalis europaea, 43
Trillium, 36, 37
Trilliums, 36, 37
Troglodytidae, 94
Troglodytes troglodytes, 95
Trout, 116
Tsuga heterophylla, 30

Turdidae, 95
Turdus migratorius, 95
Turtles, 104, 106
Typha latifolia, 15
Twinberry, black 21

Umbellularia californica, 47
Urocyon cinereoargenteus, 60
Ursidae, 58
Ursus americanus, 58

Vaccinium, 34
Vancouveria planipetala, 41
Vancouveria hexandra, 42
Vancouveria, small-flowered, 42
Vermivora celata, 97
Vespertilionidae, 74
Verbena, sand, 11
Vireonidae, 97
Vireo family, 97
Vireo, Hutton's, 97
Vireo huttoni, 97
Voles (meadow mice), 70, 71
Vulpes fulva, 60
Vulture, turkey, 81

Wake-robin, Western, 39
Warbler family, 97
Warblers, 97, 98
Water lily, yellow, 16
Waxwing family, 97
Waxwings, 97
Weasel family, 62-64
Weasels, 63
Willet, 85
Willow herb, 49
Wilsonia pusilla, 97
Woodpeckers, 90
Wren family, 94
Wrens, 94, 95
Wren-tit family, 94
Wren-tit, 94

Yarrow, 49
Yellowthroat, 97

Zapodidae, 71
Zapus princeps, 71
Zenaidura macroura, 87
Zonotrichia, 101
Zostera marina, 14

Mineral Resources and Engineering Geology

TEXTS IN EARTH SCIENCES

General Editors
Akiho Miyashiro
Seiya Uyeda
Arata Sugimura
Syn-iti Akimoto
Shinjiro Mizutani
Kazuaki Nakamura
Shohei Banno
Hitoshi Mizutani

Orogeny

Akiho Miyashiro, Keiiti Aki and A. M. Celâl Şengör

Geological Structures

Edited by Takeshi Uemura and Shinjiro Mizutani

Mineral Resources and Engineering Geology

Edited by Akira Sasaki, Shunso Ishihara and Yotaro Seki

Mineral Resources and Engineering Geology

Edited by

Akira Sasaki
Geological Survey of Japan, Ibaraki, Japan

Shunso Ishihara
Geological Survey of Japan, Ibaraki, Japan

and

Yotaro Seki
Hydroscience and Geotechnology Laboratory, Saitama University, Japan

Translated by

Norma St Clair

John Wiley & Sons

Chichester · New York · Brisbane · Toronto · Singapore

World Resources and the Development of the Earth's Surface ed. by Akira Sasaki, Shunso
Ishihara and Yotaro Seki
Copyright © 1979 by Akira Sasaki, Shunso Ishihara and Yotaro Seki
Originally published in Japanese by Iwanami Shoten, Publishers, Tokyo, 1979
This English language edition © 1985 by John Wiley & Sons Limited

Library of Congress Cataloging in Publication Data:
Main entry under title:
Mineral resources and engineering geology.
    (Texts in earth sciences)
    Includes index.
    1. Mines and mineral resources. 2. Engineering geology. 3. Geology—Japan. I. Sasaki,
Akira. II. Ishihara, Shunso. III. Seki, Yotaro, 1925– IV. Series.
TN153.M56 1985 553 84-17428
ISBN 0 471 10536 8

British Library Cataloguing in Publication Data:
Mineral resources and engineering geology.—(Texts in earth sciences)
    1. Mines and mineral resources
I. Sasaki, Akira. II. Ishihara, Shunso. III. Seki, Yotaro. IV. Series
333.8′5 HD9506.A2
ISBN 0 471 10536 8

Printed and bound in Great Britain

PART I

Introduction
Akira Sasaki
Shunso Ishihara

Chapter 1
Hidehiko Shimazaki
Shunso Ishihara
Naotatsu Shikazono
Akira Sasaki
Kazuo Sato

Chapter 2
Kazuo Taguchi
Atsuo Aihara

Chapter 3
Takeo Sato
Shunso Ishihara
Atsuo Aihara
Masao Hayashi

Chapter 4
Takeo Sato
Masao Hayashi
Shunso Ishihara

PART II

Introduction
Yotaro Seki

Chapter 5
Keiji Kojima

Chapter 6
Keiji Kojima

Chapter 7
Keiji Kojima

Chapter 8
Tomomitsu Yasue

Chapter 9
Tomomitsu Yasue

v

Contents

		Page
Preface		xi

PART I   WORLD RESOURCES

Introduction   1

Chapter 1   **The Geochemistry of Metallogenesis**   5
    1.1   The concentration of heavy metals during magmatic processes   5
        (a) The solidification of magma and the behaviour of heavy metal elements   6
        (b) Experimental research on immiscible sulphide melts .   11
        (c) Nickel-copper deposits   16
        (d) Platinum deposits   18
        (e) Chromite deposits   21
        (f) Carbonatite and anorthosite   23
        (g) Concentration of heavy metals during granitoid magmatic processes   24
    1.2   The chemistry of hydrothermal ore solutions   27
        (a) The chemical composition of ore solutions   28
        (b) Factors affecting the composition of ore solutions . . .   33
        (c) Mechanisms of migration of ore solutions   39
        (d) The sources of ore solutions   41
    1.3   Sources of water and sulphur   42
        (a) Sources of water   42
        (b) Sources of sulphur   47
    1.4   The sources of lead   51
        (a) Lead isotopes and the origins of deposits   51
        (b) Lead derived from the crust and from the mantle . . .   52

Chapter 2   **The Geochemistry of Fossil Fuel Deposit**   61
    2.1   Fossil fuel deposits   61

2.2 The geochemistry of coal deposit formation 64
  (a) Source materials for coal deposits 64
  (b) Coalification 70
  (c) Coalification as organic metamorphism 77
2.3 The geochemistry of petroleum deposit formation 80
  (a) Formation of dispersed (non-reservoir)-type
      hydrocarbons 80
  (b) Hydrocarbons from kerogens 82
  (c) Evolution of kerogens and formation of petroleum
      hydrocarbons 84
  (d) Generation mechanism of kerogen-based
      hydrocarbons 86
  (e) Petroleum source rocks 89
  (f) Migration and accumulation of petroleum 90
  (g) Evolution of petroleum and disappearance of deposits 93

Chapter 3 **Global Evolution and the Formation of Mineral Deposits** 99
3.1 Volcanogenic massive sulphide deposits 101
3.2 Nickel deposits associated with komatiite 103
3.3 Banded iron formations 106
3.4 Conglomerate-type uranium–gold deposits
    (Witwatersrand-type deposits) 109
3.5 Stratiform lead–zinc deposits in continental crust rift
    zones (McArthur-type deposits) 111
3.6 Sandstone–shale-type copper deposits 119
3.7 Mississippi Valley-type or Alpine-type deposits 124
3.8 Sandstone (Colorado plateau)- type uranium deposits ... 127
3.9 Porphyry-type deposits 129
  (a) Uneven distribution and age variation 130
  (b) Types of deposits 132
  (c) The genesis of the deposits 133
3.10 Coal deposits 135
  (a) The ages and types of coal deposits 135
  (b) Characteristics of Japanese coal deposits 139
3.11 Petroleum deposits 144
  (a) World distribution of petroleum deposits 144
  (b) Factors concerned in oilfield development 145
  (c) Development of sedimentary basins and the formation
      of petroleum deposits 147

Chapter 4 **The Development of Continents and Island Arcs and the
Formation of Mineral Deposits** 160

4.1 Continental growth and metal mineralization 160
    (a) Canadian Shield—Archaean 160
    (b) Canadian Shield—Proterozoic 163
    (c) Interior lowlands 167
    (d) Appalachian belt 171
    (e) Cordilleran belt 174
4.2 Petroleum-generating basins of North America and their
    tectonics 180
    (a) The Eastern margins of the Cordillera and the Rocky
        Mountains 180
    (b) The Mid-Continent and the Gulf of Mexico 184
    (c) Alaska—the North American frontier 186
4.3 Island arcs and mineralization 192
    (a) Regional characteristics 193
    (b) The role of oceanic plates 196
    (c) Porphyry copper deposits and Kuroko deposits 199
    (d) The importance of the continental crust 201

PART II   DEVELOPMENT OF THE EARTH'S SURFACE

Introduction 211

Chapter 5   Development of the Earth's Surface and Engineering
           Geology 215

Chapter 6   Engineering Geology Methods 221
    6.1 Changes in engineering geology methods 221
    6.2 The sequence of engineering geological surveys 224
    6.3 The geological viewpoint in engineering 225
    6.4 Physical tests of the ground and bedrock and geological
        engineering maps 233
    6.5 Geological interpretation of measured values, and models
        of the ground and bedrock—their relationship to design . 238
    6.6 Assessing the workability of the ground and bedrock ... 241
    6.7 Predicting changes in the geological environment and
        countermeasures 242

Chapter 7   Features of the Ground and Bedrock in Japan 246
    7.1 Crust movements and complex geological structures 246
    7.2 Fractures and fault shatter zones 248
    7.3 Pyroclastic rocks and solfataric clay 249

7.4   Non-calcareous rocks   252
7.5   Rain and geological actions   256

Chapter 8   **Engineering Geology—A Case Study**   259
8.1   The objectives of dams and dam construction in Japan . .   259
8.2   Engineering geology in dam construction   260
8.3   Engineering geology in dam construction—Yahagi Dam .   265
        (a) Summary of the geological survey   265
        (b) Survey of geological structures around the dam site . .   266
        (c) Rock classification at the dam site   270
        (d) Application of the results of the geological survey to
             the dam design   270

Chapter 9   **Geology and the Environment—Case Studies**   279
9.1   Silting up in reservoirs   279
9.2   River bed changes due to silt-saving dams (check dams) . .   281
9.3   Subsidence due to pumping out underground water   286
9.4   Changes in coastal topography due to offshore
breakwaters   289
General References for Part II   292

INDEX   294

Preface

Japan is endowed with small amounts of a great variety of mineral resources and in the past was self-sufficient in many of them. As Japan has now become a country which consumes vast quantities of resources, she has been forced to become an importer. To consume is easy, but the interpretation of complex geological phenomena to aid our quest for new resources is fraught with difficulties. We cannot expect to continue importing and consuming thoughtlessly. As one of the leading consumer nations, it is our duty and responsibility, not just towards ourselves but to all the peoples on earth, to contribute to the science and technology related to the discovery of mineral resources and to their efficient exploitation and utilization.

Japan is a small country but one of her characteristics is that she contains virtually all types of materials like a miniature garden. The same is true with respect to mineral resources. Complex mechanisms have led to the formation of a variety of metallic and non-metallic mineral resources in addition to coal and petroleum, even including uranium, deposits of which were originally thought to be too insignificant for economic production. To explain these complex mechanisms involves us in increasingly higher levels of geological analysis. Resource research workers in Japan have a great advantage in that, apart from the quantities, almost all kinds of mineral commodities have been recognized. Furthermore, as Japan is located in one of the world's youngest mobile belts (an island arc–ocean trench system) some materials are available in abundance here which are found only with difficulty in other areas. Recent research into Japanese deposits—a good example being the Kuroko deposits, which are Cenozoic products preserved fairly well in their original form—has provided an appropriate guide to research and exploration of similar but much older deposits abroad such as in Canada and Australia.

Great progress has been made in geological engineering in Japan since the 1950s. Because of Japan's situation in an active mobile belt there has been considerable endeavour since the Meiji period in the field of construction engineering which has now borne fruit so that Japanese technology is in the forefront of large dam construction or long tunnel excavation. In some cases it may be said to have left the rest of the world standing. Such developments in construction techniques have gone hand in hand with advances in engineering geology. Today, faced with increasing demands for the 'harmonization of national development with conservation' it has become ever more important to develop engineering geology with a thorough comprehension of the laws of natural change in the surface layers of the earth. No one denies that the earth sciences now constitute a vital and integral part of construction engineering, but the earth scientist has no room for complacency. Engineering geology faces a long hard struggle if it is to satisfactorily quantify complex geological factors such as deformation coefficients or failure strengths of the soil and bedrock.

Like all sciences, the earth sciences are also an expression of Man's instinctive search for the truth. The fruits of research must also be fed back into the discovery and exploitation of mineral resources for the benefit of society. It would give the editors more pleasure than anything else if, by reading this book, those in the various branches of the earth sciences began to think more about these problems of feedback and, in particular, if the book aroused in younger people the interest and enthusiasm for resources science and engineering geology.

We also hope that this book will assist those concerned with mineral deposits in the field, mining engineering, engineering geologists or construction engineers by deepening their understanding of the current state of mineral resources science and engineering geology. We hope at the same time that they will read more of the Iwanami Earth Science series and so gain a greater awareness of the totality of the advances in the basic branches of the earth sciences.

References particularly pertinent to the text (marked with an asterisk after the date) are collected at the end of each chapter.

PART I

World Resources

Introduction

In the very beginning of human activity Man learned to select flints and obsidian from amongst the assorted rocks around him and to use them as stone implements. This is symbolic of Man's development right up to the present day; indeed, the advances in our so-called 'material civilization' basically constitute no more than the history of our exploitation and utilization of various mineral resources. In our modern industrial society, whether we like it or not, we have become unable to sustain our daily activities without a constant supply of mineral resources, and supplies of some commodities are likely to be exhausted in the none too distant future. We must therefore not only use our proven resources with care but must also redouble our efforts to discover new ones.

Mineral resources have formed by a variety of processes and in various places throughout the over 3000 million year history of crustal development. Deposits comprise 'unusual' concentrations of specific elements or their compounds. The elements and compounds which are concentrated in deposits are also found in small amounts dispersed through the rocks, and in terms of total abundances there is much more of this dispersed material. However, our current technological level is such that we will be unable to develop and utilize it in the near future.

In order to search for deposits efficiently and to develop those discovered in a rational manner, we need to understand processes whereby individual unusual concentrations, i.e. deposits, formed. Deposits formed at different times in different places throughout the world often have many features in common. It has long been known that deposits can be classified just like rocks. Examination of the maps on the inside cover of this volume shows the remarkably uneven distribution of deposits in the world, and it seems clear that the distribution patterns are closely related to major structural elements in the crust such as orogenic belts or cratons, thus showing that deposits are no freak phenomenon but inevitable geological products related to processes intimately associated with global evolution. Strangely this fact was not really

1

appreciated in most studies of deposits until about the 1960s. A major reason for this lack of understanding was probably our then insufficient recognition of 'normal' geological phenomena from what really constituted 'unusual'. Most deposits exploited until relatively recently (about 1950) were, in part, exposed at the surface, and no real exploration technique had been necessary for their discovery. Most researchers in the field of economic mineral deposits were concerned with the then current problems of exploiting existing deposits and the saying 'they can't see the wood for the trees' was highly applicable to research projects undertaken. Very little work was undertaken to establish the genesis of deposits.

After the Second World War the technological revolution put rapidly accelerating demands on mineral resources. Getting more out of existing deposits and prospecting for new ones then became the central issues. The era in which deposits were sought patiently and painstakingly by looking for surface indications was over. The key to exploration for virgin hidden orebodies or new deposits in completely undeveloped areas with no known deposits nearby thus became a consideration of how the deposits in question might originate. An example close to home is the Kuroko boom of the 1960s. It is still fresh in the memory how, by simply beginning to consider whether it were possible that deposits that were believed to be epigenetic, metasomatic deposits could actually be syngenetic sedimentary deposits, many hidden orebodies were discovered.

To go beyond the immediate vicinity of known deposits and prospect regionally in undeveloped or virgin territories in a rational manner it is vital to have a thorough understanding of what 'mineralization' really means, not just in the narrow sense of how individual deposits came into being but also in terms of global geological processes such as the evolution of continents and island arcs. In this book we give as full an account as space permits of the current thinking about the origins of deposits seen as part of the cycle of 'normal' geological phenomena. Lack of space inevitably precludes a very extensive selection of topics and many of those included cannot be considered as fully as they deserve. We do not know whether we in fact have fulfilled the objectives set out for this book, but will be happy if it is seen as a presentation of the theories about deposits from a slightly different angle than usual.

The mineral resources we actually use are many and varied but in this book we concentrate on metallic mineral resources together with coal and petroleum deposits. Chapter 1 considers the concentration of heavy metal elements and igneous processes in its broadest sense, i.e. from magmatic to hydrothermal processes. Besides igneous processes, sedimentary and metamorphic processes also play an important part in the creation of metalliferous deposits in general. Most trace metal elements which are present at average levels of less than 0.1 per cent. by weight in the crust must increase their concentration 10^2 to 10^4 fold to become workable deposits. Igneous processes of concentration include direct crystallization from silicate melts or transportation and concentration in a water medium containing Cl, F, S, etc., contained in small amounts in magmas. Processes whereby heat supplied from magma warms meteoric, ground or sea water to create hydrothermal systems which concentrate the heavy metals are also included as igneous processes. We attempt to consider the origins of these deposits from the viewpoint of the source of the metals which accumulated in the deposits, the processes whereby they became concentrated and crystallization conditions, etc.

In Chapter 2 we examine the geochemistry of fossil fuel (coal and petroleum) deposits, which are vital to us not only as sources of energy but also as the raw materials for much of the chemical industry. Until now it has been usual to discuss such organic deposits separately from metallic and non-metallic deposits, but they are included in this chapter with the intention of providing a much more unified view of deposit formation and general geological processes. Although not touched on here, it has long been suspected that organic deposits or organic matter in sedimentary rocks could have been closely connected with the development of certain metallic mineralizations. This also suggests that we should pay much more attention to the geochemistry of organic deposit formation.

Chapter 3 is a global survey of how the evolution of the earth, and in particular more than the 3000 million years of crustal evolution, is reflected in the formation of various deposits and their particular features. Metal deposits are considered in relation to important resource materials such as iron, nickel, copper, zinc, lead and uranium, and coal and petroleum are also included. The points dealt with in this chapter and Chapter 4 are likely to be of overriding importance in future prospecting for mineral resources in undeveloped or virgin terrains.

The last chapter, Chapter 4, attempts a more concrete treatment of the time-related ore genesis discussed in the previous chapter by describing the vicissitudes in continental growth and mineralization on the continent of North America. The discussion then turns to igneous activity and metalliferous mineralization in island arc–ocean trench systems, which constitute a basic element of continental growth. This problem is explored from various angles in relation to the circum-Pacific area but concentrates on the islands of Japan. Obviously we Japanese are likely to be very involved in this field in future and we await future developments on some of the points raised in the chapter.

For reference purposes the map inside the front cover shows the 'world's major metal deposits' whereas that inside the back cover illustrates the 'world's principal coal, petroleum and uranium deposits'. An indication of coal rank is included for the coal deposits, whereas the metal deposits are divided into three types based on their formative processes from magmatic to surface genesis. The places featured in the two maps have been selected in terms of the scale of the deposits, and inevitably include many we have been unable to consider in this volume. As quantitative data are very difficult to obtain for socialist countries many deposits in such countries have been omitted. However, these distribution maps and the text go some way towards clarifying the interrelationships between tectonic environments and the location of mineral resources throughout the world.

(Akira Sasaki and Shunso Ishihara)

Chapter 1

The Geochemistry of Metallogenesis

1.1 The concentration of heavy metals during magmatic processes

The generation, eruption and solidification of magma involves bringing huge quantities of material (magma) from the deep earth to the upper crust, and is also believed to lead to the formation of many important ore deposits. The phenomena occurring in these magmatic processes and the factors controlling them are discussed in detail elsewhere in this series. In this volume we discuss the way in which heavy metal elements and sulphur, which are mere trace elements in igneous petrology, behave during magmatic processes and how they are concentrated to form deposits.

Ore deposits formed during magmatic processes are known as (ortho)magmatic deposits (the 'ortho' is often omitted). There are several types of magmatic deposit which have widely different origins but they can, for convenience, be divided into two main groups, i.e.

(1) those associated with ultrabasic–basic rocks and
(2) those associated with acidic rocks.

However, they should perhaps be classified into three groups, based on the mechanisms by which they separated from the magma and became concentrated, i.e.

(1) Separation and concentration due to immiscibility in the melt, attributable to a phenomenon in which silicate and other melts are immiscible. Nickel-copper deposits, platinum deposits, etc., are included in this group. Carbonatite also perhaps develops by this mechanism. Immiscible melts of iron and titanium oxides related to the generation of certain types of ilmenite deposits may also exist.
(2) Separation and concentration due to cyrstallization in a solid phase: chromite, ilmenite and magnetite deposits, etc.
(3) Separation and concentration due to gases and hydrothermal solutions: pegmatite deposits, etc. Hydrothermal deposits associated with igneous rocks should be treated as magmatic deposits when hydrothermal solution

5

was composed principally of liquids emitted by the solidifying magma. However, there is much debate over the sources of water, and generally these are treated separately as hydrothermal deposits. In this book, taking porphyry copper deposits and tin deposits as our examples, we outline the types of element which occur in the hydrothermal deposits related to different granitic magmas. In Sec. 1.2 we detail the chemical composition of hydrothermal solutions and the behaviour of elements in hydrothermal processes.

For a long time only physical mechanisms of solid phase separation, such as gravitative settling of crystals or filter pressing, were considered to be important in the genesis of magmatic deposits, but recently there have been many attempts to explain sudden phase separation by such causes as melt immiscibility, mixing of intermittently supplied magma, etc.

The behaviour of ore-forming elements such as heavy metals, sulphur, halogens, etc., in magmatic processes depends essentially upon (1) the type of solid phase produced when the magma (multi-consituent melt) crystallizes by cooling and (2) the partitioning of elements between the crystallizing solid phase and the magma. In relation to point (1), many experiments have been carried out using melts in simplified systems; and for point (2) we have Onuma and Nagasawa's 'Arayurunium plan' (see Chapter 5, Volume 4 of this series). Unfortunately, these studies are as yet inadequate and our knowledge remains fragmentary. The development of sulphide melts, which are immiscible with silicate magmas, is an important factor in the behaviour of heavy metal elements, and we have just begun to study the partitioning of elements between these two types of melts.

(a) The solidification of magma and the behaviour of heavy metal elements

We consider the behaviour of heavy metal elements during natural processes of magmatic crystallization and phase separation, citing the extensively studied Skaergaard intrusion. This igneous complex lies on the south-east coast of Greenland and is an accumulation of basic magma, approximately 300 km³ in volume. In its marginal phases one finds quenched fine grained gabbro which illustrates the composition of the magma when it intruded. The core became markedly differentiated as it cooled and formed the 'layered series' (see Fig. 1.1). The chemical composition of the layered series and its constituent minerals have been studied intensively and the history of fractionation of the magma has been made clear (Wager, 1960; Wager and Brown, 1967*; Wager and Deer, 1939; etc.). These studies have indicated that most of the igneous body lies hidden beneath the lowest part (lower zone) of the layered series presently exposed. The residual liquid shows almost no increase in SiO_2 until the solidification of more than 95 per cent. of the whole

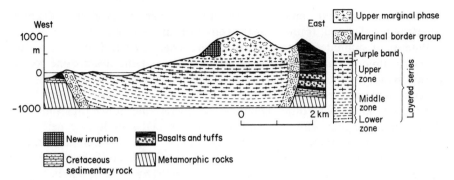

Fig. 1.1   East-west profile of the Skaergaard intrusion. (After Wager and Brown, 1967*; Wager, Vincent and Smales, 1957*.)

body, together with a decrease in MgO and an increase in total Fe. It may thus be said to be typical of fractional crystallization of basaltic magma in a closed system. However, recent research (McBirney, 1975, etc.) questions whether there is a great body hidden under the lower zone, and it is possible that the history of the solidification of Skaegaard magma may have to be rewritten.

Several studies have been made concerning the behaviour of trace elements during solidification of this intrusion (Paster, Schauwecker and Haskin, 1974*; Wager and Mitchell, 1951*; Wager, Vincent and Smales, 1957*; etc.). Principal concentration of these elements in the magma has been calculated using analytical data for each type of rock and mineral with estimates of the quantity of crystals removed as cumulates, but the results of different researchers are not in good agreement. In the following we discuss the behaviour of elements relevant to the study of ore deposits, with particular emphasis on the data relating to sulphur provided by Wager, Vincent and Smales (1957*).

We know from analyses of the chilled margin that there was only approximately 50 ppm of sulphur in the magma which formed the Skaergaard complex. This is approximately one order of magnitude less than the sulphur content of normal basaltic magmas (Moore and Fabbi, 1971; etc.). The reason why the magma which formed the Skaergaard complex was low in sulphur is not clear. There is no evidence in the lateral marginal phases for the existence of an immiscible sulphide melt produced before intrusion. We do not fully understand the hidden series but hardly any sulphur seems to have entered the silicate minerals (mainly olivine, etc.) which crystallized out. It seems that as the greater part of the magma solidified, the sulphur content of the residual liquid gradually increased. It has been calculated that the sulphur content of the magma at the time of formation of the lower zone was approximately 100 ppm. The sulphur content in the residual liquid gradually increased through the lower, middle and upper zones reaching a maximum of almost 600 ppm when the purple band, found near the top of the upper zone, was formed.

Patches of sulphides, consisting of bornite, chalcopyrite, digenite, etc., are found in minute quantities in rocks extending from the lower zone to the purple band. In the lower part of the upper zone in particular, these are concentrated to form 'melanocratic layers', indicating that the sulphides precipitated along with other minerals; i.e. there is no doubt that sulphides existed in the magma as an independent phase. From the results of experiments on sulphide melts composed principally of copper, Wager, Vincent and Smales (1957*) concluded that these patches of sulphides must have become concentrated in a molten state as immiscible melts. The sulphide patches in the portion other than the melanocratic layers would have crystallized from magma caught interstitially among the settling silicate minerals. According to the description, these sulphide patches accompany magnetite which is free of ilmenite lamellae. As we discuss below, experiments have shown that when a silicate melt coexists with an immiscible sulphide melt Ti is partitioned into the silicate melt depleting the sulphide melt (MacLean, 1976). As the magnetite in the surrounding silicate rock shows ilmenite exsolution we can possibly conclude that the patches of sulphides associated with ilmenite-free magnetite derived from an immiscible sulphide (-oxide) melt.

This indicates that the magma which contained approximately 100 ppm sulphur at the beginning of solidification of the lower zone almost certainly became saturated with sulphur, resulting in the separation of traces of an immiscible sulphide melt. The sulphur content rose to almost 600 ppm and Wager, Vincent and Smales (1957*) attribute this to the fact that the magma gradually became richer in iron thus raising the solubility of sulphur in the magma. This is supported qualitatively by the results of recent experiments. However, even though metals such as Ni, Co and Fe are known to be most readily partitioned into sulphide melts, as we shall show later, those of the Skaergaard complex at this stage are characterized by an overwhelming concentration of Cu. It is well known that Ni is selectively partitioned into olivine (see Chapter 6, Volume 4 of this series) and a possible explanation for the composition of the sulphide melt is that as crystallization began much olivine fractionated, resulting in a relatively low concentration of Ni in the residual magma. It is said (for example by Paster, Schauwecker and Haskin, 1974*) that Co is also selectively included in olivine and pyroxene, though not as strongly as Ni, thus reducing the Co content of the residual liquid. Calculations by Wager, Vincent and Smales (1957*) suggested that the Co content of approximately 55 ppm at the time of magma intrusion rose to approximately 75 ppm as the lower zone began to solidify and subsequently declined gradually. The result, therefore, is not quite consistent with the general trend stated above. It seems that Co tends to have been selectively incorporated into the sulphide patches.

Sulphides are particularly concentrated in the upper part of the purple band which is found near the top of the upper zone. This includes small patches of sulphides, about 0.5 mm in diameter at most, and the sulphur content of the rock is approximately 0.5 per cent. by weight. Because it mostly takes the form of small droplets there can be no doubt that immiscible sulphide melts were produced at this stage. The main constituent of the small droplets is pyrrhotite with small amounts of chalcopyrite. Both Ni and Co contents are of $0.0n$ per cent. According to Wager, Vincent and Smales (1957*), by the time this band was formed Cu had been selectively extracted from the remaining liquid as an immiscible sulphide melt, leaving a very low concentration of Cu in the residual liquid. However, as the sulphide melt had until then been principally composed of Cu, it seems very strange that it would suddenly change to one composed mainly of Fe.

Sulphides such as pyrrhotite, pyrite, chalcopyrite, etc., can be found above the purple band, but only in very small quantities. It is thought that as differentiation proceeded, granophyre, which is believed to have solidified last in the Skaergaard intrusion, was squeezed out of the solidifying rock by a process of filter pressing to form sheets and dykes. However, a completely different approach to the origins of granophyre has recently been suggested (see Chapter 2, Volume 3 of this series). These rocks are said to contain 3 per cent. pyrite or pyrrhotite. Wager, Vincent and Smales (1957*) deduced from their structure that patches of pyrrhotite in the acid granophyre must have been immiscible melts, but there are no positive data supporting this idea that sulphides in the rock produced in the final stages of solidification had been immiscible melts. Instead, they could be seen as having crystallized directly from the silicate magma or from hydrothermal solutions. These sulphides contain only 200 ppm of Cu and Co, and 1 ppm of Ni.

Figure 1.2 shows changes in the nickel, cobalt, copper and sulphur contents of the residual liquid and of the cumulate, as calculated by Wager, Vincent and Smales (1957*), but although the general trend is illustrated there is disagreement over the quantitative estimate of the changes in concentration of nickel, cobalt, copper and sulphur in the residual liquid among some investigators.

In consideration of other elements, Paster, Schauwecker and Haskin (1974*) investigated partition coefficients for various trace elements between liquid and solid phases (Table 1.1). As shown in Table 1.1 rare-earth elements and Ba, Cu, etc., tended to be concentrated in the remaining liquid as differentiation proceeded. With the manifestation of immiscible sulphide melts in the Skaergaard complex the concentration of Cu in the remaining liquid declined rapidly. In contrast to this, Ni, Co, Mn, etc., are thought to have been partitioned into olivine and pyroxene, and so became depleted in the remaining liquid during differentiation. Zn is usually concentrated in olivine and magnetite but in Skaergaard it has gradually increased in the residual

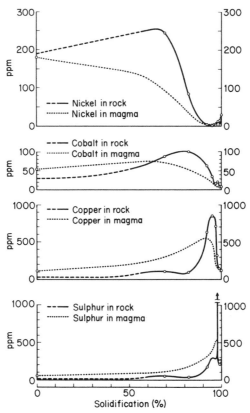

Fig. 1.2   Changes in nickel, cobalt, copper and sulphur contents in rock and the magma from which it developed, in the Skaergaard intrusion. (After Wager, Vincent and Smales, 1957*.)

magma from the lower zone to the middle of the upper zone. As and Sb have been discussed by Esson *et al.* (1965). Sb appears to have selectively entered olivine which crystallizes at an early stage, and both As and Sb began to be increasingly concentrated in the remaining liquid from the solidification of the lower to the middle zone. Although Cd can be incorporated in olivine, pyroxene and magnetite, it has been demonstrated in the Skaergaard complex to have been concentrated in the remaining liquid (Vincent and Bilefield, 1960). Interestingly, although Cd has, since the time of Goldschmidt, been classified as a chalcophile element, it does not tend to concentrate in sulphide melts rich in Cu or Fe. In this respect it resembles Zn which we discuss below. Many of the rocks in this intrusive body have Au contents close to that of magma at the time of intrusion, i.e. 0.0046 ppm, but the rocks containing sulphides of Cu have an Au content one order of magnitude higher than this

Table 1.1 Partition coefficients for trace elements between magma and minerals estimated for the Skaergaard complex. (After Paster, Schauwecker and Haskin, 1974*.)

Mineral	Plagioclase	Olivine	Pyroxene	Apatite	Magnetite	Ilmenite
La	0.069	0.0084	0.061	8.6	0.015	0.098
Ce	0.062	0.010	0.26	11.2	0.016	0.11
Nd	0.028	0.008	0.29	14.0	0.026	0.14
Sm	0.017	0.006	0.32	14.6	0.024	0.15
Eu	0.68	0.008	0.27	9.6	0.025	0.10
Gd	0.014	0.008	0.41	15.8	0.018	0.14
Tb	0.013	0.010	0.42	15.4	0.019	0.14
Ho	0.011	0.005	0.44	13.3	0.017	0.13
Yb	0.009	0.028	0.44	8.1	0.018	0.17
Ba	0.68	<0.05	<0.05	<0.05	—	—
Co	0.026	3.1	1.2	<0.03	3.4	2.2
Ga	1.70	<0.25	<0.25	<0.25	2.0	0.14
Cu	0.004	0.023	0.071	0.28	0.42	1.46
Mn	0.016	2.6	1.6	0.13	1.4	1.9
Sc	0.008	0.33	3.3	0.22	0.73	1.8
Zn	0.13	1.8	0.49	<0.25	2.6	0.38

(Vincent and Crochet, 1960), implying that Au behaved in a similar way to Cu. As we discuss below, experimental results show that Au is concentrated in sulphide melts rather than silicate magma, but it seems anomalous that none has concentrated in the upper part of the purple band. Furthermore, contrary to results obtained experimentally, no Pd concentration can be found in the sulphide melts in the Skaergaard complex (Wager, Vincent and Smales, 1957*).

As stated above, if we look at the intensely studied Skaergaard complex as an example, we find that the behaviour of elements in magmatic processes does not necessarily conform to the predictions of laboratory experiments, and we are often unable to provide an adequate explanation for what happened in nature. For a better understanding of natural phenomena it is essential to examine such factors as the composition and temperature dependence on partitioning of elements between magma and crystals.

(b) Experimental research on immiscible sulphide melts

On the genesis of nickel–copper sulphide deposits, typified by Sudbury, and platinum deposits, such as Merensky Reef in the Bushveld Complex, there has been the increasing belief that they are formed from solidified sulphide melts which separated out from basic magma due to their immiscibility. After Skinner and Peck (1969*) originally discovered small droplets consisting mainly of sulphides in quenched basalt from lava lakes in Hawaii, similar sulphide droplets were discovered in basic rocks elsewhere. The results of many laboratory experiments have also provided plausible explanations for the genesis of these nickel–copper and platinum deposits.

Experimental research into immiscible sulphide melts has been entirely related to metallurgy. This is because when smelting copper ore, for example, a silicate-based slag separates from, and rises to the surface of, a sulphide-based matte because the two melts are immiscible. Since the latter half of the 1960s earth scientists too have been performing experiments when FeS, etc., is introduced into a comparatively simple system such as $FeO-Fe_3O_4-SiO_2$. Experiments have also been carried out using natural basic and ultrabasic rocks. In these studies the solubility of sulphur (strictly speaking, the solubility of sulphides or the solubility of sulphide melts), the factors controlling the solubility, and the appearance of the liquidus surface during solidification, etc., have been considered.

The results show that factors such as temperature, sulphur and oxygen fugacity, as well as the composition of the melt, control the dissolution of sulphur in silicate melts, and in particular the amount of divalent iron in the melt is important. Sulphur dissolved in silicate melts is thought to displace oxygen, producing metal–sulphur bonds commonly with divalent iron (II). Therefore, the solubility of sulphur in silicate melts is affected considerably by the amount of divalent iron present (Haughton *et al.*, 1974; MacLean, 1969*; etc.). Figure 1.3 shows the shape of the liquidus surface in an $FeS-FeO-SiO_2$ system, whereas Fig. 1.4 shows an $FeS-Fe_3O_4-SiO_2$ system for comparison (MacLean, 1969*).

In natural magma, solidification proceeds due to falling temperature, so that the sulphur reaches saturation point and forms an immiscible sulphide melt (e.g. Fig. 1.3, a → a'). However, as clearly shown in Fig. 1.4, oxidation of the magma can also result in the formation of large quantities of immiscible sulphide melts. Similar effects may also be expected if large quantities of a solid phase crystallize out, removing divalent iron. Page (1971) could not explain the formation of immiscible sulphide melts in the Stillwater complex by a rise in oxygen fugacity and a fall in temperature, but rather explained it in terms of a rapid decline in divalent iron caused by the crystallization of chromite.

In simple systems, such as that of $FeS-FeO-SiO_2$ shown in Fig. 1.3, where silicate and sulphide melts coexist, solidification of the sulphide melt begins only after the silicate melt has completely solidified (1140 °C). Fayalite and tridymite crystallize out before it reaches the troilite region (1075 °C), and the part containing the sulphides solidifies last of all. If an alkali component or water is introduced into such a system, they generally become concentrated in the silicate melt and markedly reduce the liquidus temperature. Therefore, when immiscible melts coexist, the sequence of crystallization observed is

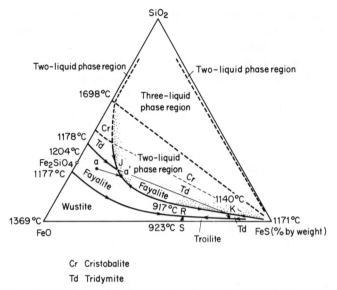

Cr Cristobalite
Td Tridymite

Fig. 1.3   The shape of the liquidus surface in an FeS–FeO–SiO$_2$ system. (After MacLean, 1969*.)

similar to the natural one; i.e. the sulphide melt also solidifies during solidification of the silicate melt, and the final product is a silicate melt which is rich in alkalis, water, etc. (Shimazaki and Clark, 1973).

Recently, in addition to these experiments, attempts have been made to investigate the partition coefficient D of various elements between immiscible melts. As shown later, in natural deposits sulphide melts contain remarkable concentrations of metals such as Ni, Cu and Co, and precious metals such as Au and Pt which can be qualitatively explained by experimental data. Table

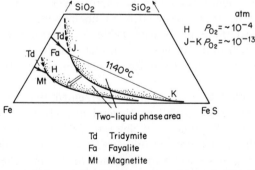

Td Tridymite
Fa Fayalite
Mt Magnetite

Fig. 1.4   Enlargement of the two-liquid phase areas shown in Fig. 1.3 due to a rise in oxygen fugacity in the system. (After MacLean, 1969*.)

1.2 shows the partition coefficients obtained to date. This type of experiment has long been carried out in the fields of smelting and metallurgy. Many papers consider the kinds and quantities of metals lost to the slag during smelting, but most of these fail to distinguish between the amount which actually dissolves in the slag and that which is lost as droplets of sulphide melt in the slag. The fact that data such as those in Table 1.2 are now appearing owes much to developments in X-ray microanalysers.

Table 1.2 The partition coefficients D for elements between silicate and sulphide melts ($D = \%$ by weight in sulphide melt/ $\%$ by weight in silicate melt)

	D			D
Ni	150^a, $231–460^c$		V	$0.4 > > 0.01^e$
Cu	50^a, $180–333^c$		Cr	0.01^e
Co	7^a, $61–80^c$		Au	176^d
Fe	1.2^a		Pt	118^d
Zn	$0.1–0.5^b$		Ir	80^d
Pb	$\geqslant 10^b$		Os	34^d
Mn	0.4^e		Pd	156^d
Ti	$0.4 > > 0.01^e$			

[a] MacLean and Shimazaki (1976*), FeS–FeO–SiO_2 system, 1150°C.
[b] Shimazaki and MacLean (1976*), FeS–FeO–SiO_2 system, mainly 1140°C.
[c] Rajamani and Naldrett (1978*), SiO_2–Al_2O_3–FeO–MgO–CaO–Na_2O–K_2O system, 1255–1325°C (synthetic andesite, basalt, olivine basalt).
[d] Rajamani *et al.* (1977), synthetic basalt, 1255°C.
[e] MacLean (1976), FeS–FeO–SiO_2 system, 1150°C.

It is well known that Goldschmidt divided the elements into lithophile, chalcophile and siderophile elements, considering smelting and metallurgical data, analyses of meteorites and free energy of formation of oxides and sulphides. Many of those designated as chalcophile and siderophile are concentrated in sulphide melts (see Table 1.2). However, there are also elements such as Zn and Cd which, although classified as chalcophile, can easily enter silicate melts under physical and chemical conditions prevailing in the earth's crust.

As shown in Table 1.2, there is some disagreement over values of D for Ni, Cu and Co, but partition coefficients depend strongly on the composition of the melts. One report (Rajamani and Naldrett, 1978*) asserts that the partition coefficients for Ni and Cu depend on whether the silicate magma is basic or ultrabasic, but it is also argued (Shimazaki and MacLean, 1976*) that partition coefficients are affected by the oxygen content of the sulphide melt. The latter argument claims that various metals enter the sulphide melt mainly in the form of sulphides, but if the oxygen fugacity is high they may also enter it as oxides, thus suggesting that the activity coefficient of these metal sulphides and oxides in sulphide melts is controlled by the oxygen content of the sulphide melt. The oxygen content of the sulphide melt is controlled by the oxygen and sulphur fugacity, etc. It has been estimated that the Sudbury sulphide magma contained 3–5 per cent. by weight of oxygen. The oxygen content of sulphide droplets in the basaltic lava lakes in Hawaii is approximately 5 per cent. (Skinner and Peck, 1969*), whereas that of basalts in the mid-Atlantic Ridge is only about 1 per cent. (Czamanske and Moore, 1977*). Further systematic experiments are needed to obtain partition coefficients close to those of natural conditions. However, as stated above, qualitative explanations of natural examples using the data given in Table 1.2 can be given.

Ni and Cu, which are of $0.0n$ per cent. in basic–ultrabasic magma, often reach up to n % of sulphide melts. However, Ni is rapidly removed from magma as olivine crystallizes as mentioned above, and therefore to achieve an effective Ni concentration immiscible sulphide melts must form early in the crystallization of the magma. Precious metals are concentrated in magmatic sulphide deposits as predicted by experimental data. Little Pb and Zn is contained in these deposits because of the low concentration of Pb in basic magma (n ppm) and, although the concentration of Zn in the magma is almost equal to that of Ni and Cu, its partition coefficient is small. The partition coefficient for Ti is also small; magnetite in Sudbury ores rarely contains ilmenite.

The partition coefficient for Cr is also low, i.e. 0.01 (Table 1.2). The compositions of the silicate melt and the immiscible sulphide melt used by MacLean and Shimazaki (1976*) and MacLean (1976) are given as J–K in Fig. 1.3. The sulphide melt contained approximately 4.3 per cent. by weight of oxygen. It is thought that the Sudbury deposits were formed from sulphide magma with a similar oxygen content. All the Cr in the Sudbury sulphide deposits is contained as traces in magnetite with no reports of chromite, in agreement with the partition coefficients given above. However, the crystallization of chromite from a sulphide melt has been confirmed in cases where it is thought the sulphide melt formed in a more reducing environment, e.g. the basaltic floor of the mid-Atlantic Ridge, nickel deposits associated with komatiite or the sulphide deposits in La Perouse stratiform gabbro in Alaska associated with graphite (Czamanske and Moore, 1977*; Czamanske *et al.*, 1976; Groves *et al.*, 1977). In the Lunnon Shoot associated with komatiite in Western Australia the Cr content of the sulphide melt has been estimated as approximately 0.4 per cent. (Groves *et al.*, 1977). The Cr partition coefficient in a sulphide melt in this sort of environment is thus thought to be considerably higher than the value given in Table 1.2. This is consistent with the chalcophile behaviour of Cr when in a reducing environment, as demonstrated by the occurrence of daubreelite ($FeCr_2S_4$) in meteorites.

(c) Nickel–copper deposits

Nickel–copper sulphide deposits associated with basic and ultrabasic rocks commonly consist of chalcopyrite and pentlandite-bearing pyrrhotite ore and have, until now, been our most important source of nickel. Almost the only other source of nickel is garnierite, which is a weathered residue of olivine containing traces ($0.n$–$0.0n$ per cent.) of nickel. As mentioned earlier, the majority of nickel–copper sulphide deposits are widely believed to have condensed and separated from the magma as immiscible sulphide melts and at present there are no strong arguments to refute this.

The area of Sudbury in Ontario, Canada, is renowned as typical of such nickel–copper deposits. Many deposits are known around the margins of the intrusion called the Sudbury irruptive or Nickel irruptive. The region has for a long time supplied more than half of the world's demand for nickel. Figure 1.5, a sketch map of Sudbury, shows the distribution of the deposits. The intrusion is funnel-shaped. The footwall is shattered and is known as Sudbury breccia, but brecciation has not affected the Sudbury irruptive or the overlying Whitewater series. The basement comprises gneiss, granitic and basic rocks of the Archaeozoic era, and the overlying Whitewater series comprises brecciated quartzite, volcanic breccia, tuffs, clay slate and arkose and cannot be correlated with any other strata in the area. The formation of the Whitewater series together with the basin structure of Sudbury has been clearly explained by the meteorite impact theory (Dietz, 1964*). (See Chapter 2, Volume 9 of this series.)

The Sudbury irruptive is a stratiform complex, the lower half consisting of norite (orthopyroxene > clinopyroxene) and the upper half of micropegmatite (Fig. 1.5). Basic rocks—called the sub-layer—have intruded irregularly near the boundary between the basement and the norite. Although discontinuous, it completely surrounds the irruptive and contains many xenoliths of basement and ultrabasic rocks in addition to sulphides. It is mainly in this sub-layer that the nickel–copper deposits developed. Some of the sub-layer, known as the offset, penetrated as dykes into the basement and is worked (see Fig. 1.5). Such basic igneous activity is believed to have been triggered by meteorite impact and the entire irruption is the result of several intrusions rather than the product of in situ differentiation of a single intrusion (Naldrett and Kullerud, 1967; Naldrett *et al.*, 1970; Peredery and Naldrett, 1975; etc.). The rising magma probably created a magma chamber at a deep level, from which it intruded intermittently to its present position. It is believed that the majority of the sulphide melts which developed because of immiscibility in the magma chamber rose and were intruded along with the silicate magma to form the sub-layer. However, as the sulphide melts were very rich in Ni, immiscibility must have occurred very early in the differentiation of the magma chamber (see Fig. 1.6). These sulphide melts rose and were intruded at a similar time to

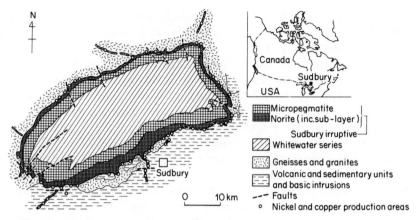

Fig. 1.5   Geological map of the Sudbury region. (After Souch *et al.*, 1969.)

magma in a fairly advanced state of differentiation, which produced norite and micropegmatite. What actually happened during this period is unclear and constitutes one of the major outstanding problems concerning the origins of the Sudbury rocks and ores (Naldrett *et al.*, 1972).

Nickel–copper deposits typified by Sudbury are associated with basic-ultrabasic intrusions. Large nickel deposits have recently been found in the Archaeozoic shields in Africa, Australia and Canada in association with

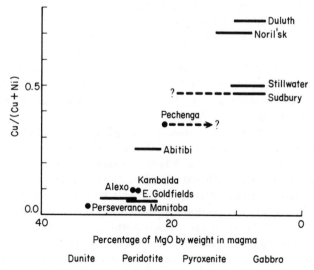

Fig. 1.6   Relationship between the Cu/(Cu + Ni) ratio of a sulphide ore and the nature of its host magma or rock. (After Naldrett and Cabri, 1976*.)

ultrabasic volcanic activity. These have recently attracted attention as sources of nickel second in importance to Sudbury. The ultrabasic rock associated with them is komatiite, and ultrabasic volcanic rock rich in MgO. The nickel deposits, and most magmatic sulphide deposits including Sudbury (1900–2000 Ma), are Archaeozoic. Exceptions to this are the young deposits found in the Duluth complex (1100 Ma) and those in the Noril'sk region (Mid-Triassic). One theory postulates that the formation of most magmatic sulphide deposits in the Archaeozoic was related to the evolution of the mantle (Naldrett, 1973*). The origins of these deposits, and the genesis of nickel deposits associated with komatiite, are discussed again in Sec. 3.4 as examples of Archaeozoic mineralizations.

As stated above, Ni is partitioned into mafic minerals more favourably than Cu during the early stages of magma differentiation. Thus the $Cu/(Cu + Ni)$ ratio is likely to vary markedly, depending on the stage of differentiation at which the immiscible sulphide melts develop. Thus the ratio and the MgO content of associated basic rocks in typical nickel–copper deposits are expected to show a linear correlation (Fig. 1.6). A similar relationship is shown by sulphide droplets in basalt collected from the mid-Atlantic Ridge (Czamanske and Moore, 1977*).

(d) Platinum deposits

Concentration of platinum group elements, mainly platinum, is almost always associated with ultrabasic–basic igneous activity. There are several theories concerning the mechanism by which they are concentrated. One view, though still debatable, is that because platinum group elements are often closely associated with chromite, they form solid solutions in chromite at high temperatures and exsolve at low temperatures (Naldrett and Cabri, 1976*; etc.). Platinum group trace minerals, found in basic rocks, are often concentrated sufficiently to be mined as sand deposits, such concentration being caused by weathering and by the natural processes of grading and deposition associated with weathering.

Another concentration mechanism is associated with sulphides and in most cases platinum group elements are thought to have been dissolved in immiscible sulphide melts. The most famous example of this type of deposit is the Merensky Reef in the Bushveld complex. The Bushveld complex is situated in the Transvaal in South Africa and is well known as the largest layered complex in the world. The complex intruded the quartzite, shales, limestones and tuffs of the Pretoria series—which form the top of the Archaeozoic Transvaal system—and a stratiform succession ranging from the peridotite to the Bushveld granites can be seen (Fig. 1.7). The exposed area of 70 000 km^2 is 650 times that of the Skaergaard complex and over fifty times that of the Sudbury irruptive. The whole body forms a large gentle basin which consists

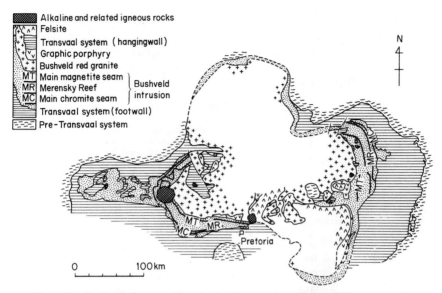

Alkaline and related igneous rocks
Felsite
Transvaal system (hangingwall)
Graphic porphyry
Bushveld red granite
MT Main magnetite seam ⎫
MR Merensky Reef   ⎬ Bushveld
MC Main chromite seam ⎭ intrusion
Transvaal system (footwall)
Pre-Transvaal system

N

0 _____ 100 km

Fig. 1.7   Geological map of the Bushveld intrusion. (After Willemse, 1969.)

of several small basin structures. One theory postulates its formation by the simultaneous impact of several meteorites (Rhodes, 1975).

The lower half of the intrusive is made up of peridotite, anorthosite and gabbro, up to 8000 m thick. In addition to the platinum deposits, there are also chromite and vanadiferous magnetite deposits. The complex is well exposed both to the east and to the west, called the Eastern and Western Mafic Lobes, which, although widely separated, show a very comparable sequence of crystallization. A simplified crystallization sequence is shown in Fig. 1.8.

The thin layer, the Merensky Reef, famous for its platinum deposits, can be traced well into the Eastern and Western Lobes, as shown in Fig. 1.7. The Merensky Reef is a layer of pyroxenite bounded above and below by thin layers of chromitite. Its structure often resembles that of pegmatite and it contains disseminated sulphides of Ni, Cu and Fe. In one sample the concentration of gold and platinum group elements is 10 g/t in a 75 cm thick layer, the proportions of precious metals being Pt 60 %, Pd 27 %, Ru 5 %, Rh 2.7 %, Ir 0.7 %, Os 0.6 % and Au 4 % (Molyneux, 1972).

There are many theories concerning the origins of the Merensky Reef, none of which is definitive. Directly above this reef lies a continuous layer of anorthosite of almost uniform thickness, in which the anorthite content of the plagioclase increases upwards, suggesting that the magma at this stage was covered with a mat of anorthosite due to the buoyancy of the plagioclase, so that there was a concentration of volatile compounds in the uppermost part of the confined magma, causing the development of a pegmatite structure. The

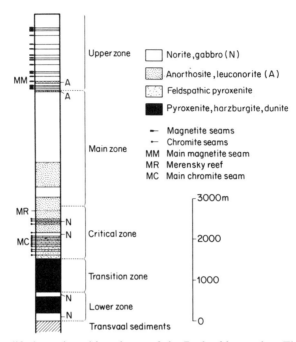

Fig. 1.8   Simplified stratigraphic column of the Bushveld complex. The boundary of zones varies slightly from one report to another. (After Vermaak, 1976*.)

iron content of the magma decreased with crystallization of chromite, causing an increase in sulphur fugacity so producing immiscible sulphide melts (Vermaak, 1976*). As shown in Table 1.2, sulphide melts readily absorb gold and platinum group elements and have played an important role in the concentration of platinum group elements in the Merensky Reef. However, the concentration of platinum group elements in the Merensky Reef (and the sulphide deposits in the upper part of the banded zone in the Stillwater complex) is much higher than in other magmatic sulphide deposits (Table 1.3). A possible explanation is that the concentration of platinum group elements in the silicate magma was exceptionally high, but it could also be that concentration of the platinum group elements was by a mechanism other than that of absorption by the sulphide melt.

The concentrations of various platinum group elements vary from deposit to deposit. Naldrett and Cabri (1976*) compared Cu/(Cu + Ni) and Pt/(Pt + Pd) ratios in various magmatic sulphide deposits excluding those associated with komatiite and found that an increase in the Cu/(Cu + Ni) ratio (thought to correspond to progression of magmatic differentiation; see Fig. 1.6) is accompanied by a decline in the Pt/(Pt + Pd) ratio. In deposits associated with komatiite the Pt/(Pt + Pd) ratio is low despite small

Table 1.3 Estimated concentrations of nickel and copper (% by weight) and platinum group elements and gold (ppm) in sulphide melts.

	Ni	Cu	Pt	Pd	Rh	Au
● Bushveld (South Africa)						
(Merensky Reef)	10.9	4.65	258	102	17	21
● Stillwater (USA) (Johns-Manville)	—	—	160–550	600–2000	—	—
● Sudbury (Canada)	4.5	4.0	1.04	1.09	0.09	0.37
● Noril'sk (USSR) (Picrite gabbro)	9.0	10.8	18.0	47.8	1.7	1.6
● Pechenga (USSR)	4.6	2.45	0.6	0.5	—	0.2
○ Marbridge (Canada) (Abitibi belt)	6.5	0.38	0.36	0.92	0.08	0.18
○ Manibridge (Canada) (Manitoba						
Ni belt)	10.0	0.75	0.95	2.6	0.26	0.24
○ Shangani (Zimbabwe)	9.75	1.20	1.3	2.0	0.20	0.10

● Indicates deposits associated with tholeiite. ○ Indicates deposits associated with komatiite. Note that both the Cu/(Cu + Ni) ratio and the Pt/(Pt + Pd) ratio are low in deposits associated with komatiite. In Bushveld and Stillwater, the concentration of platinum group elements is particularly high. (After Naldrett and Cabri, 1976*.)

Cu/(Cu + Ni) ratios (see Table 1.3). Naldrett and Cabri believed that this originated in places where komatiite magmas were produced. Nickel deposits associated with komatiite are discussed fully in Chapter 3.

(e) Chromite deposits

Concentration of chromite $(Fe^{2+}, Mg) (Cr, Al, Fe^{3+})_2O_4$ is found in various ultrabasic and basic rocks but thin layers in stratiform intrusives and those in Alpine-type ultrabasic rocks are particularly important. There are many explanations for the origins of the latter ultrabasic rocks and some workers now believe that they are ophiolites or a part of ophiolite (see the summary by Naldrett, 1973*). Thin layers of chromitite in the ultramafic cumulates which underlie the gabbro in ophiolites are thought to have an origin similar to that of stratiform intrusions; however, the origins of chromitite (massive-lenticular in form, often called podiform chromite deposits) in the dunite and harzburgite, which are stratigraphically the base of an ophiolite, have not yet been satisfactorily explained. If the Alpine-type ultrabasic rocks form part of an ophiolite with the dunite and harzburgite representing mantle residual after partial fusion, then it is likely that the podiform chromite rock formed at the same time as the host mantle.

A good example of thin layers of chromitite in a layered intrusion can be found in the Bushveld complex. Systematic changes in the composition of the chromite within each layer are apparent, e.g. the Cr/Fe ratio becomes smaller toward the upper thin layers (Cameron, 1977; Cameron and Desborough,

1969*) and the average composition in chromite-rich portions is about 49 per cent. for Cr_2O_3, 23 per cent. total iron oxides, 14 per cent. Al_2O_3, 12 per cent. MgO; Cr/Fe ratio is 1.6–1.7 (Molyneux, 1972). There are several theories relating to the origin of thin chromite layers in this type of layered intrusion. Many believe that the thin layers represent cumulate layers formed during fractionation. There are several suggestions to account for the cyclic formation of chromite layers, selective accumulation due to magmatic movements or changes in oxygen fugacity (Cameron and Desborough, 1969*). Irvine (1975) thought that thin chromite layers crystallized out and were deposited when the basic magma was extensively contaminated by granitic magma produced by the fusion of part of the felsic roof rock by the basic magma. However, a recent revision of this theory suggests that the thin chromite layers developed when fresh basic magma was supplied to the magma chamber and became homogenized (see Fig. 1.9) (Irvine, 1977*). This is clearly an attractive explanation, but as has been pointed out by Cameron (1977), it seems still rather unlikely that in a vast magma chamber, such as the Bushveld

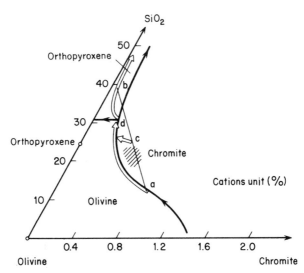

Fig. 1.9 Estimate of liquidus surface projected on the olivine, quartz and chromite join. The initial liquid a crystallizes olivine and chromite and reaches point d. Orthopyroxene, which crystallizes out, contains a considerable amount of Cr (the composition corresponds to the hatched area) and so afterwards it follows the path d→b, as indicated by the white arrow. When the composition of liquid reaches b, the liquid a is again supplied and mixes to give composition c. (The position depends on the proportion of differentiated liquid to supplied liquid.) The composition of this liquid falls in the chromite phase region and so only chromite crystallizes until it returns to the path a→d. In this way various crystallized minerals can make layers. (After Irvine, 1977*.)

complex (in the Eastern/Western Mafic Lobes it is thought that the magma was supplied from different centres), any newly supplied magma could be homogenized rapidly and completely with the pre-existed magma. Cameron (1977) abandoned his old hypothesis based on changes in oxygen fugacity and advocates pressure changes as a more likely explanation of the regional phenomenon. Debate over this issue is certain to continue.

As shown in Fig. 1.8, the Bushveld complex contains approximately 20 thin layers of vanadiferous magnetite deposits. It is known that as in the case of the thin chromite layers, these show good continuity and the V_2O_5 content of each thin layer changes from the bottom to the top (2–0.2 per cent.) (Molyneux, 1970, etc). The theories relating to the chromite layer may also be applicable to the origins of magnetite layers but many points remain obscure.

(f) Carbonatite and anorthosite

Many magmatic deposits, in addition to those discussed above, have distinctive characteristics. For example, carbonatite, which is important as a source of rare-earth elements and other elements such as Nb and Zr, is intriguing material in the origins of igneous rocks. The presence of CO_2 in the mantle and its influence on the generation of magma are discussed in detail in Chapters 3 and 4 of Volume 3 of this series. The existence of carbonatite magmas is not in doubt, but theories abound concerning the mechanisms by which they are formed. It has been suggested they are a product of fractional crystallization of magmas with low silica concentrations. However, in certain systems, such as the one rich in Na, it has been shown experimentally that carbonate becomes immiscible with silicate melts (Koster van Groos, 1975*). Many researchers have also identified immiscibility in nature (e.g. Rankin and Le Bas, 1974). Without exception carbonatite is associated with alkaline rocks such as nepheline syenite. Currently we have little proof that all carbonatite magmas are immiscible with such alkaline magmas, but this theory conforms to some descriptions of natural occurrences (see Le Bas, 1977*). Experimental results on the partitioning of elements between silicate melts and coexisting carbonate melts, such as data from Koster van Groos's (1975) experiments on Sr, throw some light on the origins of carbonatite and the mechanisms by which the elements in it are concentrated. It is thought that magmas produced by partial fusion of a CO_2-rich mantle are extremely poor in silica and rich in 'incompatible elements' such as the rare-earth elements and Ti, P, Ba, Ce, Rb, Sr, U, Th, Zr and Hf. If carbonatite magma is present in equilibrium with these magmas, these elements would tend to be partitioned into the carbonatite magma and increase the degree of enrichment still further.

Ilmenite deposits associated with anorthosite also pose major problems which cannot be ignored. It is clear that anorthosite found in layered intrusions such as the Bushveld complex is a product of a process of magmatic differentiation, whatever the mechanism of concentration. However, there is disagreement over the origin of so-called massif-type anorthosite, of which the Adirondack is a good example. Sometimes, deposits comprising mainly magnetite, ilmenite, haematite and apatite are associated with these anorthosites. Philpotts (1967) showed experimentally that such iron oxide-apatite mixtures (ratio by volume, approximately 2:1) develop a eutectic point and are immiscible with dioritic silicate melts. He thus interpreted the origins of ilmenite deposits associated with massif-type anorthosites as forming from oxide–apatite melts coexisting with silicate magmas. There are reports of oxide melts, immiscible with silicate magmas, being found in nature (Bowles, 1978), but the origins of ilmenite deposits associated with anorthosite and the origins of the anorthosite itself, including the apparent restriction of massif-type anorthosite to 1000–1700 Ma, are topics which must be considered further.

(Hidehiko Shimazaki)

(g) Concentration of heavy metals during granitoid magmatic processes

One difference between granitoid magmas and the above-mentioned basic magmas is that the former are poor in Fe, Mg, Ti and Ca, and rich in Si and K, but the critical difference is that granitoid magmas contain several per cent. of 'water' from the early stages of their development. Water greatly increases the solubility of metal compounds in melts as when compared to water-free magmas with the same composition. This could be the main reason why many trace metal deposits are associated with granitoids from orogenic belts (known as calc-alkaline rocks). Mo, Sn, Cu (porphyry type, vein type), W (skarn type, vein type, etc.), Be, Nb–Ta and Th (pegmatite, disseminated type, etc.) are typical of metals which concentrate in granitoid magmas and form ore deposits after they solidify. All these elements have low Clarke numbers; consequently these elements are well known as trace metal resources and they need to be highly concentrated to become workable deposits. It is generally believed that this concentration was achieved using a fluid of magmatic or meteoric water, etc., but there is also a possibility that a solid phase acted as the medium as in the case of Sn discussed below.

As a result of recent studies using hydrogen and oxygen isotopes, the involvement of meteoric water has been established not only in granitoids but also in mafic rocks. Nevertheless, it is believed that the type of deposit mentioned above was formed when dissolved components in the magmatic water crystallized out, the role of the meteoric water being secondary. The mechanism by which meteoric water mixed with magmatic water was important in the formation of porphyry copper deposits (see Sec. 3.9). Meteoric water is considered to have been of great significance in the development of veins of gold and silver (Hattori and Sakai, 1979*). In this instance the properties of the magmatic water underwent great changes due to interreaction between the host rock and meteoric water.

Regardless of the contribution of meteoric water when the deposits formed, there are characteristic arrangements of metal elements in granitoid bodies. The arrangements conform with the zonal distribution of magnetite and ilmenite series granitoids divided into two due to differences in oxygen fugacity (f_{O_2}) during their solidification (Ishihara, 1977*; Chapter 4, Volume 15 of this series). Ore metals associated with the magnetite series are Mo, Cu, Pb, Zn, Ag and Au, mainly occurring as sulphides. It is inferred, in this series, that there was clearly concentration of sulphur by magmatic processes and when f_{O_2} is high, these elements are more easily transported and concentrated toward later stages of solidification. Sn, W, Be, Nb, Ta, Th, etc., are important ore metals of the ilmenite series and are found mainly as oxides. Concentrations of sulphides of such elements as Mo, Cu, Pb, Zn, etc., are extremely scarce in the ilmenite series. This shows that magmatic processes for both these series were important for the concentration of ore-forming minerals and their distribution throughout the crust.

The concentration of heavy metals by granitoid magmatic processes may be divided into three stages, the source material, magmatic differentation and solidification. Magnetite series magmas are commonly associated with large-scale tectonic processes such as subduction which would have generated enough heat for large-scale zonal melting or partial fusion of mafic material at depth. The magmas then migrated long distances to reach the upper part of the earth's crust. The following points suggest that this interpretation is consistent with the concentrations of elements in the deposits (Fig. 1.10). (1) Mafic rock is generally rich in Cu, Zn, Ag, Au, S, etc. Partial melting of amphibolite and overlying stratiform sulphide deposits in a subduction zone (Sillitoe, 1972) causes further increase in their concentration. (2) In the early stages only

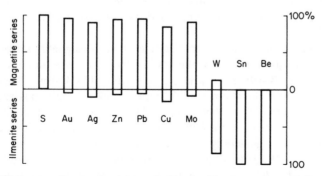

Fig. 1.10 Element ratios in deposits associated with magnetite and ilmenite series igneous rocks in Japan. Mostly based on past quantity of production associated with felsic to intermediate igneous rocks. (Revised from Ishihara, 1979.)

Mineral Resources and Engineering Geology

minor amounts of heavy metals contained in silicate minerals condense but as the process of fusion continues, elements such as Zn and Pb migrate into the melt causing their concentration in the magma to rise. On the other hand, ilmenite series magmas probably form in shallow regions of the crust and so are rich in Sn, W, Be, etc., from the start.

As magnetite series magmas are probably transported to the surface as diapirs, in addition to the concentration of heavy metals in the liquid phase due to fractional crystallization, one may also expect metal concentration in the liquid phase due to filter pressing. On the other hand, ilmenite series magmas are thought to arrive at the site of solidification via zonal melting and stoping so that heavy metals are only concentrated by fractional crystallization at high crustal levels. In this series ascent and solidification from crystal mush can often be inferred and in such cases concentration of heavy metals would not be achieved in a high degree.

Sulphur is dissolved in melts containing water bonded in the silica tetrahedron as SH^-, and is present as H_2S or SO_2 in aqueous solution. The partition of dissolved sulphur in this melt–aqueous solution system is markedly regulated by f_{O_2} (Burnham, 1979*). If the oxygen fugacity rises under constant pressure, the H_2S/SO_2 ratio falls and the partition coefficient for sulphur, $\Sigma S^v/\Sigma S^m$, rises. Burnham and Ohmoto (1980*) suggest that f_{O_2} in granitoid magmas produced from non-carbon-containing igneous rocks is higher than the quartz–fayalite–magnetite (QFM) buffer and that f_{SO_2}/f_{H_2S} for aqueous solutions in equilibrium with such a magma is 0.1–10 with an average of almost 1. On the other hand, in magmas generated from sedimentary rocks containing carbon, because f_{O_2} is lower than the QFM buffer and f_{CO_2}/f_{CH_4} is close to unity (Ohmoto and Kerrick, 1977), f_{SO_2}/f_{H_2S} is probably less than 0.01. Thus, the above results show that sulphur is fractionated in the aqueous phase and probably has a greater tendency to form sulphide deposits after separating from magnetite series magmas with high oxygen fugacity rather than ilmenite series magmas in which this is low. On the contrary, sulphur remains within the rock in the ilmenite series and so does not give rise to large sulphide deposits.

Heavy metal elements characteristically present in magnetite series granitoid may be dissolved as sulphides in the magma, but most are thought to exist as chlorides. Cl^- is an important phase in the aqueous solution associated with magmas (Kilinc and Burnham, 1972), because chloride minerals are unstable in granitoid magmas but they do produce stable neutral compounds in aqueous solution phases by combining with hydrogen, alkaline metals and heavy metals. F/Cl is generally less than 3 in magnetite series granitoids (in the ilmenite series F/Cl > 3) (Ishihara and Terashima, 1977), so it is reasonable to suppose that the F/Cl ratio in magnetite series magmas could have been low from the start, i.e. from the time they were generated these magmas were rich in ore-forming heavy metals, sulphur and chlorine and these elements became further concentrated during the processes of rising and solidifying to form ore deposits.

There is proof that in ilmenite series magmas the magma was rich in Sn, W, Be, Nb, Ta and Th. Ore deposits in this system are accompanied by fluorite and topaz. Fluorine also, like chorine, produces neutral flourine compounds during magmatic processes and condenses into aqueous solution phases. Its solubility in melts is also high. On the basis of analyses of Sn in rock-forming minerals, Ishihara and Terashima (1977*) deduced that Sn in granitoid melts is present as Sn^{4+} in the magnetite series and as Sn^{2+} in the ilmenite series. Whereas Sn^{4+} is selectively captured in solid phases (sphene, magnetite, ilmenite, etc.) which crystallize out relatively early in the process, Sn^{2+} tends to remain in the residual system, so tin deposits develop. Fluorine, which is present dissolved mainly in the melt, crystallizes in topaz and mica (where F substitutes for OH) during the later stages of ilmenite series fractionation and fluorides of tin present in aqueous solution phases precipitate out as cassiterite and fluorite.

The processes whereby ore minerals crystallize out as granitoid magmas solidify can be conceptually divided into three categories (Burnham and Ohmoto, 1980*):

Orthomagmatic process: solid phase–melt reaction
Transitional process: melt–magmatic water reaction
Hydrothermal process: (1) solid phase–magmatic water reaction
(2) solid phase–meteoric water reaction

The case of Sn, discussed above, suggests that primary concentration was achieved in magmatic processes, but that transitional and hydrothermal processes (solid phase–magmatic water reaction, e.g. the extraction of Sn from micas in host rock and its concentration in mineralizing solutions; see Tischendorf, 1978) played important roles in the formation of the final deposits. Banks and Page (1978) emphasize the role of magmatic processes for copper concentration in porphyry copper belts, but hydrothermal processes are generally considered to be more important in this type of ore deposits. In pegmatite and disseminated-type deposits magmatic and transitional processes are believed to predominate. However, the development of most deposits should be regarded as a complex combination of all three processes and future studies should pay particular regard to identifying the relative importance of these three concentration processes.

(Shunso Ishihara)

1.2 The chemistry of hydrothermal ore solutions

Hydrothermal processes, like magmatic processes (see Sec. 1.1), are important as mechanisms whereby base metal ore deposits are formed. In hydrothermal processes ore deposits are formed when base metals precipitate from high temperature aqueous solutions. Deposits formed in this manner are called 'hydrothermal ore deposits' and the solutions from which they are derived are ore solutions. Unlike magmatic deposits, the study of the genesis of hydrothermal ore deposits is hampered by the fact that the aqueous fluids no longer remain. Therefore, various indirect approaches must be used to investigate the properties of the ore solutions and the precipitation mechanism of ore-forming minerals.

Firstly we consider the chemical properties of ore solutions and the factors governing them. We then briefly discuss the migration of hot water in the earth's crust, citing present day geothermal systems.

(a) The chemical composition of ore solutions

(1) The solubility of sulphide minerals Base metal elements are mainly found as sulphides in hydrothermal ore deposits and hence base metal elements and sulphur are thought to have been dissolved to a considerable extent in ore solutions. However, the solubility of sulphides in pure water is very low and an unrealistic quantity of water should have been necessary to transport the metal precipitated even in a single ore deposit. However, solubility increases greatly when H_2S and NaCl, etc., are added to sulphide–water systems. It appears that base metal elements form various complexes in aqueous solutions, and in natural hydrothermal systems chloride complexes are often predominant. For example, it has been shown both empirically and theoretically that Pb, Zn, Cu and Fe chloride complexes are stable in high temperature aqueous solutions with high concentrations of NaCl (Helgeson, 1969*). With Au, Ag, Hg, Sb and As, not only chloride complexes but also complexes which incorporate sulphur (e.g. thio-complexes) may be important. The conditions under which Sn, W, Mo, etc., can exist in ore solutions are not yet fully understood.

The solubility of sulphides depends not only upon the chemical state of base metal elements in aqueous solution but also upon the form in which the dissolved sulphur is present (H_2S, HS^-, S^{2-}, HSO_4^-, SO_4^{2-}, $(Na, K) SO_4^-$). The concentration of the dissolved sulphur species is dependent not only upon temperature and pressure but also upon the oxygen fugacity f_{O_2}, pH, the total dissolved sulphur concentration (ΣS), and ionic strength. Therefore, the solubility of sulphides in hydrothermal solutions can be expressed as a function of temperature, pressure, ligand (Cl, S, etc.) concentration, pH, f_{O_2} and ionic strength. However, it is difficult to estimate the values of the variables mentioned above and the concentration of the base metal element is also difficult to estimate from the sulphide solubility data. It is, however, widely accepted that if chlorine, hydrogen sulphide and sulphate ions exist in sufficient quantities, base metals sufficient for the formation of deposits (more than 1 ppm for copper, lead and zinc) will dissolve in hydrothermal solutions under physicochemical conditions prevailing in natural hydrothermal systems. Chlorine, hydrogen sulphide and sulphate ions are recognized as important constituents of ore solutions.

(2) Partitioning of elements between hydrothermal ore minerals and aqueous solutions If it is assumed that the elements (chiefly cations) contained as solid solutions in the hydrothermal ore minerals were in equilibrium with the ore-forming solution, their concentration in the solution can be calculated given the necessary thermodynamic data. The chemical reaction which forms the basis of such a study is as follows:

$$AR + B = BR + A$$

where A and B are cations in aqueous solution and AR and BR are components in solid phases. When this reaction is in equilibrium, the equilibrium constant K can be expressed as $K = (a_{BR}/a_{AR})/(a_B/a_A)$, where a is the activity. Consequently, the ratio of the concentrations of these cations in the ore solution can be expressed as a function of the ratio of concentrations of the cations in the minerals, the activity coefficients of the components in the solid phase, the activity coefficients of the ions in solution, the temperature and pressure.

There has been extensive experimental research on the partitioning of elements between aqueous solutions and carbonate or sulphate minerals (Ichikuni, 1978) but little research has been directed to sulphide and silicate minerals. There are difficulties in the study of sulphide minerals; the cations produce various complexes, as has already been indicated, and it is not possible to estimate the total concentration ratio in the ore solution from the activity ratio if the experiments are conducted by buffering f_{O_2} and pH.

(3) Experiments on rock–aqueous solution interaction Base metals are extremely concentrated in sediments near ocean ridges. This unusual concentration is caused by sea water entering the earth's crust beneath the sea floor and being heated so that it reacts with basaltic rocks extracting metals to be discharged as a hot spring. Although we do not fully understand the properties of such 'modified sea water' which is discharged on to the sea floor, experiments concerning reactions between sea water and basalts at high temperatures (200–400 °C) (see Table 1.4) have shown that: (1) the concentration of base metal elements (e.g. Fe, Mn, Cu) in the sea water increases, (2) the pH decreases, (3) the K concentration increases and (4) the Mg concentration decreases.

There have been few experiments on reactions between rock (or magma) and fluids at higher temperatures and pressures, but experiments on the reactions between acidic magmas and fluids at about 600 °C have shown that: (1) base metal elements and chlorine become extremely concentrated in the fluid, (2)

Table 1.4 Chemical composition of hydrothermal solutions from experiments on basalt–sea water interaction (units in ppm)

pH	4.0[a]	6.0[b]	4.9[c]
Cl⁻			
SO_4^{2-}			
H_2S			
H_2CO_3			
HCO_3^-			
Na	14500	9814	
K	519	1026	530
Ca	1150	3263	60
Ba			
Mg	1.6	1.8	30
Sr			
Pb			
Zn			
Cu	0.35		0.3
Fe	0.12	0.23	5
$T°C$	300	300	200

[a] Hajash (1975*).
[b] Mottl, Corr and Holland (1974*).
[c] Bischoff and Dickson (1975*).

the pH of the fluid becomes very low (1–2), (3) the partitioning of alkaline elements, alkaline earth elements and base metals in the fluid shows a positive correlation with the chloride concentration (Holland, 1972*).

(4) Studies of present day hydrothermal systems In 1963 there were reports that the Salton Sea geothermal area (California, USA) contained large quantities of precipitated sulphide minerals and concentrated hydrothermal brines with high heavy metal contents. During the last decade many papers concerning the geothermal areas associated with base metal deposition have been published. Examples of these geothermal areas are: concentrated brine and large quantities of sulphide minerals precipitated on the sea floor of the Red Sea; concentrated brine and deposition of native lead in the Cheleken geothermal area (USSR); sulphide minerals in the Broadlands geothermal area (New Zealand); sediments on the East Pacific Rise which are extremely rich in heavy metals (iron, manganese, copper, chromium, nickel, lead, mercury, arsenic, uranium, silver, gold, tin, thallium, zinc, vanadium, iridium, etc.); cinnabar in the Steamboat geothermal area (USA); and on the East Pacific Rise 21°N, sulphide deposits. Thus we know that ore 'deposits' are being formed in geothermal areas both on land and on the sea floor. Table 1.5 shows

Table 1.5 Chemical composition of hydrothermal solutions in present day hydrothermal systems associated with base metal depositions (units in ppm)

	1	2	3	4	5	6	7	8	9	10
pH		6.1	5.2	5.5	8.55	6.4	6.1	6.8	7.2	6.1
Cl^-	156030	18000	155000	152110	1823	33259	19260	644	11000	824
SO_4^{2-}	840	2230	5.4	154	6	1.0	30.8	598	23	107
H_2S			16	4030			13.3	12	178	8
H_2CO_3							438			
HCO_3^-			190	220	910			3290	7390	314
Na	92600	8600	50400	73250	1300	16200	9610	1190	9140	637
K	1870	525	17500		234	3169	1348	23	460	61
Ca	5150	1030	28000	19380		3533	1530	20	1.4	16
Ba			235			59				
Mg	764	1370	54	1760			16	55	58	1.0
Sr	48		400							
Pb	6.3	0.07	102	3.6	0.005	0.2				
Zn	54	0.03	540	0.19	0.015	0.4				
Cu	2.6	0.05	8	0.9	0.012	0.1				
Fe	81	3.5	2290			187	0.5	0.1	0.1	
$T°C$	56.5	85	300–360	80		90.5	277	69.5	57	60

(1) Hot brine in the Red Sea (Brewer and Spencer, 1969); (2) Matsupi Bay (Ferguson and Lambert, 1972); (3) hot brine in the Salton Sea geothermal area (White, 1968); (4) hot brine in the Cheleken geothermal area (Lebedev, 1967); (5) hot water in the Broadlands geothermal area (Browne, 1969); (6) Arima hot spring (White, 1967); (7) hot brine in the Reykjanes geothermal area (Björnsson et al., 1972); (8) Sulfur Bank springs (White, 1967); (9) Wilbur springs (White, 1967); (10) Steamboat springs (White, 1967).

1, 3, 4, 5 and 6 are accompanied by sulphide minerals, 2 by precipitates rich in Fe and 8, 9 and 10 by cinnabar. 7 is not accompanied by any of these but is an example of a hydrothermal system formed from basalt–sea water reaction.

the results of chemical analyses of hydrothermal solutions in the geothermal systems. It is particularly noteworthy that hot water from some of these areas (Red Sea, Salton Sea, Cheleken) is extremely rich in salt, which is significant due to the important effect of chloride on the solubility of base metal compounds.

(5) Fluid inclusions Fluid inclusions in hydrothermal minerals are generally regarded as ore solution trapped in the mineral. Recent research has been directed not only to the homogenization temperature and depression of the freezing point of fluid inclusions but also to their chemical composition. However, the size of fluid inclusions is very small compared with the host mineral, and thus the analysis is difficult and rarely carried out. Table 1.6 shows the results of analyses for heavy metal elements from several localities: Creede and Hill which are vein-type deposits, Providencia and Darwin which are skarn type and Climax which is of the porphyry type.

Table 1.6 Chemical composition of fluid inclusions (analysis for heavy metal elements) (units in ppm)

	1	2	3a	3b	3c	4a	4b	5a	5b	5c	6a	6b
Cl^-			27400					128000	197000	88000	70000	14000
SO_4^{2-}									88000	(193000)		
H_2S												
H_2CO_3												
HCO_3^-												
Na			11800					36200	47500	34400	64000	20000
K			4800					15500	15900	11900	13000	10200
Ca			2500					(270000)	(68000)	(116000)	(26000)	(16000)
Ba												
Mg			120					820	0	700	2400	2000
Sr												
Pb	410	570										
Zn	1330	10900	(6200)	890	3680	870	580	(7700)	(1800)	(6300)	200	500
Cu	60	150										
Fe	140	9100	<160	340	17640	<510	200	740	<230	<340	4000	80
T°C			330								280	348

(1) Creede (Czamanske *et al.*, 1963), quartz; (2) Hill (Czamanske *et al.*, 1963), fluorspar; (3) Providencia (Rye and Haffty, 1969), a. early sphalerite, San Marcos, b. quartz, San Eligio; (4) Cave-in-Rock (Pinckney and Haffty, 1970), a. early yellow fluorspar, b. early purple fluorspar; (5) Darwin (Rye *et al.*, 1974), a., b., c. sphalerite; (6) Climax (Hall *et al.*, 1974), a., b. quartz.

(b) Factors affecting the composition of ore solutions

The chemical properties of ore solutions can be calculated on the basis of the experimental and analytical data discussed in Sec. 1.2(a), (1) to (5).

(1) pH and concentration of chlorine ions in ore solutions Assuming chemical equilibrium in rock–aqueous solution systems, we now consider the factors which govern the chemical composition of natural aqueous solutions (ore solutions) and compare the results with the chemical composition of the ore solutions given in Tables 1.4, 1.5 and 1.6.

Firstly, we consider a $Na_2O - K_2O - SiO_2 - Al_2O_3 - HCl - H_2O$ system. Albite and K feldspar are taken as mineral phases and the $NaCl-H_2O$ solution is assumed to be in equilibrium with these phases. The mass action law can be applied to the equilibrium condition, albite $+ K^+ = K$ feldspar $+ Na^+$. The total chlorine concentration is expressed as the sum of Cl^-, NaCl, KCl and HCl. Electrical neutrality is maintained, hence:

$$m_{Na^+} + m_{K^+} + m_{H^+} = m_{Cl^-} + m_{OH^-} \ (m = \text{molality})$$

Using the mass action law and given mass balance and condition of electroneutrality, a relationship between K^+ concentration and Cl^- concentration can be derived (Fig. 1.11) (Shikazono, 1978a*). A detailed study based on this theory of equilibrium in mineral–aqueous solution systems is given in Stumm and Morgan (1970).

If mica (K end member) is added to the above system, a relationship between the pH and Cl^- concentration can be derived in the same way (Fig. 1.11). If a Ca phase (e.g. calcite) or Mg phase (e.g. chlorite) is added, a relationship between the Ca^{2+} or Mg^{2+} concentration and the Cl^- concentration can also be derived (Fig. 1.12). Relationships between other alkaline elements and Cl^- concentration and between alkaline earth elements and the Cl^- concentration can again be established in a similar manner.

The composition of the natural hydrothermal solutions (shown in Tables 1.5 and 1.6) of fluid inclusions and of typical geothermal water, sea water and magmatic water are plotted on the diagram showing the cation/Cl^- concentration (Figs. 1.11 and 1.12). The composition of magmatic water is plotted on the basis of experimental results on partitioning of elements between the magma and the fluid (Holland, 1972*).

In Figs. 1.11 and 1.12 natural hydrothermal solutions appear to lie close to the equilibrium curve between silicate minerals and aqueous solutions despite some scatter. The same is true for other alkaline and alkaline earth elements. This means, therefore, that the concentrations of hydrogen ions, alkaline element ions and alkaline earth element ions are largely controlled by the concentration of chlorine ion and minerals commonly found in rocks (feldspar, quartz, mica, chlorite, calcite, etc.). The plot for sea water and

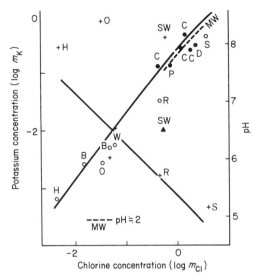

Fig. 1.11 Relationship between pH and chlorine concentration + and between potassium concentration and chlorine ion concentration ○ ● ▲. Solid lines show estimated equilibrium curves for the albite-K feldspar-mica-quartz-aqueous solution (250°C). H. Hveragerdi, Iceland, O. Otake, Japan, B. Broadlands, New Zealand, W. Wairakei, New Zealand, R. Reykjanes, Iceland, S. Salton Sea, USA, Creede, USA, P. Providencia, Mexico, D. Darwin, USA, SW. Sea water, MW. Magmatic water, ○ Present day thermal water, ● Fluid inclusion. H, B and W are corrected for increases in pH due to loss of gaseous species between collection of samples and measuring the pH. Concentration is measured in mol/kg of H_2O

magmatic water deviates from the equilibrium curve, but this is probably because the temperature of both differs markedly from that of other hot waters. Deviation is greatest for K and H, both of which are strongly temperature dependent. Taking into account the effect of temperature on the equilibrium curves, it can be seen that magmatic water and sea water are virtually in equilibrium with the surrounding rock or magma.

Figure 1.13 shows the relationship between the Cl^- concentration and the Pb and Fe concentrations in natural hydrothermal solutions. There are few data for this curve, but unlike alkaline and alkaline earth elements, the dependence upon the Cl^- concentration is not so regular. Possible reasons for this include: (1) the f_{O_2} of the hydrothermal solutions may differ, (2) these base metals form various complexes with Cl and (3) equilibrium between the hydrothermal solutions and minerals may not have been achieved. There are more factors affecting the concentration of heavy metal elements than alkaline and alkaline earth elements, but in general if the Cl^- concentration rises, the concentration of base metal elements also tends to increase, indicating the importance of Cl^- in the formation of ore deposits.

Various factors have been suggested as causes for the variation in Cl^-

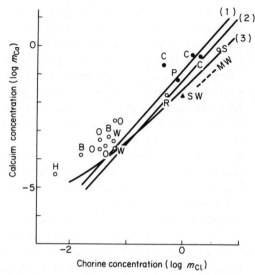

Fig. 1.12   Relationship between calcium concentration and chlorine ion concentration, where the abbreviations are the same as in Fig. 1.11. Curve (1) is the equilibrium curve for albite-Kfeldspar-mica-quartz–calcite–aqueous-solution (activity of dissolved $H_2CO_3 = 10^{-2.5}$). Curve (2) is the equilibrium curve for albite-K feldspar-mica-quartz–calcite–aqueous solution (activity of dissolved $H_2CO_3 = 10^{-2}$). Curve (3) is the equilibrium curve for anhydrite – aqueous solution (250°C)

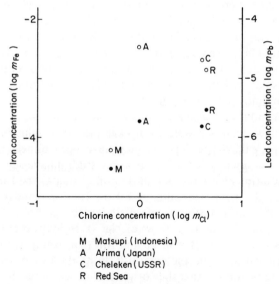

M   Matsupi (Indonesia)
A   Arima (Japan)
C   Cheleken (USSR)
R   Red Sea

Fig. 1.13   Relationship between iron and chlorine concentration ○ and lead and chlorine concentration ●

concentration which is thought to significantly control the chemical composition of ore solutions, i.e. (1) the partitioning of Cl associated with boiling of the hydrothermal solutions and the condensation of gases, i.e. the separation of liquid and gas phases, (2) the incorporation of chlorides from evaporites into the ore solutions, (3) the extraction of Cl from rocks by the ore solution, (4) differences in the partitioning of Cl between the magma and the fluid, caused by differences in the pressure, temperature and composition of the magma, (5) semi-permeable membrane filtration caused by clay minerals, etc., and (6) the formation of hydrous minerals.

With regard to point (1), experiments on NaCl–H_2O system (Sourirajan and Kennedy, 1962*) have shown that Cl becomes concentrated in the liquid phase when an ore solution boils. This may have happened during the formation of porphyry-type deposits (White *et al.*, 1971).

Large sulphide mineral deposits are even now being formed on the floor of the Red Sea. Thick layers of evaporites occur on its shores, and the high Cl content of the hot water is thought to originate in these evaporites. It is also probable that the high Cl content in the Salton Sea geothermal water derives from evaporites. They would thus seem to play an important role in the formation of ore deposits (see Chapter 3).

Experiments have been performed in which Cl has been extracted from rock by aqueous solutions in higher temperature reactions (about 200 °C), but a high NaCl concentration (several mol %) is not achieved by extraction from the rock alone. Fluid inclusion studies have shown that the Cl concentration in ore solutions for epithermal Au–Ag vein deposits is extremely low (1 mol % or less) and this may be accounted for simply by extraction from rock. The chlorine concentration in fluid inclusions in Cu, Pb and Zn vein deposits is high (several mol %), even in epithermal veins. This high concentration is probably due not only to process (3) but also involves other processes.

Process (4) is not well studied as yet, but Cl is accepted to be generally more concentrated in fluids than in magma (Holland, 1972*).

Processes (5) and (6) are also little understood, but may be important for ore solutions produced from sea water. For example, the origins of ore solutions for Mississipppi Valley-type deposits may have been oilfield brine which is itself derived from ancient sea water. Isotopic studies have suggested that the origin of ore solutions for stratabound deposits, such as the Kuroko deposits in Japan, is mainly from sea water (see Sec. 1.3 for details). The chlorine concentration of fluid inclusions is often similar to sea water, but many data show it to be slightly higher (2–5 % wt of NaCl). In hydrothermal systems on the sea floor, sediments are rich in Fe and Mn (for example, the East Pacific Rise). The chemical and isotopic composition of the hydrothermal solutions suggests a strong possibility that they originated as sea water. It is thought that the same is true of stratabound manganese and iron deposits, though in these cases the increase in the Cl concentration may not be so significant.

So far we have been concerned with ore solutions in which the Cl^-

concentration is relatively high (more than 0.01 mol/kg of H_2O). In these cases the pH correlates under constant temperature and Cl^- concentration conditions are governed by the silicate minerals. On the basis of the available data on the concentration and temperature at the time of ore formation this means that it is difficult to significantly change the pH of ore solutions rich in Cl^-. For example, at temperatures of about 200–300 °C, the pH of ore solutions ranges from almost neutral (pH = 4–6) to weakly acidic.

However, ore deposits which have been formed near the earth's surface, such as sulphur deposits, hydrothermal clay deposits (kaolin, pyrophyllite, alunite, etc.) and massive gold–copper deposits (e.g. Chinkuashih, Taiwan, and Akeshi, Japan) are considered to have formed in fairly acidic conditions from the stability of clay mineral assemblages. This is probably because H_2S reacted with oxygen near the earth's surface to form sulphate and hydrogen ions, so lowering the pH. The contribution of sulphur rather than chlorine as anions is considered to be the main control on the pH of ore solutions for these ore deposit types. Present day hydrothermal systems contain various kinds of hydrothermal solutions which affect acidity, but generally the concentration of chlorine in them is low whereas that of sulphur is high. Moreover, such hydrothermal systems are often vapour dominated, in that gas phases predominate over liquid phases (Matsukawa geothermal area, etc.).

In the hydrothermal systems associated with cinnabar and meta-cinnabar such as Wilbur Springs, Sulfur Bank and Steamboat, more HCO_3^- anions are found than those of sulphur and chlorine (Table 1.5). In such cases HCO_3^- is probably an important control of the pH of the ore solution. In the case of lower temperature, sedimentary-type uranium deposits, one cannot ignore the effects of carbon on the stability of uranium carbonate complexes in aqueous solution. Furthermore, the action of H_2CO_3 as an acid in meteoric water greatly affects weathered deposits such as bauxite.

Chloride is thus very important amongst the anions in the formation of many sulphide deposits (e.g. Cu, Pb, Zn), whereas sulphur and carbon play roles in the formation of certain other types (clay deposits, Au and Hg deposits).

(2) Oxygen fugacity The minerals in Fe–S–O systems—pyrite, magnetite, etc.—are common in ore deposits. Because the deposits are formed from aqueous solutions, we firstly consider a simple Fe–S–O–H system and consider the stability relationship between pyrite and magnetite in such a system. This relationship is determined by the following chemical reaction:

$$3FeS_2 + 6H_2O = Fe_3O_4 + 6S^{2-} + 12H^+ + O_2$$

The equilibrium constant for this chemical reaction shows that the boundary between these minerals is determined by the activity of H_2O and S^{2-} ion, pH, f_{O_2}, pressure and temperature. The activity of water does not deviate much from unity, and may be regarded as constant. In many cases the effects of

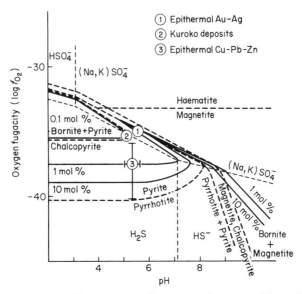

Fig. 1.14   Various types of Japanese ore-forming environments (f_{O_2} - pH ranges). For the f_{O_2} - pH diagram, $T = 250°C$, ionic strength = 1, total dissolved sulphur concentration $\Sigma S = 0.01$ mol/kg of H_2O, K^+ concentration = 0.2 mol/kg of H_2O. 0.1, 1, 10 mol % is the FeS content of sphalerite. The unit of f_{O_2} is atm. The thin broken line is the stability boundary for dissolved sulphur and the thick broken line is the stability boundary for Cu–Fe–S–O system minerals

pressure can also be neglected. The activity of S^{2-} ion is a function of temperature, pH, f_{O_2}, ΣS and ionic strength. Consequently, it is possible to plot the stability boundaries on an f_{O_2}–pH diagram at constant temperatures, ΣS and ionic strength (e.g. Barnes and Kullerud, 1961*). Similarly, the stability fields of other ore minerals and dissolved carbon and sulphur species can be represented on f_{O_2}–pH diagrams (Fig. 1.14).

If we consider the minerals as pure end members, their activity is unity. However, many minerals are solid solutions and the activity of their components is less than unity. It is possible to draw iso-activity lines (or iso-concentration lines) for particular mineral compositions on f_{O_2}–pH diagrams. Iso-concentration lines for FeS in sphalerite are shown in Fig. 1.14.

If one knows the temperature and ΣS at the time of ore deposition in addition to the mineral assemblage and chemical composition of the minerals, and if the above relationship between pH and Cl^- concentration is correct and the Cl^- concentration has been estimated, then it is possible to determine the f_{O_2}–pH range prevailing at the time of ore deposition.

Figure 1.14 shows f_{O_2}–pH ranges for various deposits at the time of formation, calculated as in Shikazono (1978b*). However, the ranges shown are no more than single cross-sections in multi-dimensional space composed of these variables. Relatively few detailed studies of individual deposits have been published to date, and it is difficult to say that environment of deposition fell within these ranges for all types of deposits. However, the environment varied depending upon the type of deposit, in particular the variation of the Cl^- concentration, pH, temperature and f_{O_2}, from one deposit to another is important.

What factors govern f_{O_2} in ore solutions? Several suggestions have been made: for example, (1) reactions between aqueous solutions and carbon compounds in the sedimentary rock through which ore solutions circulated, (2) the chemical state of sulphur in the ore solution, (3) reactions between aqueous solutions and iron minerals in the rocks which the ore solution percolated through and (4) mixing of ore solutions with underground or sea water at the site of ore deposition. Each of these points has been debated and point (1) would seem to be particularly important for the following reasons: (a) the f_{O_2} at the time of deposition of certain types of deposits (Cu–Pb–Zn vein deposits, Sn–W deposits, Skarn deposits in Japan) was close to the boundary between oxidized carbon species and reduced carbon species; (b) in many cases the estimated CO_2 fugacity at the site of deposition was higher than that of the surrounding geological environment; (c) the isotopic composition of the ore solutions seems to indicate that the source of carbon may have been organic; and (d) correspondence between the weight ratio of sedimentary and igneous rocks in the region of the deposits and the calculated f_{O_2} at the time of ore deposition.

There is a strong correlation between the oxygen fugacity at the earth's surface and the evolution of life, atmosphere and sea. Consequently the evolution of ore deposits is also closely related to that of the earth (see Chapter 3).

(c) Mechanisms of migration of ore solutions

Recently it has become apparent, mainly as a result of isotopic studies, that many of the waters which produce ore solutions are not simply of magmatic origin but have been influenced greatly by waters of meteoric and/or sea water origin. If this is so, how do these waters percolate through the ground and become ore solutions? How do they behave underground? The study of hydrodynamics is vital in answering these questions.

Geothermal areas have recently attracted attention and research, particularly theoretical, into the hydrodynamics of these hydrothermal systems has made great progress. In Wairakei (New Zealand), directions of water flow and temperature distribution have been shown in a large-scale circulating model containing many hot water whirlpools (Fig. 1.15) (Elder, 1966*). The temperature distribution widens at the top, resembling a mushroom. Furthermore, the distributions found experimentally closely resemble those predicted theoretically. Applied research has been carried out

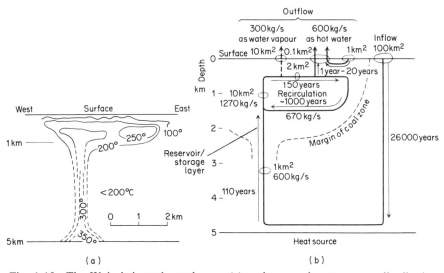

Fig. 1.15   The Wairakei geothermal area: (a) underground temperature distribution and (b) illustration of the movement of hot water in a pipe model. Years indicate the number required for the water to move the distance marked by the arrow; kg/s is water flow; km² is the area of section of the 'pipe'. (A simplified version of Elder, 1966.)

not only in Wairakei, but also in other geothermal areas such as Larderello (Italy) and The Geysers (USA). Similar studies of hydrothermal systems along oceanic ridges have shown that the scatter in heat flow results near the ridges cannot be explained by conduction of heat alone and that circulation of sea water must occur on a large scale (e.g. Wolery and Sleep, 1976*).

What factors control the movement of hot water? For example, in cases where the water is saturated in a uniform medium the Rayleigh number R will determine whether or not the water circulates by convection when there is a constant heat source from below. R is expressed as follows:

$$R = KgH\rho_w\alpha_w \frac{\Delta T}{\lambda_m/\lambda_w} \kappa_w\mu_w$$

Where K = permeability, g = acceleration gravity, H = thickness, ρ = density, α = coefficient of thermal expansion, ΔT = temperature gradient, λ = thermal conductivity, κ = thermal diffusivity, μ = kinematic viscosity coefficient, and m is the medium and w the water. Convection occurs when R is greater than $4\pi^2$. (Note that sometimes the value is not $4\pi^2$, depending on conditions; e.g. when the Boussinesq approximation is not realized.) It seems that in many cases in natural hydrothermal systems, R is greater than $4\pi^2$. For example, R has been calculated in Wairakei to be 10^4. The above formula demonstrates that when other variables are constant, convection will occur readily if the permeability or the temperature difference is large.

Numerical values for temperature distribution, pressure distribution, direction of flow and flow rate in hydrothermal systems can be calculated using a computer on the basis of the laws of conservation of mass, momentum and energy and equations of state (e.g. an equation expressing density as a function of temperature). Despite many recent studies problems still remain, the most important of these including: (1) the fact that the medium is regarded as uniform and the permeability as constant; (2) that the physical values used are those of pure water, whereas we are dealing with solutions containing dissolved NaCl, etc.; (3) that, although the water is assumed to be in a liquid state, a gas phase also exists; and (4) that, considering the actual geological structures, the boundary conditions are oversimplified. It is particularly important to remember that geological features are not homogeneous and therefore the permeability, for example, cannot be regarded as constant.

Such models of hydrothermal convection in geothermal areas can also be applied to fossil hydrothermal systems, i.e. ore deposits. For example, studies now carried out on porphyry-type deposits use convection models to calculate the flow rate and behaviour of the hot water and the temperature of the ore deposits formed in surrounding rocks, in addition to changes over time in the depth and temperature resulting from the intrusion of homogeneous magma of uniform temperature into rock saturated with water (e.g. Cathles, 1977*). These studies have shown that convection occurs when the permeability is greater than 10^{-14} cm^2.

The size of deposits which will form can be estimated from the chemical composition of the ore solution, the flow rate, direction of flow and temperature and pressure distribution of the ore solution. Because changes in temperature and pressure at the time of the circulation of the hot water can also be calculated, the depth at which condensation and boiling occur can be estimated and processes whereby salt becomes more concentrated in the ore solution will also become clearer.

(d) The sources of ore solutions

Figures 1.11 and 1.12, which show the chemical composition of ore solutions, demonstrate that the composition of sea water and magmatic water differs from that of natural hydrothermal solutions and calculated equilibrium curves. Equilibrium curves vary according to the element concerned, but in the case of K and H, temperature dependence is strong. If extrapolated to very high or low temperatures, the composition becomes more similar to that of magmatic or sea water. This suggests that both magmatic and sea water at their respective temperatures approach the equilibrium relationship between magma or the surrounding rock. Assuming that the original source of ore solutions is sea or magmatic water, the composition of a hydrothermal solution may change from its site of origin to the site where deposits form, particularly alkaline elements and alkaline earth elements. The degree of change varies with the rock/water ratio R/W which is strongly affected by geological conditions (There are various definitions of R/W. Here it is taken to be the rock/water ratio contributing to a reaction when the water and rock of a certain composition are placed in a closed system).

The mobility of material which leaves and enters ore solutions depends on the kind of element. For example, host rocks near ore deposits are sometimes enriched in potassium (K metasomatism). It is thought that reactions between the ore solutions and silicate minerals at depth produced solutions rich in K which rose and led to K metasomatism at the site of deposition. It seems that K moves relatively easily. There is a correlation between the temperature and Si concentration of geothermal water, indicating that geothermal water is likely to be saturated with quartz and amorphous silica. Hence, in the case of Si, geothermal waters are nearly in equilibrium with the surrounding rocks which were probably the source of Si. Al, however, is fairly immobile. The origins of base metals, which are important ore-forming elements, are not yet fully understood. Considering the experimental work discussed earlier, the concentration of these elements in solution are affected by rock–water reactions. In particular, when solutions with a high salt concentration react with rock, base metals become remarkably concentrated in aqueous solutions. This occurs readily, not only in magmas but also in relatively low temperature geothermal waters. Consequently, we can conclude that the source of these base metals is greatly affected by (the sources of) Cl and its concentration in the ore solution.

(Naotatsu Shikazono)

1.3 Sources of water and sulphur

As in the case of hot spring waters, there had long been little conclusive evidence to show whether the water in ore solutions was of magmatic or meteoric origin. However, hydrogen and oxygen isotopic studies, begun in the late 1950s, have contributed greatly to our understanding of this problem. Base metals, which form deposits, most commonly combine with oxygen and sulphur and solidify as oxides or sulphides. Geochemical studies of these light ore-forming elements have become practical for the first time with the introduction of stable isotope techniques. Here we discuss briefly recent isotopic studies on the origin of water and sulphur.

(a) Sources of water

(1) Isotopes and the origins of water Taking sea water, which is isotopically extremely homogeneous, as the base ($\delta D = 0\,‰$, $\delta^{18}O = ‰$), the isotopic

composition of meteoric water is generally negative for both δD and $\delta^{18}O$, and the following relationship usually pertains: $\delta D = 8\delta^{18}O + 10$. The isotopic composition of meteoric water is known to vary systematically with latitude, such that lighter water is found at higher latitudes. This is caused by the large isotopic effect involved in evaporation and condensation processes and the fact that water near the earth's surface forms a circulating system in which the ocean is the chief reservoir (Craig, 1961).

The importance of surface water, particularly meteoric water, as a source of water for ore solutions has been clarified following the discovery that many hot springs or mineral spring waters are meteoric or sea water in origin, on the basis of their isotopic composition. Figure 1.16 shows the $\delta D, \delta^{18}O$ values estimated for various ore solutions in hydrothermal deposits. For purposes of comparison, the diagram also shows the relationship $\delta D, \delta^{18}O$ for meteoric water, and shows the range of isotopic values ($\delta D = -60--80\,‰$, $\delta^{18}O = +6-+8\,‰$, Taylor, 1974*) for magmatic water, i.e. water thought to have been in equilibrium with the magma at the time the magma solidified.

As Figure 1.16 shows, many ore solutions are not simple magmatic waters as they have differing $\delta D, \delta^{18}O$ values. The hot waters, which produced sericite and other clay minerals alteration zones of the porphyry copper and molybdenum deposits in western USA, are particularly noteworthy. The δD value decreases as one goes from Santa Rita in New Mexico in the south via Bingham in Utah and Climax in Colorado, to Wickes in Montana and

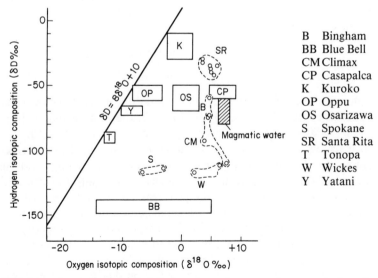

Fig. 1.16 The isotopic composition of hydrogen and oxygen in ore solutions in hydrothermal deposits. (Compiled from Hattori and Sakai, 1979*; Rye and Sawkins, 1974*; Taylor 1974*.)

Spokane in Washington in the north, i.e. towards higher latitudes. This trend is the same as that found in meteoric water, indicating a major contribution of meteoric water to these ore solutions. The fact that all these $\delta^{18}O$ values are very heavy in comparison with meteoric water is due, as in the case of thermal spring water, to the 'oxygen shift' (Craig, 1963*). This is a consequence of its reaction with high temperature rock, so that oxygen in the ore solution undergoes isotopic exchange with the oxygen in the rock. In contrast to this, the water may maintain the original δD value, since only very small amounts of hydrogen exist in normal rocks and its effect on the isotopic value of circulating water should be very small. Let us consider this problem further.

(2) Isotopes and rock-water interactions The partitioning of hydrogen and oxygen isotopes in a closed rock-water system is based on the following relationships:

$$X_i \delta_i^r + Y_i \delta_i^w = X_f \delta_f^r + Y_f \delta_f^w \tag{1}$$

$$X_i + Y_i = X_f + Y_f \tag{2}$$

where X and Y are respectively the number of atoms of hydrogen or oxygen in the rock and water participating in the reaction, δ^r and δ^w are their isotopic values and i and f are respectively the conditions before and after the interaction.

Assuming that isotopic equilibrium is achieved as a result of the reaction, the isotopic fractionation between rock and water at this temperature, $\delta_f^r - \delta_f^w$, is expressed as Δ, so from (1) and (2) we obtain:

$$\delta_f^w = \frac{\delta_i^r + (Y_i/X_i)\delta_i^w - (X_f/X_i)\Delta}{1 + Y_i/X_i} \tag{3}$$

If the rock undergoes hydrothermal alteration, it produces hydrous minerals such as mica and clay minerals and some of the water is retained by the rock. However, little change can occur in the oxygen content of the rock by this process so we may take $X_f/X_i \doteqdot 1$ in (3). In other words, the oxygen isotopic composition of the water which has reached equilibrium with the rock is determined by the temperature of the reaction, the isotopic composition of the rock and water at the time the reaction began and the rock/water ratio (Sheppard, Nielsen and Taylor, 1969*). The situation is not so simple with the hydrogen. Hydrogen in the rock is governed by the quantity of hydrous minerals and so even a slight increase in the amount of water caused by the formation of altered minerals greatly affects the X_f/Y_i ratio in (3). The degree of rock hydration has a considerable effect on the isotopic composition of the water, particularly when Y_i/X_i is small, i.e. in systems where the rock/water ratio is large (Hattori and Sakai, 1979*).

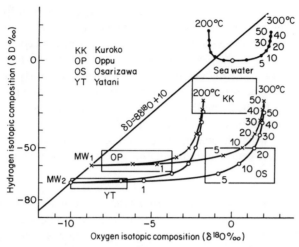

Fig. 1.17   Estimates of changes in isotopic composition (oxygen shift, hydrogen shift) of water in rock–water reactions. Sea water and two types of meteoric water, MW_1 ($\delta^{18}O = -8.75‰$, $\delta D = -60‰$) and MW_2 ($\delta^{18}O = -10‰$, $\delta D = -70‰$) react with rock ($\delta^{18}O = +7.0‰$, $\delta D = -70‰$) at 200 or 300°C and at various rock/water ratios. It is assumed that the water content of the rock increases from 1 to 3 per cent because of the reaction. The equilibrium oxygen isotopic fractionation, $\delta^{18}O_r - \delta^{18}O_w$, between the rock and the water at 200 and 300°C is taken to be similar to the fractionation value between An_{30} plagioclase and water: 8.5‰ and 4.6‰ respectively. The equilibrium hydrogen isotopic fractionation, $\delta D_r - \delta D_w$, is taken to be $-40‰$ at both temperatures. The numbers on each curve are the rock/water weight ratios (R/W); and the rectangles are the range of δD and $\delta^{18}O$ values of ore fluids in Neogene deposits in the Tohoku district of Japan. (After Hattori and Sakai, 1979*.)

Figure 1.17 shows an estimate, based on the above model, of changes in the isotopic composition of meteoric water or sea water brought about by rock–water reactions in areas of volcanic rock, with examples from the green tuff belt in north-east Japan. It is thought that in natural rock–water reactions, the water reacts whilst migrating through the rock. Thus, the actual rock/water ratio for a given mass of water increases as it migrates and the water evolves isotopically. The curves on Fig. 1.17 may be seen as expressing pathways of such isotopic evolution. The present day meteoric water in north-east Japan has $\delta D = -60 - -70$ ‰ and water during the Tertiary period is thought to have been not much different from this. Therefore the ore solutions which produced the Oppu and Yatani deposits were created by meteoric water which did not much evolve isotopically in a situation with a low rock/water ratio (weight ratio $R/W \leqslant 1$). It seems likely that much more highly evolved meteoric water contributed to ore solutions for the Osarizawa deposits.

Changes in the $\delta^{18}O$ value of circulating water, i.e. oxygen shifts at certain temperatures, are sensitive to the R/W ratio, particularly when the ratio is low

($R/W < 10$). As the rock/water ratio increases, this sensitivity rapidly decreases and the $\delta^{18}O$ value of water approaches a constant value, $\delta^{18}O_i^r - \Delta$. This may explain the fact that in the data for porphyry-type deposits (Fig. 1.16) $\delta^{18}O$ values are very similar for all deposits with the exception of Spokane. Changes in the δD value ('hydrogen shift') obviously do not become marked until the rock/water ratio is high. However, the maximum rock/water ratio $(R/W)_{MX}$ is fixed, being the value when all the water is absorbed into the rock as hydrous minerals. Simple calculations show that $(R/W)_{MX}$ is approximately 50 when the water content of the rock increases from 1 per cent. (by weight) to 3 per cent., and approximately 25 when it goes from 1 to 5 per cent.

(3) Ore solutions containing water from multiple sources Although meteoric water is often the main source of water in ore solutions, sea and magmatic water may also contribute. In fact, Fig. 1.16 gives an example suggestive of a sea water origin (Kuroko) and another indicative of magmatic water (Casapalca). Consequently, many ore solutions are probably formed by mixing of these various sources of water. Hattori and Sakai (1979*) have suggested the following explanation for the genesis of the Kuroko ore fluids.

Existing data suggest that the ore solutions which gave rise to the Kuroko deposits in the Hokuroku region had δD of $-10--30$ ‰ and $\delta^{18}O$ of $-2.5-+1.5$ ‰. These values are not very far from those of the present day sea water. However, assuming the isotopic composition of Tertiary sea water to have been much the same as today, it does not seem probable that pure sea water has evolved to the above isotopic values in the course of rock–water interaction, as can be seen in Fig. 1.17. Similarly, average magmatic water ($\delta D = -70$ ‰, $\delta^{18}O = +8$ ‰) could not have evolved to these values. Water of this isotopic composition can be obtained from meteoric water in which δD was about $-30--40$ ‰ with a high rock/water ratio ($R/W > 20$). However, the isotopic value of meteoric water in this region during the Neogene period, estimated from data for vein-type deposits, was $-60--70$ ‰ (δD). Therefore the water which produced the ore solutions for Kuroko deposits in this region was not pure sea, magmatic or meteoric water, but was probably a mixture of two or three of them.

Figure 1.18 shows the isoptic composition of sea water (SW), meteoric water (MW) and magmatic water (MGW). If we calculate (3), assuming that average volcanic rocks ($\delta D = -70$ ‰, $\delta^{18}O = +7$ ‰) react at 250 °C with $R/W < 10$, then it can be seen that water in the range enclosed by the four points a, b, c and d can evolve to reach the range of isotopic values encountered in Kuroko ore solutions. The diagram also shows lines of equal chlorine concentration in mixtures of waters taking the Cl^- level in the magmatic, sea and meteoric water as 10, 2 and 0 per cent. by weight respectively. According to existing fluid inclusions data, water with a Cl^- level of approximately 1–3 per cent. by

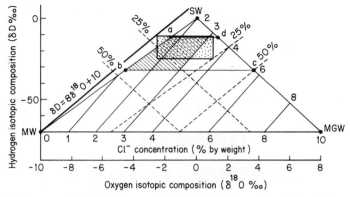

Fig. 1.18   Sources of Kuroko ore solutions. ▓ is the range of δD, δ^{18}O values in Kuroko ore solution in the Hoburoku area. ▨ shows the possible range for sea water (SW), meteoric water (MW) and magmatic water (MGW) mixtures which may have formed Kuroko ore solutions at 250°C with rock/water ratios (R/W) < 10, on the basis of available data of δD, δ^{18}O and Cl$^-$ concentrations for fluids inclusion. (After Hattori and Sakai, 1979*.)

weight is common in Kuroko ore solutions. Thus, water lying within the area marked by hatches is most likely to be the source water in this case. This corresponds to sea water combined with an average of 20–30 per cent. meteoric water, and it may also contain up to 20 per cent. magmatic water. Determination of the types and proportions of different waters which constitute ore fluids undoubtedly is very important in estimating the sources of ore-forming materials in general.

(b) Sources of sulphur

Isotopic techniques have also been successfully applied to the study of sources of sulphur, which is one of the most important ore-forming elements. Sulphur in the earth exhibits changes in δ^{34}S values in excess of ± 50 ‰ compared to the sulphur in meteorites which is isotopically almost homogeneous (δ^{34}S = 0 ‰). The main cause of variation is the occurrence of sulphur in both oxidized and reduced forms. Initially it may have had a homogeneous isotopic composition similar to that in meteorites, but various geological processes, including the evolution of the atmosphere and hydrosphere, are considered to have led to the isotopic fractionation of the earth's sulphur. As a result, various materials on earth are characterized by particular isotopic composition (Fig. 1.19).

Igneous rocks, in particular mafic rocks whose origins have a fairly direct mantle origin, have average δ^{34}S values of about + 1 ‰, which is close to the marine evaporites are of overriding importance as reservoirs of heavy sulphur.

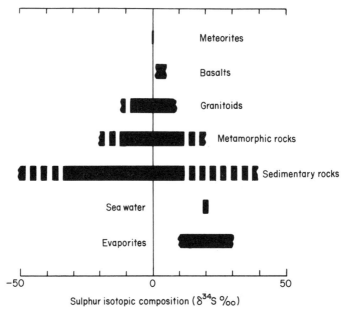

Fig. 1.19   Changes in the isotopic composition of sulphur in meteorites and various
terrestrial materials

The current $\delta^{34}S$ value for sea water is almost $+20$‰ in the middle of the
range for evaporites from the geological record which ranges from $+10$ to
$+30$ ‰. Sulphides in sedimentary rocks which precipitated due to the activity
of sulphate-reducing bacteria in an anaerobic environment are generally rich in
light sulphur. However, as reduction progresses in closed systems, heavy
isotopes concentrate in the remaining sulphate with the result that the sulphur
in sulphides produced in this late stage is very much heavier than that of the
earlier stage.

   The sulphur isotope composition of ore deposits formed as a direct result of
such geochemical processes will obviously manifest individual characteristics.
For example, many of the magmatic sulphide deposits, such as Sudbury,
formed in association with mafic igneous activity, have $\delta^{34}S$ values close to
those of the host mafic rocks. The barite layers in Meggen and Rammelsberg
in Germany and gypsum and barite deposits in Kuroko-type deposits in Japan
are examples, other than evaporites, where sea water sulphate has solidified.
The Permian copper-bearing shales in Europe (Kupferschiefer) and the
Proterozoic White Pine deposits in Michigan are famous examples of deposits
in which sulphur produced by bacterial reduction was connected directly with
deposit formation.

   However, it is interesting to note that, like the water for the mineralizing
solutions discussed above, the sources of sulphur which produced many

'igneous' deposits were not simply magmatic as was originally thought. Instead some, or indeed most, of the sulphur was supplied from materials with no direct connection with magma. Furthermore, even in the case of a magmatic origin, one finds clear instances of the contribution of sea water sulphate and sedimentary sulphides to the source of materials. Sulphur in stratabound-type deposits provides a good example in this respect.

Not only in such sedimentary deposits as the cupriferous shale deposits discussed above, where there is clear evidence suggesting bacterial reduction of sea water sulphate, but also in many stratabound sulphide deposits, the $\delta^{34}S$ shows a direct correspondence to the $\delta^{34}S$ value of sulphate at the time of deposition (Fig. 1.20). Sangster (1968, 1971*) believed this demonstrated that the sulphur in such deposits was mainly supplied from sea water sulphate by bacterial reduction. However, it seems unreasonable to apply the same interpretation to sulphur in volcanogenic stratiform or massive sulphide deposits, typified by Kuroko deposits. One theory is that the isotopic parallelism between ore sulphur and sea water sulphur in these deposits should be regarded as the result of isotopic exchange in hydrothermal systems with sea

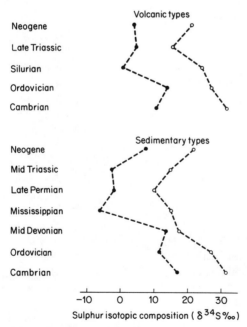

Fig. 1.20 The parallelism between the isotopic composition of sulphur in stratabound-type sulphide deposits (●) and that of those in marine sulphate (○) from various geological ages. Volcanic types are stratabound-type sulphide deposits which are closely linked with volcanic rock and volcanogenic sedimentary rock; sedimentary types are deposits associated with sedimentary rock containing little volcanic-origin material. (After Sangster, 1968, 1971*.)

water origins (Sasaki, 1970). This led to a more advanced theory that Kuroko sulphur originated exclusively in sea water (Kajiwara, 1971*; Kajiwara and Date, 1971*; Ohmoto *et al.*, 1970). In any case, neither theory conflicts with the suggestion from Fig. 1.20 that sea water is deeply involved in the genesis of these deposits.

Recent research on sulphur isotopes in granitoids and associated deposits has revealed some interesting features concerning the sulphur cycle in the outer layers of the earth, including the upper mantle (Sasaki and Ishihara, 1979*, 1980*). The $\delta^{34}S$ values of Japanese granitoids can clearly be divided into two after the rock series types—i.e. magnetite series and ilmenite series—and whilst the former are generally positive, $+1 - +9‰$, the latter almost always show negative values of $-11 - +1‰$ (Fig. 1.21). Similarly, the values of associated deposits such as contact metasomatic deposits and Sn, W and Mo veins vary in a similar fashion, i.e. $-2 - +7‰$ in the magnetite series and

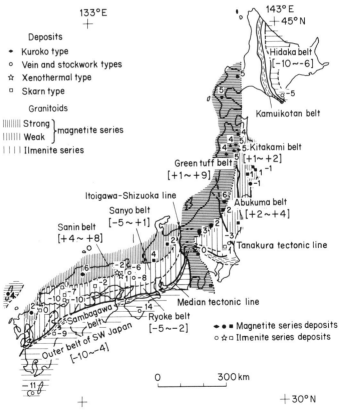

Fig. 1.21 The correlation between the isotopic composition of rock sulphur and ore sulphur established in magnetite series and ilmenite series granitoids and related ore deposits of Japan. (After Sasaki and Ishihara, 1980*.)

− 14- + 2 ‰ in the ilmenite series, implying that sulphur in these deposits is derived from the same source as sulphur in granite, i.e. magma. Ore sulphur tends to be somewhat lighter than rock sulphur and this probably reflects the fact that a proportion of the heavy isotopes concentrated in the oxidized sulphur species had not become fixed in the deposit. The difference in the values of the two rock series can be explained as follows.

The magnetite series is believed to be formed from mantle material incorporated heavy sulphur, probably of sea water origin, which had been transported to the site of magma genesis, perhaps by a subducting oceanic plate. However, most of the sulphur in ilmenite series magma, which has a dominantly crustal source, was supplied from isotopically light crustal sulphur, typically sulphides in sedimentary rock. The importance of sea water sulphur in the earth's sulphur system would thus seem to be far greater than might be anticipated.

(Akira Sasaki)

1.4 The sources of lead

In the group of light elements, such as hydrogen, oxygen and sulphur discussed in the preceding section, various isotopic effects due to slight mass differences are the cause of isotopic fractionation during geochemical processes. Another factor responsible for changes in the isotopic composition of elements in nature is, needless to say, the decay of radioactive elements; isotopic ratios of such elements as lead and strontium are controlled by this mechanism.

Approximately one third of the earth's lead is radiogenic, produced from the decay of uranium and thorium. Any lead has an isotopic composition reflecting the whole history of evolution of the U–Th–Pb system in which it has been placed. In general, lead in lead minerals such as galena can be considered as 'fossilized' in terms of isotopic composition because when it crystallized it became completely separated from the system of radioactive decay. Because of this characteristic, and the fact that lead is one of the most common ore-forming metals, research into lead isotopes has a unique importance for our understanding of the ore genesis.

(a) Lead isotopes and the origins of deposits

A general tendency is found for lead in younger deposits to be richer in radiogenic nuclides, but it is not unusual for considerable differences to exist in the lead isotope ratios of deposits thought to be of the same age. This reflects the diversity of geochemical history prior to the point when the lead became fixed in the lead ore and thus enables us to assess the origins of lead from its isotopic ratio. In this type of study, the isotope ratio of ore lead is often compared with the lead isotope ratio of rocks thought to have contributed to the formation of deposits. Feldspars are most commonly used to measure non-radiogenic lead, since they contain practically no uranium or thorium. Let us consider one example. Stacey, Zartman and Nkomo (1968*) found that the isotope ratio of galena in Tertiary hydrothermal deposits in Utah, North America, was similar to that of feldspar in the intrusion thought to have participated directly in its formation. In the same area many small-scale deposits are found with far greater proportions of radiogenic lead. They therefore concluded that almost all the lead in the main deposits was derived from the intrusive magma, whilst the lead in the minor deposits may have incorporated varying amounts of radiogenic lead extracted from country rocks by ascending ore fluids. This trend, that the lead in the main deposits contains the smallest proportion of radiogenic lead whereas that in surrounding minor deposits is more radiogenic, is also found in deposits such as Broken Hill and Sudbury and their surrounding vein deposits (Stanton and Russell, 1959). It appears that this is a common feature in deposits found in old basement terrains.

It is generally accepted that the radiogenic components of the surrounding minor deposits in Broken Hill and Sudbury were supplied from radiogenic lead produced in the country rocks between the formation of the main deposits and later regional metamorphisms (Kanasewich, 1962, 1968*; Stanton and Russell, 1959). However, because of its old age, it is not easy to ascertain the source of the lead in the main deposits. Simple comparison between ore lead and the rock lead is not possible in most instances. Techniques similar to the Rb–Sr isochron method are needed if we are to estimate the isotope ratio of rock lead in the surrounding rocks at the time of the main mineralization. In other words, the concentration of lead and uranium (thorium) must be determined together with the lead isotope ratio and, as in the Rb–Sr method, a sort of isochron is drawn with the lead isotope ratio such as $^{206}Pb/^{204}Pb$ on the vertical axis and the ratio of parent nuclide to non-radiogenic lead isotope such as $^{238}U/^{204}Pb$ on the horizontal axis. Thus, an 'initial ratio' of the lead can be found. In Broken Hill, the initial lead isotopic ratio calculated from whole rock isochrons for several gneiss specimens was almost the same as the isotopic ratio of the main deposits (Reynolds, 1971). This seems to impose one constraint on the origins of lead in the main deposits. On the contrary, in Mount Isa in Australia where there is a similar type of deposit, none of the granites or volcanic rocks has an initial ratio equal to the isotope ratio of the main deposits (Farquharson and Richards, 1974*).

(b) Lead derived from the crust and from the mantle

We now leave aside attempts to assess the direct sources of lead to deposits and consider how to ascertain in what type of global geochemical environment the isotopic evolution of lead occurred. To do this we need to examine the isotopic evolution of lead in the earth's crust and mantle, which form the main reservoir of lead in the earth, in addition to a detailed isotopic study of deposits of varying geological age.

The lead isotope ratios of many major lead orebodies (conformable orebodies), including Broken Hill and Mount Isa, vary in a regular fashion in accordance with the age of the deposit. In other words, when plotted on a graph of $^{207}Pb/^{204}Pb-^{206}Pb/^{204}Pb$ or $^{208}Pb/^{204}Pb-^{206}Pb/^{204}Pb$, the distribution of isotope ratios in these deposits closely follows a single growth curve. When examined in detail, this growth curve is found to differ slightly from those obtained from any 'single stage model'. Thus, there is a tendency for younger deposits to have a higher proportion of radiogenic lead than that predicted by the model. There has been much discussion about this regularity as well as another characteristic of the major lead orebodies, namely that each deposit is isotopically very homogeneous (Cumming and Richards, 1975*; Ostic *et al.*, 1967; Oversby, 1974; Stacey and Kramers, 1975).

The thesis that this type of ore lead has come from a crustal source is now widely accepted. The composition of materials in the earth's crust is very diverse and thus lead isotope ratios should vary widely. Consequently, samples of lead taken from different localities cannot be expected to have the same isotopic ratio, even if they were formed in the same geological period. One explanation to account for the extensive isotopic homogeneity is a large-scale circulation of 'mineralizing solutions' in the earth's crust. For instance Richards (1971*) has suggested that as hot brine passes through crustal materials it extracts several types of lead which subsequently mix completely to an isotopic ratio more or less representative of the average crustal lead of that time.

Another explanation is incorporated in Armstrong's (1968*) 'dynamic earth' model of the isotopic evolution of lead and strontium. This presupposes the idea that the different types of crustal lead become mixed during weathering and erosion, and consequently lead in pelagic sediments derived from the crust has an isotopic ratio equal to the average ratio in the coeval upper crust. It also assumes that pelagic sediments become involved in volcanic activity in island arc areas due to the subduction of oceanic plates. Stanton (1960) had previously pointed out that major lead orebodies have formed in island arc environments and this thought gave the basis of Armstrong's model. It may also be possible to use this model to explain the isotopic characteristics of Kuroko lead in Japan (Sato and Sasaki, 1973). However, doubts have been expressed about the likelihood of the involvement of pelagic sediments associated with oceanic plate subduction. Nevertheless, it is generally accepted that the growth curve of major lead orebodies is a reasonable approximation for the isotopic evolution of average crustal lead.

Isotopic data from rock lead in oceanic basalts, which may represent the present day mantle, give us information concerning the evolution of mantle lead. However, samples of mantle lead from different geological periods corresponding to the ore lead samples in the crust have not been established yet. Doe and Zartman (1979*) proposed a model establishing various evolutionary environments such as continental crust, island arc and mantle as reservoirs of ore lead, and suggested that the isotopic ratio of individual deposits would equal that of its evolutionary environment. This would render assessment of the origin of the lead possible. However, more work is necessary in order to characterize the individual evolutionary environments. A contradiction is found, for instance, in that one sample chosen as being most typical of mantle lead deposits, from Cyprus, almost overlap those for the Japanese Kuroko deposits which are thought to be derived from continental crust. There is actually disagreement as to whether or not the Troodos ophiolite, which gave rise to the Cyprus deposits, derived simply from mantle sources. Lead isotope ratios, mentioned here, rather lend support to Miyashiro (1973), who regarded this ophiolite as an island arc product.

Studies of Besshi-type deposits in Japan have revealed a possibility that a group of deposits exists with isotopic characteristics clearly differing from those of most lead–zinc stratiform sulphide deposits which probably derive from continental crust. One of the features of the above major lead orebodies is that all deposits of the same age have similar isotopic compositions, but the lead isotope ratios in Besshi-type deposits, belonging to the same period, commonly show considerable variation (Sato and Sasaki, 1976). Furthermore, the $^{207}Pb/^{204}Pb$ ratios in these deposits are generally lower than those in major lead orebodies of the same age (Fig. 1.22) (Sato and Sasaki, 1978*). Thus, it is inferred that this type of lead must have evolved in a different geochemical

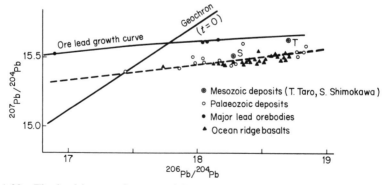

Fig. 1.22   The lead isotope features of Japanese Besshi-type deposits (after Sato and Sasaki, 1978*). The growth curve for major lead ore bodies is based on Cummin and Richards (1975*)

environment from the major lead orebodies, from a relatively early period of the earth's history—perhaps 2000 million or more years ago (see Sato, 1974*). Figure 1.22 shows a comparison of the isotopic ratios of several Besshi-type deposits, including the Mesozoic Shimokawa deposits, with recent measurements of major lead orebodies and modern ocean ridge basalts. It also shows results for the Taro deposits—pre-tertiary stratiform sulphide deposits—in Japan characterized by particularly high lead and zinc levels. Lead in Besshi-type deposits possesses isotopic characteristics similar to those of ocean ridge basalts and the linear trends they show appear to be essentially similar to those of ocean ridge basalts, i.e. to lead in the present day oceanic mantle. This is possible due to the fact that the formation of Besshi-type deposits is closely associated with mafic magmatic activity and that, without exception, the deposits have low lead concentrations. It seems certain that the source of this lead was the mantle.

In contrast, the lead isotope data for Mesozoic Taro deposits plot very close to the growth curve of major lead orebodies. This lead is known to be isotopically very homogeneous. When combined with the fact that the deposits are of lead–zinc stratiform sulphide type and that related igneous activity is calc-alkaline, one may conclude that they are of crustal origin, like many major lead orebodies.

Sato and Sasaki (1978*) reexamined existing data on 'major lead orebodies' and concluded that some of them were formed from mantle materials from a consideration of their isotopic ratios. This seems to be true, particularly of deposits in regions of volcanic activity in the Archaean, i.e. in 'greenstone belts' such as Barberton in South Africa and Manitouwadge in Canada (Fig. 1.23). Many other major lead orebodies exist chiefly in sialic continental areas with ages ranging from the Proterozoic to the lower Palaeozoic. Engel *et al.* (1974*) divided the chemical evolution of the earth's crust into three main

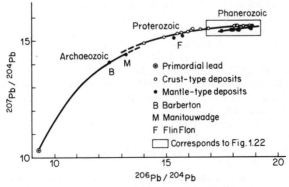

Fig. 1.23   The two types of lead in stratiform sulphide deposits

periods: (1) the Archean, (2) the Proterozoic–Palaeozoic and (3) the Mesozoic–Cenozoic. In terms of significant geological episodes, these three may be specified respectively by: (1) greenstone belt magmatism, (2) growth of continental crust and (3) continental rifting and the rise of mantle material. If we consider the two different series of lead found in stratiform sulphide deposits in these terms, then 'mantle origin' lead would be connected with periods (1) and (3) and 'crust origin' lead with period (2).

(Kazuo Sato and Akira Sasaki)

References

Armstrong, R. L. (1968). A model for the evolution of strontium and lead isotopes in a dynamic earth, *Rev. Geophys.*, **6**, 175–199.
Barnes, H. L., and Kullerud, G. (1961). Equilibria in sulfur-containing aqueous solution in the system Fe–S–O, and their correlation during ore deposition, *Econ. Geol.*, **56**, 648–688.
Bischoff, J. L., and Dickson, F. W. (1975). Seawater–basalt interaction at 200 °C and 500 bars: implications for origins of sea-floor heavy metal deposits and regulations of seawater chemistry, *Earth Planet. Sci. Lett.*, **25**, 385–397.
Burnham, C. W. (1979). Magmas and hydrothermal fluids, in *Geochemistry of Hydrothermal Ore Deposits* (Ed. H. L. Barnes), 2nd ed., pp. 71–136, John Wiley, New York.
Burnham, C. W., and Ohmoto, H. (1980). Late-stage processes of felsic magmatism, *Mining Geol. Spec.*, Issue No. 8, 1–11.
Cameron, E. N., and Desborough, G. A. (1969). Occurrence and characteristics of chromite deposits—Eastern Bushveld Complex, in *Magmatic Ore Deposits* (Ed. H. D. B. Wilson), Vol. 4, pp. 23–40, Econ. Geol. Monogr.
Cathles, L. M. (1977). An analysis of the cooling of intrusives by ground-water convection which includes boiling, *Econ. Geol.*, **72**, 804–826.
Craig, H. (1963). The isotopic geochemistry of water and carbon in geothermal areas, in *Nuclear Geology on Geothermal Areas* (Ed. E. Tongiorgi), pp. 17–53, Consiglio Nazionale delle Ricerche, Laboratorio di Geologia Nucleare, Spoleto, Pisa.
Cumming, G. L., and Richards, J. R. (1975). Ore lead isotope ratios in a continuously changing earth, *Earth Planet. Sci. Lett.*, **28**, 155–171.
Czamanske, G. K., and Moore, J. G. (1977). Composition and phase chemistry of sulfide globules in basalt from the Mid-Atlantic Ridge rift valley near 37°N lat., *Bull. Geol. Soc. Am.*, **88**, 587–599.
Dietz, R. W. (1964). Sudbury structure as an astrobleme, *J. Geol.*, **72**, 412–434.
Doe, B. R., and Zartman, R. E. (1979). Plumbotectonics, the Phanerozoic, in *Geochemistry of Hydrothermal Ore Deposits* (Ed. H. L. Barnes), 2nd ed., pp. 22–70, John Wiley, New York.
Elder, J. W. (1966). Heat and mass transfer in the earth, hydrothermal systems, N.Z. Dept. Sci. Industr. Res. Bull., No. 169, 114 pp.

Engel, A. E. J., Itson, S. P., Engel, C. G., Stickney, D. M., and Cray, E. J., Jr., (1974). Crustal evolution and global tectonics: a petrogenic view, *Geol. Soc. Am. Bull.*, **85**, 843–858.

Farquharson, R. B., and Richards, J. R. (1974). U–Th–Pb isotope systematics related to igneous rocks and ore Pb, Mount Isa, Queensland, *Mineral. Deposita (Berl.)*, **9**, 339–356.

Hajash, A. (1975). Hydrothermal processes along mid-ocean ridges: an experimental investigation, *Contrib. Mineral. Petrol.*, **53**, 205–226.

Hattori, K., and Sakai, H. (1979). D/H ratios, origins and evolution of the ore forming fluids for the Neogene veins and Kuroko deposits of Japan, *Econ. Geol.*, **74**, 535–555.

Helgeson, H. C. (1969). Thermodynamics of hydrothermal systems at elevated temperatures and pressures, *Am. J. Sci.*, **267**, 729–804.

Holland, H. D. (1972). Granites, solutions and base metal deposits, *Econ. Geol.*, **67**, 281–301.

Irvine, T. N. (1977). Origin of chromitite layers in the Muskox intrusion and other stratiform intrusions: a new interpretation, *Geol.*, **5**, 273–277.

Ishihara, S. (1977). The magnetite-series and ilmenite-series granitic rocks, *Mining Geol. (Japan)*, **27**, 293–305.

Ishihara, S., and Terashima, S. (1977). The Sn content of granitoids in Japan and its significance to Cretaceous granitic activity, *Chishitsu Gaku Zasshi (Journal of Geological Society of Japan)*, **83**, 657–664.

Kajiwara, Y. (1971). Sulfur isotope study of the Kuroko-ores of the Shakanai No. 1 deposits, Akita Prefecture, Japan, *Geochem. J.*, **4**, 157–181.

Kajiwara, Y., and Date, J. (1971). Sulfur isotope study of Kuroko and Kieslager-type strata-bound massive sulfide deposits, Japan, *Geochem. J.*, **5**, 133–150.

Kanasewich, E. R. (1968). The interpretation of lead isotopes and their geological significance, in *Radiometric Dating for Geologists* (Eds. E. I. Hamilton and R. M. Farquhar), pp. 147–223, Interscience.

Koster van Groos, A. F. (1975). The effect of high CO_2 pressures on alkalic rocks and its bearing on the formation of alkalic ultrabasic rocks and the associated carbonatites, *Am. J. Sci.*, **275**, 163–185.

Le Bas, M. J. (1977). *Carbonatite–nephelinite Volcanism*, John Wiley, pp. 347.

MacLean, W. H. (1969). Liquidus phase relations in the FeS–FeO–Fe_3O_4–SiO_2 system, and their application in geology, *Econ. Geol.*, **64**, 865–884.

MacLean, W. H., and Shimazaki, H. (1976). The partition of Co, Ni, Cu, and Zn between sulfide and silicate liquids, *Econ. Geol.*, **71**, 1049–1057.

Mottl, M. J., Corr, R. E., and Holland, H. D. (1974). Chemical exchange between seawater and mid-ocean ridge basalt during hydrothermal alteration, an experimental study, *Geol. Soc. Am. Abstracts with Program*, **6**, 879.

Naldrett, A. J. (1973). Nickel sulphide deposits; their classification and genesis, with special emphasis on deposits of volcanic association, *Canadian Mining Metal. Bull.*, **66**, No. 739, 45–63.

Naldrett, A. J., and Cabri, L. J. (1976). Ultramafic and related mafic rocks; their classification and genesis with special reference to the concentration of nickel sulfides and platinum-group elements, *Econ. Geol.*, **71**, 1131–1158.

Norton, D., and Knight, J. (1977). Transport phenomena in hydrothermal systems; cooling plutons, *Am. J. Sci.*, **277**, 937–981.

Paster, T. P., Schauwecker, D. S., and Haskin, L. A. (1974). The behavior of some trace elements during solidification of the Skaergaard layered series, *Geochim. Cosmochim. Acta*, **38**, 1549–1577.

Rajamani, V., and Naldrett, A. J. (1978). Partition of Fe, Co, Ni, and Cu between sulfide liquid and basaltic melts and the composition of Ni-Cu sulfide deposits, *Econ. Geol.*, **73**, 82-93.

Richards, J. R. (1971). Major lead orebodies—mantle origin?, *Econ. Geol.*, **66**, 425-434.

Rye, R. O., and Sawkins, F. J. (1974). Fluid inclusion and stable isotope studies on the Casapalca Ag-Pb-Zn-Cu deposit, Central Andes, Peru, *Econ. Geol.*, **69**, 181-205.

Sangster, D. F. (1971). Sulphur isotopes, stratabound sulphide deposits, and ancient seas, *Soc. Min. Geol. Japan*, Spec. Issue, **3**, 295-299.

Sasaki, A., and Ishihara, S. (1979). Sulfur isotopic composition of the magnetite-series and ilmenite-series granitoids in Japan, *Contrib. Mineral. Petrol.*, **68**, 107-115.

Sasaki, A., and Ishihara, S. (1980). Sulfur isotope characteristics of granitoids and related mineral deposits in Japan, *Proc. 5th IAGOD Symp. E. Schweizerbart'sche Verlag. (Nägele u. Obermiller), Stuttgart, pp. 325-335.*

Sato, K. (1974). *A review of lead isotope geochemistry, Mining Geol.* (in Japanese), **24**, 237-266.

Sato, K., and Sasaki, A. (1978). Two major evolutionary systems for stratiform ore leads as exemplified by Japanese samples, in *Short Papers of the Fourth International Conf., Geochronology, Cosmo-chronology, Isotope Geology*, (Ed. R. E. Zartman), USGS Open File Report 78-701, pp. 378-379.

Sheppard, S. M. F., Nielsen, R. L., and Taylor, H. P., Jr. (1969). Oxygen and hydrogen isotope ratios of clay minerals from porphyry copper deposits, *Econ. Geol.*, **64**, 755-777.

Shikazono, N. (1978a). Possible cation buffering in chloride-rich geothermal waters, *Chem. Geol.*, **23**, 239-254.

Shikazono, N. (1978b). Selenium content of acanthite and the chemical environments of Japanese vein-type deposits, *Econ. Geol.*, **73**, 524-533.

Shimazaki, H., and MacLean, W. H. (1976). An experimental study on the partition of zinc and lead between the silicate and sulfide liquids, *Mineral. Deposita (Berl.)*, **11**, 125-132.

Skinner, B. J., and Peck, D. L. (1969). An immiscible sulfide melt from Hawaii, in *Magmatic Ore Deposits* (Ed. H. B. D. Wilson), Vol. 4, pp. 310-322, Econ. Geo. Monogr.

Sourirajan, S., and Kennedy, G. C. (1962). The system H_2O-NaCl at elevated temperatures and pressures, *Am. J. Sci.*, **260**, 115-141.

Stacey, J. S., Zartman, R. E., and Nkomo, I. T. (1968). A lead isotope study of galenas and selected feldspars from mining districts in Utah, *Econ. Geol.*, **63**, 796-814.

Taylor, H. P., Jr. (1974). The application of oxygen and hydrogen isotope studies to problems of hydrothermal alteration and ore deposition, *Econ. Geol.*, **69**, 843-883.

Vermaak, C. G. (1976). The Merensky Reef—thoughts on its environment and genesis, *Econ. Geol.*, **71**, 1270-1298.

Wager, L. R., and Brown, G. M. (1967). *Layered Igneous Rocks*, Oliver and Boyd, 588 pp.

Wager, L. R., and Mitchell, R. L. (1951). The distribution of trace elements during strong fractionation of basic magma—a further study of the Skaergaard intrusion, East Greenland, *Geochim. Cosmochim. Acta*, **1**, 129-208.

Wager, L. R., Vincent, E. A., and Smales, A. A. (1957). Sulphides in the Skaergaard intrusion, East Greenland, with an appendix by P. Bartholomé, *Econ. Geol.*, **52**, 855-903.

Wolery, T. J., and Sleep, N. H. (1976). Hydrothermal circulation and geochemical flux at mid-ocean ridges, *J. Geol.*, **84**, 249-276.

Further reading

Barnes, H. L., (Ed.) (1967). *Geochemistry of Hydrothermal Ore Deposits*, Holt, Rinehart and Winston, New York, 670 pp.

This book deals with the behaviour of heavy metals in granitoid magmatic processes. The book also discussed all the important issues in the study of deposits and so it is useful as a comprehensive textbook. The 2nd edition was published in 1979.

There are many textbooks on the basic chemistry of solutions, and of these the following are outstanding, dealing with the statistical mechanics and chemistry of aqueous solutions at high temperatures:

Harned, H. S., and Owen, B. B. (1958). *The Physical Chemistry of Electrolitic Solutions*, Reinhold, Am. Chem. Soc. Monograph Series, 803 pp.
Robinson, R. A., and Stokes, R. H. (1965). *Electrolyte Solutions*, Butterworth, London, 571 pp.

There are also many books on the foundations of thermodynamics, for example:

Prigogine, I., and Defay, R. (1954). *Chemical Thermodynamics*, Longmans Green, New York, 543 pp.
Garrels, R. M., and Christ, C. L. (1965). *Solutions, Minerals and Equilibria*, Harper and Row, New York, 450 pp.

This applies thermodynamics and the chemistry of solutions to geochemistry, and the book includes many Eh–pH diagrams.

Stumm, W., and Morgan, J. J. (1970). *Aquatic Chemistry*, John Wiley, New York, 584 pp.

This deals in detail with acid–base and oxidation–reduction reactions in mineral-aqueous solution systems and the book also includes examples of calculations based on equilibrium models for mineral-aqueous solution systems.

Helgeson, H. C. (1964). *Complexing and Hydrothermal Ore Deposition*, International Series of Monographs on Earth Sciences, Vol. 17, Pergamon Press, Oxford, 128 pp.

This deals in detail with the solubility and chemical forms of heavy metal elements (especially PbS) under the temperature and pressure conditions prevailing when deposits were formed.

Krauskopf, K. B. (1979). *Introduction to Geochemistry*, 2nd ed., McGraw-Hill Book Co., New York, 617 pp.

This deals more fully with deposits than do general textbooks on geochemistry and brings together factual explanations. It is thus a convenient textbook for those interested in deposits.

Tatsumi, Tatsuo (Ed.) (1977). *Fundamental Aspects of the Study of Deposits*, Todai
   Shuppan Kai (University of Tokyo Press), 258 pp. (in Japanese).

This book covers topics currently of interest in the study of deposits. It also
discusses the chemistry of solutions, including an introduction to isotopes.

Nakamura, Takeshi (Ed.) (1976). *Genesis of Vein-type Deposits in Japan—The
   Mechanisms and Conditions of Their Formation*, Kozan Chishitsu (Mining
   Geology), Special Issue No. 7., 131 pp. (in Japanese).

This issue deals with problems in the chemistry of ore solutions; e.g. fluid
inclusions, isotopes and a chemical model of the formation of deposits.

Elder, J. W. (1966). Heat and mass transfer in the earth, hydrothermal systems, *N.Z.
   Dept. Sci. Industr. Res. Bull.*, No. 169. 114 pp.

This gives an easily comprehensible hydrodynamic model of present
geothermal areas, e.g. Wairakei (New Zealand) and Larderello (Italy), which
can be applied to ore-forming hydrothermal systems in the past.

Yuhara, K., and Seno, K. (1970). *The Study of Hot Springs*, Chijin Shokan, 294 pp.(in
   Japanese).

This book discusses several questions concerning hot springs, in particular
research on hydrodynamics applied to hot spring regions, and it is also useful
for research on the genesis of deposits.

Hall, W. E. (Ed.) (1974). Stable isotopes as applied to problems of ore deposits, *Econ.
   Geol.*, **49**, No. 6, 755–1006.

This is a collection of papers given at the 1973 Symposium of the Soc. Econ.
Geologists, and it includes research on the genesis of ore deposits using stable
isotopes including hydrogen, oxygen, carbon, sulphur, lead and strontium.

Chapter 2

The Geochemistry of Fossil Fuel Deposit

2.1 Fossil fuel deposits

Fossil organic material may be classified in terms of the way in which it developed into 'condensed types' which form actual deposits and 'dispersed types' which are finely dispersed throughout sedimentary rocks. They take solid, liquid or gaseous forms. Condensed fossil organic material has been utilized since the beginning of civilization and is readily identifiable in the field, obvious examples being coal, petroleum, oil shale or solid bitumen. Table 2.1 shows a classification of condensed fossil organic materials concentrating on their chemical properties.

The amount of condensed organic material which forms in deposits is negligible compared with the total quantity of dispersed organic material. Estimates of organic carbon in sedimentary rocks, classified by type and environment, are shown in Table 2.2, which gives a total quantity of as much as $12\,000 \times 10^{18}$ g. In contrast to this, inherent primary reserves of coal, which is quantitatively the most common fossil organic material, are equivalent to no more than about 15×10^{18} g as carbon.

Estimates of the total amount of dispersed organic material existing in the form of hydrocarbons have indicated an abundance of nearly 200×10^{18} g. In contrast, the inherent primary reserves of condensed hydrocarbons which form oil and gas deposits are thought to be 7.2×10^{12} bbl (Weeks, 1965*), corresponding to almost 1×10^{18} g when converted to the carbon equivalent. If the source of petroleum hydrocarbons is taken to be sedimentary organic material, then less than 2 per cent. of the sedimentary organic carbon has formed hydrocarbons, of which less than 0.5 per cent. has condensed in reservoir rocks to form petroleum. In other words, less than 0.01 per cent. of the original organic matter has condensed to form petroleum deposits.

Many factors are involved in the formation of these diverse condensed fossil fuel (deposits) near the surface of the crust, as shown schematically in Fig. 2.1. These include differences in the source organic materials, variations in the

61

Table 2.1 Classification of condensed fossil organic matter

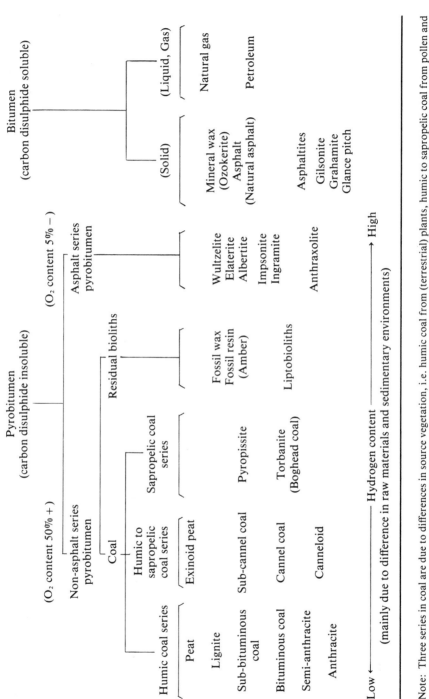

Note: Three series in coal are due to differences in source vegetation, i.e. humic coal from (terrestrial) plants, humic to sapropelic coal from pollen and resin durable to oxidation decomposition and sapropelic coal from aquatic plants. 'Oil shale' is a commercial name given to what includes asphalt series pyrobitumen to natural asphalt that generate large quantity of oily materials by cracking, but may include mineral wax. 'Natural solid bitumen' is a general name given to asphalt series pyrobitumen, mineral wax, natural asphalt and asphalt.

Table 2.2 Distribution of sedimentary organic carbon in the crust (prepared from Hunt, 1972*)

	Mass (10^{18} g)	Organic carbon		Petroleum hydrocarbon (Carbon mass 10^{18} g)		Coal (Carbon mass 10^{18} g)
		Wt %	Mass (10^{18} g)	Dispersed type	Condensed type	
Continent, shelf and slope						
Clays and shales	830 000	0.99	8200	} 166		
Carbonates	250 000	0.33	800			
Sandstones	320 000	0.28	900	16		
Total	1 400 000		9900			
Oceanic						
Clays and shales	340 000	0.22	700	} 21		
Carbonates	350 000	0.28	1000			
Siliceous sediments	150 000	0.26	400			
Total	840 000		2100			
Totals by sediment type						
Clays and shales	1 170 000		8900			
Carbonates	600 000		1800			
Sands and siliceous sediments	470 000		1300			
Total	2 240 000		12 000	203 ($\fallingdotseq$ 200)	1	15[a]

[a] This value shows the total quantity of all coaly materials in sediments on the earth, and is greater than the coal reserves which is recoverable by mining in the coalfield as shown in the Table 3.2.

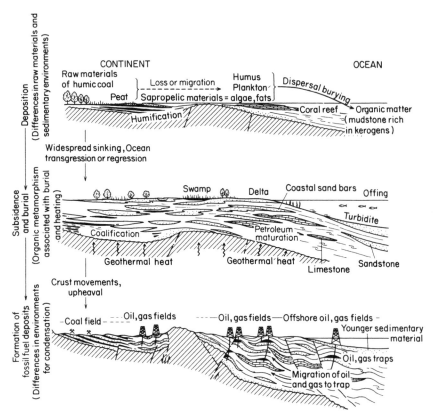

Fig. 2.1 Geological model of fossil fuel deposit formation. For coal deposit formation see Sec. 2.2(a); for coalification see Sec. 2.2(b), (c); for petroleum deposits see Sec. 2.3(a); for petroleum formation see Sec. 2.3(d); and for petroleum migration see Sec. 2.3(f)

sedimentary environment where they accumulated and differences in the processes of condensation, maturation and metamorphism which takes place after the commencement of deposition and before final formation of the deposits. We discuss below various geochemical aspects of the formation of organic reserves, citing coal deposits as a typical example of solid materials and oil deposits as typical of fluid reserves.

(Kazuo Taguchi and Atsuo Aihara)

2.2 The geochemistry of coal deposit formation

(a) Source materials for coal deposits

Any geochemical explanation of coal deposits must attempt to establish the chemical composition of the ancient vegetation from which coal has been derived. However, identifying the chemical makeup of the source material is very difficult as the ancient vegetation has been completely transformed into various ranks of coal. Hence, we can only make deductions on the basis of our knowledge of the chemical composition of vegetation still extant today. Most terrestrial vegetation consists mainly of cellulose (50+ per cent.) and lignin (about 30 per cent.), with small amounts of proteins, fats and resins. As the majority of coal in workable deposits is composed of humic coal derived from terrestrial vegetation, cellulose and lignin are thus believed to be its principal contributors.

Cellulose is the principal component of cell membranes and is formed from polymers on to which glucose is glucoside bonded with oxygen bridges. Its structural form may be represented as follows:

It is chemically stable but is easily decomposed biochemically, or hydrolysed by acids to become carbohydrates with low degrees of polymerization. Ultimately it breaks down to glucose ($C_6H_{12}O_6$). Lignin, the next most important consituent, binds plant tissue composed of cellulose. Its structure is highly complex and still not fully understood, but it is known to consist of polymers produced in the plant by polymerization of various alcohols with phenylpropane carbon skeletons such as *p*-coumaryl, coniferyl or sinapir alcohols:

p-coumaryl alcohol	coniferyl alcohol	sinapir alcohol

Broad-leaved and coniferous plants produce lignin of differing compositions. Unfortunately, our understanding of its bonding mechanisms is still poor. Lignin is chemically very stable and is considerably more stable biochemically than cellulose.

The remains of the vegetation, unless broken down and incorporated into soil as humus, are turned into the source material for coal deposits by accumulation in suitable locations, current peat areas being formed in this way. Similarly, reducing environments with a low supply of oxygen in the ground water have probably existed in the geological past. Climatically peat areas are found in the sub-arctic to parts of the temperate zones, and in tropical rain forests with luxuriant vegetation. Because the breakdown of vegetable matter by microorganisms is so vigorous in the latter case, the topography is a particularly important factor in the preservation of peat. The pH of modern peat areas tends to be 3–5 owing to humic acids produced from the breakdown of vegetation in water. The acidic environment then suppresses the activity of microorganisms. It seems likely that the chemical conditions during the early stages of coal-forming basins were similar to this in the geological past.

The environment of coal deposition may also be assessed by considering such sedimentary features as parting laminae or single layers of inorganic clastic material other than coal in the coal seams and the sediments immediately underlying the coal seam. Under-clay or seat earth rich in kaolinite sometimes develops beneath coal seams and its high alumina contents (Al_2O_3, 30–40 per cent.) have attracted particular attention as fire clay. The under-clay was once believed to be paleosol produced by ancient vegetation and was the subject of debate between the autochthonous and the allochthonous coal deposition theories in the first half of this century. Moreover, the chemical composition and trace element distribution do not always correspond with the soil under modern peat; more often they resemble products of weathering and leaching of silica in stagnant water, with low pH and Eh. Thus the possibility that the under-clay represents the paleosol itself is increasingly remote.

The initial chemical changes in vegetable matter in such chemical environments, i.e. humification, have been debated since the beginning of this century, with a cellulose theory (Bergius, 1912; Erasmus, 1938; etc.) and a lignin theory (Eller, 1920; Fischer and Schrader, 1920; Waksman, 1938; etc.). The cellulose theory considers the formation of coal in terms of natural processes of breakdown in vegetation together with the results of simulated coalification experiments with higher temperature and pressure conditions, and postulates that when water is added to cellulose and lignin, the lignin disappears in the following manner:

$$
\text{Vegetation}
\begin{cases}
\text{cellulose} \longrightarrow \underset{\text{hydrolysis}}{\text{sugars}} \longrightarrow \text{humic acid} \longrightarrow \text{humins} \\
\text{resins} \longrightarrow\joinrel\longrightarrow \text{bitumen} \\
\text{lignin} \longrightarrow \left\{\begin{array}{c} CO_2 \\ H_2O \\ CH_4 \end{array}\right\} \to \text{disappears}
\end{cases}
\left.\begin{array}{c}\\ \\ \end{array}\right\} \text{coal}
$$

Conversely, the lignin theory believes that the lignin remains stable because it is such a chemically stable material and that the relatively more unstable cellulose will break down and disappear by the following route:

$$
\text{Vegetation}
\begin{cases}
\text{cellulose} \rightarrow \begin{Bmatrix} CO_2 \\ CH_4 \\ \text{fatty acids} \end{Bmatrix} \longrightarrow \text{disappears} \\[2em]
\text{resins} \longrightarrow \text{bitumen} \\[1em]
\text{lignin} \longrightarrow \underset{\downarrow}{\underset{CH_3COOH}{\text{(methoxyl-cont.)}}} \underset{\downarrow}{\underset{CH_2OH}{\text{humic acid}}} \longrightarrow \underset{}{\text{(methoxyl-free)}} \underset{\downarrow}{\underset{H_2O}{\text{humins}}}
\end{cases} \Big\} \text{coal}
$$

Numerous variables which complicate the process of humification can be imagined; they are, for example, variations in the activity of aerobic and anerobic bacteria owing to ancient climatic changes or variation in the water level in peat swamp during decomposition of the plant material, the diversity in the chemical composition of various constituent plants in addition to the principal components or changes in the sedimentary environment which may lead to variations in sapropelic or humic properties over wide areas.

Since coal, which we now observe as the final reaction product, is a high polymer compound with a chemically non-uniform character, obviously the humification reaction had to be a complex process and is difficult to explain in terms of a single chemical change. Unsolved chemical problems still remain at many stages in the coalification process.

Recent knowledge of coal petrology has contributed greatly to our geochemical appreciation of the formation of coal deposits. When detailed macroscopic examinations of the profiles of minable coal seams are made, one is able to trace a sequence of changes that took place during coal sedimentation. For example, favourable sedimentary conditions for accumulating source materials developed in the underlying sediments, whereupon parting and banded ingredients, distinguishable macroscopically, were variably accumulated, reflecting changes not only in the source material but also in the sedimentary environment. Finally, the favourable sedimentary conditions for peat-accumulation have disappeared when the overlying strata are reached. Coal petrology based on such macroscopic and microscopic observations rests basically on the premise that coal is composed of the minimum units of various vegetable parts that can be identified microscopically; the minimum units are called 'macerals'. Those are analogous to the minerals which make up rocks. The microlithotype observed microscopically is determined by the combination of unit constituents (maceral or mineral type). A coal microscope, examining their sections with transmitted light, was used to observe coal structures, but commonly reflected light techniques are now used on polished specimens. Standards for classification and examination are being laid down by the International Committee for Coal Petrology (ICCP) based on oil-immersion reflected light observations. The basic premise established long ago by Stopes (1919) (extreme right column, Table 2.3) has been revived as the basis for lithotype classification in the ICCP standards, and her name has therefore been combined with the name of the location of the first committee meeting to give us the Stopes–Heerlen System.

(1) Lithotypes Vitrain is usually banded or lenticular, forming layers several millimetres to centimetres thick with a glassy lustre, occurring within coal seams. Orientated cleats frequently develop at right angles to the bedding so it readily crumbles with conchoidal fractures. It is the principal constituent of humic coal.

Clarain normally forms fine alternating laminae several millimetres to centimetres thick. It is harder than vitrain, without the glassy lustre, but silky

Table 2.3 Outline of coal petrography

Macerals	Maceral (group)	Microlithotype	Lithotype
Collinte Telinite	Vitrinite (V)	Vitrite (V > 95%)	Vitrain
Sporinite Cutinite Resinite Alginite	Liptinite (L) or Exinite	Clarite (V + L > 95%) Liptite (L > 95%) Vitrinertite (V + I > 95%) Duroclarite (V > L + I)	Clarain
Micrinite Macrinite Fusinite Semifusinite Sclerotinite	Inertinite (I)	Clarodurite (I > L + V) Durite (I + L > 95%) Inertite (I > 95%)	Durain Fusain

in cross-sections at right angles to the bedding. It is the second most important constituent of humic coal.

Durain exhibits no banding and often exists as hard blocks with a duller lustre. Fractures are irregular and rough. It is only a minor constituent of humic coal.

Fusain has a fibrous structure like natural charcoal, occurring in lenticular or banded forms of a few millimetres to centimetres. It is extremely friable and powders easily. Its hardness is increased when inorganic material has infiltrated into the structure.

(2) Macerals Macerals are named by adding the suffix 'nite' to the name of the plant tissue left in the coal. Combining their physical and chemical properties, source materials and structure, they are classified into three groups of vitrinite (V), liptinite (L) or exinite and inertinite (I). These groups are further subdivided as follows.

Vitrinite (V) is derived from wood. It may be divided into non-structured collinite and telinite in which the woody structure is still apparent. Collinite may also be classified into telocollinite in which a structureless band is seen under the microscope, and desmocollinite which forms a matrix for other macerals. Reflectance measurements for determining the rank of coalification are executed on the former.

Liptinite (L) is divided into pollen and spore-derived sporinite, cuticle-derived cutinite, wax and resin-derived resinite, and algae-derived alginite. Alginite is particularly rich in hydrogen and is the major component of sapropelic coal.

Inertinite (I) forms a maceral group in which the concentration of carbon has proceeded further during the processes of humification or coalification than in other macerals, and which has become thermally inactive and inert. It is composed of fusinite which is a charcoal-like maceral produced in the humification; semifusinite which is intermediate between the earliest stage of fusinite and vitrinite; sclerotinite derived from fungal sclerotia; micrinite, structureless maceral of small particles—masses showing a high reflectance; and macrinite, a highly reflective structureless material dispersed in a matrix.

(3) Microlithotypes The microlithotype is determined by the combination of macerals. If a single or multiple maceral with a minimum size of 50 µm accounts for 95 per cent., it is given a name with the suffix 'ite', as shown in Table 2.3. The number of macerals from which the material is composed is used to identify a monomaceral group such as vitrite, liptite and inertite, a bimaceral group such as clarite, durite or vitrinertite, and a trimaceral group such as duroclarite or clarodurite. Observation and microlithotype analysis are usually performed on a polished plug specimen (2.5–3.0 cm in diameter) prepared by forming a coagulated sample of pulverized coal (750 µm) with a

synthetic resin (particulate specimen). The maceral composition is counted using a 20-point graticule (in an eyepiece). Macerals per intersection (5 per cent.) are assessed in order to determine the microlithotype of the particles.

The above-mentioned petrological methods of classification and examination of coal enables one to trace the transformation from the initial deposition of material to the many diverse coal deposits found today. There are two significant processes, i.e. physical and chemical, during the early stages of deposition which affect the structure and composition of the coal and chemical changes in the crust after deposition (organic metamorphism).

(b) Coalification

(1) The concept of coalification Coalification is a process of geochemical change in which the remains of vegetation are initially fixed and buried in the earth as peat deposits, whereupon they change into lignite, sub-bituminous coal and bituminous coal. Finally, they change from anthracite to graphite. As coal consists of non-crystalline high-polymer compounds whose chemical structure is difficult to ascertain, it is usual to employ a statistical treatment of the analytical data for C, H and O—the principal elements of coal—and to express these as an atomic numerical ratio—H/C:O/C (van Krevelen, 1950). Figure 2.2 illustrates the chemical composition of modern plant material which corresponds to the source materials of the principal macerals, together with the distribution of analytical results for coal at various stages of the coalification process. This clearly shows quite remarkable differences in the chemical structure and composition of macerals derived from various plant components. The fact that the many analytical data which have stopped at various ranks or stages of coalification show continuous band distributions (called 'coal bands') implies that chemical changes in coalification reaction progressed in this direction in nature. Figure 2.2 records the typical direction of changes in atomic H/C:O/C ratios, together with experimental results for artificial coalification reactions using brown coal or lignite as the starting material. It also shows the results of heating experiments using Japanese vitrinite at various ranks of coalification (performed in a nitrogen atmosphere at 1 atmosphere pressure). We can use these data to trace the chemical changes during coalification, concentrating mainly on vitrinite genesis.

In the early stages, when peat changes to lignite, dehydration occurs due to physical compression at low reaction temperatures. As the material becomes more deeply buried, coalification proceeds under temperature and pressure conditions corresponding to the depth of burial, so that absorbed water is removed and division into functional groups takes place. Humic acid changes to humins and becomes gelatinous. As the reaction time lengthens, rises in temperature cause dehydration and rises in pressure, decarboxylation. As the reactions proceed still further, dissociation of aliphatic or hydrogenous

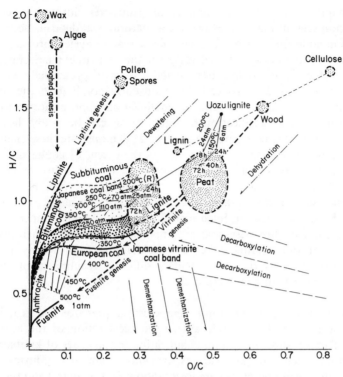

Fig. 2.2 H/C: O/C (atomic ratio) showing the chemical evolution of coal and associated materials during coalification. The effects of temperature, pressure and reaction time on chemical composition can be seen from artificial coalification experiments and heating experiments on Japanese vitrinite of various ranks.

reactive side chains occurs, whilst condensation and cyclization reactions proceed simultaneously in the aromatic rings. These are ringed at the sub-bituminous coal stage, increasing to about six rings at the bituminous coal stage. Subsequent reactions are accelerated markedly by rises in temperature and proceed towards demethanizing reactions based on the removal of aliphatic or hydrogenous reactive side chains. However, still greater effective reaction temperatures and times are required for coalification to proceed from bituminous coal to anthracite. The number of aromatic rings which continue to condensate during this phase reaches over a few tens. The arrangement of molecules gradually becomes parallel to the bedding plane, so that the distance between layers is reduced until the material finally becomes graphite.

(2) Properties of the products of coalification reactions (coal rank) Products with quite specific physical and chemical properties are obtained at each of the above-mentioned stages of coalification. Vitrinite, a typical maceral in humic

coals, manifests the several changes in properties during the course of coalification seen in Fig. 2.3. However, as natural coal deposits contain other macerals in addition to vitrinite, their chemical and physical properties will be determined by the compositional ratios of the constituent macerals and the level to which the coalification reactions have proceeded. Qualitative assessment of coal deposits can be made corresponding to the degree of organic metamorphism if a rank of coalification appropriate to individual applications such as gasification or liquefaction can be established. If one selects properties of the reaction products that demonstrate these changes, one mày develop a geochemical index to assess the extent of coalification and to establish the degree of organic metamorphism (see (c)). In this connection vitrinite in Japanese coal is clearly far richer in hydrogen than Euramerican coals, which gives it its characteristic properties of thermal activity (e.g. high fluidity) (Figs. 2.2 and 2.3). Such high fluidity and a wide temperature range of plastic stage of Japanese coal are important properties which permit the production of outstanding coke for steelmaking, even when mixed with various foreign coals that have widely differing inactive components, or softening and hardening temperatures.

(3) Factors affecting coalification Temperature, pressure and reaction time may all be cited as factors relevant to the acceleration of the coalification process. The pressures in natural coalification in the order of kilobars are far higher than that of artifical experiments. Similarly, during natural coalification, the temperatures are lower (about 200 °C max.) and the reaction times incomparably longer. The effects of reaction time on coalification are now appreciated, following various long-term experiments at relatively low temperatures (e.g. 200 °C, 2 years, Friedel, 1970; 100–600 °C, 1 month, Bostick, 1973*).

On the other hand, one general principle in coalfield surveying is that the rank of coal will be more advanced the deeper the coal layer. Decreases in the moisture content (Schüllman's rule) and volatile content (Hilt's rule) also occur. Karweil (1956*) took samples from boreholes in the Ruhr coalfield and was the first to establish a clear relationship between geological reaction time and rank of coalification. The diagram he proposed to illustrate the relationship between temperature, time and rank of coalification found in many coalfields is often referred to. In Fig. 2.4 we apply Karweil's approach to Japanese vitrinite to demonstrate the relationship between coal rank and depth of burial, taking into account the geothermal gradient needed to reach that reaction temperature. Figure 2.4 also correlates the degree of petroleum maturity with the temperature, depth of burial, etc.

The reflectance of vitrinite is often considered to be a useful indicator of the degree of coalification. Surveys using this technique have been carried out, particularly when testing boreholes for oil. In general, the reflectance is

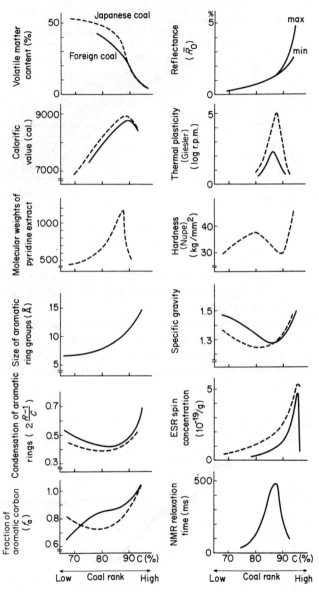

Fig. 2.3 Changes in physical and chemical properties of Japanese vitrinite during coalification

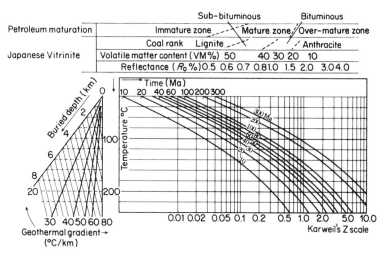

Fig. 2.4   Correlation of temperature, time, depth and coalification based on Karweil's diagram. (After Karweil, 1956*.)

plotted on a logarithmic scale in the horizontal axis against depth of burial on the vertical axis (e.g. Fig. 2.5). In many cases the data are plotted on a characteristic reflectance gradient.

Figure 2.5 summarizes the changes in reflectance obtained from heating experiments under 1 atmosphere of nitrogen on timber (Correia *et al.*, 1974) and Japanese vitrinite at various stages of coalification (Sugimura *et al.*, 1969). An increase in temperature has a clearly marked effect. Differences in

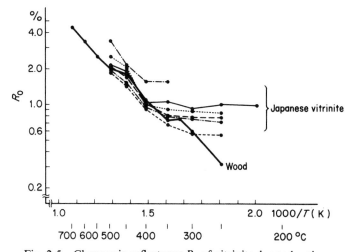

Fig. 2.5   Changes in reflectance R_o of vitrinite due to heating

reflectance between samples of the same geological age, i.e. with the same reaction time, are therefore thought to reflect variations in ancient temperatures which accelerated the coalification reactions. A recent study by Buntebarth (1979*), drawing together the results for borehole samples of differing geological age, suggests that reflectance R_0, corresponding to the degree of acceleration of coalification in reaction time t at a depth of z in an area where the function of the geothermal gradient T is shown by f_T, may be expressed thus:

$$R_0^2 = f_T \int z(t) \, dt$$

Because the depth of the sample for which R_0 is measured is known, its $\int z(t) dt$(km.ma) can be assessed for a given geological age so that R_0^2 can be plotted as shown in Fig. 2.6. In Germany, for several bore-holes in which the geothermal gradient T(°C/km) had been established, the relationship for T and $\int z(t) dt = I$, when $R_0^2 = 1.0$ was given as $T(°C/km) = 98.7 - 14.6 \ln I$ (km.Ma) (Buntebarth, 1977). This result is also recorded on Fig. 2.6 on the line $R_0^2 = 1.0$. By this means one may deduce an ancient geothermal gradient which would be the most effective in bringing about coalification or the maturation of petroleum.

At one time it was thought that lateral pressure associated with orogenic movements had the effect of deforming coal beds and of generating heat in folded and faulted areas, thus accelerating the coalification process. In the folded coalfields of the Ruhr, however, coalification was already advanced before the deformation of coal measure, resulting isorank lines (isovol lines in

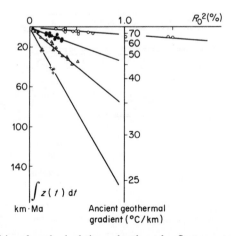

Fig. 2.6 Relationship of geological time, depth and reflectance to ancient geothermal gradient. (Prepared from Buntebarth, 1977, 1979*.)

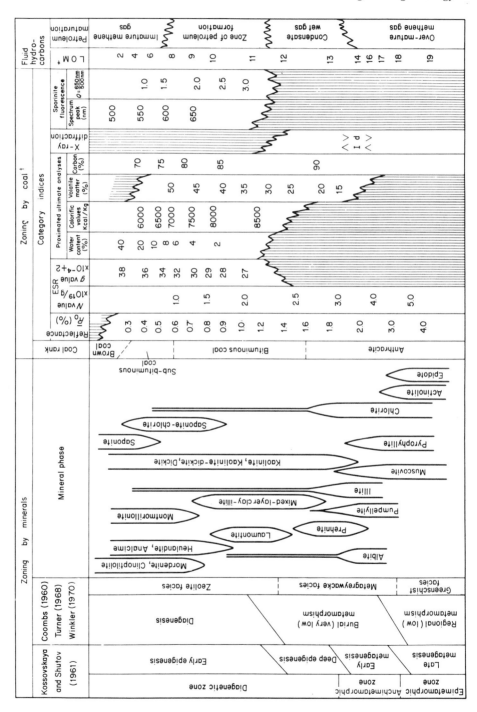

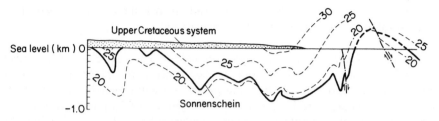

Fig. 2.7 Relationship of folds and isorank lines in Ruhr coalfield. Figures (%) represent volatile matter content. (Prepared from Teichmüller, 1962, 1966.)

this case) folded in the same way as the strata (Fig. 2.7). The idea that lateral pressure must have accelerated coalification has, thus, been abandoned.

(c) Coalification as organic metamorphism

(1) Parameters of organic metamorphism The geochemical changes which affect plant residues fixed in the crust may be viewed as a type of organic burial metamorphism. On the basis of works on low grade metamorphism of zeolite facies and coalification of phytoclast- or coal-bearing strata containing zeolites or clay minerals (Ammosov, 1968; Bostick, 1971; Buryanova, 1967; Kisch, 1969; Kossovskaya *et al.*, 1964; Quinn, 1958; etc.), the degree of coalification for Japanese coal corresponding to metamorphic mineral phases can be set out as in Fig. 2.8.

The most effective of the many coalification indicators which can be related to the degree of organic metamorphism is the reflectance of vitrinite, in particular of tellecollinite. Identification of macerals is made under an oil-immersion reflecting microscope (refractive index $n = 1.515$). In recent years this technique has gained wide acceptance by many researchers following the international standardization of measuring methods (ASTM, 1972; ICCP, 1963, 1971). The processes by which the principal carbon atoms become concentrated during coalification can be traced continuously from increases in vitrinite reflectance. The technique is extremely effective when applied in

---

Fig. 2.8 Comparison of mineral phases in progressive diagenesis and burial metamorphism with coalification indices for organic metamorphism and degrees of petroleum maturation

† Humic coals. Data are for vitrinite, except for sporinite fluorescence analysis. Coal rank divisions do not correspond with existing divisions for those including various macerals.

‡ LOM = level of organic metamorphism (see Taguchi, 1978b*).

conjunction with other methods to the study of organic metamorphism. It is also useful in assessing the maturity of petroleum.

(2) Geological setting for organic metamorphism The coal basins where peat accumulated sink very slowly, and the temperature and pressure conditions which govern early organic metamorphism are controlled by the depth of burial. The temperature is governed by the geothermal gradient, increases in which considerably accelerate organic metamorphism by encouraging the condensation of aromatic rings, and cyclization, together with the split-off of functional side chains. Under such conditions, coal seams that were deposited at the earlier stages were apt to be buried deeper, then the more advanced were the coalification reactions. Over a region of uniform geothermal gradient, organic metamorphism tends to be more advanced at the centre of a sedimentary basin, even along the same time plane (i.e. coal layer), due to the greater depth of burial. A close relationship may also be found between the bed thickness, rock facies and depth of sediments in coal-bearing formations. Coarser sediments frequently develop around margins of sedimentary basins or more slowly sinking areas, and organic metamorphism may often be retarded in such places. On the other hand, if the depth of burial decreases due to uplift, this lowers the temperature and pressure and inhibits organic metamorphism. If the material reaches the surface, as when it was initially deposited, metamorphism will cease altogether. Where lift is caused by orogenic movements, so that the coal-bearing formations are deformed as they are uplifted, the initially developed patterns of coalification will be deformed like the strata, with no acceleration of the coalification process. If uplift is associated with intrusion of plutonic bodies along the central axes of orogenic belts, the geothermal gradient at the time of upheaval will vary and additional rises in temperature will be reflected in a new pattern of metamorphism, showing an overprinting on the rank of coalification.

A concentric zonal distribution of organic metamorphism has been found around subterraneous intrusive bodies revealed by geophysical prospecting near Bramsche in north-west Germany (Bartenstein *et al.*, 1975; Stadler *et al.*, 1971). A profile of this area is shown in Fig. 2.9. The geological setting of organic metamorphism is thus closely related to the thermal structure of the crust in that area, but thermal effects from dykes intruding coal beds are quite local and cannot be detected at a distance of more than three times the width of the dyke (Bostick, 1973; Mackowsky, 1968).

(3) The types of organic metamorphism If we imagine two different coalfields of the same geological age but formed in different places with differing geothermal structures, a particular reaction temperature condition in the region of higher heatflow must have been in a much shallower position than in lower heatflow regions. Had they been at the same depth higher heatflow

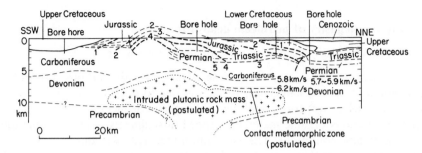

Fig. 2.9 Progress of organic metamorphism due to a postulated intrusive in Bramsche. 1–5 = reflectance of phytoclasts in sediments (%). (Prepared from Bartenstein *et al.*, 1975, and Stadler *et al.*, 1971.)

regions would have reached higher temperatures than the lower heatflow regions. Therefore organic metamorphism in regions of high heatflow should reflect conditions of higher temperatures and lower pressures than in lower heatflow regions. For example, if we compare the degree of organic metamorphism of vitrinite formed under higher temperature and/or lower pressure conditions with that formed under lower temperature and/or higher pressure conditions, we may expect the differences in the chemical progress of coalification. In such a case, the chemical composition of vitrinite from high heatflow regions will tend towards a lower H/C value compared to that from low heatflow regions because it would probably have been easier for aliphatic or hydrogenous active side chains and functional groups cut off by the rise in temperature to break away under conditions of lower pressure. Conversely, vitrinite from low heatflow regions will tend more towards a higher value for H/C than that from the high heatflow regions, and aliphatic or hydrogenous functional group will remain in its chemical structure. Its aliphatic carbon content will also be higher. From this viewpoint, consideration of organic metamorphism is possible from both the chemical composition and the structure of the reaction products. Such a geochemical view of organic metamorphism is conveniently highly applicable to the Japanese Islands, where we find the Ishikari coalfield in Hokkaido, composed of thick sediments in a low heatflow region on the Pacific side, and coalfields in north-west Kyushu in the continent side of south-west Japan composed of relatively thin sediments in what is even now a high heatflow region. The results of investigations of Palaeogene coal-bearing strata based on such observations (Aihara, 1977, 1978*, 1980*) have revealed a pair of organic metamorphism with relatively low temperatures and/or high pressure on the Pacific side of north-east Japan and relatively high temperatures and/or low pressure on the continent side of south-west Japan (see Sec. 3.10 for more details).

(Atsuo Aihara)

2.3 The geochemistry of petroleum deposit formation

(a) Formation of dispersed (non-reservoir)-type hydrocarbons

Three types of source may be envisaged for the hydrocarbons distributed throughout the crust, namely (1) formation due to the biosynthesis of living things themselves; (2) formation due to diagenetic or metamorphic processes acting on various organic materials trapped in sediments; and (3) formation under inorganic conditions. The assumption that hydrocarbons from sources (1) and (2) contribute to petroleum formation leads to the so-called 'organic origin' theory, whereas emphasizing hydrocarbons from source (3) leads to the 'inorganic origin' theory. The latter, however, cannot reasonably explain formative processes for petroleum in reservoir rocks, and it is of little account today. Various pathways for the formation of petroleum hydrocarbons which are thought to be of biological origin may be envisaged, but there are considerable differences in the degree to which they contribute to the development of petroleum deposits.

Various hydrocarbons, formed directly from living creatures due to biosynthesis (1 in Fig. 2.10), are detected in crude oil, but these are quantitatively quite limited. The majority decompose during deposition and

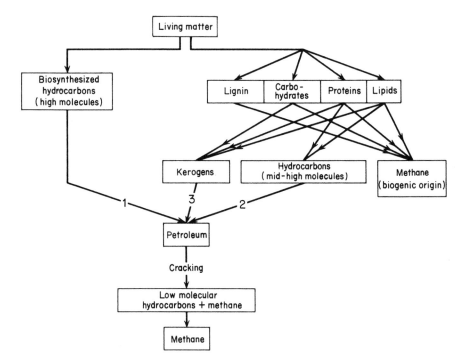

Fig. 2.10   Formation of petroleum hydrocarbons

their contribution to petroleum deposit development is thus regarded as minor. However, one type of these 'biosynthetic' hydrocarbons, namely isoprenoid hydrocarbons which show characteristic carbon bonding (Fig. 2.11), is regarded as important proof of the organic genesis of petroleum. They also form indispensable 'fingerprints' in identifying and correlating oil with oil, or oil to source rock, despite their low abundance. Study of biosynthetic hydrocarbons is an important field of research for the future development of petroleum geochemistry (Taguchi, 1979*).

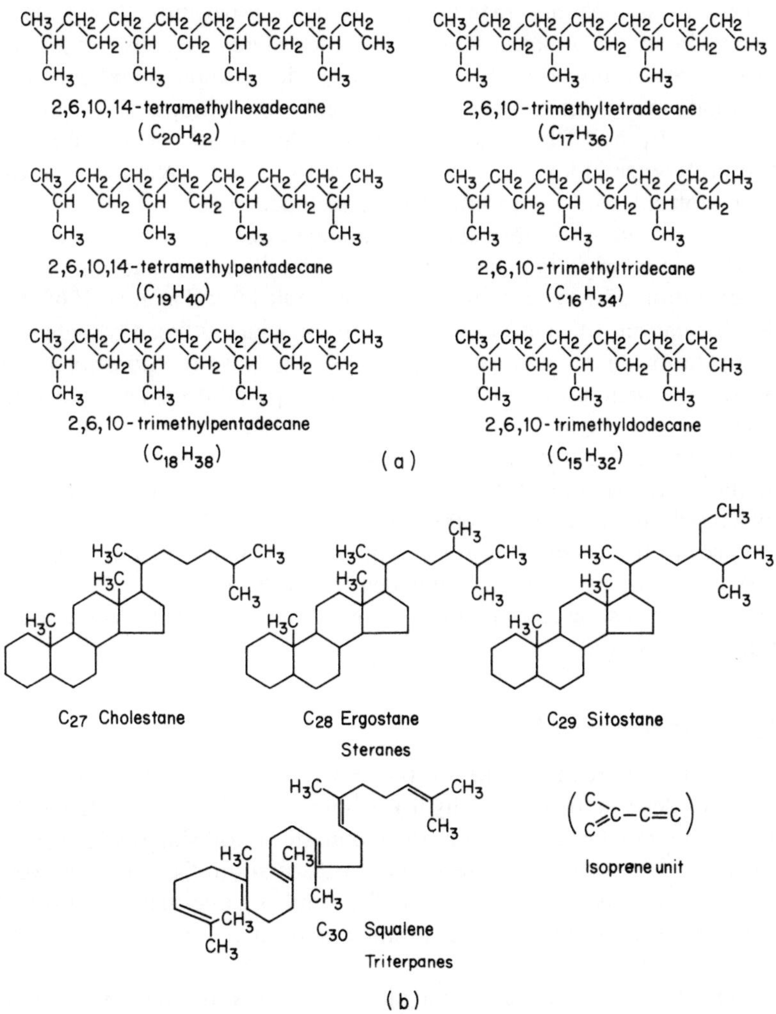

2,6,10,14-tetramethylhexadecane
($C_{20}H_{42}$)

2,6,10-trimethyltetradecane
($C_{17}H_{36}$)

2,6,10,14-tetramethylpentadecane
($C_{19}H_{40}$)

2,6,10-trimethyltridecane
($C_{16}H_{34}$)

2,6,10-trimethylpentadecane
($C_{18}H_{38}$)

(a)

2,6,10-trimethyldodecane
($C_{15}H_{32}$)

C_{27} Cholestane

C_{28} Ergostane

C_{29} Sitostane

Steranes

C_{30} Squalene

Isoprene unit

Triterpanes

(b)

Fig. 2.11 Isoprenoid hydrocarbons: (a) isoparaffin; (b) polycyclic type (steranes, triterpanes)

Fats and proteins from the remains of organisms readily form hydrocarbons and at the very beginning of deposition form hydrocarbons as a result of the metabolic activities of bacteria, and in the early stages of diagenesis by decarboxylation and deamination (2 in Fig. 2.10). However, these also only make a relatively small contribution, of perhaps a few per cent., to the formation of petroleum deposits.

Fats constitute a large proportion of the bodies of the lower animals and amongst the biopolymers have structures most reminiscent of hydrocarbons. Jurg and Eisma (1964*) have shown that the alcohols and fatty acids which constitute these fats are readily converted to *n*-paraffin. The fatty acids contained in living organisms and recent sediments or soils predominantly possess even carbon numbers, whereas odd carbon numbers tend to predominate in ancient sediments or in oilfield brine. Cooper and Bray (1963*) linked this with the CPI problem of dispersed hydrocarbons in sediments (i.e. carbon preference index, the quantitative ratio between odd and even carbon number molecules in *n*-paraffin). They concluded that the fact that the CPI declined from recent to more ancient sediments was due to the production of odd carbon number fatty acids and even carbon number *n*-paraffin, caused by decarboxylation of even carbon number fatty acids (see Taguchi, 1968*).

The formation of hydrocarbons from proteins is readily achieved by decarboxylation and deamination proocesses because the constituent amino acids contain structures which correspond to paraffin-system hydrocarbons for pentanes or higher. Thompson and Creath (1966*) established that hydrocarbons in recent to ancient mollusca shells are derived from amino acids in the shells because there was a rapid rise in the amounts of low molecule C_1–C_5 hydrocarbons at about 11 000 years. Philippi (1977*) also demonstrated that hydrocarbons themselves are present as side chains in some of the amino acids which make up proteins (equivalent to 11.26 per cent. by weight of the protein). He also showed that cracking egg albumin yields hydrocarbons with carbon numbers of C_1–C_7.

(b) Hydrocarbons from kerogens

Kerogens are regarded as one of the most important source materials of biologically derived petroleum hydrocarbons (3 in Fig. 2.10). Kerogen was originally the name given to solid organic matter in oil shales which produces petroleum-like substances as a result of dry distillation. Currently, however, it has come to be used as a general title for solid organic material insoluble in alkaline aqueous solutions and organic solvents, found finely dispersed through sediments.

The term 'kerogen' includes some plant fragments, but mostly these cannot be identified as such, and are complex amorphous high polymer organic substances composed principally of C, H and O, but including small amounts

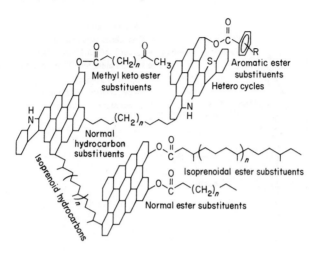

Fig. 2.12 Schematic model of chemical structure of immature kerogens. Nucleus composed of aromatic structure, sometimes contains naphthene or heteromolecules. Each nucleus is bonded to form a network structure with alkyl chains, and possesses various side chains readily hydrolysed or oxidized

of N and S. They are not specific chemical compounds. Figure 2.12 shows a model of their chemical structure. Their nucleus is normally built up from several aromatic sheets with condensed polycyclic structures, and occasionally may include naphthenes or heteromolecules. These nuclei are bonded together by alkyl chains, various functional groups or naphthene rings to form a three-dimensional network structure. In sediments they can be bonded to clay minerals perhaps by ion exchange or by chemisorption.

Kerogens have been classified into three principal types on the basis of element analysis, hydrolysis, pyrolytic analysis, spectral analysis, infrared absorption, refractive index, reflectance and microscopic observation. Each type changes characteristically as the burial depth increases. The three types of kerogen and their evolution are expressed by plotting their principal elements, C, H and O, on an H/C, O/C diagram as in Fig. 2.13 (see Taguchi, 1975*).

Type I is known as oil shale, sapropelic, lipid or algal types. These are rich in chain structures, whereas the nucleus possesses few condensed polycyclic aromatic or hetero compounds when compared with other types. Most of the oxygen is present as esters. Immature types exhibit high H/C but low O/C ratios. This type of kerogen is derived from amorphous elements such as algae or lipid constituents contained in pollens and spores. The majority of kerogens in oil shales fall into this categoy.

Type II is known as coaly-oil shale type, liptinite type or intermediate type. These are thought to originate in organic material from plankton or bacteria which accumulated in a reducing marine environment.

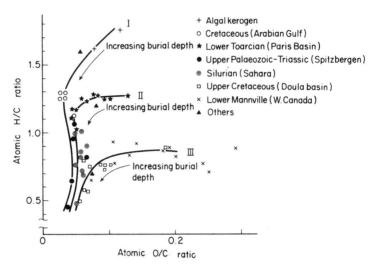

Fig. 2.13 Evolution of the three types of kerogen: I, II, III. See Fig. 2.2 for coalification. (After Tissot *et al.*, 1974*.)

Type III is known as coal, humic or carbohydrate lignin types. The nuclei of these are rich in polycyclic aromatic structures and contain large amounts of ketones and heterorings. They possess low H/C and high O/C ratios. This type of kerogen is thought to derive from nitrogeneous and humic constituents of marine and continental plants.

Hydrocarbons originating from kerogens do not differ from those derived from fatty acids, or amino acids in the respect that they are of biomonomer origin, but they are different in the respect that they are formed via kerogens which are a kind of complex polymer formed from carbohydrates, amino acids and fatty acids of biomonomer origin. The reason why we particularly differentiate hydrocarbons from this source is because they are currently believed to be the largest contributors to reservoir petroleum formation. The revival of the kerogen origin theory, about which argument has raged since the 1920s, has depended on our rapidly expanding knowledge about the changes of sedimentary organic matter with increasing depth of burial, together with the results of research into kerogens themselves (see Taguchi, 1972*, 1978a*, 1978b*).

(c) Evolution of kerogens and formation of petroleum hydrocarbons

The progressive changes in kerogens with increasing depth of burial have already been indicated in Fig. 2.13, but marked changes in their infrared absorption spectra (Fig. 2.14) and vitrinite reflectance (Fig. 2.15) are also apparent. Although experiments on the pyrolysis of kerogens have

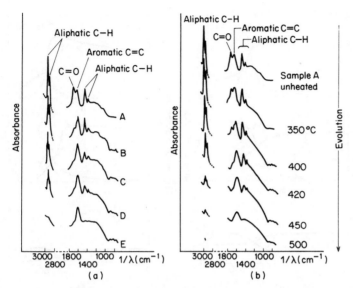

Fig. 2.14   Evolution of type II kerogens seen by IR spectrum. Comparision of (a) natural samples and (b) artificially heated samples. A and B in (a) are from Paris Basin; C, D and E from Sahara. Samples in (b) are lower Toarcian shales. Gradual disappearance of C = O and aliphatic CH_2, CH_3 is similar in both. (Prepared from Tissot *et al.*, 1974*.)

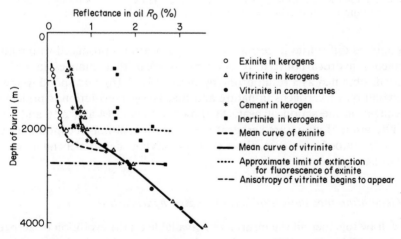

Fig. 2.15   Reflectance changes in type III kerogens associated with increasing depth (after Durand and Espitalié, 1976*). Also shown is reflectance of other component macerals (see Sec. 2.2a) contained in identical kerogens, as well as vitrinite reflectance

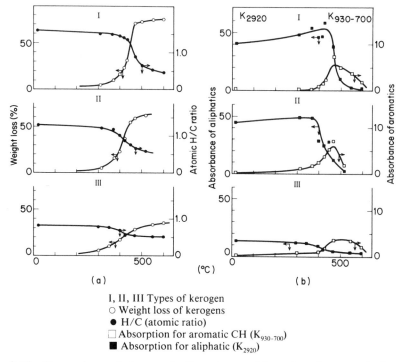

I, II, III Types of kerogen
○ Weight loss of kerogens
● H/C (atomic ratio)
□ Absorption for aromatic CH ($K_{930-700}$)
■ Absorption for aliphatic (K_{2920})

Fig. 2.16 Comparison of changes in three types of immature kerogens in heating experiments (after Robin, Rouxhet and Durand, 1977*). (a) Changes in weight (%) of atomic H/C ratio and kerogens due to heating. (b) Changes in IR absorption bands related to aliphatic groups (K_{2920}) and to aromatic CH ($K_{930-700}$). Although changes are continuous they can be divided into three zones: < 350; 350–500; > 500°C

encountered difficulties in correlating the hydrocarbons produced with natural petroleum hydrocarbons, it is nevertheless clear that changes in residual kerogens obtained as a result of the pyrolysis (Fig. 2.16) correspond well with the evolution of kerogens in nature and that kerogen evolution is principally dependent on the action of heat. As shown in Figs. 2.14 and 2.16 and Table 2.4, alteration of immature kerogens due to heating, although continuous, can be divided into three stages, these changes varying slightly depending on the type of kerogen involved.

(d) Generation mechanism of kerogen-based hydrocarbons

If we draw together all the information available on the evolution of kerogens based on field observation and pyrolysis experiments, and in particular examine studies which compare changes in the properties of kerogens in response to increasing depth with changes in the properties of hydrocarbons in

Table 2.4 Changes associated with heating type II kerogens (prepared from Robin, Rouxhet and Durand, 1977*)

Temperature stage	I 150–350°C	II 350–500°C	III 500–600°C
Kerogen weight loss	Slight	Max.	Very slight
H/C	1.25 ±	0.5 ±	0.48–0.5 ±
Oxygen containing functional groups	Decrease in C = O	Decrease in C = O Decrease in ketones	Almost disappeared
Chain and aromatic structures	Slight change	Decrease in CH_2, CH_3 Appearance of aromatic CH	Almost disappeared
Reflectance $R_0\%$	0.3 ±	2.0 ±	3.0 ±

sediments containing those kerogens, we may give the following explanation for the generation of kerogen-based hydrocarbons (see Figs. 2.14 and 2.17).

(1) Early diagenetic stage The initial removal of various functional groups (unstable carbonyl and carboxyl groups) causes removal of O, together with H_2O or CO_2 and gaseous components such as N_2 or CH_4 (particularly in type III kerogens). As a result several kerogen nuclei, which were linked by chain structures, dissociate and may simultaneously produce N, O and S compounds (B in Fig. 2.17) which are soluble in organic solvents. Those remaining become A′ kerogens with rather higher aromaticity. Most B components function as a type of intermediate compound in petroleum formation.

(2) Later diagenetic stage As the kerogens enter the next stage in which the burial depth increases with an associated rise in temperature (50–200 °C),

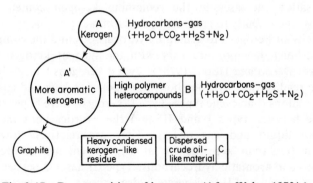

Fig. 2.17 Decomposition of kerogens. (After Welte, 1972*.)

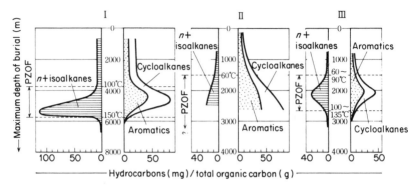

Fig. 2.18   Kerogen types and the formation of oil-producing zones (after Tissot, Deroo and Hood, 1978*). Weight ratio of hydrocarbons/total organic carbon changes as depth increases, reaching a maximum at a certain depth. Type I kerogens (Uinta Basin, America, Eocene-Palaeocene). Type II kerogens (Paris Basin, Lower Toarcian system). Type III kerogens (Nigeria Doula Basin, Upper Cretaceous). PZOF: principal zone of oil formation

more of the various bonds in the kerogens are severed and they separate into smaller and smaller fragments. Esters and C–C bonds present in B components break down and B components lose their heteromolecules of, for example, N, O and S, whilst at the same time produce C components consisting of hydrocarbons and chain compounds. This stage corresponds to the 'principal zone of oil formation' (Vassoyevich *et al.*, 1970*; see Fig. 2.18). Hydrocarbons produced at this point differ from those of biosynthetic origin, which are rich in relatively high molecular weight hydrocarbons, in that they have low to medium molecular weights. They characteristically occur accompanying *n*-heptane, 1-2 ring cycloparaffin, toluene or xylene.

(3) Metamorphic stage At burial depths where the temperature is in excess of 200 °C C–C bonds break down and the area becomes a dry gas-producing zone with methane as its principal component. Aromatization and polycondensation increases in the remaining kerogen content and they gradually lose their ability to generate hydrocarbons.

The capacity of kerogens to generate hydrocarbons and the composition of the hydrocarbons they produce vary with the type of kerogen (Laplante, 1974*; Tissot, Deroo and Hood, 1978*). Type I kerogens have 6–10 per cent. H and these readily yield hydrocarbons in response to heat and contain more iso- and *n*-paraffins than cyclic types. Type II kerogens have H per cent. values intermediate between types I and III and the hydrocarbons they produce possess both liquid and gas phases. They are relatively low in chain hydrocarbons (less than 20 per cent.) but rich in cyclic hydrocarbons such as cycloparaffins and aromatic hydrocarbons. Type III has 3–5 per cent. H and is less able than types I and II to generate hydrocarbons. These kerogens tend to produce gaseous hydrocarbons readily, composed predominantly of cyclic compounds. The proportion of iso- and *n*-paraffin is higher than is the case with type II.

Data have gradually been accumulating concerning the importance of reaction time to the generation of petroleum hydrocarbons from kerogens. Connan (1974*) established the existence of an almost linear relationship between the logarithm of time (log t_0) and the inverse of the absolute temperature $(1/T)$ by analysing data of the ages of strata and underground temperature at depths where hydrocarbons would rapidly form from kerogens (i.e. the depth of the oil-formation zone in its earliest stage). He regarded this reaction as being in accordance with the Arrhenius first order reaction. Hood, Gutjahr and Heacock (1975*), whose research into hydrocarbon generation from kerogens was conducted from a quite different perspective, also demonstrated that this reaction followed the Arrhenius equation. On the other hand, Connan (1974*) obtained a value of 11 000–14 000 cal/mol and Hood, Gutjahr and Heacock (1975*) a value of 18 000 cal/mol for the apparent activation energy when hydrocarbons are produced from kerogens. Studies by Tissot (1969*) gave a result of 20 000 cal/mol. Connan attributed these differences to the effects of catalytic activity by clay minerals, etc. This is clearly an area which requires more work.

(e) Petroleum source rocks

Condensed petroleum hydrocarbons, i.e. reservoir oils, are formed when dispersed hydrocarbons in sedimentary rocks somehow migrate from those rocks and accumulate in reservoir rocks with high porosity and permeability. In such cases the hydrocarbon-producing rock thought to have made the greatest contribution to the formation of the oil deposits is called the 'petroleum source rock'. Geochemical and geological studies have indicated the following basic criteria for good petroleum source rocks.

(1) Organic carbon content One of the most important criteria for petroleum source rocks is the amount of organic carbon present. Hunt (1961*) gave average organic carbon contents in shales and carbonate rocks of about 1.72 per cent. and 0.24 per cent. respectively. By comparison, Ronov (1958*) looked separately at oil-producing and non-oil-producing zones and gave values for the former of 1.5 per cent. for shale and 0.5 per cent. for carbonate rocks, as opposed to 0.41 per cent. for shale and 0.2 per cent. for carbonate rocks in the latter. Carbonate rocks generally contain less organic carbon than shales, but they commonly become good petroleum source rocks.

(2) Extractive organic matter (bitumen) and hydrocarbon contents The amounts of these present are also important in assessing petroleum source

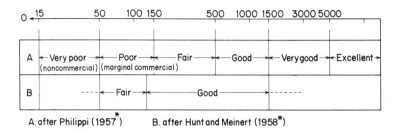

A. after Philippi (1957*)   B. after Hunt and Meinert (1958*)

Figures represent ppm relative to dry sample

Fig. 2.19   Source rock evaluation based on hydrocarbon content

rocks. Figure 2.19 shows the criteria proposed by Philippi (1957*) and Hunt and Meinert (1958*).

(3) Kerogen type As discussed earlier, the quantity of petroleum hydrocarbons generated from a particular sedimentary rock is obviously affected by the amount of kerogens present in it, but is also controlled by their type and maturity. Suitability as petroleum source rocks deteriorates in the order type I, II and III, given the same kerogen content. The maturity of kerogens is easily determined from the reflectance of vitrinite in the kerogens (Fig. 2.15) and from H/C, O/C diagrams (Fig. 2.13). Sedimentary rocks containing immature or highly metamorphosed kerogens are not regarded to be suitable as petroleum source rocks.

(f) Migration and accumulation of petroleum

Because petroleum is usually fluid, its behaviour after formation is a very important factor in the development of deposits. Looking firstly at migration, there is primary migration from the source rock to a highly permeable carrier bed, and secondary migration from there to a trap. The migration of oil may take place through diffusion or water-flow. In any case, water is the principal transporting medium, and pressure and temperature differences are thought to be the cause of migration. Kerogen-origin hydrocarbons are generally formed at depths in excess of about 1500 m, but as most pore water capable of migration is lost at shallower depths than 1000 m due to compaction, the migration of hydrocarbons is thought to occur because of the expulsion of inter-layer water from clay minerals without recourse to compaction current water. Such water originating from clay minerals is thought to be the principal factor causing abnormally high pressures (encountered when pore fluid pressure in sedimentary rock is considerably higher than the hydrostatic water pressure which would be expected at that depth). Some authors believe these abnormally high pressures are the trigger causing petroleum migration.

Various models have been proposed for the removal of water from sediments associated with compaction and diagenetic changes in clay minerals (Burst, 1969*; Perry and Hower, 1972*; Powers, 1967*). In these models the depth at which water is expelled from clay minerals corresponds well with the depth providing the temperature conditions necessary for the formation of kerogen-origin hydrocarbons, suggesting that primary migration of hydrocarbons is achieved by water from this source.

Petroleum droplets, micelles, colloids, molecular solutions and gas dissolution have all been cited as the forms in which petroleum hydrocarbons may migrate with a water medium. Despite variations between individual sedimentary basins, Welte (1972*) estimated general changes in porosity and average pore size as 15 per cent. and 50–100 Å at 2000 m depth, and 9 per cent. and 20–30 Å at 3000 m depth. Asphaltene, which is the largest of the oil components, readily forms micelles in water, but is normally larger than 300 Å. It would therefore be difficult for it to migrate through depths in excess of 2000 m in this form; therefore, most petroleum migration is believed to take place in molecular solution and partly in gas solution.

The solubility of migrating hydrocarbons in water was formerly overlooked because of the immiscibility between oil and water, but many workers reconsidered it once its significance had been pointed out by Baker (1959*). As shown in Table 2.5, hydrocarbons will dissolve in water in molecular solution even though only in small amounts. Price (1976*) also demonstrated that the solubility of hydrocarbons in water increases rapidly once the temperature exceeds 100 °C and that barely soluble high molecular weight components become relatively much more soluble than low molecular weight components as the temperature rises. Such improved solubility in response to increasing temperature is an important property for the migration of kerogen-origin hydrocarbons at large burial depths.

If it is assumed that hydrocarbons migrate, dissolved in water as described above, they must also separate from the water by some process if petroleum deposits are to form. Baker (1968*) regarded the concentration of salts in the water as an important factor in the deposition of petroleum. He claimed that as brine, containing the hydrocarbons, migrated through the strata from coarse sediments (e.g. reservoir sandstone) once more to fine sediments, salt would be removed from the water by a type of membrane effect and accumulate in the coarse sediments. The changes in the ion concentration produced there would then lead to separation of the hydrocarbons from the water.

Price (1976*) investigated changes in the solubility of benzene accompanying changes in the concentration of NaCl solutions at 25 °C under 1 atmosphere of pressure. He found a remarkable decrease in benzene solubility when the concentration of NaCl was high. He further linked temperature-related changes in hydrocarbon solubility with the fact that the

Table 2.5 Dissolution of hydrocarbons in distilled water (ppm at 25 °C). (After Price, 1976*.)

Compound		Price	Authority Baker	McAuliffe
n-paraffins	Pentane	39.5	40.0	38.5
	Hexane	9.47	9.52	9.5
	Heptane	2.24	2.19	2.93
	Octane	0.431	0.493	0.66
	Nonane	0.121	0.098	0.220
Iso-paraffins	2,2-Dimethylbutane	21.2	—	18.4
	2-Methylpentane	13.0	—	13.8
	3-Methylpentane	13.1	—	12.8
Cyclo-paraffins	Cyclopentane	160.0	—	156.0
	Methylcylopentane	41.8	—	42.0
	Cyclohexane	66.5	—	55.0
Aromatics	Benzene	1740.0	—	1780.0
	Toluene	554.0	—	515.0

NaCl concentration in interstitial water in sediments off the Gulf Coast is low in the shales which are apt to become source rocks but high in the sandstones which are more favourable for reservoir rocks. He gave the following explanation for the migration of petroleum from deeply buried source rocks and its subsequent accumulation. In brief, because petroleum source rocks found at great depth possess interstitial water low in NaCl but at relatively high temperature, this water can contain relatively large amounts of dissolved hydrocarbons. If this interstitial water is affected by compaction, it will migrate to shallower positions along faults or fractures and if it then encounteres sandstone layers rich in NaCl, the solubility of the hydrocarbons will further decrease, assisted by the drop in temperature, so they dissociate from the water and condense. McAuliffe (1979*), however, whilst agreeing with the kerogen-origin theory, totally refuted the idea of primary migration based on the dissolution of petroleum in water, and claimed that petroleum and gas produced in the kerogen overflowed out of the source rock through the three-dimensional network structure of the kerogens. There are many such arguments surrounding the migration and accumulation of petroleum and many points need clarifying by future research.

(g) Evolution of petroleum and disappearance of deposits

Petroleum deposits, formed as outlined above, are affected by the same changes due to time and temperature that affect any organic matter in sediments. Ultimately these lead to their breakdown and disappearance.

The phenomenon whereby heavy oils turn into light oils as a result of temperature and time is known as petroleum 'evolution' or 'maturation'. Statistically speaking, the greater the depth of burial of reservoir rocks of the same geological age, or the older the reservoir rocks at the same depth, the

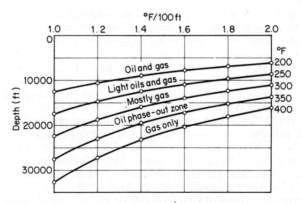

Fig. 2.20 Relationship between underground temperature and the presence of oil and gas. (After Landes, 1967*.)

higher the proportion of light oils. This is because cracking oil hydrocarbons results in the formation of hydrocarbons with smaller molecules. Thus the evolution of petroleum is fundamentally regulated by time and temperature. If the time taken for sediments to reach a certain depth is known, then the occurrence of the petroleum hydrocarbons will be determined by the depth and temperature gradient (Landes, 1967*). For example, with a temperature increase of $1.5°F/100$ ft ($2.15\ °C/100$ m) hydrocarbons will exist in gaeous forms only at depths in excess of about 5500 m. At very deep sites with high temperatures, the gas produced will consist only of CH_4 and the presence of ordinary petroleum deposits cannot really be expected.

If petroleum deposits become exposed at the surface or come into contact with rainwater, low grade hydrocarbons are lost by evaporation or dissolution in water and some may be oxidized to become tar sands or natural asphalt, both causing the deposits to break down. Microorganisms can also affect the breakdown of hydrocarbons and we know of examples in which originally light oils of the paraffin type are altered to medium–heavy oils of the napthene system in reservoir rocks. The properties of microorganisms, which utilize particular petroleum hydrocarbons as their energy sources for living or source materials in cell growing, are known as microbial metabolism of hydrocarbons and are used in reverse in oil-related industries (e.g. desulphurization, protein manufacture) and in oil exploration.

(Kazuo Taguchi)

References

Aihara, A. (1978). Stratigraphic coalification pattern and its implication to the geologic development of the Ishikari coalfield, Japan, *Mem. Fac. Sci., Kyushu Univ.* (D), **24**, No. 1, 33–46.
Aihara, A. (1980). Coalification pattern and organic metamorphism of Paleogene systems in Japanese Island arc, in *Prof. S. Kanno Memorial Volume* (Ed. H. Igo and H. Noda), Memorial Assoc. Prof. S. Kanno's Retirement, Tsukuba Univ., pp. 497–510.
Baker, E. G. (1959). Origin and migration of oil, *Science*, **129**, 871–874.
Baker, E. G. (1968). Evaluation of petroleum migration and accumulation, in *Fundamental Aspects of Petroleum Geochemistry* (Eds. B. Nagy and U. Colombo), pp. 299–329, Elsevier, Amsterdam.
Bostick, N. H. (1973). Times as a factor in thermal metamorphism of phytoclasts (coal particles), *C.R.7. Congr. internat. strat. Géol. Carbonifère*, **2**, 183–193.
Buntebarth, G. (1979). Eine empirische Methode zur Berechnung von paläogeothermischen Gradienten aus dem Inkohlungsgrad organischer Einlagerungen in Sedimentgesteinen mit Anwendung auf den mittleren Oberrhein-Graben, *Fortschr. Geol. Rheinld. u. Westf.*, **27**, 97–108.
Burst, J. F. (1969). Diagenesis of Gulf Coast clayey sediments and its possible relation to petroleum migration, *Am. Assoc. Petrol. Geol. Bull.*, **53**, 73–93.

Connan, J. (1974). Time-temperature relation in oil genesis, *Am. Assoc. Petrol. Geol. Bull.*, **58**, 2516-2521.

Cooper, J. E., and Bray, E. E. (1963). A postulated role of fatty acids in petroleum formation, *Geochim. Cosmochim. Acta*, **26**, 1113-1127.

Durand, B., and Espitalié, J. (1976). Geochemical studies on the organic matter from the Douala Basin (Cameroon)—II. Evolution of kerogen, *Geochim. Cosmochim. Acta*, **40**, 801-808.

Hood, A., Gutjahr, C. C. M., and Heacock, R. L. (1975). Organic metamorphism and the generation of petroleum, *Am. Assoc. Petrol. Geol. Bull.*, **59**, 986-996.

Hunt, J. M. (1961). Distribution of hydrocarbons in sedimentary rocks, *Geochim. Cosmochim. Acta*, **22**, 37-49.

Hunt, J. M. (1972). Distribution of carbon in crust of earth, *Am. Assoc. Petrol. Geol. Bull.*, **56**, 2273-2277.

Hunt, J. M., and Meinert, R. N. (1958). *Petroleum Prospecting*, U.S. Patent, No. 2, 854, p. 396.

Jurg, J. W., and Eisma, E. (1964). Petroleum hydrocarbons: generations from fatty acids, *Science*, **144**, 1451-1452.

Karweil, J. (1956). Die Metamorphose der Kholen vom Standpunkt der physikalischen Chemie, *Z. Deutsch. Geol. Ges.*, **107**, 132-139.

Landes, K. K. (1967). Eometamorphism and oil and gas in time and space, *Am. Assoc. Petrol. Geol. Bull.*, **51**, 828-841.

Laplante, R. E. (1974). Hydrocarbon generation in Gulf Coast Tertiary sediments, *Am. Assoc. Petrol. Geol. Bull.*, **58**, 1281-1289.

McAuliffe, C. D. (1979). Oil and gas migration—chemical and physical constraints, *Am. Assoc. Petrol. Geol. Bull.*, **63**, 761-781.

Osawa, Y., *et al.* (1969). Chemical structure and properties of heat treated coal in the early state of carbonization, XVII, XVIII, XIX, Infrared spectra (1-3), *Nenryo-Kyokai-Shi*, (in Japanese) **48**, 303-309, 694-702, 703-711.

Perry, F. A., Jr., and Hower, J. (1972). Late stage dehydration in deeply buried pelitic sediments, *Am. Assoc. Petrol. Geol. Bull.*, **56**, 2013-2021.

Philippi, G. T. (1957). Identification of oil source beds by chemical means, *20th International Geol. Congress*, Mexico, Sec. 3 pp. 25-38.

Philippi, G. T. (1977). Proteins as a possible source material of low molecular weight petroleum hydrocarbons, *Geochim. Cosmochim. Acta*, **41**, 1083-1086.

Powers, M. C. (1967). Fluid release mechanism in compacting marine mudrocks and their importance in oil exploration, *Am. Assoc. Petrol. Geol. Bull.*, **51**, 1240-1254.

Price, L. C. (1976). Aqueous solubility of petroleum as applied to its origin and primary migration, *Am. Assoc. Petrol. Geol. Bull.*, **60**, 213-244.

Robin, P. L., Rouxhet, P. G., and Durand, B. (1977). Caracterisation des kérogènes et de leur évolution par spectroscopie infrarouge, in *Advances in Organic Geochemistry 1975* (Eds. R. Campos and J. Goni), pp. 693-716, Madrid.

Ronov, A. B. (1958). Organic carbon in sedimentary rocks (in relation to the presence of petroleum), *Geochemistry*, **5**, 510-536.

Sugimura, H. *et al.* (1966). Studies on the early stages of coalification. I. Japanese coal seen from the results of compositional, industrial and element analysis, *Nenryo-Kyokai-Shi*, (in Japanese) **45**, 199-208.

Taguchi, K. (1968). Problems of *n*-paraffin in relation to the origins of petroleum—with special reference to the carbon preference index, *Sekiyu Gakkai Zassi* (*Jour. Jap. Pet. Inst.*), (in Japanese) **11**, 414-428.

Taguchi, K. (1972). The origin of petroleum—a biogeochemical approach, *Kagaku* (*Science*), **42**, 58-65.

Taguchi, K. (1973). Organic geochemistry of hydrocarbons, *Japan Jour. Geol. Soc.*, (in Japanese) **79**, 569–584.

Taguchi, K. (1975). Trends in 'Late Diagenetic Theory of Petroleum Genesis'. A review, *Sekiyu Gikyo-shi* (*Jour. Jap. Assoc. Petrol. Tech.*), (in Japanese) **50**, 7–23.

Taguchi, K. (1978a). Chemical fossils as indicators of sedimentary environment, *Kaiyo Kagaku* (*J. Marine Science*), (in Japanese) **10**, 255–262.

Taguchi, K. (1978b). Organic maturation—a review, with special reference to its significance in the inorganic process of diagenesis and incipient metamorphism, *Memoirs of Geol. Soc. Japan*, No. 15, (in Japanese), pp. 165–190.

Taguchi, K. (1979). A geochemical approach to petroleum exploration, *Memoirs in Commemoration of 50th Anniversary of Japan. Assoc. Min. Petrol., and Geologists*, (in Japanese), pp. 179–188.

Thompson, R. R., and Creath, W. B. (1966). Low molecular weight hydrocarbons in Recent and fossil shells, *Geochim. Cosmochim. Acta*, **30**, 1137–1152.

Tissot, B. (1969). Première données sur les mécanismes et la cinetique de la formation du pétrole dans les sédiments. Simulation d'un schéma réactionnel sul ordinateur, *Inst. Francais Pétrole Rev.*, **24**, 470–501.

Tissot, B., Durand, B., Espitalié, J., and Combaz, A. (1974). Influence of nature and diageneis of organic matter in formation of petroleum, *Am. Assoc. Petrol. Geol. Bull.*, **58**, 499–506.

Tissot, B., Deroo, G., and Hood, A. (1978). Geochemical study of the Uinta Basin; formation of petroleum from the Green River formation, *Geochim. Cosmochim. Acta*, **42**, 1469–1485.

Vassoyevich, N. B., Korchagina, Yu I., Lopatin, N. V., and Chernyshev, V. V. (1970). Principal phase of oil formation, *Moskov Univ. Vestnik*, No. 6, 3–27. English translation, *Internat. Geology Rev.*, **12**, 1276–1296.

Weeks, E. L. (1965). World offshore petroleum resources, *Am. Assoc. Petrol. Geol. Bull.*, **49**, 1680–1693.

Welte, D. H. (1972). Petroleum exploration and organic geochemistry, *J. Geoch. Expl.*, **1**, 117–136.

Further reading

One of the best treatments of the chemical aspects of coal is contained in:

van Krevelen, D. W. (1961). *Coal*, Elsevier, Amsterdam, 514 pp.

We can also recommend:

Francis, W. (1961). *Coal*, E. Arnold Limited, London, 806 pp.

Murchison, D. G., and, Westoll, T. S. (Ed.) (1968). *Coal and Coal-bearing Strata*, Oliver and Boyd, London, 418 pp.

The latter is excellent as a general reference text dealing with the geology, palaeontology, sedimentology and geochemistry relating not just to coal but to coal-bearing formations in general. The most recent and detailed treatment of coal itself in terms of coal petrology is:

Stach, E., Mackowsky, M., Teichmüller, M. and R., Taylor, G. H., and Chandra, D. (Eds.) (1975). *Coal Petrology*, Borntraeger, Berlin, 428 pp.

There are also many reference books on coal in Japan. Relatively recent ones include:

Murata, T. (1964). *Sekitan Kagaku* (*Coal Chemistry*), Keiso Shobo, 334 pp.
Kurokawa, M., *et al.* (1963). *Sekitan, Sekitan Kagaku* (*Coal and Coal Chemistry*), Nikkan Kogyo, 230 pp.
Fueki, K., *et al.* (1980). *Shigen, Enerugi no Kagaku* (*The Chemistry of Energy and Resources*), Iwanami Series 'Modern Chemistry'.

However, virtually none deal with coal geology, although the only relatively recent reference volume:

Sakakura, K. (1964). *Sekitan Chishitsugaku* (*Coal Geology*), Gijutsu Shoin, 218 pp.

is a collection of the then available data, but now seems somewhat out of date in view of the subsequent progress in this field.

Specialist textbooks on geochemical aspects of petroleum include:

Nagy, B., and Colombo, U. (Eds.) (1967). *Fundamental Aspects of Petroleum Geochemistry*, Elsevier, Amsterdam, 388 pp.
Tissot, B. P., and Welte, D. H. (1978). *Petroleum and Occurrence*, Springer-Verlag, Berlin, 538 pp.
Hunt, J. M. (1979). *Petroleum Geochemistry and Geology*, W. H. Freeman & Company, San Francisco, 617 pp.

The last two are particularly recommended as they were published after completion of this volume.

For a better understanding of petroleum geochemistry, a fundamental knowledge of organic geochemistry is vital. The following textbooks are recommended as concurrent reading:

Breger, I. A. (Ed.) (1963). *Organic Geochemistry*, International Series of Monographs on Earth Science, Vol. 16, Pergamon Press, Oxford, 658 pp.
Eglinton, G., and Murphy, M. T. J. (Eds.) (1969). *Organic Geochemistry*, Springer-Verlag, Berlin, 828 pp.

General textbooks on petroleum geology which is a basic subject in the petroleum geochemistry include:

Russel, W. L. (1960). *Principles of Petroleum Geology*, 2nd ed., McGraw-Hill Book Company Inc., New York, 503 pp.
Chapman, R. E. (1973). *Petroleum Geology*, Elsevier, Amsterdam, 304 pp.
Kinoshita, K. (1973). *Sekiyu Shigen no Kagaku* (*Science of Petroleum Resources*), Kyoritsu Shuppan, 173 pp.

A more specialized but slightly outdated work:

Levorsen, A. I. (1967). *Geology of Petroleum*, 2nd ed., W. H. Freeman & Co., San Francisco, 724 pp.

is famous as treating oil principally as a reservoir fluid.

Recent treatments of petroleum geochemistry from the viewpoint of sites of deposition include:

Fischer, A. G., and Judson, S. (Eds.) (1975). *Petroleum and Global Tectonics*, Princeton University Press, Princeton, New Jersey, 322 pp.
Hobson, G. D. (Ed.) (1977). *Developments in Petroleum Geology 1*, Applied Science Publishers Limited, London, 335 pp.

Chapter 3

Global Evolution and the Formation of Mineral Deposits

Throughout the 3800 million or so years of the earth's geological history the styles of igneous activity and sedimentation, the composition of the sea and atmosphere and the forms of life have been changing (Fig. 3.1). The types of mineral deposits and the elements which accumulated in them have also changed in response to such global evolution. The formation of mineral deposits is a phenomenon which results from the combination of various

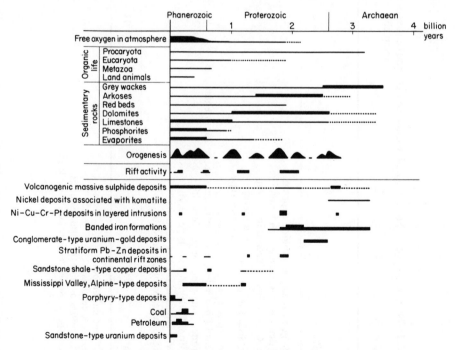

Fig. 3.1   Relationship between the history of global evolution and periods of deposit formation. (Prepared from Cloud, 1972*; Gastil, 1960; Vezier, 1976*.)

99

Table 3.1 The proportions (%) of estimated world resources and output accounted for by metal deposits of the types considered in this chapter

Deposit type	Cu[a]	Pb[a]	Zn	Fe	Ni[b]	U[a]	Principal associated metals[c]
Volcanogenic massive sulphide deposits	11	6	22				Au, Ag
Nickel deposits associated with komatiite					27		
Ni–Cu–Cr deposits in layered intrusions	2				63		**Cr, Pt**
Banded iron formations Algona type				12			Au
Superior type				48			
Conglomerate-type U–Au deposits						36	**Au**
Stratiform Pb–Zn deposits in rift zones in the continental crust		19	12				Ag
Sandstone, shale-type copper deposits	27	33	32				**Co**
Mississippi Valley, Alpine-type deposits							
Porphyry-type and related deposits	53	7	8				**Mo**, Au
Sandstone-type uranium deposits						24	
Total	93	65	74	60	90	60	

[a] Excl. Communist Block.
[b] Excl. laterite deposits.
[c] Bold type: 50% or more of world resources.
Roman type: a few per cent or more of world resources.

factors involving the mantle, crust, hydrosphere and atmosphere. The distinctive features of each era in the context of global evolution are reflected sensitively by differences in the genetic types of mineral deposits.

Various systems can be devised from classifying mineral deposits, and, in the case of metalliferous deposits, factors such as the type of accumulated metal, the rock which hosts it or the conditions of temperature or pressure under which the deposits developed can be used for classification (e.g. Lindgren, 1933; Stanton, 1972*). However, as these classifications are not necessarily suitable for the purposes of this chapter, we classify important resources such as iron, nickel, lead, zinc, copper and uranium by the 'site' of mineralization. Below we discuss the origins of these metalliferous deposits as well as coal and petroleum deposits in turn. The ages of formation of each type of mineral deposit, based on this classification, are shown in Fig. 3.1, and their importance as resources in Table 3.1. We will mention briefly some of the mineral deposits not covered by this classification in Chapter 4.

3.1 Volcanogenic massive sulphide deposits

Volcanogenic massive sulphide deposits are deposits composed principally of sulphide of iron, copper, lead or zinc formed in association with submarine volcanic activity. Within single areas (e.g. the Green Tuff Region in Japan) they are commonly found only in specific types of strata and hence are referred to as 'stratabound' types. Such deposits comprise material deposited with exhalative or hot spring activity on the sea floor and hence are also known as 'submarine exhalative sedimentary deposits'. In many cases volcanic rocks associated with volcanogenic sulphide deposits are calc-alkaline acidic volcanic rocks of the island arc type, but sometimes they consist of oceanic basalts (part of the ophiolite-suite ophiolites), the former being of overwhelming importance in terms of resources. A typical example of the former is the Kuroko deposits occurring in the Green Tuff Region of Japan, whereas the latter have come to be known as the 'Cyprus-type' because they have been extensively studied in the ophiolites of Cyprus. As Kuroko-type deposits which formed in the Archaean era differ in terms of their mineral composition from those dating from the Phanerozoic, they are sometimes called the 'Noranda' type (see Chapter 4).

The upper half of the orebody in Kuroko-type deposits is stratiform or lenticular. Sedimentary structures are often seen in the ore and the deposits are thus taken to be sedimentary ores which settled on the sea bed. In the lower half of the deposits, mineralization occurred in vein or disseminated forms in pyroclastic rock or autobrecciated lava, interpreted as fossilized vents for mineralizing solutions. Studies of the Kuroko deposits in Japan suggest that mineralizing solutions were emitted from the sea bed at temperatures of 200–300 °C.

Kuroko-type deposits have been formed in almost all geological periods from the Archaean to the Tertiary times. Numerous Archaean deposits have been found on the Canadian Shield, the oldest being more than 3000 million years old. Volcanic accumulations on the Canadian Shield (so-called 'greenstones') contain thick sequences of basalt containing komatiite near the base, whereas in the upper part they contain dacite or rhyolites of the upper volcanic layers, and where there is repetition of similar basic–acidic cycles, the deposits are generally associated with only one of these cycles. Exactly the same tendency is seen in Kuroko-type deposits of the Proterozoic and Phanerozoic eras (Fig. 3.2); thus Kuroko-type deposits are described as stratabound.

In the case of the Japanese Kuroko deposits, the deposits formed in subsiding basins during the Mid-Miocene period. As the basins sank, large quantities of acidic volcanic material extruded into them together with basaltic lavas and dykes. As the volcanic rocks were all subjected to hydrothermal alteration, few petrological studies have been made. However, the chemical composition of the least altered rocks indicates that volcanic material in the form of lava domes associated with the Kuroko deposits are the most highly differentiated of all the acidic volcanic rocks in the basin (Tatsumi and Clark, 1972). Although one cannot be absolutely certain in the case of older deposits,

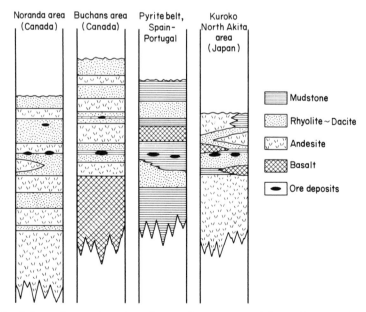

Fig. 3.2 Schematic stratigraphy of several areas containing volcanogenic massive sulphide deposits. (After Sato, 1974*; Spence and de Rosen-Spence, 1975*; Strauss *et al.*, 1977; Thurlow, Swanson and Strong, 1975*.)

the subsidence appears to have been genetically closely related to the extrusion of acidic volcanic rocks and the formation of deposits (Hodgson and Lydon, 1977*). Suggestions for the origin of this structure include: (1) a submarine caldera, (2) pushing up of acidic magma from magma which differentiated in the uppermost mantle or lower cust and (3) a graben zone in a regional extensional stress field, i.e. an aborted rift.

Isotopic studies concerning the origin of the mineralizing solutions which created the Kuroko deposits have shown that they were a mixture of waters from various sources (see Sec. 1.3). However, we do not really know which particular source of water was the most important for the accumulation of metals, or whether the fact that it was a mixture from several sources was, in itself, important. The very good correlation between the isotopic ratios of ore sulphur and oceanic sulphur (Sangster, 1968, 1971) suggests a process whereby sulphur derived from sea water could become fixed in the deposits (Sec. 1.3b). The sources of ore-forming elements in volcanogenic massive sulphide deposits are currently actively debated in connection with the origins of subsiding basins.

For whatever reason, there is certainly a close genetical relationship between the Kuroko deposits and calc-alkaline acid volcanism of the island arc type. The formation of this type of deposit in many places of all geological ages reflects the fact that calc-alkaline volcanism has been relatively common throughout geological time. One may therefore suppose that properties of the sea and atmosphere or evolution of life forms, which are thought to have considerably changed during the past 3000 million years, were not of fundamental significance to the formation of this type of deposit.

On the other hand, the formation of Cyprus-type deposits is restricted to the Phanerozoic era, and no exhalative sedimentary deposits of base metals are found amongst the extensive basalts in Archaean greenstone belts. Because the deposits are associated with ophiolites, which are thought to be fragments of the oceanic crust, there is wide support for a model whereby Cyprus-type deposits formed due to the circulation of heated sea water, below an ocean ridge under extensional stress. Unlike Kuroko-type deposits, some factor connected with global evolution in addition to the extrusion of basaltic volcanic rocks is thought to have played an important role in the formation of Cyprus-type deposits.

3.2 Nickel deposits associated with komatiite

Orthomagmatic nickel–copper sulphide deposits are associated with various basic and ultrabasic rocks. The most important of these are those of the Sudbury type found in huge differentiated intrusions and those in association with komatiite. According to estimates of nickel resources by Naldrett (1973), the Sudbury deposits contain by far the largest amount of nickel of all known

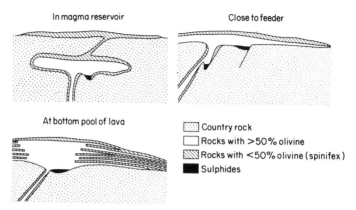

In magma reservoir　　　　　Close to feeder

At bottom pool of lava

☐ Country rock
☐ Rocks with >50% olivine
▨ Rocks with <50% olivine (spinifex)
■ Sulphides

Fig. 3.3　Position of nickel sulphide deposits in komatiitic rocks. (After Naldrett, 1973*.)

differentiated intrusions, but if this special case is excluded, far more deposits are associated with komatiite than with differentiated intrusions. Komatiite is an ultrabasic lava found characteristically in Archaean greenstone belts. A high degree of partial fusion of mantle material due to high geothermal gradients in the Archaean era is thought to have been essential to its formation. Sulphides for lenticular deposits near the base of komatiite lava flows or shallow intrusives, and in particular large deposits, develop topographical hollows in rocks lying beneath komatiite (Fig. 3.3). Peridotitic rocks above the deposits contain little sulphur, but small amounts of sulphides are found as one approaches the deposit, until a zone of disseminated nickel sulphide ore is reached. The ores are composed of almost equal amounts of sulphide minerals (chiefly pyrrhotite and pentlandite) and silicate minerals (chiefly serpentinized olivines), with sulphide minerals incorporated as a network between euhedral crystals of olivine. Underneath the disseminated ores, delineated by a sharp boundary, are massive ores composed of almost 100 per cent. sulphides. The massive ores may directly cover the underlying rocks or peridotite rich in pyroxene may be interposed between them.

　This mode of occurrence and the fact that there is no proof for in situ differentiation of the komatiite lavas suggests that when komatiite magma erupted, sulphides were already suspended in it as an immiscible liquid phase, and rapidly sank to the bottom of lava flows or magma pools in the very short time between eruption and solidification. This idea also provides a very credible explanation for the high Ni/Cu ratios associated with komatiite by comparison with sulphide deposits in differentiated intrusions. That is, nickel is incorporated in silicate minerals, particularly olivine, which crystallize out in the initial phases of fractional crystallization of basic–ultrabasic magmas, whereas copper concentrates in the residual liquid phase, hardly entering those rock-forming minerals. If the partition coefficient for copper and nickel between liquid silicate phase and liquid sulphide phase is not much affected by temperature, pressure or the composition of the magma, a large amount of fractional crystallization before separation of an immiscible sulphide phase leads to a low Ni/Cu ratio in the sulphide. In fact there is an extremely low nickel content in sulphides found in the Skaergaard intrusion (see Sec. 1.1) which had a low level of sulphur in the original magma and in which the sulphide phase appeared as an immiscible liquid phase only after differentiation had become quite advanced.

How then are ultrabasic magmas saturated with a sulphide phase produced? Naldrett (1973*, 1976) proposed the following model. In Fig. 3.4 the fusion curve for Ni-bearing sulphides intersects the Archaean geothermal gradient at a depth of about 100 km. Because there is about 10 per cent. partial fusion of mantle material at this depth, liquid sulphide with its relatively high specific gravity sinks to a deeper level. At a depth of about 200 km the degree of partial fusion of the Archaean mantle was less than 5 per cent. (near point A in Fig. 3.4) so that the liquid sulphides would have been unable to sink any further with the result that the mantle become enriched in sulphides near this depth. However, when the degree of partial fusion of mantle material is about 5 per cent. there is a strong tendency for diapiric upwelling. Such a diapiric rise of mantle material can be considered to be an adiabatic system, so that its route would follow ABCD in Fig. 3.4. Therefore, once it had begun to ascend, its rise would be accelerated further due to adiabatic expansion. If the diapir reached point B where partial fusion was 25–30 per cent., the liquid phase would have a basaltic composition. At point C there would be an additional 30

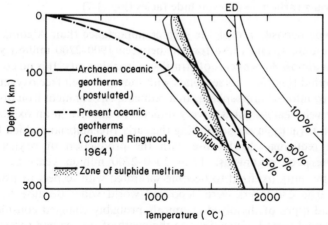

Fig. 3.4 The relationship of the degree of melting of mantle material (pyrolite II + 0.2% wt H_2O) with Archaean and modern geotherms. (After Naldrett and Cabni, 1976*.)

per cent. liquid phase, and if the liquid phase is separated at this point, it would erupt or intrude as high temperature komatiite magma via CE.

The model of Naldrett discussed above is based on the supposition of a much steeper geothermal gradient in the Archaean era than at present (e.g. Green, 1975). It gives a plausible explanation for the formation of sulphide deposits associated with komatiite, by linking the development of a sulphide-rich zone at a particular depth in the mantle, caused by a type of filtration, with the development of komatiite magma in that zone.

3.3 Banded iron formations

Banded iron formations (BIF) developed from the Archaean until the early Proterozoic eras (Fig. 3.5). Those from the Archaean era are associated with volcanic rocks in greenstone belts and are known as 'Algoma' types, whereas those dating from the Proterozoic era and associated with sedimentary rocks are known as 'Superior' types. As the characteristics of the deposits are very similar, however, we consider them together.

The following features are common to banded iron formations:

(1) Cherts and iron-bearing minerals form finely banded structures.
(2) The formations are distributed over a wide area. In Algoma types, they may be traced across the whole of a sedimentary basin several hundred kilometres wide, and in the Superior type, for several thousands of kilometres. The latter type appear to have formed at about the same time in many localities world wide (Fig. 3.6).
(3) There is a progressive change in the principal iron minerals from an oxide facies via a carbonate to a sulphide facies (Fig. 3.7).

Superior-type deposits are of far greater importance than Algoma types in terms of resources, and those formed between 1900–2200 million years ago account for almost 80 per cent. of stratiform iron deposits. It is no coincidence that this period (Fig. 3.1) corresponds with the time when free oxygen became incorporated into the atmosphere. In a reducing environment iron dissolves in water relatively readily but it is very difficult to dissolve in an oxidizing one. The oxygen fugacity in the sea during the early Precambrian, which had been sufficiently reducing, slowly rose with the production of oxygen due to photosynthesis of organisms. Then 2000–2200 million years ago the sea became sufficiently oxidized to become saturated with respect to iron so that enormous iron ore layers were deposited world wide. Because the oxygen fugacity and types of dissolved chemicals probably changed considerably in this transitional period, depending on the depth of the sea and topography of the ocean bed, it is likely that oxide, carbonate and sulphide facies were deposited in response to different local environments.

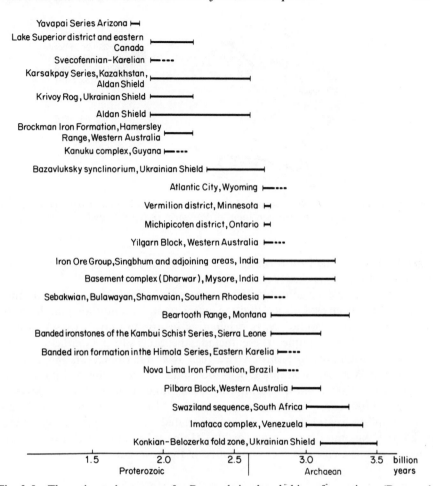

Fig. 3.5   The estimated age range for Precambrian banded iron formations. (Prepared from Goldich, 1973*.)

The distribution of Algoma-type deposits is restricted to relatively small sedimentary basins, and their age varies from basin to basin. Therefore the phenomena which resulted in the deposition of iron must also have operated on a sedimentary basin scale. As Algoma-type deposits are closely associated with volcanic rocks (Fig. 3.7), volcanic activity may have been a factor in their development. Volcanic activity could induce deposition of iron in the following ways: (1) the supply of H_2S and CO_2 from volcanic gases, (2) introduction of iron by reactions between magma and sea water and/or volcanic exhalation, and (3) the rise of abyssal water rich in Fe^{2+} to shallower depths due to warming as a result of volcanic activity. Sulphide and carbonate mineral phases are better developed in Algoma- than in Superior-type

Mineral Resources and Engineering Geology

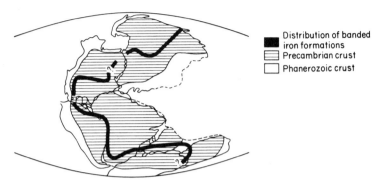

Fig. 3.6   Distribution of banded iron formations in the early Proterozoic (1900–2100 million years ago) on the continent of Pangaea. (After Goodwin, 1973*.)

deposits. Because the iron formations are found where the volcanic rocks are thickest factor (1) was clearly of considerable importance.

Let us now consider gold deposits associated with banded iron formations. It has recently been established that the majority of Precambrian gold deposits are so-called 'stratabound' types originating in iron ore layers (Sawkins and Rye, 1974*). For example, these include the Steynsdorp Goldfield in the Barberton Mountains in South Africa (ca. 3400 million years), the Yilgarn Goldfield in Western Australia (2600–3000 million years), the Abitibi area in Canada (ca. 2700 million years), the Homestake mine in South Dakota, America (1700–2200 million years), and the Morro Velho area in Brazil (>2800 million years). Iron ore layers associated with these gold deposits are all of the Algoma-type except for the Homestake mine. However, small amounts of basic volcanic rocks are found in the host rocks here too.

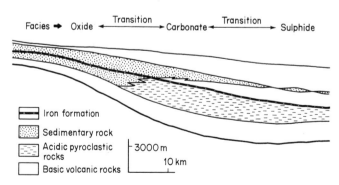

Fig. 3.7   Changes in mineral facies in Algoma-type banded iron formations in the Michipicoten sedimentary basin of the Canadian Shield (after Goodwin, 1973*). Superior-type iron deposits exhibit similar changes

Because gold in those areas has concentrated in secretional veins contained in the iron ore layers (principally carbonate facies), it is considered likely that it initially collected in the iron ore layers but was later reconcentrated to the level of an ore by subsequent deformation and metamorphism. In fact, extremely high gold contents have been detected in certain banded iron formations (0.1–0.01 ppm in Krivoy Rog in USSR, 0.075 ppm in Steynsdorp Goldfield in South Africa). These are much higher than the value (0.003 ppm) for sedimentary materials rich in iron and maganese currently found in the East Pacific Rise. The accumulation of gold in banded iron formations was possibly due to high levels of gold in Archaean komatiite and basalts associated with them (0.02–0.005 ppm; current ocean ridge basalts; 0.0006–0.0009 ppm) (Viljoen, Saager and Viljoen 1969*).

3.4 Conglomerate-type uranium–gold deposits (Witwatersrand-type deposits)

Gold–uranium deposits known as Witwatersrand or Rand types are found in conglomerates and sandstones from the early Proterozoic era. Typical examples include Witwatersrand in South Africa, Blind River in Canada and Jacobina in Brazil, all being found in sedimentary basins in cratons (Fig. 3.8). Conglomerates and sandstones around the deposits are thought to be fluviatile or deltaic sediments, and the deposits are present in the conglomerates chiefly as stratiform or thin lenticular forms. The ore minerals consist of native gold, uraninite and brannerite (U, Ca, Th, Y) (Tc, Fe)$_2$O$_6$ and also contain sulphide

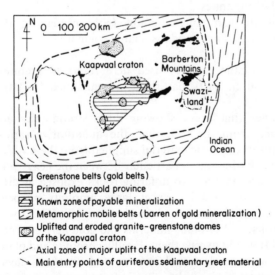

Fig. 3.8 Relationship between the greenstone belts and the placer gold basin in Kaapvaal craton, S. Africa. (After Viljoen, Saager and Viljoen, 1970*.)

minerals such as pyrite or pyrrhotite. They are associated with so-called 'heavy' detrital minerals such as ilmenite, magnetite or chromite. Large quantities of carbonaceous material is also frequently encountered in the ore zones in Witwatersrand.

There has been a lengthy controversy concerning the origin of the deposits between supporters of the hydrothermal and placer theories. However, it is now well established that the uraninite and pyrite are detrital in origin, and the placer theory is widely accepted. This theory has been given more support by the work of Viljoen, Saager and Viljoen (1970*) in Witwatersrand who compared 'heavy minerals' in the ore-bearing conglomerates and sandstone layers with the rock facies of the surrounding Archaean rocks which are thought to have formed their source of supply.

Viljoen, Saager and Viljoen (1970*) took Archaean rocks in the Barberton Mountains to the east of Witwatersrand sedimentary basin as their model, and divided them into the following four units according to their rock facies, starting from the base:

Unit I: Basalts, komatiites and small amounts of acidic tuffs; low volatile tonalite plutons.

Unit II: Balatic lavas, intermediate or acidic lavas, pyroclastic rocks; chert (including gold deposits); low volatile tonalites and the root zones of high volatile granites.

Unit III: Shales, greywacke sandstones, small amounts of banded iron formation (including gold mineralization); the root zones of high volatile granites.

Unit IV: Quartzite and conglomerates (gold present at the base); high volatile granites and associated pegmatites.

The term high volatile granites used here refers to granites subjected to metasomatism and in particular those accompanied by large amounts of pegmatites.

If one assumes that areas showing such stratigraphy arose and were gradually eroded from the top, then the quantitative ratios between the constituent minerals of clastic material supplied from there which accumulated in a neighbouring basin, and in particular between the heavy mineral suite, are bound to vary corresponding to differing rocks exposed at differing levels of erosion. That is, one would expect large amounts of pegmatite-derived uraninite, monazite and cassiterite brought from unit IV at the very bottom of the clastic deposits, and sulphide minerals and gold derived from gold deposits in units III and II would overlie them. Finally chromite and platinoid minerals, which are typical minerals found in basic and ultrabasic lavas as in unit I, would be uppermost. This explanation is fully borne out as demonstrated in Table 3.2.

Sulphide minerals and uraninite are unstable in our modern oxidizing atmosphere. They are readily completely oxidized and hence are not deposited as detrital minerals. It would therefore only be possible for Witwatersrand-type deposits to have formed in a reducing atmosphere such as existed prior to the early Proterozoic.

The three deposits mentioned earlier all possess different ratios of uranium to gold, and Blind River contains very little gold at all. This undoubtedly reflects compositional differences in the source areas. In Witwatersrand carbonaceous materials are characteristically associated with high grade gold. These are thought to be Proterozoic fossil algae, and it has been pointed out that such algae were capable of concentrating gold. The high gold content at Witwatersrand may well have been due at least in part to such biological activity.

3.5 Stratiform lead–zinc deposits in continental crust rift zones (McArthur-type deposits)

Large stratiform lead and zinc deposits are found in continental rift zones. Typical examples of those include Sullivan in Canada and Broken Hill, McArthur and Mount Isa in Australia. All of them were formed during the Proterozoic. As small quantities of tuffs occur in the strata surrounding most of these deposits, some authors placed them in the same category as volcanogenic massive sulphide deposits (see Sec. 3.1). However, one may cite the following characteristics which enable this type of deposit to be distinguished from volcanogenic sulphide deposits.

(1) The host rocks for the deposits are carbonate rocks and/or fine grained clastic sediments such as mudstones or silts. If volcanogenic material is present, it is only in limited quantities.
(2) The structural location of deposits is in aulacogens or troughs produced in intracontinental rift zones.
(3) The lateral extent of the deposits is large compared to their thickness.
(4) In the case of non-metamorphosed or weakly metamorphosed deposits, the grain size of the ore minerals is extremely fine and they form distinct layers clearly alternating with the clastic sediments.
(5) The $Cu/(Pb + Zn)$ and Au/Ag ratios in the deposits are extremely small.

These deposits with the above features will be referred to as 'McArthur-type deposits'.

Those who believe in an affinity between McArthur-type deposits and volcanogenic massive sulphide deposits (e.g. Hutchinson, 1973*) think that the latter were formed proximally to the volcanic activity and the former settled distally from it. This would explain the paucity of volcanic material in the host rocks for McArthur-type deposits, and resulted in the production of ores rich

Table 3.2 Comparison of heavy minerals in sediments hosting Witwatersrand gold–uranium deposits with original corresponding strata in the Barberton Mountains. (After Viljoen, Saager and Viljoen, 1970*.)

Position in stratigraphic sequence	Detrital minerals									Provenance units	Main rock types in provenance units
	Uran- inite	Garnet	Mon- azite	Cassiter- ite	Zircon	Gold	Sulph- ides	Chrom- ite	Platin- oids		
Kimberley- Elsburg Series	+				++	++	++	+++	+++	Top I Bottom II	I *Ultramafic unit* 'Primitive' mafic and ultramafic lavas Minor felsic tuffs and porphyries Low volatile tonalitic granite
Main- Bird Series	++				++	+++	+++	++	+	Top II Bottom III	II *Mafic to felsic unit* Mafic lavas Andesitic to felsic lavas Felsic to mafic pyroclasts Banded chert Mainly low volatile tonalitic granite Some high volatile granite (root zone)

	III *Argillaceous unit*						IV *Arenaceous unit*			
	Shales	Greywackes	Banded ironstone	Low volatile tonalitic granite	High volatile granite (root zone)	Top III / Bottom IV	Quartzites	Conglomerates	High volatile 'hood' granite (potash-rich leucogranite)	Pegmatites
Lower Wits System	++	++	+	+	+					Bottom IV
Dominion Reef System	+++	+++	+++	++	+	+				

Relative abundances of heavy mineral constituents: + generally not abundant, + + generally fairly abundant, + + + generally very abundant.

in lead, zinc and silver which are relatively soluble at low temperatures. However, the fact that there are such fundamental structural differences between the sites of deposition and that there are no known examples of volcanogenic massive sulphide deposits coexisting with McArthur-type deposits, suggest there are major differences in the mechanism by which they formed.

The McArthur deposits in the Northern Territories of Australia which are taken as the model for this type of deposit have hardly been affected by deformation or metamorphism, so it is a very useful example for examining the depositional environment.

The host rocks in which the McArthur deposits occur comprise sedimentary material more than 5000 m thick composed principally of carbonate rocks, shales, silts and sandstones deposited in the Mid-Proterozoic Batten trough (Fig. 3.9a). Similar strata, also seen in the Mount Isa trough to the south, host the Mount Isa and Hilton deposits.

Mineralization 55 m thick is seen in shales in the centre of the Batten trough (Fig. 3.9b), where seven layers of ore alternate with dolomitic shale. Individual ore layers consist of lamina of fine grained sulphides and tuffaceous shale. The lateral extent of the deposits is about 1.5 km², but as they have been eroded on the west and their eastern boundary is indistinct, we do not know their original extent. Isotopic studies of sulphur and lead have indicated the following ideas concerning the depositional mechanism.

The sulphur isotopic composition (δ^{34}S) of sulphide minerals from the McArthur deposits (Smith and Coxford, 1973), sphalerite ($+3.3-+8.9‰$) and galena ($-1.2-+5.7‰$), shows a relatively narrow spread within the orebody. Moreover, the difference in δ^{34}S values between sphalerite and galena from the same sample is generally nearly constant, and both seem to have maintained isotopic equilibrium during deposition. On the other hand, the δ^{34}S of pyrite is from -3.9 to $+14.3‰$, showing the characteristically wide variation of biogenic sulphur. δ^{34}S of pyrite gradually becomes heavier towards the top of the deposits irrespective of variations in the δ^{34}S values for sphalerite and galena. In other words, unlike volcanogenic massive sulphide deposits, pyrite and sphalerite–galena in the McArthur deposits show a different isotopic trend and thus the sulphur appears to have originated from two different sources. In terms of the lead isotopic ratios (Gulson, 1975) pyrite and sphalerite–galena show similar differences, the former having a multi-stage origin and being richer in radiogenic lead than the latter.

This strongly suggests that the sphalerite–galena and pyrite settled or were deposited in the same place but from separate systems, i.e. from mutually independent Pb–Zn– and Fe– solution systems. One hypothesis is that pyrite formed initially and was deposited with the shales, whereas sphalerite and galena were formed subsequently replacing the pyrite. However, the texture and genesis of the ores suggests this hypothesis is unlikely (Lambert, 1976*).

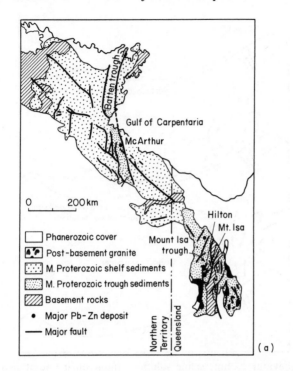

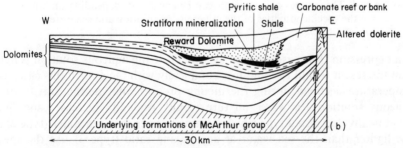

Fig. 3.9 (a) Geological map of NE Australia showing position of Batten and Mt. Isa troughs. (Simplified from Lambert, 1976*.) (b) Schematic EW section through the McArthur area during deposition of the Reward dolomite

Thus one would have to envisage a mechanism whereby deposits from two differing aqueous solution systems settled simultaneously on the same part of the sea floor. The author's model is as follows.

An aqueous solution (mineralizing solution) with a salt concentration different from that of the sea and at a higher temperature is ejected into the sea (Fig. 3.10). When the specific gravity of this aqueous solution is higher than that of the surrounding sea, it flows along the sea bed and finally accumulates

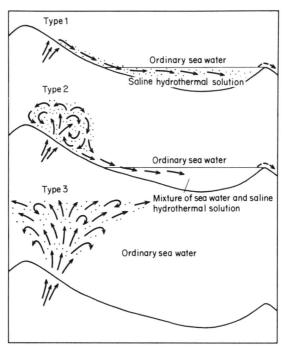

Fig. 3.10 Behaviour of hot, saline solutions (mineralizing solutions) when emitted onto sea bed. Three types of behaviour can be envisaged, depending on differences in the specific gravities of the mineralizing solution and sea water

in a depression (this case is taken as type 1). If the aqueous solution is lighter than the sea, it would rise and mix completely with the sea. In this case, as its temperature declined during the mixing process, the specific gravity of the aqueous solution–sea water mixture would gradually increase, and finally could be divided into a type which became heavier than sea water (type 2) and one lighter than the sea water at any mixing ratio (type 3). As the specific gravity of aqueous solutions is a function of temperature and salinity, and assuming these to be constant in sea water, the subsequent behaviour shown by a mineralizing solution is determined by its temperature and salinity at the time when it entered the sea (Fig. 3.11). Obviously the higher the salinity and the lower the temperature, the more likely it is to exhibit type 1 behaviour; and the lower the salinity and higher the temperature, so its behaviour will be more in accord with type 3.

If the mineralizing solutions exhibited type 1 behaviour, this provides a very plausible explanation for various features of McArthur-type deposits. First of all, such deposits are almost always found in depressions near the centre of sedimentary basins. Except in the case of the Sullivan deposits, the stratiform

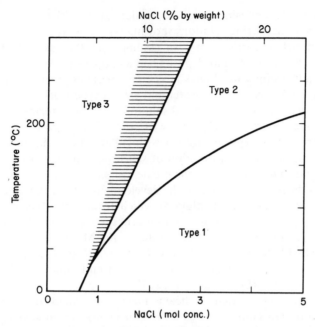

Fig. 3.11   Relationship between salinity and temperature when hot concentrated saline solutions flow out into the sea, and types of behaviour therein (see Fig. 3.10). If the effects of thermal conduction are strong the shaded section will come under type 2

deposits are not underlain by stringer zones which can be interpreted as an outlet for the mineralizing solution. Secondly, a particular feature of ore minerals in this type of deposit is their frequent alternation with layers of fine grained clastic material. Because type 1 mineralizing solutions create stable reservoirs of warm mineralizing solution in sea bed depressions, clastic material such as mud or volcanic ash supplied to them is likely to form clearly alternating layers, corresponding to their rate of supply, with ore minerals settling out from the mineralizing solutions at a more or less constant rate. On the other hand, when ore minerals settle out from a type 2 solution, the violent motion of the solution probably results in a uniform mixture of sulphide minerals with clastic material rather than alternating layers. The third point is that a type 1 mineralizing solution which collects in a sea bed depression is gravitationally stable, and will scarcely mix with the sea water. Therefore hydrothermal galena and sphalerite will be precipitated from the mineralizing solution in the depression whereas biogenic pyrite will settle out from the overlying sea water or slide down from nearby highs so that both are deposited in the same place. This provides a credible explanation for the differing sulphur and lead isotopes in the two. The characteristics of volcanogenic massive sulphide deposits discussed earlier suggest that they could have derived from mineralizing solutions showing type 2 or type 3 behavior.

If this model is correct, and we assume that the mineralizing solution responsible for the McArthur deposits had a temperature of 150 °C (Lambert, 1976*), then its salinity would have to be several times greater than that of the sea for it to be denser than sea water and exhibit type 1 behaviour (Fig. 3.11). How could such highly concentrated solutions have been formed?

Plumb and Brown (1973) showed that halite casts and dolomite pseudomorphs after gypsum together with collapsed breccia, thought to have formed as a result of the dissolution of salt layers, are frequently seen in the dolomites and shales underlying the ore deposits. This suggests that evaporites had formed during early stages of the development of the Batten trough, so it is possible that mineralizing solutions which formed the McArthur deposits have dissolved the salt layers in such evaporites to become highly saline. There is no proof for the presence of evaporites in the Mount Isa and Broken Hill deposits which have been subjected to regional metamorphism, but pseudomorphs of celestine after gypsum have been found in the host rocks of the Sullivan deposits (Edmunds *et al.*, 1977).

Similarly, sediments rich in heavy metals deposited from mineralizing solutions with high salinity caused by evaporite dissolution have recently been found on the bed of the Red Sea (Fig. 3.12). The same origin may also be attributed to the Pliocene Boleo deposits in Baja California, Mexico (Wilson, 1955). Thus such deposits are not restricted to the Proterozoic. However, Phanerozoic deposits generally possess much lower concentrations of lead than their Proterozoic counterparts, and are associated with large amounts of basic or intermediate volcanic rock. These will now be referred to as Red Sea-type deposits.

Tectonically, McArthur-type deposits are found in troughs and aulacogens in the continental interior and Red Sea-type deposits in areas associated with continental breakup or marginal sea development. This is probably because such areas are suitable for the development of thick evaporite deposits and the high heatflow is conducive to the formation of hydrothermal solutions with high salinity. The paucity of copper in McArthur-type deposits may be attributed to the greater instability of chloride complexes of copper compared with lead and zinc complexes at relatively low temperatures (e.g. Lambert, 1976*). However, Red Sea-type deposits are rich in copper and zinc but deficient in lead, a contributory factor probably being the concentrations of the metals in the host rocks. That is to say, sedimentary rocks predominate in the aborted rifts where McArthur-type deposits occur, whereas Red Sea-type deposits are predominantly associated with basalts in well-developed rifts leading to the formation of oceans.

The cupriferous pyrite deposits (Kieslager) which developed principally in the Sanbagawa belt in Japan, typified by the Besshi mine, are known as

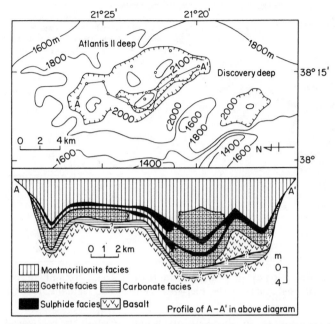

Fig. 3.12   Sea bed topography near Atlantis II Deep in the Red Sea and profile of sediments rich in heavy metals. (After Hackett and Bischoff, 1973*.)

Besshi-type ore deposits. The tectonic settling of the site of deposition of the Besshi deposits is thought to resemble that of the Red Sea (Sugisaki *et al.*, 1970) and the form of the deposits is also similar to Red Sea sediments, being rich in heavy metals. Thus they can probably be classified as Red Sea-type deposits.

3.6 Sandstone–shale-type copper deposits

Sandstone–shale-type copper deposits are stratiform deposits, principally of copper, which generally occur in conglomerates, sandstones, mudstones and dolomites. Typical examples are found in Central Africa, such as in Zambia and Zaire (Fig. 3.13), and in Europe, particularly in Germany (Fig. 3.14). The former are the famous 'copper belt' and the latter, the Kupferschiefer, but the 'copper belt' is by far the more important in terms of ore.

Sandstone–shale-type copper deposits resemble McArthur-type lead–zinc deposits in that they form stratiform orebodies in fine grained clastic rocks. However, they are distinctly different in that the host rocks are shallow marine or lagoon sediments deposited close to a coastline, and the mineralized zone extends continuously for several hundreds of kilometres. Copper is the major metal recovered from the deposits, but substantial quantities of lead and zinc

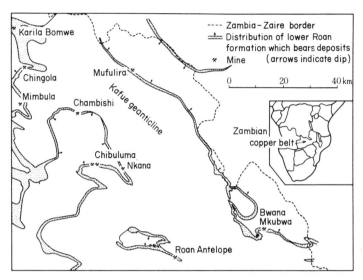

Fig. 3.13 Distribution of ore-bearing strata (Lower Roan) in Zambian copper belt and principal mines. (After Fleischer, Garlick and Haldane, 1976*.)

are also encountered in the Kupferschiefer. Cobalt is recovered as a by-product in the copper belt.

Figure 3.15 is a schematic stratigrapgic column showing the principal deposits in the Zambian copper belt. The basement consists of gneisses and granites, overlain by schists and quartzites. The Katanga formation, which hosts the copper deposits, overlies the basement with an extremely irregular

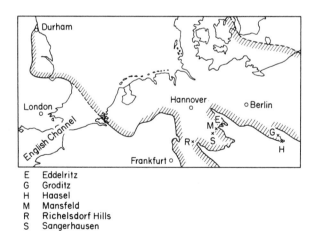

E Eddelritz
G Groditz
H Haasel
M Mansfeld
R Richelsdorf Hills
S Sangerhausen

Fig. 3.14 Extent of Kupferschiefer basin and principal mines. (Simplified from Dunham, 1964.)

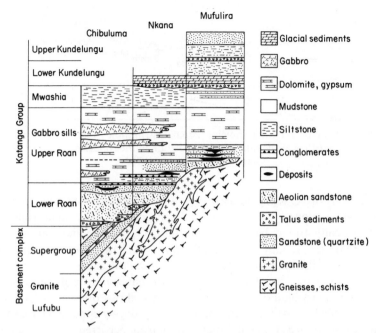

Fig. 3.15 Schematic stratigraphic column showing principal deposits in Zambian copper belt. (After Fleischer, Garlick and Haldane, 1976*.)

unconformity. It is divided into three: the Lower Roan group with basal talus deposits and aeolian sandstones, giving way to conglomerates and sandstones; the Upper Roan group which is principally composed of dolomite containing anhydrite or dolomitic mudstones; and the Mwashia group composed of dolomites and shales. These are overlain unconformably by the Kundelungu Series which contains glacial deposits. The mineral deposits occur as tabular layers in the sandstones and mudstones near the boundary between the Upper and Lower Roan.

As mentioned earlier, the mineralized zone extends for large distances parallel to the ancient coastline, but is only a few kilometres wide. It is interesting to note that with increasing distance from the palaeo coastline, there is a zonal distribution of chalcocite→bornite→chalcopyrite→pyrite (Fig. 3.16). Such a zonal distribution of sulphide minerals suggests that the site of mineral desposition gradually became more reducing further offshore. The 'Kupferschiefer' are shales, rich in organic matter, which concentrated heavy metals, principally copper and then lead and zinc. It is found in the lower Zechstein of the Mid-Permian which extends across northern Europe. The Kupferschiefer and its equivalents are distributed across an enormous area from the north of England across Germany as far as Poland, but by no means

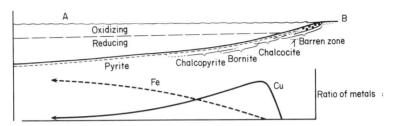

Fig. 3.16   Schematic diagram showing zonal distribution of minerals according to distance from coastline at the time of ore deposition in the copper belt. (After Fleischer, Garlick and Haldane, 1976*.)

all of it attains ore grade. There are only a few places where it has been viably mined and exploited (Fig. 3.14). 'Rotliegendes' (red sandstones) are characteristically found beneath Kupferschiefer, and aeolian sandstones or basal conglomerates may occasionally form its base. The overlying strata consist of dolomitic limestone (Zechsteinkalk) and these are further covered by thick layers of evaporites. This implies that the environment of Kupferschiefer deposition was lagoonal or shallow marine basinal just offshore, as in the case of the copper belt. Fossils are indicative of a hot drying climate. Here, too, the concentration of heavy metals apart from iron occurred at the margin of basins. Another similarity with the copper belt is that the distribution of copper, lead and zinc and the copper mineral assemblages appear to have been governed by the distance from the ancient coastline and the submarine topography, i.e. the depth of the sea at the time of deposition (Jung and Knitzschke, 1976*).

In summary, the formative environments for the Kupferschiefer and copper belt had the following important points in common:

(1) Heavy metals accumulated in shallow marine deposits near the coastline.
(2) Much organic carbon was present in the host rocks, suggesting a stagnant reducing environment in the area of mineral deposition.
(3) Evaporites are found above and below the deposits and around the mineralized zone. The ancient climate appears to have been hot and arid.

Other deposits with similar features include so-called 'Red Bed'-type copper deposits (Permian) which extend from New Mexico through Texas and Oklahoma to Kansas in the USA (Smith, 1976), Triassic lead–zinc deposits in France (Samama, 1976), Udokan in the USSR (Early Proterozoic) (Bakun *et al.*, 1971) and Corocoro-type copper deposits in Bolivia (Triassic) (Shiroishi *et al.*, 1972). Amongst these deposits are some in which precipitation of the heavy metals is thought to have occurred after deposition of the host rocks, but the formative mechanisms for such deposits in essence probably resemble those of the copper belt and Kupferschiefer.

Among the three characteristics detailed above, as Renfro (1974*) and Rose (1976*) pointed out, particular importance should be placed on the close association of evaporites and the ore deposits. The reason for this, as with McArthur-type deposits, is that saline solutions originated from dissolution of rock salt or condensation of sea water by evaporation are capable of transporting large amounts of heavy metals, even at low temperatures. The site of copper belt and Kupferschiefer deposit formation was continental rift zones (Sawkins, 1976*). The Udokan deposits, another major example of this type of deposit, also seem to have been formed in a Proterozoic aulacogen in eastern Siberia (Burke and Dewey, 1973*). Thus the tectonic regime in which these deposits formed is the same as that of McArthur-type deposits, implying that such areas are favourable for the formation of large-scale evaporite basins.

However, as stated above, the differences between these two types of deposit lie in the shape of the orebodies, the metal species concentrated and the presence or absence of a zonal distribution of minerals.

What could have been the cause of such differences? The author suggests the following hypothesis. In McArthur-type deposits, mineralizing solutions would have been brought in from reducing subterranean hydrothermal systems. As demonstrated by sulphur isotopic studies, the sulphur present was not the result of bacterial reduction of the sulphate acid in sea water, but was certainly transported there together with the heavy metals in the same hydrothermal solutions.

On the other hand, when the copper belt and Kupferschiefer developed, heavy metals derived from oxidized ore exposed on the land surface would have been brought in by saline surface water. The metals precipitated when they entered the stagnant evaporating marine basin and bonded with bacteria-derived reduced sulphur. This theory can explain the zonal distribution of minerals as the distribution of sandstone–shale-type deposits was governed by the coastline at that time, so that there were changes in the stable combinations of sulphide minerals as the oxidizing environment became a reducing one at greater depths and distance from the coastline. The zonal distribution of deposited metals was in order of increasing solubility of their respective sulphides so that deposition would probably have begun with the least soluble nearest the shore. The concentration and ratios of metals in the weathered and eroded rocks in the hinterland were obviously also of importance.

If this model is correct, necessary conditions for the formation of sandstone–shale-type ore deposits are the oxidation of already existing sulphide deposits in an arid climate and the presence of biogenic sulphur in a stagnant shallow marine basin. In terms of global evolution such environments seem to have existed since the Proterozoic era. In fact, the host rocks of the Udokan deposits are Early Proterozoic in age, but other deposits were formed from the Late Proterozoic onwards. Cloud (1972*) has proposed that the amount of atmospheric oxygen increased rapidly 700 million years ago, which would obviously intensify processes of surface oxidation and could have brought about conditions favourable for the formation of sandstone–shale-type deposits.

3.7 Mississippi Valley-type or Alpine-type deposits

The forms and derivation of the group of deposits known as Mississippi Valley-type or Alpine-type deposits show great variety, but they are all lead–zinc deposits hosted by limestone or dolomite. They are sometimes referred under the general title of 'carbonate-hosted Pb–Zn deposits' (Sangster, 1976*). The majority of deposits have the following features in common:

(1) The deposits consist mainly of lead and zinc, with very minor amounts of copper but with abundance associated baryte and fluorite in the majority of deposits.
(2) The carbonate host rocks are reef or marginal-reef limestones which are frequently dolomitized.
(3) The deposits formed at the margins of basins containing thick sedimentary sequences, these basins often yielding petroleum and evaporites.

Mississippi Valley-type deposits are found mostly in North America centring on the Mississippi Valley region (see Fig. 4.6), and are produced by limestone replacement chiefly along unconformities or faults. Ancient karsts, dissolved breccias or reefs are also known as structural traps for the deposition of minerals (Fig. 3.17). The host rocks for the deposits range from Cambrian to Carboniferous in age.

Alpine-type deposits are lead–zinc deposits in carbonate host rocks from the so-called Alpine geosyncline in Central Europe, and particularly in the eastern Alps. A few deposits of this type also occur in Ireland. They differ from Mississippi Valley-type deposits in being stratiform and possessing sedimentary structures which indicate that at least some of the ores were contemporaneous with the surrounding rocks (Sangster, 1976*). Their host rocks are commonly carbonates deposited in back reefs (Fig. 3.18). A feature common to this type of deposit in the Alps and Ireland is the presence of volcanic material in the host rocks.

So what kind of processes were involved in the formation of deposits like these? Three important points have been established from fluid inclusions and isotopic studies:

(1) The mineralizing solutions had high salt concentrations with temperatures ranging from 70 to 160 °C.
(2) The mineralizing solutions were isotopically very similar to oilfield brine.
(3) The source of sulphur for the sulphide minerals was bacterial.

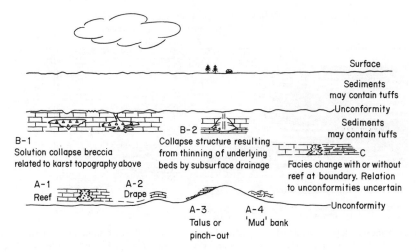

'Basement' may be igneous, sedimentary or metamorphic

Fig. 3.17 Geological and structural location of Mississippi Valley-type lead-zinc deposits. (After Callahan, 1967*.)

Carpenter *et al.* (1974) suggested that in addition to high salinity, oilfield brine in the Mississippi region has characteristically high concentrations of lead, zinc and barium which are the metals found in Mississippi Valley-type deposits. Oilfield brine, interstitial water contained within the strata in sedimentary basins, is believed to be sea water condensed by evaporation (Carpenter *et al.*, 1974).

Mississippi Valley-type deposits probably develop when saline interstitial water rich in lead and zinc migrate from the centre of a sedimentary basin towards the edge depositing minerals in 'traps' such as reef limestone. This is similar to the source reservoir relationship for petroleum. Recent studies have suggested that dehydration of clay minerals, such as montmorillonite, is the driving force for petroleum migration (see Sec. 2.3). For example, dehydration of clays composed principally of montmorillonite occurs at 80–120 °C in the oilfield zone in the Gulf of Mexico forming overpressure of a hydrostatic head of water (Jones, 1970). This temperature is similar to that at which Mississippi Valley-type deposits were formed. Oil is present in fluid inclusions in Mississippi Valley-type deposits, so it is likely that migration of the mineralizing solution responsible for the Pb–Zn deposits and migration of petroleum are achieved by the same mechanism.

Isotopic studies suggest that the source of sulphur is from sulphur-reducing bacteria. Jackson and Beales (1967*) and Beales (1975) pointed out that there is abundant biogenic hydrogen sulphide (sour gas) in petroleum gases in limestone reservoir rocks. They suggested that heavy metals were transported

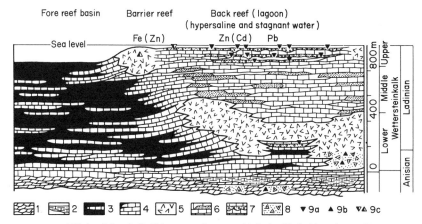

1 = uppermost, 'Alpine Muschelkalk': wavy-clumpy, thinly bedded, bituminous limestone with chert nodules; 2 = andesitic green tuffs (ash and crystal tuffs, few lapilli with thin layers of marl and limestone); 3 = 'Partnach-shales': marls, shales with lenticles of layered limestone (like 4) (Ladinian basin facies); 4 = 'Partnach-lime-stone': bituminous, marly, layered limestones (Ladinian basin facies); 5–8 = different types of 'Wetterstein-limestone' (Ladinian reef facies): 5 = massive limestone and dolomite, partly cavernous with relict patterns of bioherms (often coral colonies); 6 = well-layered gray limestone (mainly calcarenite), with debris and colonies of algae (Dasycladaceae), single algal patch reefs; 7 = predominantly thinly layered limestone, with intercalations of the 'special facies' in distinct sequences (back-reef units, tuffaceous marls, slump structures, 'ore sediments', etc.); 8 = late, diagenetic alteration of the cavernous reef body by recrystallization of dolomite, quartz and different Fe dolomites; 9a = Pb–Zn(Fe) sulphide ores with sedimentary fabrics; 9b = Pb–Zn sulphide ores primarily enriched in metasomatic replacement bodies, locally associated with small amounts of Cu–Sb–As minerals; 9c = predominantly Fe dolomite and Fe sulphide ores, with small amounts of ZnS(PbS).

Fig. 3.18 Diagrammatic location of occurrence of Alpine-type lead-zinc deposits in northern limestone Alps (Bavaria, N. Tyrol). (After Maucher and Schneider, 1967*.)

in solutions containing little or no reduced sulphur, but when they mixed with hydrogen sulphide in limestone they precipited as sulphide minerals. In this case, limestone which contains pore spaces suitable for precipitation of the minerals is thus an inevitable location for ore deposition because of the presence of hydrogen sulphide. This provides a most convincing explanation for restriction of mineralizing limestone.

If the dehydration of clay minerals was the driving force for the migration of interstitial water containing the heavy metals, a depth of 3 km or more would have been necessary for this to occur, given an average geothermal gradient of 30 °C/km. Such depths would probably not have been reached until a comparatively late stage in the development of the basin. The overpressurized interstitial water thus produced would have been forced towards the periphery of the basin along highly porous layers such as sandstone, and would thus have migrated into carbonate reefs, etc., when they were already buried and consolidated. If there was a high geothermal gradient due to volcanic activity, dehydration of clay minerals could occur even at quite shallow depths, so that interstitial water of the basin would flow out on to the sea bed on the margins. This probably accounts for the fact that the Mississippi Valley-type deposits, which formed on the edges of sedimentary basins in the continental interior lacking volcanic activity, are epigenetic deposits produced in previously consolidated carbonate rocks, whereas at least part of the Alpine-type deposits associated with volcanic activity were formed as syngenetic sedimentary ores.

3.8 Sandstone (Colorado plateau)-type uranium deposits

Sandstone-type uranium deposits generally have a sandstone host and their genesis is strikingly similar to the sandstone–shale-type copper deposits discussed in Sec. 3.6. This type of deposit may in fact contain significant amounts of copper. Vanadium is frequently encountered as well as small amounts of molybdenum or selenium. The deposits are distributed world wide and in particular almost 100 per cent. of the uranium resources currently economically viable in the United States are of this type. Most of the deposits date from the Mesozoic onwards.

The sandstones, which form the host rocks for the deposits, are generally fluvial or deltaic sediments. The distribution of the deposits is governed by palaeo river channels with uranium being particularly concentrated in sandstones rich in carbonaceous material, enclosed above and below by impermeable, fine grained layers of clastic material. Broadly speaking the deposits have one of two forms, i.e. roll or tabular form.

A roll-type deposit has a crescent-shaped profile with the convex side towards the direction of the dip of the host rocks (Fig. 3.19). The host rock contains pyrite and carbonaceous material towards the down-dip side of the deposits whereas the up-dip side is oxidized to a red colour and the pyrite and carbonaceous material have decomposed. This oxidation was caused by permeation of oxidizing ground water, and the position of the roll deposits shows the front of the oxidizing water table. Therefore the deposits are often scattered along several kilometres in a system which follows the boundary between oxidized and non-oxidized zones parallel to the strike of the host rocks (Fig. 3.19).

Tabular deposits are almost parallel with the bedding plane and may be stratiform or lenticular. The sandstones surrounding the deposits are commonly fluviatile, and are rich in carbonaceous material such as fossilized trees, but they have none of the locational specificity encountered with roll-type deposits due to the oxidizing water table (Fig. 3.20). Tabular deposits often contain economically viable amounts of vanadium.

Uranium has a valency of 6 in an oxidizing environment and is readily soluble, but in a reducing environment has a valency of 4 and is insoluble. The

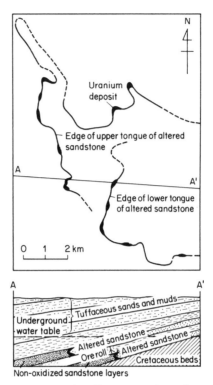

Fig. 3.19 Mode of occurrence of roll-type uranium deposits (Shireley basin in Wyoming). (After Fischer, 1974*.)

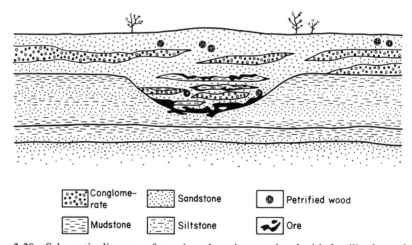

Fig. 3.20 Schematic diagram of uranium deposits associated with fossilized woods in a 'paleochannel'. (After Mitcham and Evensen, 1955.)

forms of the deposits described above therefore imply that 6-valent uranium was transported in oxidizing river or ground water, but became 4-valent when it encountered a reducing environment and so precipitated. The presence of extensive, exposed uranium-bearing rocks in the hinterland subject to weathering and erosion is a necessary prerequisite for the development of large uranium deposits. Most uranium deposits of this type are located in inland basins with hinterlands comprising uplifted blocks of uranium-rich granites. Another important source of uranium could be from acidic tuffs where these extensively cover the sandstone layers.

The relationship between the time when the host rocks were deposited and when uranium deposits formed differs depending on whether the deposit is of the tabular or roll type. The former developed immediately after deposition of the host rocks, whilst deposition of the overlying strata was still in progress. The latter, however, probably developed long after deposition of the host rocks when the overlying layers had been eroded away (Fischer, 1974*). Therefore there could be cases in which areas possessing tabular deposits were lifted, the overlying layers were then eroded so that the water table fell, resulting in oxidation of the tabular orebodies to develop roll orebodies (Granger, 1968).

The process whereby heavy metals carried in oxidizing ground or meteoric water form deposits by being fixed in a reducing environment is very similar to the formation of sandstone–shale-type copper deposits discussed earlier. However, the uranium deposits are not associated with evaporites, and the humid conditions which prevailed when the host rocks were deposited seem to have been of great significance. This may be attributed to the fact that the solubility of uranium is virtually independent of the salinity of aqueous solutions and that abundant vegetation was an important source of the carbonaceous material which acted as a reducing agent for the uranium. Thus sandstone-type uranium deposits could not form until there was terrestrial vegetation.

There are some instances in which a limited amount of uranium has accumulated in reducing marine strata. Examples of this include Alum shale (Cambrian) in southern Sweden and the Chattanooga shale (Devonian) in Tennessee. Uranium also collected in phosphorite. All these are of a low grade, but as they exist in large quantities, they will be important as uranium resources in the future.

(Takeo Sato)

3.9 Porphyry-type deposits

Porphyry-type deposits are those in which useful minerals are produced in disseminated or stockwork forms at, or near, the tops of porphyritic granitoids or porphyry. They are low grade, enormous size deposits and have rather recently begun to be exploited. Deposits discovered up until now have yielded copper, molybdenum, tin and tungsten. Tin and tungsten have not yet been exploited commercially but are of considerable interest in terms of future resources. Porphyry-type deposits may be divided into the following categories based on their mineral types:

Copper	Cu–Au (island arc type)
	Cu–Mo (Cordillera type)
Molybdenum	Mo (Rockies type)
Tin	Sn, Sn–Ag (Potosi, Bolivia)
Tungsten	W–Mo (Yangchuling, China)

Porphyry copper deposits account for about 50 per cent. of world wide copper resources and are economically of enormous significance. They may also contain gold (1 ppm or less) and molybdenum (0.015 per cent. or less) which can be recovered as by-products. Because of the large quantities of ore to be treated, the economic aspects of these by-products cannot be ignored. Almost all the world supply of molybdenum is from porphyry-type deposits. In this section we discuss some genetic problems of this type of deposit, chiefly with reference to porphyry copper deposits.

(a) Uneven distribution and age variation

The distribution of porphyry copper deposits is remarkably heterogeneous. They developed in the Mesozoic and Cenozoic orogenic belts which were widely distributed around the Circum Pacific belt, with particular concentration on the American side (Fig. 3.21). This distribution may be compared with the greisen-type tin–tungsten deposits found in Eastern Asia, which similarly belonged to the Circum Pacific orogenic belt and predominantly developed from the Malay peninsula to China and Russia. On the Asian side, porphyry copper deposits predominate only in young SW Pacific island arcs which are in oceanic environments. Porphyry molybdenum deposits are concentrated on the North American continent. Porphyry-type deposits are associated with magnetite series granites (see Sec. 1.1) so in order to understand the genesis of this type of deposit it is necessary to consider the genesis of magnetite series granitoids which occur abundantly in the American continent side and in island arcs.

The tectonic setting of granitic activity may broadly be divided into the following three types, i.e.

(1) hotspot or rift types,
(2) subduction types,
(3) collision types.

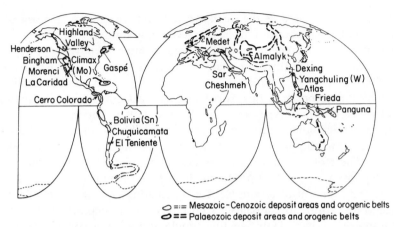

○ =:= Mesozoic – Cenozoic deposit areas and orogenic belts
○ == Palaeozoic deposit areas and orogenic belts

Fig. 3.21 Distribution of porphyry-type deposits. (Author's additions to Sutherland Brown, 1976*). (Mo), (Sn), (W) = porphyry molybdenum, tin and tungsten deposits. If not specified, then porphyry copper is meant

The ratio of magnetite/ilmenite series granitoid declines from type (1) to type (3). Most porphyry-type deposits develop in subduction-type orogenic belts and the ratio of the two series of granitoids within the orogenic zones affects the distribution of the deposits. It has also been suggested that around the Japanese archipelago the expansion of the marginal basin (Japan Sea) is closely connected with the formation of the magnetite series and the field of compression on the Pacific side with the formation of ilmenite series (Ishihara, 1979).

The distribution of porphyry copper deposits is also of considerable interest in terms of global evolution, and it appears that there are practically no Precambrian deposits. The same is true of porphyry molybdenum deposits. The enormous deposits of porphyry copper date predominantly from the Mid-Palaeozoic (e.g. Appalachia, Russia), the Mid–Late-Mesozoic (North America, China, etc.) and the Cenozoic (North and South America, Central Asia, South West Pacific, etc.). The amounts produced per geological period from the quantity of metal in the deposits are shown in the table below. One significant factor could possibly be that the ratio of magnetite/ilmenite series

	Cenozoic	Mesozoic	Palaeozoic	Precambrian
Copper (ton/year)	2	0.4	Little	Virtually 0
Molybdenum (kg/year)	44	3	Virtually 0	Virtually 0

granitoid has increased as the earth evolved, but we still are ignorant of the detail of global distributions of the two series of granitoid.

Not all areas of magnetite series granitoids contain porphyry-type deposits, e.g. in Japan, where there are many instances of vein-type or Kuroko-type deposits. In general, pyroclastic rocks are not found in the vicinity of porphyry-type deposits so that association with calderas is virtually unknown in obvious porphyry-type deposits. Sillitoe (1980) believes that volatile components, including heavy metals, would probably accumulate at the top of the magma chamber in this type of volcanic activity and be ejected with the magma. Therefore, even if there was subsequent plutonic activity, porphyry-type deposits would not be produced. Because structural forms such as ring dykes, etc., are also unsuitable for circulating volatile components in concentrated forms, the absence of porphyry copper deposits in Japan (the green tuff belts), Nevada or San Juan would appear to be connected with the eruptive mechanism of the magma.

(b) Types of deposits

Most porphyry-type deposits are found at the base of strato-volcanoes and were produced as a result of intrusive and hydrothermal activity after the principal eruptive activity had ceased. A good example is the Henderson deposits in the United States. Here mining development has revealed that a surface plug of rhyolite porphyry is connected with the lower granites over 1 km or more. Sillitoe (1973*) attempted to reconstruct deposits in the volcanic belt in Argentina, and his proposals are embodied in Fig. 3.22.

This type of deposit is generally associated with porphyritic intrusive rocks belonging to the calc-alkaline series. They are widely distributed across the North and South American continents and may be called the 'Cordillera type'. A particular feature of porphyry copper deposits associated with calc-alkaline rocks is a concentric distribution of the constituent minerals centred upon the porphyry. Lowell and Guilbert (1970*), who initially summarized this feature, described a barren core, accompanied by small amounts of magnetite and sulphide minerals. Chalcopyrite (bornite) and molybdenite increase away from this core, forming workable deposits, and further out still pyrite accumulates and the chalcopyrite declines. Zonal distribution can also be recognized in altered minerals, and, in general, from the centre outwards one finds a potassic alteration zone (potassium feldspar, biotite), a phyllic alteration zone (sericite, quartz), an argillic alteration zone (kaolinite, montmorillonite) and a propylite alteration zone (chlorites, epidote, calcite).

On the other hand, porphyry copper deposits rich in gold have been found in association with alkaline rocks between the Alaska–Idaho batholiths, the diorite model of Hollister (1978*). A diorite–monzonite–syenite complex accompanied by deposits intrudes sub-marine volcanic rocks. This type of pophyry copper deposits may be described as an island arc type. Frieda in New Guinea is another example of this type (Asami and Britten, 1980). In addition to the potassic alteration zone, sodium metasomatism (albitization) is seen in the centre of the deposits, and a propylite alteration zone rich in chlorite is found around it; i.e. the phyllic and argillic alteration zones are generally absent and zonal arrangements indistinct. Furthermore, they are not accompanied by pyrite halos. Chalcopyrite–bornite–magnetite or bornite–gold–magnetite are found in the centre and chalcopyrite–pyrite in the propylite

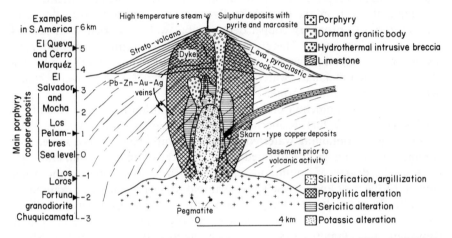

Fig. 3.22   Schematic profile of porphyritic copper deposits. (After Sillitoe, 1973*.)

zone. These minerals appear in disseminated and stockwork form, but unlike the calc-alkaline types, no quartz is found in the networks of fine veins. Instead epidote, chlorite, calcite, prehnite and zeolite, etc., may be seen.

(c) The genesis of the deposits

The two particular features of porphyry-type deposits are the concentric distribution of minerals, typified in the above calc-alkaline rocks and the disseminated–stockwork ore structure. The concentric distribution is also remarkable in temperature of formation and salinity of fluid inclusions, both being high at the centre and declining towards the edges. Stable isotopic studies have shown that magmatic water was the chief component of hydrothermal ore solutions from the phyllic alteration zone inwards and ground water from the argillic alteration zone outwards. This phenomenon can be accounted for by a hydrothermal plumbing system between magmatic water centring on the porphyry stock and meteoric water. Great effort is currently being directed towards finding a concrete explanation for this mechanism.

Meteoric water plays two roles in igneous processes, namely to lower and dilute the temperature and salinity, respectively, of extremely hot ore solutions. In either case this causes a remarkable reduction in the solubility of metal sulphides and therefore is a principal factor in deposit formation. This is clearly indicated by the frequent occurrence of workable porphyry-type deposits near the surface of contact between magmatic and meteoric water. Hot circulating meteoric water plays another important role in extracting ore-forming material from the host rocks. Rocks rich in copper occasionally form the wall rocks to prophyry copper deposits, but wall rocks rich in Cl such as evaporite are unknown. Therefore the high salt concentrations must have derived from magmatic water, and the high salinity may be the result of a process in which magmatic water boiled due to differences in vapour pressure between the water and chlorine.

The boiling phenomenon provides a tidy explanation for the origins of the stockwork texture which is another characteristic of porphyry-type deposits. As the magma containing water cooled, there would be a marked increase in volume, when the H_2O saturated melt dissociated to form mineral + gas phases. The degree of volume increase would be proportional to the water content of the melt and inversely proportional to the pressure. For example, if a granite–diorite melt containing 2.7 per cent. by weight of water crystallized 2 km below the surface, there would be a 50 per cent. increase in volume (Burnham and Ohmoto, 1980*). As such shallow roof rocks do not exhibit plasticity, this volume increase is equivalent to a pressure increase of several kilobars. This pressure would be greater than the strength of the wall rocks by a factor of 10. Therefore failure of the rocks would occur, first laterally in the direction of minimum stress and then upwards and downwards, resulting extensive development of minute fractures. Stockworks of veins would be produced as minerals precipitated from the aqueous solutions in the fractures thus formed.

Calc-alkaline porphyry-type deposits probably formed when granitic magma, originally rich in heavy metals, Cl and S, but undersaturated with water, rose and intruded into a tectonic environment from which volatile components could not readily escape. Separation of the aqueous solution phase from the melt and boiling drew in ground water, thus creating a large-scale hydrothermal circulation system which led to the development of deposits. On the other hand, the alkaline rock series type is poor in sulphur, and it is thought that magma saturated with water perhaps cooled without any significant reaction with meteoric water to form the deposits.

(Shunso Ishihara)

3.10 Coal deposits

(a) The ages and types of coal deposits

As minable coal deposits are chiefly composed of humic coal, the major coal deposits are associated with the following three geological periods, when continental vegetation flourished particulary well; viz. the Palaeozoic from the Carboniferous to the early half of the Permian periods when vascular cryptogams flourished; the Mesozoic until the early half of the Cretaceous period typified by Pteridophyta and Gymnospermae; and the Cenozoic from the latter half of the Cretaceous period typified by Angiospermae. The larger coalfields are generally Palaeozoic in age.

An essential condition for the development of coalfields is the presence of gradually or intermittently sinking swamps or marshes in land areas with lush vegetation or watery areas adjacent to these. As the process of subsidence and development of a sedimentary basin is controlled by the structural history of the terrain, it is possible to develop a structural classification of coalfields (summarized in Table 3.3). On the basis of this different approach, their world-wide distribution is shown in 'Principal deposits of coal, oil and uranium' on the back cover. Coalfields will now be discussed on the basis of the three principal types.

(1) Cratogen type The structure of cratogen-type coalfields is fairly simple with little variation in the coal beds. They are generally very extensive. Where the basement rocks are Precambrian in age and the thermal structure of the crust has been stable, the coalification process is not very well advanced, even in coalfields with extremely long reaction times (i.e. geologically ancient coalfields) (see Chapter 2, Fig. 2.4).

The Tungusk coalfield, which covers a large area (about 1 million km²) of the western Siberian plateau on the Angara shield, consists of a Permo-Carboniferous coal-bearing sequence of 200–300 m thick resting directly on the Precambrian system, and derived from Angaran flora. Its rank of coalification is about that of sub-bituminous. The Kuznetsk coalfield located at the western edge of the Angara geosyncline south-west of the Tungusk field was formed at the same time, but here the sediments reach 2500 m thick and the rank of coalification has advanced to bituminous. The Lensk coalfield, which extends over a large part of the east of the same Siberian plateau (about 750 000 km²) is composed of Jurassic sediments about 500 m thick, and here again the rank of coal has only reached lignitic to sub-bituminous. In the Verhoyansk geosyncline further east where Jurassic sediment increases to 2000 m and the Cretaceous sediments to 1500 m thick, coalification has reached bituminous coal in the Cretaceous Zyryansk coalfield.

A similar example where coalfields formed in small semi-grabens or depressions over the Precambrian system is the Collie coalfield over the

Table 3.3 Geotectonics, coal basins and coal deposits

| Geotectonic classification | Coal basin | | | Coal deposit | | | | | | |
| | | | | Coal seam | | | | | Coalification | |
	Sedimentary facies	Thickness of sediments	Shape of basin	Distribution	Number of coal seam	Thickness of coal seam	Variation of coal thickness	Structure	Rank	Variation
Foredeep or subduction side	Littoral	Thick	Elongated	Medium to narrow	Many	Thin to thick	Variable (gradual change)	Complex	Low to high	Much
Orogen type In orogenic zone	Limnic to brackish	Thin	Small basin to semi-graben	Narrow	Few	Thin to thick	Variable (rapid change)	Simple to complex	Low to high	Much
Intermediate type Orogenic belt side Continent mass side	Litoral to brackish	Thick to thin	Elongated to graben	Wide to medium	Many to medium	Thick to medium	Medium	Complex to simple	High to low	Medium
Cratogen type In cratonic continent	Limnic	Thin	Basin to semi-graben	Narrow to wide	Few	Medium to thick	Little	Simple	Low	Little

Yilgarn block in the south-western corner of Australia. This is an Upper Permian (Gondwana series) coalfield of 200 m thick forming a gentle monocline towards the steep faults crossing its south-west margin. The sedimentary overburden is thin so the degree of organic metamorphism is low. Coal exploited by strip mining on the surface has developed only to the rank of sub-bituminous coal. The enormous Bowen and Sydney coalfields on the eastern Australian continent date from the same period but belong to the following intermediate type.

(2) Intermediate type The intermediate type corresponds to the cratogen or labile shelf type described by Bubnoff (1937*), and develop between or across cratonic and geosynclinal zones.

The Tasman geosyncline in eastern Australia, which opened towards the east, began to be infilled from the Cambrian onwards. By the end of the period of coal deposition, both the Bowen and Sydney coalfields had formed between stable blocks on the west. These resemble many other coalfields in the southern hemisphere, being derived from Gondwana flora, most of it *Glossopteris*. The type of vegetation and the occurrence of glacial deposits have led to a belief that they developed in cold dry climatic conditions. They are rich in inert components, particularly fusinite, so that their carbon content may sometimes be greater than the degree of organic metamorphism assessed by vitrinite reflectance, etc. In areas overlying cratonic blocks where they are thin, coarse grained sediments, the rank of coalification is sub-bituminous, whereas in the east-facing centre of the geosyncline, where thick sediments and muds develop, the lower or more easterly the coal beds, the higher is the rank of coalification, reaching bituminous and even anthracite levels in places. Vitrinite reflectance, determined from many boreholes (Diessel, 1975; Shibaoka *et al.*, 1973, 1977), is high due to the influence of igneous activity in the east of the continent at the end of the Palaeozoic.

Coalfields are widely distributed in the North American continent, with the Appalachian and Pennsylvanian coalfields in the east, many more in Illinois and the Mid-West, and Mesozoic–Cenozoic coalfields from the Cordilleran orogenic belt on the Pacific side to the west of the Canadian Shield (see Fig. 3.23).

The coalfields in the eastern part of North America are of global importance and like the principal European coalfields derived from Euramerican flora, which flourished in the warm humid environment of the Carboniferous period. Sediments are thinner in the west with correspondingly fewer coal seams, whereas the Pennsylvanian and Appalachian coalfields in the east have both thicker sediments and a greater number of coal seams. There may be 60 or more designated seams in the 1700 m of coal-bearing strata. With low-volatile bituminous coal being found in the lower horizons in these coalfields, with high-volatile bituminous coal upper, the coalification is clearly more

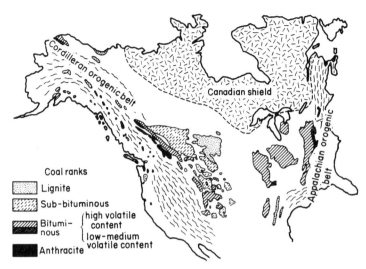

Fig. 3.23   North American geological structure and the distribution of coalfields and
coal ranks

advanced the deeper one goes, and a pattern of coalification ranks prior to
orogenic movements can be established. Basically, the closer a region was to
the eugeosynclines in the east, where vigorous igneous activity occurred prior
to the opening of the Atlantic ocean, the greater the total layer thickness. Also
the deeper the coal layers are buried, the higher the rank of coalification (see
Fig. 3.23). The structures are also more complex towards the east, but the
pressures accompanying structural deformation may not have accelerated the
coalification reaction, since the pattern of coalification ranks is similarly a
deformed version of that existing prior to orogenic movements (Damberger,
1974*).

The Mesozoic coalfields of the western North American continent show
more stable structures and lower ranks of coalification (sub-bituminous
lignite) as we go further away east or south-east from the Cordilleran orogenic
belt, as exemplified by the coalfields in the eastern foothills of the Rocky
Mountains. In the Rockies, the structures become remarkably complex due to
numerous reverse faults, thrusts or recumbent folds, and the rank of
coalification increases from bituminous coal to anthracite in places on the
Canadian side. The thickness of Mesozoic sediment, including the Cretaceous
which constitutes the main coal-bearing unit, increases towards the W or
WNW of the centre of subsidence, the number of coal seams also increasing in
the same direction. On the Canadian side, where the number of coal seams and
thickness of the coal-bearing strata are greater, the rank of coalification also
increases with depth so that the pattern of coalification ranks prior to the
orogenic movements remains intact. The nearer an area is to the central axial

zone of the Cordillera in the west, the higher the rank of coalification. However, there is no observed correlation between the rank of the coal and the severity of deformation, as inferred from the frequency of faults and folds, i.e. with the effects of lateral pressure (Aihara, 1971).

(3) Orogen type Coalfields located in orogenic belts are generally small and show complex variations in their structure and coal rank.

Thin horizontal bedded Tertiary coalfields which have suffered virtually no deformation are widely distributed between the Mesozoic coalfields in the foothills of the Rockies and the Canadian Shield. These are of the cratogen type and provide lignite–sub-bituminous coal. Contemporaneous deposits occur sporadically further west than the Rockies on the Pacific side of the Cordilleran orogenic belt. They are small in scale and are deformed by faults and folds with extreme variation in the rank of coalification. Anthracite is found towards the inside of this zone centring around intrusions (e.g. Mt. Rainier) associated with igneous activity in Cascade orogeny, but the rank of coalification decreases steadily towards the west. This pattern of coalification rank change was produced after the orogenic movements occurred.

Orogen-type coal deposits are often found in the Cenozoic. This may be attributed to the factor that coal deposits form and are buried at fairly shallow levels, so that coalfields in older orogenic belts would often have been completely eroded away. In most cases, therefore, these are only remnants of coal deposits in ancient or orogenic belts which may occur as extensions to intermediate coalfields, for example the Pennsylvanian anthracite field in the Appalachian orogenic belt on the East Coast of North America.

In Table 3.4 we summarize the distribution and reserve (approximate) of world-wide coalfields by area (continent and country) and age, also considering the type of deposit.

(b) Characteristics of Japanese coal deposits

Japanese coal deposits are found mainly in the Palaeogene, and are associated with the Circum-Pacific Cenozoic orogenic belt. The complexity of their geotectonic structures is also very characteristic, as is the high volatile matter and hydrogen contents and high fluidity of the coal. These properties are influenced in part by the large amount of liptinite in the coal and by the inherent character of its vitrinite which is evident by comparison with foreign vitrinite. This must be the result of some specific feature of the coalification process in the Japanese Cenozoic.

Figure 3.24 illustrates depth-related changes in the reflectance of vitrinite (R_0) obtained from borehole samples dating from the Cenozoic to the Upper Cretaceous for the area of Tertiary coalfields and adjacent areas in the Japanese Islands. Depth-related changes in the progress of coalification shown

Table 3.4 Age, coalfield type and reserves (estimated) of major coalfields throughout the world. + 100 million tons or less. Large variation in accuracy of statistics between countries; table indicates relative trends only. Total world reserves: 6 615 500 million tons (after World Energy Conference, 1963)

Region	Country	Devonian	Carboniferous	Permian	Triassic	Jurassic	Cretaceous	Palaeogene	Neogene	Reserves (100 million tons)
North	America		⊙○●				○⊙	⊙●	○	11,000
America	Canada		⊙				⊙	○		610
	Mexico			⊙●			⊙●	⊙●		35
Central	Peru					⊙	●			23
and	Venezuela						⊙●			1
South	Chile							●		2
America	Columbia						●	●		125
	Argentine			⊙		⊙		●		5
	Brazil			○						107
Oceania	Australia			○⊙	⊙	⊙		○		160
	New Zealand						⊙●	●		8
	Mozambique			○⊙						7
	Madagascar			○⊙						+
	Nigeria						⊙			+
	South Africa			○⊙						725
Africa	UAE			⊙						+
	Zambia			○						1
	Zimbabwe			○						66
	Kinshasa			○⊙						1
	Swaziland			⊙						50
Middle	Turkey	⊙		⊙					●	13
and Near	Afghanistan					⊙●				1
East	Pakistan							●	●	17
	Iran					⊙●				10
	India			⊙		⊙		●	●	1,063
	Burma					●			●	+
	Indonesia							●	●	8
	Malaysia								●	+
	Philippines							●	●	+
Asia	Thailand							●		+
	China (Taiwan)								●	3
	Korea		●			●		○		12
	Vietnam				⊙●					10
	China (Mainland)		○⊙	⊙	○	⊙		○		10,110
	Japan				●			●	●	192
	Russia (Asia, Europe)	○	○⊙	○⊙		○⊙	○⊙	○⊙●		42,216
	Hungary					⊙		⊙	●	7
	United Kingdom		⊙			⊙	⊙			155
	France		⊙	⊙						28
	Czechoslovakia		○⊙						○	116
	West Germany		⊙	⊙				○		700
	Portugal		⊙							+
	Holland		⊙							24
Europe	Poland		○⊙					○⊙		457
	Bulgaria		⊙							15
	East Germany		⊙							1
	Rumania					⊙		●		6
	Norway						⊙	○		2
	Austria							●		+
	Spain		⊙							+
	Yugoslavia		⊙							3
	Belgium		⊙	⊙						18
	Sweden		⊙							1
Coalfield type		○ Cratogen type						Total		68,114
		⊙ Intermediate type								
		● Orogen type								

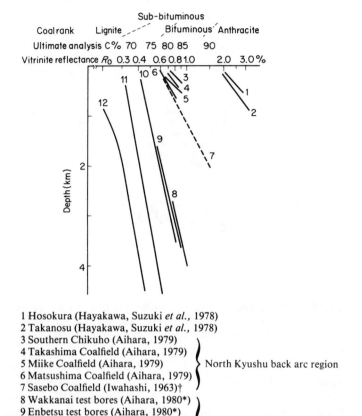

1 Hosokura (Hayakawa, Suzuki *et al.,* 1978)
2 Takanosu (Hayakawa, Suzuki *et al.,* 1978)
3 Southern Chikuho (Aihara, 1979)
4 Takashima Coalfield (Aihara, 1979)
5 Miike Coalfield (Aihara, 1979)   } North Kyushu back arc region
6 Matsushima Coalfield (Aihara, 1979)
7 Sasebo Coalfield (Iwahashi, 1963)†
8 Wakkanai test bores (Aihara, 1980*)
9 Enbetsu test bores (Aihara, 1980*)
10 Masuhoro test bores (Aihara, 1977) } Hokkaido Hidaka fore arc region
11 Hamayuchi test bores (Ujiie, 1978)
12 Niikappu (Morishima *et al.,* 1978)

† Ultimate analysis results (%) by depth and area of vitrinite in main workable layers is converted to R_o and shown by restoring displacement due to Sasagawa fault.

Fig. 3.24   Depth-related changes in vitrinite reflectance in Cenozoic (and part Mesozoic) systems in Japan

by R_o, i.e. the R_o depth gradient, are themselves diverse, but in general may be classified into a high R_o depth gradient group typified by the Northern Kyushu coalfields and a low R_o depth gradient group found in the Cenozoic deposits in the mid-western Hokkaido. Places where the R_o depth gradient is large also tend to have a large R_o value at the surface. Comparing the same R_o value for the two groups, i.e. the depth at which the same degree of organic metamorphism is reached, indicates a much shallower depth for North Kyushu back arc basins than for Hokkaido Hidaka fore arc basins. The reasons for such a major difference in the degree of organic metamorphism between

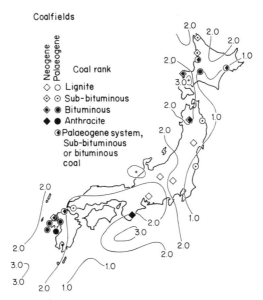

Fig. 3.25   Coalfield and coal rank classification in Cenozoic Japan and variations in terrestrial heat flow. Figures = HFU (10^{-6} cal/cm²s). If one coalfield contains two ranks of coal, half the relevant symbols are shown

deposits of the same geological age, i.e. deposits which would have the same reaction time, are thought to result from differences in the ancient thermal structure of the crust at the time of metamorphism (Aihara, 1980*).

Figure 3.25 outlines the current pattern of terrestrial heatflow and ranks of coalification in the major Cenozoic coalfields of Japan. The terrestrial heatflow is higher in the inner zones of south-west Japan, covering the coalfields of the north-west Kyushu back arc basins and in the so-called green tuff region (Miocene volcanic region) in north-east Japan, than in the coalfield areas of central western Hokkaido (Hidaka fore arc depression). As the thermal structure of the crust in the Tertiary age appears to have been similar to the current situation, this may be combined with the results in Fig. 3.24 to demonstrate that R_0 and the R_0 gradient are larger in areas of higher heatflow and lower in areas of lower heatflow. This means that the Palaeogene coalfields which form the principal coal deposits in Japan were involved in a pair of organic metamorphic reactions, viz. a lower temperature and/or higher pressure type on the Pacific side of north-east Japan and a higher temperature and/or lower pressure type towards the south-west Japan inner zone (Aihara, 1978*).

This pattern of organic metamorphism in Cenozoic Japan is also reflected by differences in the chemical properties of the vitrinite—a reaction product. As shown in Fig. 3.26 the value of H/C in coalfields which are geologically

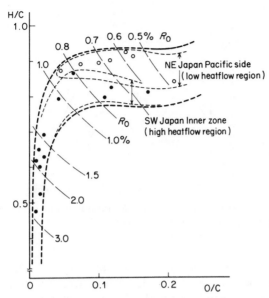

Fig. 3.26 Chemical composition of Japanese vitrinite demonstrating two types of organic metamorphism. (Author's additions to Sugimura *et al.*, 1966*.)

classified as the lower temperature and/or higher pressure type is generally higher than for the higher temperature and/or lower pressure type. Lines of equal R_0 values are also included in the diagram. Because R_0 is governed to a great extent by the atomic refractive index of carbon it correlates with variations in carbon content (C%), but it is difficult to infer the behaviour of functional groups and side chains which split off and dissociate under rising temperatures and falling pressures during the coalification process; analysis of the chemical structure of vitrinite has been attempted by various means. One approach is shown in Fig. 3.27, which illustrates the results of infrared absorption spectrum analysis (Osawa, Sugimura and Fujii, 1969*).

When C%, taken as an index of coalification, is plotted against the specific extinction coefficient at 2920 cm^{-1}, an indicator of aliphatic absorption, it can be seen that the low heatflow areas have a higher specific absorption coefficient. Thus, the high H/C value in low temperature and/or high pressure coalfields may be due to the presence of aliphatic side chains. In other words, in low heatflow areas with remarkable subsidence of the coal basin and thick sediments, the effects of the increasing pressure without large temperature increases may allow aliphatic or hydrogenous side chains to remain. In high heatflow areas, however, where the temperature rose markedly even at shallow depths, they would split off and dissociate far more readily. The more an area tended towards higher temperatures and lower pressures and the longer the reaction time, the more this tendency would be emphasized.

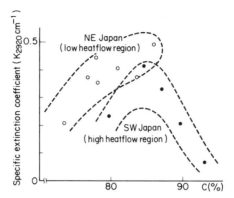

Fig. 3.27 Paired organic metamorphic belts and changes in specific extinction coefficient in IR spectrum of Japanese vitrinite (2920 cm^{-1}). (Author's additions to Osawa, Sugimura and Fujii, 1969*.)

In young orogenic belts, such as the Japanese Islands where the geological data have been examined in detail, such differences in temperature and pressure conditions are reflected in the degree of organic metamorphism. It is thought that similar variations in the degree of coalification may perhaps have also been produced in Mesozoic and Palaeozoic coalfields of the cratogen and intermediate types. Any such ancient coalfield will have experienced much longer reaction times than those in Japan and is more likely to have been affected by geological events, and so is thus likely to have endured a much more complex thermal history. However, if we supplement our organic geochemical data with geological data obtained by prospecting for and developing coal resources in the future, we may expect to improve our understanding of organic metamorphism and its relationship with geological structures in the thermal structure of the crust.

(Atsuo Aihara)

3.11 Petroleum deposits

(a) World distribution of petroleum deposits

Much time has elapsed since Man first began to utilize petroleum. In Japan, which has virtually no oil resources of her own, even the Nihonshoki (one of the oldest Chronicles of Japan) took note of oil as a kind of combustible water. When subsequently it became clear that the various components of petroleum with different boiling points could be separated by heating, petroleum became one of the most vital commodities to human existence, not just as a simple energy source but also as the material on which the whole of petrochemistry is based. Numerous oilfields have been discovered across the

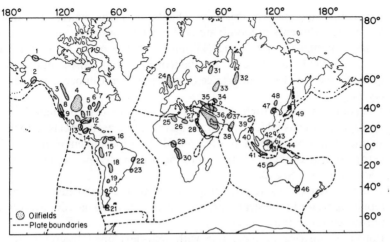

1 North Slope (P ~ T), 2 Cook Inlet (T), 3 Alberta (D), 4 Rocky Mountains (O ~ T), 5 Illinois basin (O ~ C), 6 Michigan basin (O ~ C), 7 Appalachia basin (€ ~ C), 8 San Joaquin (T), 9 Los Angeles (T), 10 Delaware (€ ~ ℞), 11 Wichita (€ ~ P), 12 Gulf of Mexico (T), 13 Tampico (K), 14 Chiapas-Tabasco (K), 15 Maracaibo (T), 16 E. Venezuela (T), 17 Oriente (K), 18 Bolivia (D ~ C), 19 Mendoza (℞), 20 Neuquen (K), 21 Tierra del Fuego (K), 22 Riconcabo (K), 23 Campos (K), 24 North Sea (J,T), 25 Algeria (€ ,D,C), 26 Sirte (Pre € ~ T), 27 Western Desert (T), 28 Gulf of Suez (K, T), 29 Niger delta (T), 30 Gabon, Congo, Angola (K, T), 31 Timan-Pechona (C,K), 32 Volga-Ural (C), 33 W. Siberia (K), 34 Emba (T), 35 N. Caucasus (T), 36 Middle East (J, K, T), 37 Potwar (J, K, T), 38 Gulf of Cambay (T), 39 Assam (T), 40 Irrawaddy (T), 41 Sumatra, Java, (T), 42 Brunei, Sarawak (T), 43 Mahakam delta (T), 44 W. Irian (T), 45 W. Australia (℞ , J, K), 46 Bass Strait (K, T), 47 North China basin (T), 48 Sungliao basin (T), 49 N.E. Japan (T)

Fig. 3.28   World-wide oil-producing zones and ages of oil-bearing strata. (T—Tertiary, K—Cretaceous, J—Jurassic, ℞ —Triassic, P—Permian, C—Carboniferous, D—Devonian, O—Ordovician, € —Cambrian, Pre € —Precambrian.)

world as a result of intense exploration, mainly on the basis of surface indication of oil and the favourable geological structures. One feature of oilfields is that they rarely exist independently, but tend to occur as groups spread over fairly wide areas to form oilfield belts (Fig. 3.28). (Chinese oil-producing areas other than in the Taching field and the North China basin have been omitted for lack of data.)

(b) Factors concerned in oilfield development

Once petroleum became a vital commodity to mankind, the geology of oil-producing zones was surveyed in great detail and the origins of petroleum and its accumulative processes were studied intensely so that greater quantities could be discovered more efficiently. The following factors attracted much attention as the distinctive geoscientific features of areas where petroleum deposits form:

(1) Petroleum appears to originate chiefly in areas where Tertiary and Mesozoic sediments predominate (sedimentary basins of several thousand square kilometres and several kilometres deep) or in areas adjacent to them. Oilfields are found in Palaeozoic strata also, but these are quantitatively of less significance than deposits in Cenozoic and Mesozoic layers.

(2) The source material for petroleum is taken to be organic materials called sapropel kerogens which are extracted from fine grained clastic rocks such as mudstones or shales deposited mainly in a marine environment. These kerogens are thought to turn into petroleum by processes of thermal maturation (see Sec. 2.3).

(3) The petroleum thus formed migrates from the petroleum source rocks replacing water in the strata (primary migration) and moves upwards along porous strata or fault planes (secondary migration).

(4) Porous sandstone or limestone with well-developed fractures (reservoir rocks) must be of a form suitable for accumulation of the petroleum if this is to accumulate. These are known as 'traps', and 80 per cent. of all oilfields are found in anticlinal traps which have a bowl-shaped geological structure.

(5) The trap must be covered with extremely fine grained rocks (cap rocks) to enclose the oil and prevent it from migrating elsewhere.

(6) Crustal movements are thought to play a major role in the formation of traps, from minor deformation to deltas, synchronous with deposition, to major orogenic movements.

(7) If there is deformation after the petroleum has migrated and accumulated, the petroleum may migrate and reaccumulate, but most will probably escape through fissures to the surface, or the oil may break down completely due to igneous activity associated with the deformation. This might explain why Palaeozoic oilfields are quantitatively less significant than more recent ones.

Oil exploration has proceeded on the basis of such observations, and many major fields with recoverable reserves in excess of 500 million barrels (1 kl = 6.29 barrels) were discovered in the latter half of the 1920s and 1930s and also in the early 1960s (Nehring, 1978*). In the mid-1970s exploratory wells were drilled successively in large-scale anticlinal structures (long axis several tens of kilometres, short axis several kilometres) such as in the Bay of Bengal (off Bangladesh and Burma) and the Gulf of Alaska, but no petroleum was found. One reason for this could be the immaturity of the petroleum source material due to low geothermal gradients. Temperature conditions are very difficult to ascertain from surface surveys during the early stages of exploration. However, temperature is one of the fundamental factors in petroleum deposit development, and it must be closely connected with the geological situation underground. Explaining the causes of remarkable temperature variation between areas is thought to hold the key to the enigma of the genesis of petroleum-producing areas. This may also be connected in some way with the origins of sedimentary basins, which will be considered in the next section.

(c) Development of sedimentary basins and the formation of petroleum deposits

For petroleum deposits to form there must be a sedimentary basin and a supply of heat, sufficient to mature them. Geological situations such as this in the Mesozoic and Cenozoic periods are closely associated with plate tectonics (Fig. 3.28). Clearly it is very difficult to establish the movements of plates during the Palaeozoic era, but we have been able to identify some ancient plate boundaries from our improved knowledge of ophiolites and metamorphic zones. The mechanisms of orogenic movements are now explained in terms of relative plate movements. As a result we can provide a global and unified explanation for the genesis of petroleum deposits originating in Palaeozoic strata in the same way as for Mesozoic and Cenozoic deposits.

(1) Development of sedimentary basins The mechanisms whereby sedimentary basins develop may be sought in the three types of plate boundary; namely the convergent, divergent and transform types. Large sedimentary basins develop at convergent plate boundaries associated with folding of the crust and erosion of new continental crust produced by igneous activity. They are thus found around island arcs or continental margins where an oceanic plate is being subducted. If this proceeds further the two continents will collide. Divergent plate boundaries are initiated at a triple junction, and the one 'failed arm', an aulacogen, can form a site for the development of a sedimentary basin in the same way as the continental margins which subsequently diverge and separate. The transform type is initially based on lateral slippage but its subsequent development will follow that of the divergent type.

(2) Convergent-type plate boundaries and petroleum deposits The potential for petroleum development in sedimentary basins along the convergent plate boundaries shows extreme variation, dependent upon the igneous activity caused by the subduction and the location of mélanges. Looking at the basin from the subducting plate, the area which develops to the rear of the zone of igneous activity is termed a back arc basin and that at the front a fore arc basin (Fig. 3.29).

Back arc basins tend to provide the geological conditions necessary for petroleum deposit formation and they frequently develop into major oil-producing zones, i.e. they tend to contain quartz-rich reservoir rocks formed

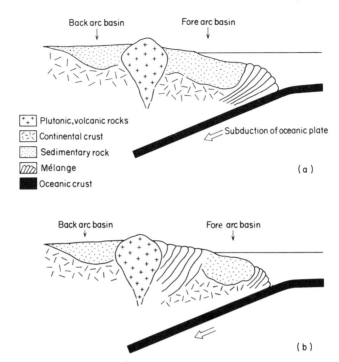

Fig. 3.29   Sedimentary basin developing at convergent-type plate boundaries

from the erosion of granitic rocks, and the heat necessary for petroleum maturation is supplied from igneous activity or the granitic rocks themselves. Folding of the sedimentary strata due to orogenic movements is common, thus producing numerous traps. Such back arc basins are thus of tremendous importance for oil exploration.

The Appalachian basin, the oldest petroleum-producing area in North America, is thought to have developed as a back arc basin in an area of igneous activity (Taconic orogeny) produced in response to the subduction of an oceanic plate. Maturation of the petroleum source materials is believed to have commenced at that time. Continental collison subsequently occurred (Acadian orogeny) and petroleum probably migrated and accumulated in the numerous traps formed as a result of these two series of crustal movements.

The oil-producing areas of Java and Sumatra in Indonesia are also examples of back arc basins. There is great variation in the sizes of oilfields with the largest being the Minas field (discovered 1944, recoverable reserves 600 million kl, ranking 40th in the world), so the area is thus thought to possess great potential. The Oriente basin which extends from southern Colombia to Ecuador and north Peru can also probably be termed a back arc basin. The origin of this sedimentary basin is thought to be a Cretaceious to Tertiary delta formed before the Andes orogeny occurred. Maturation of the petroleum and formation of traps were probably dependent on these orogenic movements. The Shushufindi oilfield discovered in the Amazon jungle in Equador in 1969 ranks 158th in the world with recoverable reserves of 130 million kl.

The Japan Sea side of north-eastern Japan also contains back arc basins with petroleum source materials. There is also the desirable thermal conditions for petroleum formation. Despite this, however, the tuffs formed by subsequent igneous activity have caused a remarkable decline in the reservoir characteristics of the rocks. However, this area is still important as an oil-producing zone to Japan, and there is a strong possibility that new fields will be discovered in future, even if they are only small.

When a fore arc basin is adjacent to a zone of igneous activity, it may become an important oil-producing area in the same way as a back arc basin (Fig. 3.29a). However, if the basin becomes separated from the igneous activity by a mélange (Fig. 3.29b), the heat source would perhaps be removed preventing further maturation of the petroleum. Moreover, both subsidence and deposition proceed rapidly in fore arc basins which are adjacent to active subduction zones, so that a steady rise in temperature is hindered. The reservoir rocks often consist primarily of poorly sorted turbidites, and because rapid deposition impedes dewatering processes, drilling problems often result. As fore arc basins are normally kept cool as a result of the subduction of a cool oceanic plate, they tend not to be of much interest for oil exploration (Fig. 3.29b).

However, the Cook Inlet in Alaska, San Joaquin basin in California and Irrawaddy basin in Burma are examples of oil-producing fore arc basins located between the zone of igneous activity and a mélange.

On the other hand, the northern Gulf of Alaska and the Bay of Bengal referred to earlier are both fore arc basins separated from zones of igneous activity by immensely thick mélanges. It would appear that petroleum has not yet matured at exploitable depths (4–5 km).

The Indian Ocean sides of Java and Sumatra, the Pacific side of Canada and the Pacific side of north-eastern Japan are all similar sedimentary basins, and the results of exploration undertaken so far are not encouraging.

(3) Collision-type plate boundaries and petroleum deposits A collision-type plate boundary represents the final stage of a convergent type. Plate boundaries in the Middle East, where most of the world's major oilfields are found, belong to this category. In such areas maturation of the petroleum is encouraged by heat from igneous activity preceding the plate collision as well as those generated by the collision itself (Fig. 3.30).

From the Palaeozoic to Mesozoic in the Middle East, a sea extended from southern Turkey to the present Persian Gulf, and vast amounts of petroleum source material accumulated there. The sea was quite shallow towards the

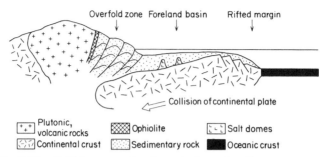

Fig. 3.30   Collision-type plate boundaries and sedimentary basins

Arabian Peninsula and evaporites and limestones formed. Migration of the Afro-Arabian plate towards the north-east began in the Mesozoic era, and the margins of the Eurasian continent became a site of plate convergence. Orogenic movements produced by subduction of the oceanic plate formed the Zagros Mountains in Iran and induced maturation of the petroleum source materials to petroleum. The petroleum thus formed migrated upwards and became caught in numerous massive traps on the Arabian peninsula side (anticlinical structures associated with salt domes or gentle anticlines produced by strata compaction). Following subduction of the oceanic plate, continental collision took place, which turned the front line of the Zagros Mountains into a shallow sea. Thick limestones formed here, to be covered with clastic rocks supplied from the Zagros Mountains. Expansion of the Red Sea accelerated the north-easterly migration of the Arabian plate, and an overfold zone was produced in the forefront of the Zagros Mountains. The thick layers of limestone developed countless fissures during folding and became ideal reservoir rocks. This, we believe, is how the series of oilfields from Iran and Iraq to Turkey developed.

In this connection, in the Red Sea where sedimentary strata reach 3000 m thick, exploration undertaken so far has not yet found them to be of interest. This is thought to be an area where the intense heat due to rifting movements caused petroleum, which had probably already formed, to break down.

The world's largest oilfield, Ghawar, was discovered in Saudi Arabia in 1948. It has recoverable reserves of 13 200 million kl and size-wise is in a class by itself, together only with the Burgan field in Kuwait which has reserves of 11 500 million kl and ranks 2nd in the world. Besides these, the Khafji oilfield discovered by Japanese industry has recoverable reserves of 5000 million kl when combined with the Safaniya field on its southern extension (4th in the world). These massive oilfields are concentrated in the Middle East countries of Iran, Iraq and the United Arab Emirates and have been calculated to account for some 45 per cent., i.e. 82 000 million kl, of the proven world-wide reserves of 180 000 million kl.

The Prudhoe Bay field on the northern edge of Alaska (1500 million kl, 18th in the world) has also been interpreted as the result of continental collision and we discuss this in more detail in Chapter 4.

(4) Divergent aulacogen-type plate boundaries and petroleum deposits The Delaware and Wichita Basins in the mid-continent of the United States, including the east Texas oilfield with slightly under 900 million kl (31st in the world), are thought to derive from an aulacogen.

The Benue trough carved out by the Niger River in Nigeria on the West Coast of Africa is an aulacogen dating from the breakup of Pangaea in the Mesozoic. The Niger delta developed along the Atlantic coast and a major oil-producing zone was formed. Heat supplied from the aulacogen caused maturation of petroleum source material in the adjoining delta. The petroleum was subsequently trapped in traps formed by roll-over folds associated with the growth faults peculiar to the delta. Nigeria possesses recoverable reserves of 3000 million kl, ranking 11th in the world, with the largest field, Jones Creek, accounting for 130 million kl.

The Bombay High oilfield discovered off the Gulf of Cambay in India in 1974 ranks 80th in the world with recoverable reserves of 240 million kl. This too is probably associated with an aulacogen.

(5) Plate boundaries of the interrupted divergent type and petroleum deposits If subsequent movements cease in places where continental breakup has been initiated and thick sedimentary layers have developed, isostatic movements simultaneous with deposition may cause folding or faulting, leading to the formation of traps. In places where divergent plate motions have led to thinning of the crust there is a resultant higher surface heatflow allowing maturation of petroleum source material. The North Sea bounded by Britain and Norway is such a sedimentary basin (Pegrum and Mounteney, 1978*). Britain follows China and ranks 10th in the world with recoverable reserves of more than 3000 million kl. The largest field in the North Sea is the Statfjord field, discovered in 1974 and on a scale to rank 47th in the world with recoverable reserves of 400 million kl.

The Michigan and Illinois basins, which have been important oil-producing zones in the United States, are also examples of interrupted continental separation in the Palaeozoic. In China, the North China basin including the Gulf of Pohai and Sungliao basin, where the Taching field is located (1000 million kl, 30th in the world), seem to be further examples of this type. The Sirte basin in Libya, with reserves of 4000 million kl, and ranking 8th in the world, is also a case of aborted continental breakup. The oil layers extend from the Precambrian right up to the Tertiary systems and comprise several fields, the largest of which is the Sarir field with a capacity of over 1100 million kl (24th in the world), and others in the 600 million kl class. The origin of the

Mineral Resources and Engineering Geology

Hassi Messaud field (25th in the world, 1100 million kl) in Algeria is again thought to be similar. The Gulf of Suez in Egypt also belongs to this group.

(6) Complete separation-type plate boundaries and petroleum deposits If separation at the divergent plate boundaries proceeds fully, continent-derived clastic material can accumulate on the continental margin. As separation continues, the ocean ridge, which provided the heat source, becomes more distant and the petroleum potential of the newer strata is lessened. Oilfields of this type, found on the Atlantic coasts of Brazil, the Congo, Angola and Cabinda, where the supply of heat must have been sufficient in the early stages of dispersal, are on a much more limited scale, the largest being the Malongo West field in Angola (140 million kl).

The Gulf of Mexico on the North American continent corresponds to this type of oil-producing zone. On the other hand, countless exploratory wells have been drilled along the Atlantic coast of North America, but no commercial oilfields have been revealed so far. The reasons for this are thought to lie not only in the low abundance of petroleum source materials but also in the low geothermal gradient (Franks, 1977*).

(7) Transform-type plate boundaries The Los Angeles basin and Ventura basin form an oil-producing zone containing numerous fields, the largest of which is the Wilmington field with a capacity of 450 million kl. Their original form was a Cretaceous fore arc basin but the crust was subsequently disrupted by the transform movement of the North American and Pacific plates. The area developed as a sedimentary basin and petroleum formed probably due to igneous activity associated with thinning of the crust. The oil-producing area cutting across beneath the Bass Strait between Australia and Tasmania (Elliot, 1972*) and the Maui gasfield in New Zealand are also believed to have been located in a similar type of mobile belt.

We have attempted to classify some of the world's oil-producing zones by the origins of their sedimentary basins and to outline the factors which predisposed them to the formation of petroleum deposits. By carefully applying such considerations to as yet unexplored areas, or even areas where exploration has failed, oil-producing zones may yet be revealed. The most important factor in achieving this must be first to gather a detailed scientific dossier on the area concerned and then interpret it correctly.

(Masao Hayashi)

References

Aihara, A. (1978). Stratigraphic coalification pattern and its implication to the geologic development of the Ishikari coalfield, Japan, *Mem. Fac. Sci. Kyushu Univ. Ser. D*, **24**, No. 1, 33–46.

Aihara, A. (1980). Coalification pattern and organic metamorphism of the Paleogene system in the Japanese Islands, in *Prof. S. Kanno Memorial Volume* (Ed. H. Igo and H. Noda), Memorial Assoc. Prof. S. Kanno's Retirement, Tsukuba Univ. pp. 497–510.

Bubnoff, S. (1937). Kohlenbildung in Raum and Zeit, *Glückauf*, **73**, 641–652.

Burke, K., and Dewey, J. F. (1973). Plume generated triple junctions; key indicators in applying plate tectonics to old rocks, *J. Geol.*, **81**, 406–433.

Burnham, C. W., and Ohmoto, H. (1980). Late-stage processes of felsic magmatism. *Mining Geo. Spec. Issue*, **8**, 1–11.

Callahan, W. H. (1967). Some spatial and temporal aspects of the localization of Mississippi Valley-Appalachian type ore deposits, in *Genesis of Stratiform Lead–Zinc–Barite–Fluorite Deposits* (Ed. J. S. Brown), Vol. 3, pp. 14–19, Econ. Geol. Monogr.

Cloud, P. (1972). A working model of the primitive earth, *Am. J. Sci.*, **272**, 537–548.

Damberger, H. H. (1974). Coalification patterns of Pennsylvanian coal basins of the Eastern United States, *Geol. Soc. Am. Sp. Paper*, **153**, 53–74.

Elliot, J. L. (1972). Continental drift and basin development in South East Australia, *Australian Petroleum Exp. Assoc. J.*, **12**, pt. 2, 46–51.

Fischer, R. P. (1974). Exploration guides to new uranium districts and belts, *Econ. Geol.*, **69**, 362–376.

Fleischer, V. D., Garlick, W. G., and Haldane, R. (1976). Geology of the Zambian copperbelt, in *Handbook of Strata-bound and Stratiform Ore Deposits* (Ed. K. H. Wolf), Vol. 6, pp. 223–350, Elsevier, Amsterdam.

Franks, S. G. (1977). *AAPG/SEPM Annual Meeting, Program and Abstracts*, pp. 74–75.

Goldich, S. S. (1973). Ages of Precambrian banded iron formations, *Econ. Geol.*, **68**, 1126–1134.

Goodwin, A. M. (1973). Archean iron-formations and tectonic basins of the Canadian Shield, *Econ. Geol.*, **68**, 915–933.

Hackett, J. P., and Bischoff, J. L. (1973). New data on the stratigraphy, extent and geological history of the Red Sea geothermal deposits, *Econ. Geol.*, **68**, 533–564.

Hodgson, G. J., and Lydon, J. W. (1977). Geological setting of volcanogenic massive sulphide deposits and active hydrothermal systems: some implications for exploration, *Can. Inst. Mining Metall. Bull.*, **70**, 95–106.

Hollister, V. F. (1978). *Geology of the Porphyry Copper Deposits of the Western Hemisphere*, Soc. Mining Engineers, AIME, New York, 219 pp.

Hutchinson, R. W. (1973). Volcanogenic sulfide deposits and their metallogenic significance, *Econ. Geol.*, **68**, 1223–1247.

Jackson, S. A., and Beales, F. W. (1967). An aspect of sedimentary basin evolution, the concentration of Mississippi Valley-type ores during late stages of diagenesis, *Bull. Can. Pet. Geol.*, **15**, 383–433.

Jung, W., and Knitzschke, G. (1976). Kupferschiefer in the German Democratic Republic (GDR) with special reference to the Kupferschiefer deposit in the southeastern Harz foreland, in *Handbook of Strata-bound and Stratiform Ore Deposits* (Ed. K. H. Wolf), Vol. 6, pp. 353–406, Elsevier, Amsterdam.

Lambert, I. B. (1976). The McArthur lead–zinc–silver deposits: features, metallogenesis and comparison with some other stratiform ores, in *Handbook of Strata-bound and Stratiform Ore Deposits*, (Ed. K. H. Wolf), Vol. 6, pp. 535–585, Elsevier, Amsterdam.

Lowell, J. D., and Guilbert, J. M. (1970). Lateral and vertical alteration-mineralization zoning in porphyry ore deposits, *Econ. Geol.*, **65**, pp. 373–408.

Maucher, A., and Schneider, H.-J. (1967). The Alpine lead–zinc ores, in *Genesis of Stratiform Lead–Zinc–Barite–Fluorite Deposits* (Ed. J. S. Brown), Vol. 3, pp. 71–89, Econ. Geol. Monogr.

Naldrett, A. J. (1973). Nickel sulphide deposits—their classification and genesis with special emphasis on deposits of volcanic association, *Can. Mining Metall. Bull.*, **66**, 45–63.

Naldrett, A. J., and Cabri, L. J. (1976). Ultramafic and related mafic rocks: their classification and genesis with special reference to the concentration of nickel sulfides and platinum-group elements, *Econ. Geol.*, **71**, 1131–1158.

Nehring, R. (1978). *Giant Oil Fields and World Oil Resources*, CIA Report R-2284 RAND Corp.

Osawa, Y., Sugimura, H., and Fujii, S. (1969). Chemical structures and properties of heat treated coal in the early state of carbonization XVII, XVIII, XIX. Infra red spectra 1, 2, 3, *Nenryo-Kyokai-Shi*, (in Japanese), **48**, 303–309, 694–702, 703–711.

Pegrum, R. M., and Mounteney, N (1978). Rift basins flanking North Atlantic Ocean and their relation to North Sea area, *Am. Assoc. Petroleum Geologists*, Bull. **62**, 419–441.

Renfro, A. R. (1974). Genesis of evaporite-associated metalliferous deposits: a sabkha process, *Econ. Geol.*, **69**, 33–45.

Rose, A. W. (1976). The effect of cuprous chloride complexes in the origin of red-bed copper and related deposits, *Econ. Geol.*, **71**, 1036–1048.

Sangster, D. F. (1976). Carbonate-hosted lead–zinc deposits, in *Handbook of Strata-bound and Stratiform Ore Deposits* (Ed. K. H. Wolf), Vol. 6, pp. 447–456, Elsevier, Amsterdam.

Sato, T. (1974). Distribution and geological setting of the Kuroko deposits, in *Geology of Kuroko Deposits* (Ed. S. Ishihara *et al.*), pp. 1–14, Soc. Mining Geol. Japan, Tokyo.

Sawkins, F. J. (1976). Metal deposits related to intracontinental hotspot and rifting environments, *J. Geol.*, **84**, 653–671.

Sawkins, F. J., and Rye, D. M. (1974). Relationship of Homestake-type gold deposits in iron-rich Precambrian sedimentary rocks, *Inst. Mining Metall. Trans.*, **83**, sec. B, B56–B59.

Sillitoe, R. H. (1973). The tops and bottoms of porphyry copper deposits, *Econ Geol.*, **68**, 799–815.

Spence, C. D., and de Rosen-Spence, A. F. (1975). The place of sulfide mineralization in the volcanic sequence at Noranda, Quebec, *Econ. Geol.*, **70**, 90–101.

Stanton, R. L. (1972). *Ore Petrology*, McGraw-Hill, New York, 713 pp.

Strauss, G. K., Madel, J., and Fdez. Alonso, F. (1977). Exploration practice for stratabound volcanogenic sulphide deposits in the Spanish Portuguese Pyrite Belt: geology, geophysics and geochemistry, in *Time- and Strata-bound Ore Deposits* (Eds. D. D. Klemm and H.-J. Schneider), pp. 55–93, Springer-Verlag, Berlin.

Sugimura, H., *et al.* (1966). Chemical structure and properties of heat treated coal in the early state of carbonization I. Characteristics of Japanese coal in view of petrographic, proximate and ultimate analyses (in Japanese), *Nenryo-Kyokai-Shi*, **45**, 199–208.

Sutherland Brown, A. (1976). *Porphyry Deposits of the Canadian Cordillera*, CIM Spec. Vol. 15, 510 pp.

Thurlow, J. G., Swanson, E. A., and Strong, D. F. (1975). Geology and lithogeochemistry of the Buchans polymetallic sulfide deposits, Newfoundland, *Econ. Geol.*, **70**, 130–144.

Vezier, J. (1976). Evolution of ores of sedimentary affiliation through geologic history:

relations to the general tendencies in evolution of the crust, hydrosphere and biosphere, in *Handbook of Strata-bound and Stratiform Ore Deposits* (Ed. K. H. Wolf), Vol. 3, pp. 1–42, Elsevier, Amsterdam.

Viljoen, R. P., Saager, R., and Viljoen, M. J. (1969). Metallogenesis and ore control in the Steynsdorp Goldfield, Barberton Mountain Land, South Africa, *Econ. Geol.*, **64**, 778–797.

Viljoen, R. P., Saager, R., and Viljoen, M. J. (1970). Some thoughts on the origin and process responsible for the concentration of gold in the early Precambrian of Southern-Africa, *Mineral. Deposita*, **5**, 164–180.

Further Reading

A good overall textbook on metal deposits is:

Stanton R. L. (1972). *Ore Petrology*, McGraw-Hill, New York, 713 pp.

As its title implies, it intends to treat ore deposits as specific types of rocks (not altogether successfully) and would be useful for geologists not familiar with ore deposits. It also provides important coverage of the various opposing ideas concerning the genesis of ore deposits which lack of space prevented this chapter from discussing.

There are virtually no discussions of the correlation between global evolution and metal deposits apart from the short article:

Watson J. (1973). Influence of crustal evolution on ore depositions, *Trans. Inst. Mining Metall.*, sec. B, **82**, B107–B113.

However, Cloud (1972*) and Vezier (1976*) contain many suggestions relating to their consideration of the evolution of particular sedimentary deposits. Below we cite the major references for each category of deposits discussed.

Volcanogenic massive sulphide deposits

Essential reading for students of this type of deposit relating to the collected research on the Kuroko deposits up to the early 1970s is:

Ishihara, S. *et al.* (Eds.) (1974). *Geology of Kuroko Deposits*, Mining Geol., Spec. Issue 6, 435 pp.

Subsequent developments in the theory of the origins of Kuroko deposits are contained in:

Kozan Chishitsu (*Mining Geology*), Vol. 28 (1978), Nos. 4 and 5.

The following is an excellent account of Precambrian deposits in North America concentrating on the Noranda type:

Sangster, D. F., and Scott, S. D. (1976). Precambrian stratabound massive Cu–Zn–Pb sulfide ores of North America, in *Handbook of Stratabound and Stratiform Ore Deposits (HSSOD)* (Ed. K. H. Wolf), Vol. 6, pp. 129–222, Elsevier, Amsterdam.

Hutchinson (1973*) is perhaps the only general treatment of temporal changes in volcanogenic massive sulphide deposits but its conclusions and method of deposit classification do not correspond with this chapter.

Komatiite-associated nickel deposits

Essential reading for generalized theories about Komatiite-associated nickel deposits is contained in Naldrett (1973*).

Although slightly old, magmatic deposits are dealt with in:

Wilson, H. D. B.(Ed.) (1969). *Magmatic Ore Deposits*, Econ. Geol. Monogr., No 4.

A recent discussion of the origins of magmatic deposits with special reference to platinoids is:

Econ. Geol., **71** (1976), No. 7, An issue devoted to platinum group elements.

Banded iron formations

Econ. Geol., **68** (1973), No. 7, Precambrian iron formation of the world

is to be recommended. This gives an overall perspective of the genesis and recent theories of the formation of globally important banded iron deposits.

A detailed account of the classification, description and economic significance of iron deposits is contained in:

United Nations (1970). *Survey of World Iron Ore Resources*, UNESCO, New York, 479 pp.

Conglomerate-type uranium–gold deposits

The following two papers by Pretorius are useful accounts of the Witwatersrand deposits:

Pretorius, D. A. (1976). Gold in the Proterozoic sediments of South Africa, systems, paradigms and models, *HSSOD*, **7**, 1–28.
Pretorius, D. A. (1976). The nature of the Witwatersrand gold–uranium deposits, *HSSOD*, **7**, 29–88.

On Blind River, there is the following:

Robertson J. A. (1966). The relationship of mineralization to stratigraphy in the Blind River area, Ontario, *Geol. Assoc. Can.*, Spec. Paper 3.

Stratiform lead–zinc deposits in rift zones in the continental crust

A detailed description of McArthur deposits and comparison with similar deposits are found in Lambert (1976*).

A thorough treatment of metalliferous sediments in the Red Sea is contained in:

Degens, E. T,. and Ross D. A. (Eds.) (1969). *Hot Brines and Recent Heavy Metal Deposits in the Red Sea*, Springer-Verlag, New York, 600 pp.

Sandstone shale-type copper deposits

Fleischer, Garlick and Haldane (1976*) and Jung and Knitzschke (1976*) are recent summaries about the copper belt and Kupferschiefer, though the view of the genesis of the deposits is not wholly in agreement with this chapter.

Tourtelot, E. B., and Vine, J. D. (1976): *Copper Deposits in Sedimentary and Volcanogenic Rocks*, USGS Prof. Paper 907 C, 34 pp.

is a neat description of copper deposits in sandstone and shale world wide (including Red Sea-type deposits as classified in this chapter). The bibliography at the end of the volume is also useful.

Mississippi Valley, Alpine-type deposits

The following monograph gives a generalized collection of papers:

Brown, J. S. (Ed.). *Genesis of Stratiform Lead–Zinc–Barite–Fluorite Deposits (Mississippi Valley Type Deposits)*, Econ. Geol. Monogr., No. 3.

Studies of one particular area from many angles are dealt with in:

Econ. Geol., *72* (1977), No. 3, An issue devoted to the Viburnum Trend, South-east Missouri.

Sandstone-type uranium deposits

The following symposium proceedings provide the most complete discussion of the origins of uranium deposits:

IAEA (1974). *Formation of Uranium Ore Deposits*, Intern. Atomic Energy Agency, Vienna, 750 pp.
Packley, R. I. (1976). Origin of western-states type uranium mineralization, *HSSOD*, *7*, 89–156

clearly illustrates the formative environments for sandstone-type uranium deposits in the United States.

A recent special issue on uranium is contained in:

Econ. Geol., **73** (1978), No. 8.

Porphyry copper deposits

A general bibliography for porphyry copper deposits is as follows:

Gustafson, L. B., and Titley, S. R. (Eds.) (1978). Porphyry copper deposits of the south-western Pacific islands and Australia, *Econ. Geol.*, **73**, 597–985.

Hollister, V. F. (1978). *Geology of the Porphyry Copper Deposits of the Western Hemisphere*, Soc. Mining Engineers, AIME, New York, 219 pp.

Ishihara, S. (1969, 1970). *Introduction to Porphyry Copper Deposits* (in Japanese), Lattice Book Co., Tokyo, I Examples 260 pp, II Summary 252 pp.

Sutherland Brown, A. (Ed.) (1976). *Porphyry Deposits of the Canadian Cordillera*, CIM Spec. Vol. 15, 510 pp.

Titley S. R. and Hicks, C. L. (Eds.) (1966). *Geology of the Porphyry Copper Deposits—Southwestern North America*, Univ. Arizona Press, 287 pp.

The following are worth reading together as detailed descriptions and discussion of the genesis of single particular deposits:

An issue devoted to the Bingham mining district, *Econ. Geol.*, **73**, No. 7, 1215–1365.

Gustafson, L. B., and Hunt J. P. (1975). The porphyry copper deposit at El Salvador. Chile. *Econ. Geol.*, **70**, 857–912.

Field, C. W., and Gustafson, L. B. (1976). Sulfur isotopes in the porphyry copper deposit at El Salvador, Chile, *Econ. Geol.*, **71**, 1533–1548.

Sheppard, S. M. F., and Gustafson, L. B. (1976). Oxygen and hydrogen isotopes in porphyry copper deposit at El Salvador, Chile, *Econ. Geol.*, **71**, 1549–1559.

Besides the following essays on porphyry molybdenum deposits, Southerland Brown (above) also includes Canadian examples:

Clark, K. F. (1972). Stockwork molybdenum deposits in the western Cordillera of North America, *Econ. Geol.*, **67**, 731–758.

Wallace, S. R., Muncaster, N. K., Jonson, D. C., Mackenzie, W. B., Bookstrom, A. A., and Surface, V. E. (1968). Multiple intrusion and mineralization at Climax, Colorado, in *Ore Deposits of the United States, 1933–1967* (Ed. J. R. Ridge), pp. 605–640, AIME, New York.

Up to date information on porphyry tin and tungsten deposits is contained in:

Ishihara, S., and Takenouchi, S. (Eds.) (1980). *Granitic Magmatism and Related Mineralization*, Mining Geol. Spec. Issue 8.

Coal deposits

There are virtually no treatments which link coal deposits with the evolution of the crust. The following are general reference volumes dealing with the formation of and changes in coal:

Francis, W. (1961). *Coal, Its Formation and Composition*, 2nd ed., Arnold, London.

van Krevelen, D. W. (1961). *Coal*, Elsevier, Amsterdam, 514 pp.

Murchison, D. G., and Westoll, T. S. (Eds.) (1968): *Coal and Coal-bearing Strata*, Oliver & Boyd, Edinburgh and London, 418 pp.

There are very few works on this in Japan. A relatively recent discussion on coal geology are:

Sakakura, K. (1964). *Coal Geology* (in Japanese), Gijutsu Shoin, 218 pp.
Tanai, T. (1972). *A Consideration on the Formation of Coal Deposits* (in Japanese), Mining Geology, Special Issue, No. 4, Part II, pp. 271–283.

Petroleum deposits

The only major comprehensive although somewhat old textbook on the origin of petroleum deposits, methods of exploration and exploitation written in Japanese is the Japanese Association of Petroleum Technologists' *Petroleum Mining Manual* (1963).

The origins of sedimentary basins in relation to plate tectonics is dealt with in:

Dickinson, W. R. (1974). Plate tectonics and sedimentation, in *Tectonics and Sedimentation* (Ed. W. R. Dickinson) soc. econ. Paleon. Miner. Spec. Pub. No. 22, 1–27.

A discussion of the relationships between the crust and major oilfields is contained in:

Klemme, H. D. (1975). Giant oil fields related to their geologic setting—a possible guide to exploration, *Bull. Canadian Petroleum Geol.*, **23**, 30–66.

The origins of petroleum deposits are discussed in terms of plate tectonics in:

Bullard, E. (1975). Plate tectonics and oil accumulation in Canada's Continental Margins, *Canadian Soc. Petroleum Geol., Memoir*, **4**, 1–7.
Dickinson, W. R., and Yarborough, H. (1976). *Plate Tectonics and Hydrocarbon Accumulation*, Am. Assoc. Petroleum Geol., Continuing Education Course Note Series No. 1.
Thompson, T. L. (1976). Plate tectonics in oil and gas exploration of continental margins, *Bull. Am. Assoc. Petroleum Geol.* **60**, 1463–1501.

Chapter 4

The Development of Continents and Island Arcs and the Formation of Mineral Deposits

In Chapter 3 we made a global survey of the formation and characteristics of several types of mineral deposits in relation to earth's evolution. The formation of mineral deposits must never be discounted as an abnormal geological phenomenon, but always seen as an integral part of general geological processes. It would thus be of considerable value to our understanding of mineralizing processes if we were to look at mineralization in relation to the growth of a single continent. In this chapter we concentrate on North America, for which a wealth of data is available.

Continents have experienced island arc activity in the processes of divergence and collusion, and a wide variety of deposits has been formed. The type of activity in island arc–oceanic trench systems is thought to have varied over geological time, but in order to understand ancient island arc systems we need to study modern examples if our approach is to be consistent. We thus consider arc-trench systems in the Circum Pacific region.

4.1 Continental growth and metal mineralization

In this section we look at when and how the deposits whose origins were discussed in Chapter 3 formed throughout the geological evolution of a single continent, in this case, North America. We discuss petroleum deposits in detail in Sec. 4.2, but mention them briefly here if they occur at the same locality as metalliferous deposits. (The general geology and structures of North America are discussed in Volume 16 of this series.) Lack of space precludes us from a detailed discussion of individual deposits, but interested readers should consult Ridge (1968*) or Douglas (1970*).

(a) Canadian Shield—Archaean

Precambrian rocks of the North American continent crop out widely over the Canadian Shield, which can be structurally divided into several provinces. Of these, Archaean rocks have typically developed in the Superior Province, an area which has been the subject of extensive research. Hence we examine the characteristics of Archaean mineralization with particular reference to this area.

The Superior Province is a single Archaean tectonic unit centred on Hudson Bay and extending to the Great Lakes. Granites and migmatites are ubiquitous but we will concentrate on supracrustal rocks which occur in zones composed chiefly of sedimentary rocks (greywackes, shales) alternating with zones composed mainly of volcanic rocks (Fig. 4.1). Due to the fact that the volcanic rocks become young in a southerly direction (2950–2750 Ma), Goodwin (1972) concluded that the Superior Province had grown from north to south. The principal types of mineral deposits in Superior Province are volcanogenic massive sulphide deposits (Noranda type), nickel deposits associated with komatiite, Algoma-type iron formation and associated gold deposits. In addition to these, copper–gold deposits occur in sheared zones in anorthosites in the Chibougamou area (Fig. 4.1) adjacent to the Grenville Province. All of these deposits are found in the zones of volcanic rocks.

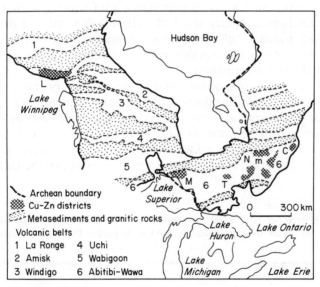

Fig. 4.1   Distribution of volcanic zones in the Superior Protocontinent and copper-
zinc districts. (Simplified from Douglas, 1970*.)

Accumulations of Archaean volcanic rocks are known as greenstone belts and are composed of the products of marine volcanic activity such as komatiite, basalt, andesite, dacite and rhyolite. These belts show one or several basic acidic cycles from the bottom upwards. There are at least five such cycles in the Noranda district (Fig. 4.1) where volcanogenic massive sulphide deposits have accumulated (Spence and Rosen-Spence, 1974), but the main deposits are associated only with acidic volcanic activity in just one of the cycles (see Fig. 3.1). Goodwin (1972) estimated the volcanic rocks in Superior Province to be from 12 000 to 18 000 m thick and put the ratio of basalts : andesites : dacites + rhyolites at about 6 : 3 : 1 overall.

As discussed in Chapter 3, nickel deposits are associated with komatiite or ultrabasic intrusives and Algoma-type iron formations are accompanied by various types of volcanic rock. In Superior Province, iron formations are associated with acidic volcanic rocks (Goodwin, 1973*).

Gold deposits are present as gold–quartz veins in sheared zones or around acidic intrusives, or may be stratabound associated with chemical sediments such as banded iron formations. Gold–quartz vein-type deposits, when plotted regionally, seem to be restricted to certain specific stratigraphic horizons and chemical sediments such as cherts rich in iron are frequently included in these horizons. Hutchinson, Ridler and Suffel (1971*) deduced that the gold was initially concentrated in tuffs and chemical sediments by exhalative processes during volcanic activity and was then redistributed due to subsequent intrusive igneous activity and deformation.

The distribution of gold, nickel and iron ore deposits (or showings) is fairly uniform in all the greenstone belts of the Superior Province but copper–zinc deposits (or showings) are concentrated in the most southerly, i.e. the youngest, greenstone belt, the Abitibi-Wawa zone (Fig. 4.1). This is clearer when one examines the proportions of each type of ore deposit (showings) in each volcanic zone (Table 4.1). As there are suggestions that the La Ronge and

Table 4.1 Relative percentages of the number of mineral occurrences of gold, copper-zinc, nickel and iron in each volcanic zone in Superior Province. (After Goodwin, 1971.)

	Gold	Copper-zinc	Nickel	Iron
Windingo	50	10	15	25
Uchi	48	14	9	30
Wabigoon	52	21	7	20
Abitibi-Wawa	34	50	4	12

Amisk zones in Fig. 4.1 belong to the Churchill Province and that the massive sulphide deposits in the Lynn Lake–Snow Lake areas were formed in the Proterozoic (Sangster, 1972), these areas are not included in Table 4.1.

There is no reasonable explanation as to whether or not such variations in metal species in temporally different Archaean volcanic zones are related to the chemical evolution of mineralization. Globally, however, it is interesting to note that the relative proportion of acidic volcanic rocks is low in older Archaean greenstone belts (e.g. Southern Africa) and no significant copper–zinc deposits are found in them.

No important mineralization is associated with the vast expanse of granites on the Canadian Shield except in small-scale pegmatites which contain some molybdenum, lithium and beryllium.

(b) Canadian Shield—Proterozoic

The boundary between the Archaean and Proterozoic in the Canadian Shield is placed within the Kenoran orogeny, 2500 Ma. Proterozoic sediments consist generally of orthoquartzites, sandstones and carbonate rocks, and appear to be shallow marine sediments deposited on a stable craton. Volcanic activity was less than in the Archaean, and in general tholeiitic basalts were produced. The intrusion of large layered basic–ultra basic sills and anorthosite were other forms of igneous activity which characterized this era.

Volcanic massive sulphide deposits, very similar to those from the Archaean, were formed in areas where calc-alkaline intermediate acidic volcanic rocks had developed (i.e. Lynn Lake–Snow Lake area in Canada, Jerome area in the United states, both aged about 1800 Ma). Proterozoic deposits other than these reflect the differences in sedimentary and igneous activity described above, and tend to have origins different from those formed during the Archaean. The metal species which accumulated were also very different.

The principal mineralizations which occurred in the Canadian Shield during the Proterozoic were as follows: (1) three types of uranium deposit, i.e. conglomerate-type deposits in the Blind River area, vein and disseminated-type pitchblende deposits in the north-west of the Shield and pegmatite deposits in the Grenville Province; (2) Superior-type banded iron formations; (3) nickel–copper deposits in the Sudbury intrusion; (4) Ni–Co–Ag–As deposits in the Cobalt area; (5) copper deposits in and around the Keewatin basalts in the Great Lakes area; (6) stratiform lead–zinc deposits in Sullivan; (7) ilmenite deposits in anorthosite bodies in the Grenville Province. The distribution of these deposits is shown in Fig. 4.2. The characteristics of deposits, which are of interest because their origins are considered to reflect the history of global evolution during the Proterozoic era are discussed below in more detail.

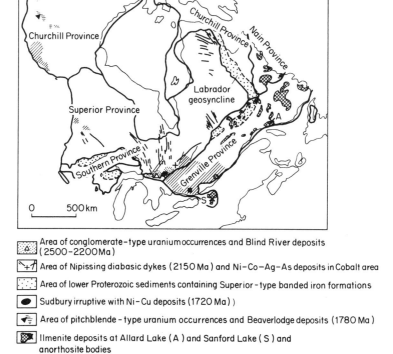

Area of conglomerate-type uraniumoccurrences and Blind River deposits (2500-2200Ma)

Area of Nipissing diabasic dykes (2150 Ma) and Ni-Co-Ag-As deposits in Cobalt area

Area of lower Proterozoic sediments containing Superior-type banded iron formations

Sudbury irruptive with Ni-Cu deposits (1720 Ma)

Area of pitchblende-type uranium occurrences and Beaverlodge deposits (1780 Ma)

Ilmenite deposits at Allard Lake (A) and Sanford Lake (S) and anorthosite bodies

Area of Pegmatite-type uranium occurrences and Bancroft deposits

Fig. 4.2   Proterozoic mineralization and principal deposits in Canadian Shield. (Prepared from Douglas, 1970*.)

The host rocks for the Blind River deposits are conglomerates and sandstones of the early Huronian period (2500–2200 Ma) (Robertson, 1966*). These are alluvial fan or deltaic sediments and clastic material for them was derived from Archaean rocks to the north. As discussed in Chapter 3, their origins are similar to those of the Witwatersrand deposits in South Africa.

The concentration of uranium in the hinterland played an important role in the formation of the deposits, in addition to the uplift of the Archaean basement due to the Kenoran orogenic movements, with the development of stable cratons. Gold is of far less economic significance in the Blind River area, however, than it is in Witwatersrand.

Deposits of uranium around Beaverlodge in Saskatchewan are found as disseminations or veins of pitchblende in gneisses of the Aphebian period (2500–1800 Ma). Mineralization is thought to have occurred in several stages since 1780 Ma (Koeppel, 1968). There is some disagreement as to the origins of these deposits, but the author finds the hypothesis of Langford (1977*) the most credible. This suggests that uraninite, existed primarily in pegmatites in the Aphebian gneisses, was oxidized by the atmosphere, which had then been sufficiently oxidizing. The uranium dissolved in meteoric water then permeated underground to be redeposited in a reducing environment.

At about 2000 and 1200 Ma, major rifting occurred on the North American continent (Burke and Dewey, 1973*).

The Labrador trough was created by a rifting at nearly 2000 Ma, and banded iron formations developed. At about the same time sedimentation was also taking place in the Great Lakes region, accompanied by the development of banded iron formations including the famous Mesabi deposits. Veins of Ag-Ni-Co-As in the Cobalt area of Ontario were formed around the Nipissing dolerite dykes (2150 Ma) which are thought to be precursors to the rifting. The origin of these veins, with their highly specific combination of elements, is not fully understood, but Hutchinson, Ridler and Suffel (1971*) pointed out that deposits formed in places where the dolerite dykes cut across Archaean chemical sediments rich in pyrite. They postulated that silver and sulphur were supplied from the chemical sediments and nickel and cobalt from dolerite.

The rifting that occurred at about 1200 Ma (Fig. 4.3) also led to the

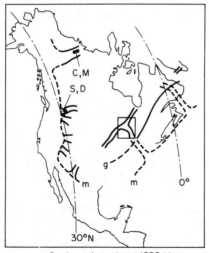

m	Continental margins at 1200 Ma
C	Coppermine R.
D	Coeur d'Alene
g	Grenville front
M	Muscox
S	Sullivan

Fig. 4.3 Rift-aulacogen zones at about 1200 Ma and associated deposits. (Author's additions to Burke and Dewey, 1974.) Broken lines: ancient latitude at about 1300 Ma (after Seyfert and Sirken, 1973*). ☐—see Fig. 4.4.

Mineral Resources and Engineering Geology

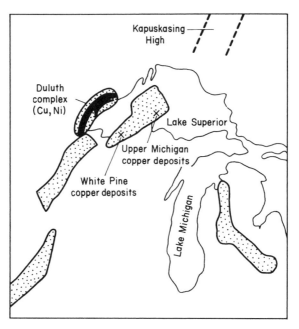

Fig. 4.4 Mineralization near Michipicoten hotspots at about 1200 Ma. (From Sawkins, 1976**.) Dotted areas indicate high gravity areas

development of important ore deposits. Thick tholeiitic plateau basalts typified by the Keweenawan formation erupted onto the Great Lakes region. This type of basalt usually has a high copper content (Sawkins, 1976*), and copper extracted from the basalts by saline connatic water (White, 1968) or by metamorphic water accumulated on top of the basaltic pile or in overlying sediments. The White Pine and Upper Michigan deposits in Michigan (Fig. 4.4) are amongst those formed in this way. Although as yet undeveloped, the same process of mineralization in this period is thought to have occurred in the Coppermine River area in northern Canada (Fig. 4.3).

Enormous quantities of basic rock derived from magma with the same source as the plateau basalts, mentioned above, was intruded along the central axis of the rift zone, with the accumulation of nickel, copper and chromite. The Duluth intrusive body in the Great Lakes region and the Muskox intrusive body in northern Canada are examples of intrusions which formed on the North American continent at about 1200 Ma. Copper and nickel mineralization occurred in the Duluth complex, and chromite has accumulated in the Muskox. Neither has yet been exploited because of quality, location and environmental constraints, but they have considerable potential as future resources.

The largest lead–zinc–silver deposits in Canada—the Sullivan deposits—formed in an aulacogen which developed on the western margin of the continent during this period (Kanasewich, 1968*) (Fig. 4.3). The Coeur d'Alene deposits in Idaho, USA, which are adjacent to the Sullivan deposits, constitute the largest lead–zinc–silver resources in the United States. The mineralization occurs as veins or disseminations, and data such as lead isotope ratios have indicated that they might possibly be regenerated Sullivan-type deposits.

As yet the Sudbury irruptive, which contains the largest nickel–copper deposits in the world, has not been mentioned. The reason for this is that if the theory of Dietz (1964) is correct in claiming it to be a meteorite crater, the formation of the Sudbury irruptive is not pertinent to the history of tectonic development in North America. However, because the age of its formation (1950 Ma) corresponds with the period of rifting at about 2000 Ma, it has also been regarded as an intrusion along the central axis of a rift like the Duluth and Muskox intrusions (e.g. Sawkins, 1976*).

Figure 3.1 indicates that carbonate rocks formed increasingly during the Proterozoic and from about the middle of the era evaporites also developed. The importance of these two rock types to the development of Mississippi Valley-type deposits has already been discussed and several deposits, thought to be of this type, are found on the North American continent at the end of the Proterozoic (Sangster, 1976*). These include zinc deposits in the Balmat-Edwards area of New York State and the Franklin-Sterling zinc deposits in New Jersey which are famous for the occurrence of various minerals. Both of these deposits are stratiform–massive deposits occurring in marble. Anhydrite layers, believed to have originated from evaporites, have developed around the Balmat-Edwards deposits.

(c) Interior lowlands

Several marine transgressions and regressions since the beginning of the Palaeozoic over the Precambrian basement of the interior lowlands of North America have built up Phanerozoic strata which have been virtually unaffected by deformation. Various economic resources have developed there, viz. petroleum and coal, rock salt, sandstone-type uranium deposits and Mississippi Valley-type Pb–Zn deposits, etc. The genesis of these ore deposits was closely bound up not only with processes of sedimentation but also with the ancient climate and the tectonics of the surrounding orogenic zones. A summary of these is shown in Fig. 4.5.

The first marine transgression in the Palaeozoic occurred from the Mid-Cambrian to the Ordovician. When the transgression was at its maximum virtually the whole of the North American continent was under water except for the Canadian Shield and the Transcontinental Arc which extended from it.

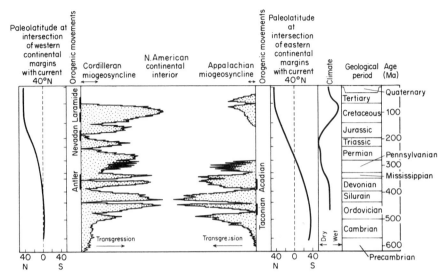

Fig. 4.5 Phanerozoic transgression and regression, paleolatitudes, climate, etc., in North American interior lowlands. (Author's additions to Seyfert and Sirkin, 1973*.)

The regression of the Mid-Ordovician coincided exactly with the Taconic orogenic movements in the Appalachian geosyncline, and part of the Appalachian miogeosyncline appeared as land. Limestone karsts produced along unconformities became sites for the deposition of Mississippi Valley-type deposits in the Appalachian belt, such as in East Tennessee-Austinville and Timberville (Hoagland, 1976*). Heat supplied by the igneous activity associated with orogenesis was important in the formation of petroleum in the Appalachian belt, as discussed in Sec. 4.2. This heat must also have contributed to the formation and migration of the mineralizing solutions which created the Mississippi Valley-type deposits. The Appalachian belt was then uplifted during the Devonian in response to Taconic and Acadian orogenic movements. Finally, large quantities of clastic material were supplied to the interior lowlands. The Silurian hematite ores in Clinton and low grade uranium found in lower Mississippian Chatanooga shales are the results of sedimentary mineralization processes in shallow marine sediments.

Sedimentary mineralization in the interior lowlands was not uniform, and Palaeozoic basin structures may be found (Fig. 4.6). Palaeozoic sediments, including evaporites, up to several kilometres thick were deposited in these basins. The sediments are particularly thick in the Allegheny, West Texas and Williston basins found on the continental margins. Large quantities of petroleum and coal have developed in these basins (see Sec. 4.2) and many Mississippi Valley-type deposits have developed in the surrounding limestone (Heyl, 1969*).

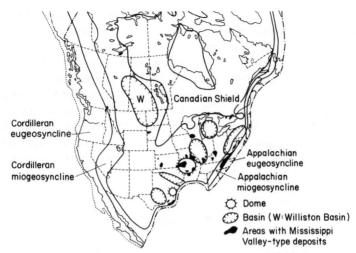

Fig. 4.6   Structural elements of North America in the early Palaeozoic and location of Mississippi Valley-type deposits. (Author's additions to Seyfert and Sirkin, 1973*.)

The enormous Williston basin which runs along the Cordillera from the northern United States into Canada contains the Alberta oilfield and oil sands in its western extension (Elk Point basin). The world's largest sylvite (KCl) deposits are also found in its thick Devonian evaporites. Almost total evaporation of sea water is required for sylvite to be deposited. In addition to appropriate climatic conditions, another essential factor for the development of such thick evaporites must have been the formation of a closed marine basin when the Cordillera belt was uplifted during the Antler orogeny. The origins of these basins will be discussed in Sec. 4.2, and one should note particularly that evaporites, Mississippi Valley-type deposits and petroleum are found together in each case.

A major marine regression occurred from the end of the Palaeozoic to the Triassic. Remarkably thick deposits of red sandstone and evaporite developed in the interior lowlands, due to the dry climate of the period. Mineralization in the lowlands was limited to small-scale sandstone-type copper deposits.

However, at the end of the Palaeozoic the continent began to drift northwards following the breakup of Pangea. By the Jurassic the whole of North America had entered central latitudes (see Fig. 4.5). Great changes in sedimentation patterns in the so-called 'forelands' of the Mesocordillera belt were caused by orogenic movements associated with Nevadan orogeny in the Triassic–Jurassic periods, and Laramide orogeny in the Cretaceous–Palaeogene periods. As outlined below, together with the changes in life forms, these changes in sedimentation helped to provide conditions ideal for the formation of sandstone-type uranium deposits such as those on the Colorado plateau or Wyoming basins.

   The principal strata containing uranium deposits are Triassic–Jurassic on the Colorado plateau and Palaeogene in the Wyoming basins. Both deposits are composed of deltaic sediments brought down by rivers from uplifted blocks. They contain fossilized vegetation, such as carbonized trees. The presence of such carbonaceous material is vital for uranium liberated from uranium-rich rocks in exposed Precambrian basement to be fixed and concentrated as ore deposits. The Jurassic Morrison formations, which contain the uranium-bearing layers of the Colorado plateau, are also famous for their dinosaur fossils—indicating that the climate at that time was temperate and relatively damp. Figure 4.7 illustrates both the relationship

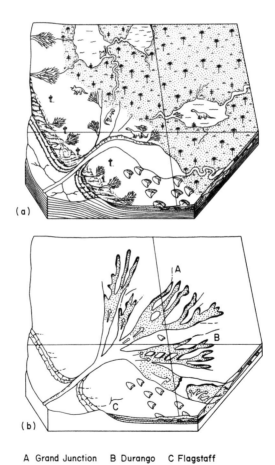

A Grand Junction   B Durango   C Flagstaff

Fig. 4.7   (a) Palaeogeography and (b) location of uranium deposits during deposition of Morrison formation at Colorado Plateau. (Stippled area—oxidation and elution zone; thick black areas—uranium deposits.) (After Packley, 1976*.)

between the palaeogeography and life forms when the Morrison formation was deposited, and the sites where uranium accumulated.

(d) Appalachian belt

The claim by Wilson (1966) that North America split away from Eurasia at the end of the Proterozoic so producing the proto-Atlantic Ocean has now gained general acceptance. At the beginning of the hotspot and rift activity (ca. 800 Ma) which initiated the continental breakup, carbonatite and basaltic lavas and dykes were produced in the Appalachian belt. No remarkable mineralizations are associated with this igneous activity but stratiform copper (zinc) deposits (Fig. 4.8) in the Ducktown area of Tennessee and Ore Knob in

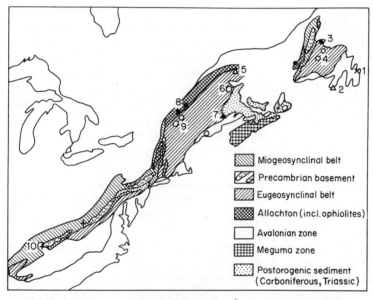

Miogeosynclinal belt

Precambrian basement

Eugeosynclinal belt

Allochton (incl. ophiolites)

Avalonian zone

Meguma zone

Postorogenic sediment
(Carboniferous, Triassic)

+ Massive sulphide deposits in upper Precambrian sediments. 10—Ducktown (Cu)
× Sedimentary hematite deposits in Ordovician shallow marine sediments. 1—Wabana
○ Massive sulphide deposits in acidic volcanic rocks of Cambrian–Ordovician periods (Kuroko-type). 4—Buchans (Cu–Pb–Zn–Au–Ag), 6—Bathurst–Newcastle area (Cu–Pb–Zn–Ag), 9—Eastern Townships
● Massive sulphide deposits in Cambrian–Ordovician ophiolites. 3—Betts Cove area (Cu)
■ Asbestos deposits in ophiolites of Cambrian–Ordovician periods. 8—Thetford area
△ Deposits associated with Devonian granites. 2—St. Lawrence (CaF₂), 5—Gaspé Copper (Cu-Mo)
▲ Deposits in Carboniferous continental volcanic rocks. 7—Mt. Pleasant (W-Mo-Sn-Bi-Cu-Zn).

Fig. 4.8   Principal deposits in Appalachian orogenic belt (excl. Mississippi Valley-type deposits). (Structural divisions after King, 1977.)

North Carolina are thought to be mineralizations in such rift zones or their associated aulacogens (Sawkins, 1976*). If this is the case we can classify them as Red Sea-type deposits (discussed in Chapter 3).

Eugeosynclines in the southern Appalachians correspond to the Blue Ridge and Piedmont zones, but whereas there is extensive exposure of upper Precambrian sediments containing the Ducktown deposits, and of basement rocks involved in Grenville orogeny, lower Palaeozoic rocks are rare. These lower Palaeozoic rocks comprise sediments with few of the island arc-type submarine volcanic rocks which produced significant volcanogenic massive sulphide deposits in the northern Appalachians. Therefore no significant mineralization occurred in the eugeosynclinal zone of the southern Appalachians.

In the lower Palaeozoic, thick sediments, mainly carbonate rocks, accumulated in the Valley and Ridge belt on the inner side of the Blue Ridge zone, which corresponds to a miogeosyncline. As mentioned earlier, this miogeosynclinal zone and the Palaeozoic basins formed further towards the continental interior yield petroleum, evaporites and Mississippi Valley-type Pb–Zn deposits, forming one of the most important mineral-producing areas in the southern Appalachians. These sedimentary basins are interpreted to be places where continental breakup has been interrupted mid-way (see Sec. 4.2), and provided favourable conditions for the simultaneous development of petroleum, evaporites and Mississippi Valley-type deposits.

The eugeosyncline in the northern Appalachian belt runs from central Newfoundland across the New Brunswick and Quebec Province boundaries into New England. Extensive Cambrian–Ordovician island arc-type volcanic rocks from this belt are found containing many volcanogenic massive sulphide deposits. The principal deposits are concentrated in the Bathurst–Newcastle area of New Brunswick, the Eastern Townships of Quebec and the Central Mobile belt of Newfoundland.

Many lead–zinc-(copper) deposits have developed in the Mid-Ordovician acidic volcanic rocks in the Bathurst–Newcastle area. These deposits are reminiscent of the Kuroko deposits in Japan in terms of the combinations of sulphide minerals and their close association with acidic volcanic rocks, but there are differences also, particularly in the fact that they lack sulphate minerals such as barytes or gypsum, and thick iron layers are found overlying the deposits.

The volcanic rocks which gave rise to the Eastern Townships deposits are Mid-Ordovician, but these are relatively deficient in acidic rocks and rich in basic rocks. The ore deposits are associated with small amounts of acidic volcanic rocks (mainly rhyolitic tuffs) but in comparison with the Bathurst–Newcastle deposits they lack lead but are rich in copper.

According to Bird and Dewey (1970*) the island arc in the northern Appalachians at the beginning of the Palaeozoic resembled the double-arc system of the Philippines–Marianas today, the Bathurst–Newcastle area corresponding to the outer and the Eastern Townships to the inner island arcs. Julian and Hubert (1975) proposed that the basement for the Palaeozoic volcanics of the Eastern Townships area is oceanic crust. Such differences in the island arc structure and properties of the basement are thought to have determined the composition of the volcanic rocks and their associated mineral deposits.

The Appalachian belt was subjected to Taconic orogeny in the late Ordovician and to Acadian orogeny in the Devonian, by which time the proto-Atlantic Ocean is thought to have closed completely. Both series of orogenic movements were associated with granitic intrusions, but copper, molybdenum, tungsten and fluorite mineralization is particularly pronounced in those that were intruded at Acadian orogeny. Amongst these, Gaspé Copper in Quebec is the only example of porphyry copper deposits in the Appalachian belt, and the St. Lawrence deposits in Newfoundland are also important for fluorite.

With the final closure of the proto-Atlantic Ocean, oceanic crust thrust over the continental crust and formed an ophiolite zone extending from the north of Newfoundland to eastern Quebec, which contains small Cyprus-type deposits such as Betts Cove and podiform chromite mineralization. Thetford and Asbestos in Quebec contain the world's largest asbestos mines.

The Wabana haematite deposits are found in shallow marine sediments of Early Ordovician age in the Avalonian zone, which lies on the outer side of the eugeosyncline. These closely resemble the Clinton deposits and are interpreted as shallow marine sediments on the continental margins of the palaeo-African continent or as a microcontinent which existed in the palaeo-Atlantic.

Figure 4.9 provides a schematic representation of the tectonic setting of each type of deposit mentioned above.

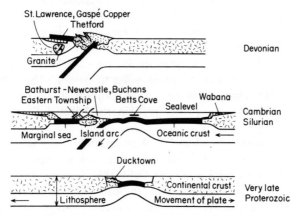

Fig. 4.9 Schematic diagram showing Palaeozoic plate tectonics in Appalachian orogenic zone and sites of mineralization

The Mt. Pleasant deposits in Nova Scotia, with a highly characteristic metal combination of W–Mo–Bi–Sn–Cu–Zn, are the result of mineralization in the caldera of a continental volcano of Mississippian age. No other similar deposits are known in the Appalachian belt, and the tectonic situation which led to the volcanic activity is also obscure.

The reopening of the Central Atlantic is thought to have been initiated at about 180 Ma (Pitman and Talwani, 1972). Contemporaneous rifting produced numerous graben along the eastern side of the North American continent (Burke, 1976). Extrusion of basaltic lavas and dyke intrusion occurred in and around these graben, mainly in the Triassic, the famous Palisade diabase being an example of this. In cases where dykes crosscut lower Palaeozoic limestone, Cornwall-type magnetite deposits (containing small amounts of copper) were formed in the limestone. The Canadian Shield also contains graben of the same age, regarded as the failed arms of rift zones (Dewey and Burke, 1974), which have minor amounts of carbonatite and kimberlite. The Oka deposits in Quebec, which are the largest source of niobium in North America, are found in such carbonatites.

By the end of this period, the Appalachian belt formed a continental margin of the so-called 'Atlantic' type and no further notable metallogenesis occurred.

(e) Cordilleran belt

The Cordilleran belt, from the Precambrian to Mesozoic, has a complex history, including the formation of rift zones, the development of island arcs and marginal seas associated with the subduction of the oceanic plate and collisions with microcontinents and island arcs (e.g. Burchfield and Davis, 1972, 1975; Monger *et al.*, 1972). The major ore deposits produced during this time are illustrated in Figs. 4.10 and 4.11.

Stratiform lead–zinc deposits occur in the Anvil area in the Canadian Cordillera within sediments of the Tintina geosyncline which is of Eocambrian or Cambrian age. The host rocks principally consist of clastic sediments, but also contain small quantities of basic volcanic rocks. The sediments are thought to have been deposited in a rift zone (Burchfield and Davis, 1975) and the origin of the deposits is probably akin to the Red Sea or McArthur deposits.

Other mineral deposits shown in Fig. 4.10, excluding Reeves-Salmo, are all massive sulphide deposits associated with island arc volcanism. The copper–zinc deposits in the East Shasta area of California developed in the Devonian period, whereas Triassic deposits rich in lead and barytes are found in neighbouring West Shasta. Where island arc activity was repeated in the same area in this way, the massive sulphide deposits associated with the younger island arc are richer in lead and barium. This has been reported from several

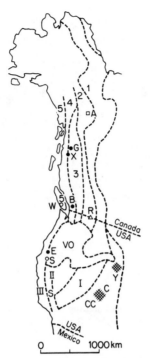

I Miogeosynclinal belt, II Eugeosynclinal belt, III Coastal mountains, S Sierra Nevada Mts., VO Columbia plateau + Cascade Mts., CC Colorado plateau + central southern Rockies
Structural zones in Canadian Cordillera (1–5) as Fig. 4.11.
○ Cu–Pb–Zn deposits in island arc volcanic rock (W—Western, S—West Shasta)
● Cu–(Zn) deposits in island arc volcanic rock (G—Granduc, X—Anyox, B—Britania, E—East Shasta)
□ Pb–Zn–(Cu) deposits in shelf sediments (A—Anvil)
△ Pb–Zn deposits in carbonate rocks (R—Reeves-Salmo)
※ Sandstone-type U deposits (C—Colorado Plateau, Y—Wyoming Basins)
Fig. 4.10   Structural divisions of N. American Cordillera and major deposits (excl. porphyry-type)

other areas and may be taken as an indication of the 'evolution' of the ore deposits associated with the development of the island arc (Hutchinson, 1973*).

The Cordilleran orogenic belt developed into a geanticline as a result of Nevadan (Jurassic period) and Laramide (Late Cretaceous–Early Palaeogene periods) orogenic movements. As previously mentioned, continental clastic sediments from the uplifted blocks became the host rocks for uranium deposits in the Colorado plateau and Wyoming basins.

The Nevadan orogeny caused strong deformation and metamorphism of the eugeosynclinal sediments, resulting in the intrusion of many large granitic batholiths. The Laramide orogeny caused some deformation in the foreland to

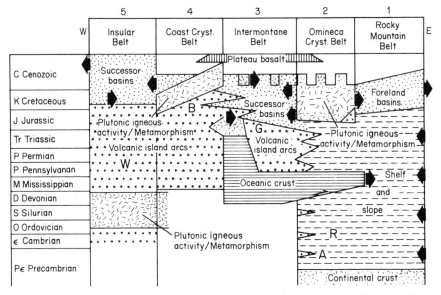

Fig. 4.11   Variations in igneous and sedimentary activity in the Canadian Cordillera. (After Eibacher, 1974.) B, G, W, A, R as Fig. 4.10.

the east, forming small granitoid bodies, but no intrusion of batholiths occurred.

The prophyry copper deposits which are one of the most important mineral resources in the United States, are mainly associated with the small granitic intrusives of the Laramide period (see Sec. 4.2 for a plate tectonic interpretation of the Laramide orogeny). The majority of the intrusive rocks related to the ore deposits have been dated at 80–35 Ma. Their ages tend to become younger from the Yerington deposits (111 Ma) on the east of the Sierra Nevada batholith towards those found in northern Mexico to the south-east (59, 53 Ma) (Fig. 4.12).

Porphyry copper deposits in western Canada are also found principally in the Intermontane belt where similar small-scale granitoid rocks are found. Very few ore deposits occur in the Coast Crystalline or Omineca Crystalline belts on either side of the batholith (Fig. 4.13). Porphyry copper–gold deposits are associated with alkaline granitoids, and prophyry copper or copper–molybdenum are associated with calc-alkaline granitoids. The former date from the Late Triassic–Early Jurassic periods (200–175 Ma) whereas the calc-alkaline granitoids formed during several periods: Early Jurassic (200–175 Ma), late Jurassic (155–140 Ma), Late Cretaceous–Palaeogene (80–35 Ma) and Neogene (26–18 Ma). The Early Jurassic and Late Cretaceous–Palaeogene deposits are the most important in terms of resources. There is a tendency for the deposits to become younger towards the interior of the continent.

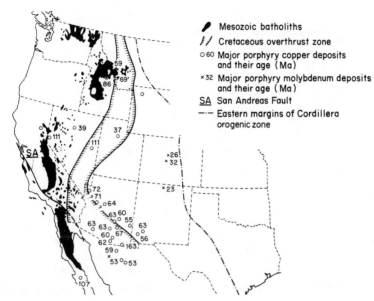

Fig. 4.12 Age and distribution of major porphyry copper deposits in Southern Cordillera. (After Hollister, 1978.)

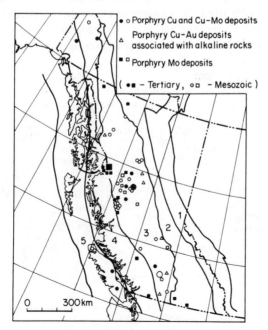

Fig. 4.13 Distribution and age of porphyry copper deposits in Canadian Cordillera (After Christopher and Crater, 1976.) 1–5 correspond to structural zones in Fig. 4.11.

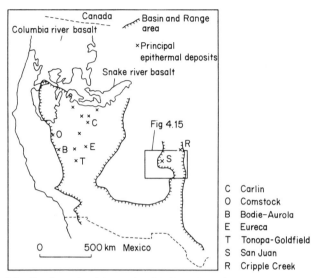

Fig. 4.14   Distribution of epithermal gold-silver deposits in Basin and Range area

During the Cenozoic the Cordillera was characterized by intermediate and acidic volcanic activity until the beginning of the Miocene, and by basaltic volcanic activity from the Late Tertiary to the Quaternary and an extensional tectonic regime led to the formation of Basin and Range topography. The reason for such an extreme change in the type of igneous activity and tectonic

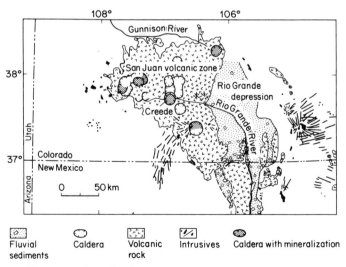

Fig. 4.15   Epithermal mineralization associated with calderas in San Juan. (After Lipman *et al.*, 1976*.)

situation is probably due to the subduction of the East Pacific rise under North America which began in the Middle Tertiary (e.g. Menard, 1964).

Intermediate to acidic igneous activity in the Basin and Range zone during the Eocene, Oligocene and Early Miocene periods mainly involved the eruption of ignimbrites with the formation of numerous calderas. Numerous epithermal gold and silver veins formed in these calderas (Figs. 4.14 and 4.15).

Several hot springs, associated with Quaternary volcanic activity, formed hot spring deposits containing mercury, silver or antimony, as shown in Fig. 4.16. White (1974*) considered that the water in Steamboat Springs was derived from circulating meteoric water and that the hot spring activity was a surface manifestation of ephithermal gold–silver mineralization. The hot spring deposits in and around Sulfur Bank are exploited as mercury ore, and the source of the hot spring water is thought to be metamorphic water, this area overlying the Franciscan formation. Imperial Valley (Salton Sea) is a geothermal area which follows the San Andreas fault. The salinity of the very hot underground water is extremely high, and it contains large quantities of

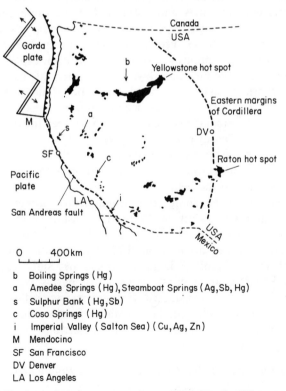

b Boiling Springs (Hg)
a Amedee Springs (Hg), Steamboat Springs (Ag,Sb, Hg)
s Sulphur Bank (Hg,Sb)
c Coso Springs (Hg)
i Imperial Valley (Salton Sea) (Cu,Ag, Zn)
M Mendocino
SF San Francisco
DV Denver
LA Los Angeles

Fig. 4.16 Distribution of Quaternary volcanoes in the Cordillera and hot springs associated with deposition of heavy metals

silver, zinc and lead. The water is assumed to derive from meteoric water, with the high salinity being attributed to the dissolution of rock salt (Craig, 1966*).

(Takeo Sato)

4.2 Petroleum-generating basins of North America and their tectonics

Petroleum exploration carried out to date indicates that petroleum deposits are restricted to sedimentary basins. Although there are many sedimentary basins containing petroleum, there are also many which do not, so an understanding of the reasons has become one of the most important topics of research in petroleum geology.

The long history of exploration has shown the following conditions to be essential to the formation of petroleum deposits: the emergence of a place where sedimentary strata can form; the deposition of petroleum source materials; the presence of heat to convert these into petroleum; the deposition of porous reservoir rocks to collect the petroleum; the presence of traps to which the petroleum migrates and accumulates; the presence of fine 'cap' rocks to prevent the accumulated petroleum from escaping to the surface.

Although some of these geological phenomena are the result of deformation, particular emphasis in practical petroleum exploration is placed on the thickness of the sedimentary layers and the size of the trap. Therefore the standard criteria of assessment used by the petroleum geologists tend to rely on the size of the basin and presence or absence of traps, and no criteria based on global and systematic considerations have been introduced.

However, Bird and Dewey (1970*) have explained the two series of orogenic movements which occurred in the Appalachia of North America during the Palaeozoic era in plate tectonic terms. Adapting this theory on the basis of scientific evidence led to the belief that plate tectonics could perhaps play an important role in establishing the fundamental directions petroleum exploration should take (Dickinson, 1976*; Thompson, 1976*). In this section we look at several areas in North America (Fig. 4.17) and consider their petroleum geology against a background of plate tectonics. As oil-producing areas of Appalachia, Illinois, Michigan, Cook Inlet, San Joaquin, Southern California and the Atlantic coast sedimentary basins were mentioned in Chapter 3, they are not considered further. As we believe that the oil-producing areas of Canada can be explained in the same manner as the Cordilleran areas these too are omitted from this section.

(a) The Eastern margins of the Cordillera and the Rocky Mountains

The North American Cordillera extends from Canada to Mexico, and its eastern margins are characterized by countless groups of overthrust faults and

Fig. 4.17   Oil-producing zones in North America

their associated overfolds. The Rocky Mountains lie further to the east of this zone and here, instead of overthrusts and overfolds, the basement has been uplifted to a height of several thousand metres (Fig. 4.18). The overfold zone and the intermontane basins in the Rockies are major areas for petroleum

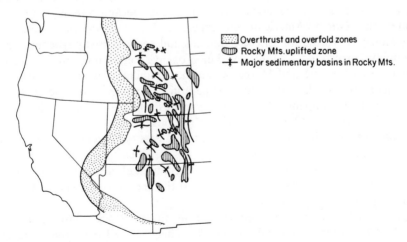

Fig. 4.18   Eastern margins of the Cordillera and Rocky Mts

prospecting, and the detailed crustal changes, both temporal and spatial, that occurred have been studied intensely. Major events in this respect were the development of the Cordillera in response to igneous activity in the Early Mesozoic, mid-period movements, principally overthrust faulting and overfolding, along the eastern margins of the Cordillera, and uplifting of the basement in the Rockies between the Late Mesozoic and Early Tertiary periods. These are known respectively as the Nevadan, Sevier and Laramide orogenies.

The relationship between the tectonics of these three series of orogenic movements and the formation of petroleum deposits is not yet fully understood. However, recent interpretations which attempt to explain the orogenic movements systematically on the basis of plate subduction seem to go some way to solving the problem. This approach is examined below.

Marine sediments, dating from the Late Precambrian (1200–800 Ma) to the Mesozoic, increase in thickness rapidly on the western edge of the overfold zone of the Cordillera named the Wasatch Line by Marshall Kay (1951). Precambrian metamorphic basement blocks enclosed by these strata remain as mountain chains or highlands in Utah and Nevada. The process whereby such a geological situation evolved could be as follows: the North American continent split around the Wasatch Line in the Precambrian. A new oceanic plate was produced and a sea developed. Sedimentation and subsidence continued until the Mesozoic, forming great thicknesses of marine strata. Fragments of the continental crust left behind after the continental split occurred are now mountain chains and highlands composed of metamorphic rocks, and one margin of the rifted continent now corresponds to the Wasatch Line.

The breakup of Pangea subsequently occurred during the Mesozoic and the oceanic plate mentioned above formed in the Precambrian was subducted under the North American continent, which was drifting westwards. Consequent deformation of the sediments and accompanying igneous activity probably correspond to the Nevadan orogeny. Petroleum source materials from the Palaeozoic and Mesozoic marine sediments were transformed into petroleum as a result of the rising temperature associated with igneous activity and burial of sediments. Horizontal compression due to subduction of the plate and intrusion of large quantities of igneous material gradually pushed the Precambrian to Mesozoic rocks towards the east, producing overthrust and overfold belts. This is the Sevier orogeny. Petroleum, which had probably already formed and migrated, finally accumulated in traps made by the anticlines in these overfolds, so leading to the creation of some of the most important deposits in North America.

Furthermore, many sedimentary basins in the Rocky Mountains were enclosed by uplifted Precambrian blocks. This occurred from the Cretaceous to the Eocene, resulting in heights of several thousands of metres. A particular feature of this deformation (the Laramide orogeny) was that it was unaccompanied by igneous activity.

According to Lowell (1974a*, 1974b*), deformation in the Rocky Mountains is attributable to folding and strike-slip faulting due to horizontal compression, and to the vertical movements mentioned above, all of which have been superimposed over each other, this deformation being caused by the subduction of a plate from the western margins of North America underneath the Rocky Mountains. In short, in the early stages of subduction (Fig. 4.19a) horizontal compression produced folds and strike-slip faults, and as the plate was subducted further, its own buoyancy brought about the vertical movements of the crust. As the subducted plate would not have been uniformly thick, there would have been variations in its buoyancy, so producing relative uplift and depression (Fig. 4.19b). The final result was the distinctive topography seen in the Rocky Mountains today.

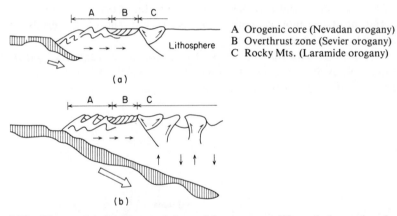

A Orogenic core (Nevadan orogany)
B Overthrust zone (Sevier orogany)
C Rocky Mts. (Laramide orogany)

(a)

(b)

Fig. 4.19 Diagrammatic representation of basement uplift and depression in the Laramide orogeny in the Rocky Mts. accounted for by non-uniformity in the thickness of the subducted plate (Lowell, 1974b*). (a) Initial stage of plate subduction. (b) Buoyancy difference due to variations in thickness of subducted plate and resulting deformations of lithosphere

Block movements in the basement produced faults and folds in the overlying sediments which can exceed 10 000 m in depth in depressed blocks. The increase in temperature associated with such a great depth of burial probably provided enough heat to transform petroleum source materials into petroleum. The migration of this petroleum through the strata and its accumulation in traps formed by the faulting and folding generated the oilfields.

(b) The Mid-Continent and the Gulf of Mexico

Plate tectonics can also probably account for the genesis of oilfields in the mid-continent which stretch from northern Texas to Oklahoma, and also of the oil-producing zone to the south in the delta along the Gulf of Mexico. In order to do this we rely on data on the geology of the Ouachita Mountains and from numerous exploratory wells.

It appears that three triple junctions developed near the present southern margin of North America between the end of the Precambrian and Early Cambrian periods (Fig. 4.20a). Following enlargement of the fractures due to igneous activity and faulting, the North and South American continents split and three failed arms were left at the southern extremity of North America: the Delaware, Wichita and Reelfoot aulacogens (Fig. 4.20b). Vertical and horizontal expansion continued in these aulacogens until the Devonian period and more than 10 000 m of Palaeozoic clastic sediments accumulated (Walper, 1976*, 1977*). The aulacogens were of the mid-oceanic ridge type and provided sites for igneous activity. Heat from this source is believed to have been the motive force in converting petroleum source materials in the sediments to petroleum.

The South American plate, alias the continent of Llanoria, which had migrated relatively southwards, collided with North America between the Devonian and Mid-Carboniferous. A convergent-type plate boundary had

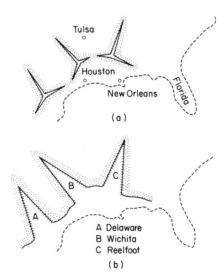

Fig. 4.20   (a) Three triple junctions which developed in the early Palaeozoic on the present southern margin of North America. (b) Aulacogens growing with continental separation

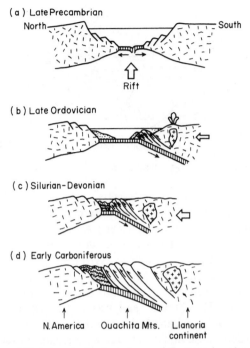

(a) Late Precambrian

North — South

Rift

(b) Late Ordovician

(c) Silurian-Devonian

(d) Early Carboniferous

N. America   Ouachita Mts.   Llanoria continent

Fig. 4.21   Collision of Palaeozoic N. America and S. America showing the view that N. America subducted under the northwards-migrating S. America plate (Llanoria continent). (After Walper, 1977*.)

developed between the two continents, and the Ouachita Mountains represent the suture. Both subduction of North America southwards (Briggs and Roeder, 1975*) and subduction of Llanoria northwards (Burgess, 1976*) have been proposed. However, as in the Ouachita Mountains, deformation of Palaeozoic deposits is dominated by overthrust faults towards the north (Fig. 4.21), which suggests that the first proposal is more reasonable.

The compressional forces generated by the relative movement of the two plates probably extended into the Palaeozoic deposits in the aulacogens, forming numerous folds. These folds then provided the traps which collected the previously matured and migrated petroleum. On the other hand, reefs which had developed at the margins of the aulacogens were also ideal traps due to their very porous nature. The identification of reefs buried 3000 m below the surface is therefore a very important aspect of exploration.

After the oilfields in the mid-continent had formed a mid-oceanic-type plate boundary formed to the south of the Ouachita Mountains at the beginning of the Triassic. This expanded and grew into the Gulf of Mexico. The extensive development of salt at this time suggests that it was probably a closed shallow

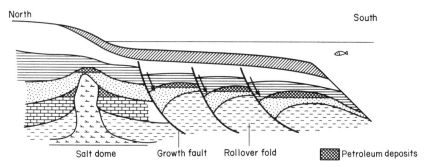

Fig. 4.22   Trap formation in the Gulf of Mexico

sea initially. Subsequent rifting of the oceanic plate enlarged the Gulf of Mexico and from the Jurassic through Tertriary and up until the present day it has remained a site for the deposition of large amounts of clastic material derived from North America. Many river systems, principally the Mississippi, transport the debris and the deltas which formed at the individual river mouths ultimately aggregated to form an enormous delta covering the north shores of the Gulf of Mexico. The Triassic salt was buried deeply as sedimentation proceeded and eventually began to rise again as salt domes. As these pushed aside the overburden, anticlinal structures were created. Independent of these movements, locally produced faults deepened due to subsequent sedimentation (growth faults) and formed numerous traps associated with rollover folds (Fig. 4.22). The thickest sediments in the Gulf of Mexico exceed 15 000 m so that deeply buried petroleum source materials matured. The petroleum thus formed migrated to traps associated with salt domes or rollover folds, and thus the largest oil-producing zone in North America was generated.

(c) Alaska—the North American frontier

In this section we review the development of geological structures in the Arctic area, where prospecting for oil has met with success, the northern Gulf of Alaska, where high initial hopes proved unfounded, and the Bering Sea, which is as yet unexplored.

In early 1968 the Prudhoe Bay oilfield, which is the largest single-trap oilfield in North America, was discovered under the permafrost, on the northern edge of Alaska. Subsequently several hundred exploratory wells were drilled to depths of 3000–5000 m, which, when combined with a wide variety of geophysical explorations undertaken at the same time, gave a tremendous boost to our understanding of the geological history of the Alaskan arctic zone.

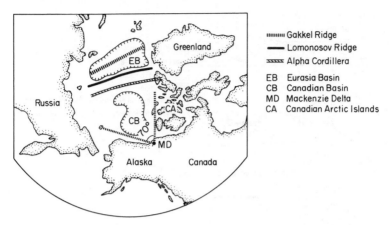

ıııımıı Gakkel Ridge
━━ Lomonosov Ridge
xxxxx Alpha Cordillera

EB Eurasia Basin
CB Canadian Basin
MD Mackenzie Delta
CA Canadian Arctic Islands

Fig. 4.23   Outline of geological structures around margins of the Arctic Ocean

The main geological structures around the Arctic Ocean are shown in Fig. 4.23. The northern edge of Alaska and the Canadian Arctic Islands form an angle of about 70 ° measured from the Mackenzie Delta, but a comparison of the two areas shows that sediments from the Devonian to the lowest Cretaceous have lithofacies, indicating deposition mainly in a continental shelf environment. These are termed the Ellesmerian (Tailleur and Blosge, 1970*). In northern Alaska this group of strata thicken towards the south with a predominance of marine facies, but they thin gradually towards the north and disappear off the coast. In contrast the upper Cretaceous and Tertiary sediments thicken and overlap the underlying Ellesmerian. The Ellesmerian in the Arctic islands also thins towards the Canada basin, being overlapped by the Tertiary sediments. Glaucophane schists are distributed in a linear fashion along the Kobuk River which runs east–west through the south of the Brooks Range in northern Alaska, suggesting the former presence of a plate boundary (Forbes *et al.*, 1977*). The northern slopes of the Brooks Range are about 200 km wide with series of overthrust faults to the north. If the strata are 'unfolded' there appears to have been a contraction of as much as 240 km in a north–south direction (Tailleur and Blosge, 1970*). The position of the Devonian–Carboniferous palaeomagnetic pole in northern Alaska differs from that deduced from elsewhere in North America, but if northern Alaska is isolated and turned clockwise through 70 °, this difference disappears (Newman, Mull and Watkins, 1977*).

Figure 4.24 shows the tectonic development of arctic Alaska considering the evidence mentioned above. A similar sedimentary environment was maintained around the ancient continent of Innuitia (Tailleur and Blosge, 1970*) which was thought to have formerly existed in the Arctic. The Ellesmerian deposits particularly close to the continent form good reservoir

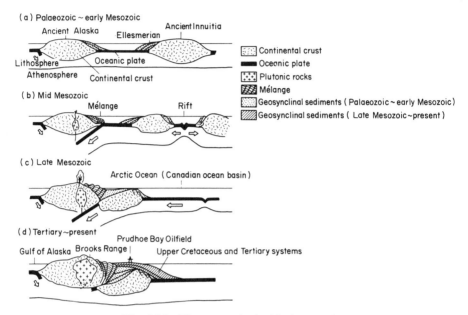

Fig. 4.24   Plate tectonics in Alaskan arctic

rocks with well-sorted deltaic facies. A different facies, mudstone, was deposited at the same time further offshore, providing petroleum source materials, which were preserved without being oxidized. The continent of Innuitia then broke off in the Late Jurassic as a result of rifting. The broken segment turned anticlockwise as it migrated and at the same time subduction of the oceanic plate on the northern margin of ancient Alaska was initiated. Subsequently the fragment of Innuitia collided with ancient Alaska to complete the skeleton of modern day Alaska. Igneous activity associated with these movements provided heat to encourage maturation of the petroleum source materials which had been preserved without being oxidized. The petroleum produced migrated upwards through porous strata, to be trapped in the Permian-Triassic deltaic sandstones now unconformably overlain by upper Cretaceous-Tertiary sediments. Thus the Prudhoe Bay oilfield was created.

We now examine the Gulf of Alaska. The basement of this Tertiary basin is a mélange, the Yakutat formation, of Jurassic to Cretaceous age (Plafker, Jones and Pessagno, 1977*), which extends from the hinterland of the Gulf of Alaska Tertiary province to the Shumagin Islands close to the tip of the Alaskan Peninsula (Fig. 4.25b). The mélange consists of a low temperature-high pressure type of metamorphic rock containing glaucophane and is linked with the underlying Palaeozoic layers by a series of overthrust faults.

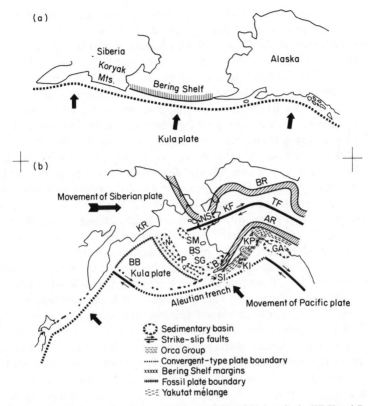

AR Alaskan Range, BB Bering Sea Basin, BS Bering Shelf, KF Kaltag fault, KP Kenai Peninsula, N Navarin Basin, P Pribilof Canyon, SI Shumagin Island, TF Tintina fault, B Bristol Basin, BR Brooks Range, GA Gulf of Alaska Basin, KI Kodiak Island, KR Koryak Mts., NS Norton Basin, SG St. George Basin, SM St. Matthew Basin

Fig. 4.25 (a) Margins of Mesozoic Bering Sea. (b) Deformation around Alaska brought about by 800 km eastwards migration of Siberian plate

The Aleutian trench where the Pacific plate is being subducted today disappears to the south-east off Kodiak Island, and does not extend as far as the north of the Gulf of Alaska. This mélange indicates that during the Mesozoic era a destructive plate boundary existed in the north of the Gulf of Alaska.

Accretionary prisms, the Orca formation of Palaeocene to Eocene age, occur seawards of the Yakutat formation extending from Kenai peninsular in south-west Alaska to Kodiak Island (Lyle *et al.*, 1978*; von Huene *et al.*, 1976*). They do not occur in the northern part of the Gulf of Alaska. The Siberian plate may have moved eastwards by as much as 800 km (Patton and Tailleur, 1977*), so this fact in addition to the location of the early Tertiary accretionary prisms and the Mesozoic mélange, must be considered in any evaluation of the structural history of the Gulf of Alaska.

During the Mesozoic the Gulf of Alaska had an almost straight margin (Fig. 4.25a) with a destructive plate boundary at its southern margin. It was here that subduction of the Kula plate occurred and accretionary prisms resulting from this subduction are now Yakutat formation mélange. From the end of the Mesozoic to the Early Tertiary the Siberian plate, which had drifted eastwards, collided with Alaska with its westward projecting peninsular (Fig. 4.25a). This is thought to have produced two slightly differing types of deformation (in particular, deformation expressed by the hatching in Fig. 4.25b). In essence a massive flexure developed throughout the whole of Alaska, the Kaltag-Tintina fault (the boundary of the north and south Alaska plates, which corresponds almost exactly to the Kobuk River), which developed into a slip place with southern Alaska, including the Bering Sea, showing slightly more severe deformation than the northern part. Furthermore, at 40 Ma the Pacific plate changed its direction of motion from north to north-west, as shown by the angle between the Emperor Seamounts and Hawaiian Islands. Consequently the Kenai Peninsula–Kodiak Island area took virtually the full force of this movement with the development of the Orca Group, a remarkably deformed accretionary prism. As the eastern part of the Tertiary province was oblique to the subduction of the Pacific plate, large anticlinal structures consisting of more gentle folds than the Orca Group were formed (Bruns and Plafker, 1975*). The presence of these structures generated enormous interest when in 1976 the US Federal Government sold petroleum leases for the northern Gulf of Alaska. Subsequently ten exploratory wells were drilled to depths of up to 5400 m but no petroleum was found in the huge anticlinal structures. The bottom hole temperatures of the wells, measured when they were drilled, indicated that the temperature gradient was extremely low. This could be because the cool subducting oceanic plate cooled the overlying sedimentary strata. This may be the reason why petroleum source materials have not been matured in the area, as observed in the fore arc basins elsewhere.

Finally, we consider the last frontier in petroleum exploration, the Bering Sea. Seismic exploration in recent years on the Bering Sea continental shelf has demonstrated the presence of several large sedimentary basins possessing clastic rocks 5000–10 000 m thick. No exploratory wells have yet been drilled into any of these basins, but in this section we discuss the structural development of two large basins, the St. George and Navarin, and consider whether they could be likely sites for the development of petroleum. An outline of the topography and geology around the Bering Sea is shown in Fig. 4.25b. Firstly, we consider its structure and characteristics.

The Koryak Mountains in the USSR are formed from a Mesozoic mélange of the Franciscan type (Marlow *et al.*, 1976*), and are probably comparable to the Yakutat formation which extends from the northern Gulf of Alaska to Shumagin Islands. The Bering Sea shelf connects the Koryak Mountains and Shumagin Islands. Late Cretaceous rocks gathered from the Pribilof Canyon (Fig. 4.25b), which cuts deeply into the Bering Sea shelf, seem to have been subject to forces much greater than those due to current loading; original grain boundaries can no longer be seen and clays have recrystallized (Hopkins *et al.*, 1969*). Similar examples may be recognized in the Pleistocene rocks sampled from the northern walls of the Aleutian trench through the DSDP (deep sea drilling project). This is thought to indicate that they were once buried to much greater depths before being brought to their present positions (von Huene *et al.*, 1971*). As the Cretaceous rocks found around the margin of the Bering Sea shelf are the same as the Yakutat formation or the Koryak Mountains mélange it is likely that the rocks were taken to great depths as a result of northerly subduction of the plate at the edge of the continental shelf, and subsequently ascended to shallower positions due to overthrust faulting. The north–south magnetic lineations in the Bering Sea basin correspond to M_1–M_{13} in the Mesozoic and are thought to be from the Kula plate and older than the magnetic pattern found in south side of the Aleutian trench (Cooper *et al.*, 1976 a*, 1976b*). The virtual absence of earthquakes suggests that this plate does not subduct under the Bering Sea shelf any more.

The Siberian plate moved eastwards from the Late Mesozoic to Early Tertiary, causing an extensive bend in southern Alaska. At about the same time the Pacific plate changed direction from north to north-west, and these two series of movements brought about enormous changes in the geological structures around the Bering Sea. The ocean trench south-east of the Alaskan Peninsula was positioned such that the north-west advancing Pacific plate collided head on, and it continued to be a site of subduction. However, the structural trend of the margin of the Bering Sea shelf suggests that, where a big bend had developed, subduction ceased. The Alaskan Peninsular trench propogated south-westwards, in response to the subduction, forming the framework of the modern Aleutian trench system. The Kula plate, which had been subducting under the Bering Sea shelf, now subducted into the Aleutian trench, located further south. The remnant of the Kula plate in the Bering Sea basin lost the propulsion necessary to drive it further north, so that the forces acting on the Bering Sea shelf changed from compressional to tensional due to rebound in the continental crust. These forces produced large sags around the continental shelf, which became infilled and enlarged by vast quantities of clastic material derived from the north, forming huge sedimentary basins such as the St. George and Navarin basins (Figs. 4.25, 4.26).

With the cessation of the subduction of the Kula plate at the margin of the Bering Sea shelf, the low geothermal gradient which had prevailed would gradually have disappeared. There is evidence of igneous activity from the Late Mesozoic to Early Tertiary on the islands of St. Matthew and St.

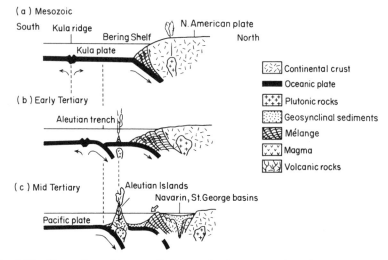

Fig. 4.26   Formation of large sedimentary basins on margins of Bering Sea shelf

Lawrence (Patton *et al.*, 1975*). This was probably due to the early stages of Kula plate subduction at the margins of the continental shelf and may well have provided the thermal conditions necessary for petroleum maturation. Seismic profiles of the area have failed to reveal anticlinal structures in the sedimentary strata which exceed 10 000 m, but there are numerous potential traps related to faults or basement rocks. The development of this area as a centre for oil exploration is likely in the not too distant future.

The author wishes to acknowledge the enormous assistance he received from exploration data provided by Idemitsu Oil Development Co., Limited, in the preparation of this section.

(Masao Hayashi)

4.3 Island arcs and mineralization

Almost all metal resources are produced in orogenic zones, in close association with intermediate to acidic plutonic or volcanic rocks. Examples do exist of important deposits developing in non-orogenic cratonic blocks, such as stratiform uranium deposits, banded iron formations or Mississippi Valley-type lead–zinc deposits, but major deposits of the porphyry, vein or skarn types are always found in orogenic zones. As many orogenic zones can be interpreted as resulting in part from former island arcs associated with subduction of oceanic plates, it is extremely important to examine the distribution and common features of such deposits with particular reference to the geologically young island arcs of the Circum Pacific belt in order to establish how they developed.

(a) Regional characteristics

Intermediate to acid igneous rocks dating from the Late Palaeozoic onwards are distributed widely throughout the Circum Pacific belt, and are referred to collectively as the Circum Pacific igneous belt. However, the following features are found to the east and west of the Chukotsk-Alaska zone (Fig. 4.27)

(1) Sulphide deposits, typified by porphyry copper in orogenic zones on continental margins (continental-type island arcs), are concentrated on the American side. Remarkable deposits of cassiterite, an oxide ore, are found on the Asian side.

(2) Porphyry and Kuroko types are found in island arcs between oceans accompanied by marginal seas, but the two rarely coexist.

The most fundamental reason for the above global inequalities lies in differences in the ratio between magnetite series and ilmenite series igneous rocks (see Sec. 3.9). Figure 4.27 gives some indication of these ratios.

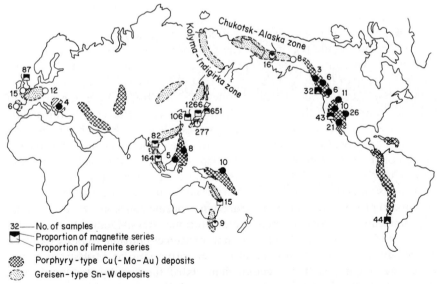

32——No. of samples
Proportion of magnetite series
Proportion of ilmenite series
Porphyry-type Cu(-Mo-Au) deposits
Greisen-type Sn-W deposits

Fig. 4.27 Distribution of magnetite series/ilmenite series granitoids and the characteristics of deposits (additions to Ishihara, 1977*). Results for ☐ major batholith and ○ minor rock units

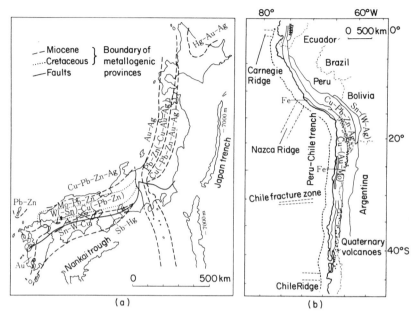

Fig. 4.28   Metallogenic provinces in (a) Japanese Islands and (b) Andean orogenic zone. (After Ishihara, 1978*, and Sillitoe, 1974*.)

Some features can also be recognized in orogenic zones common to the whole Circum Pacific region, e.g. the presence of asymmetrical metallogenic formation. A frequently cited example is that of the Japanese islands where in south-west Japan (Miocene) the association of Sn–W–Cu is seen in the Outer Zone, Sb–Hg in the Seto volcanic zone and Cu–Pb–Zn–Ag in the green tuff belt (Sanin area). On the other hand, the Cretaceous–Palaeogene Inner Zone of south-west Japan reveals an arrangement of W–Cu→Mo–Pb–Zn from the barren centre towards the Japan Sea. In the Mesozoic–Cenozoic orogenic belt of the north central zone of the Andes, deposits developed from Fe→Cu–(Mo–Au)→Cu–Pb–Zn–Ag→Sn–(W–Ag–Bi) towards the interior (Fig. 4.28).

Such asymmetrical changes are believed ultimately to originate in the asymmetry of the continental crust and mantle at sites of ocean plate subduction, but a more concrete explanation has been provided in the case of Japan. It is postulated that the magma in south-west Japan was more oxidizing in the direction of the Japan Sea irrespective of the geological period. Oxidizing magma is much better than reducing magma at concentrating sulphur and metals bonded to it (see Sec. 1.1) so that ore deposits which precipitated as the sulphides of Mo, Cu, Pb, Zn, Ag, etc., formed on the Japan Sea side. There has not yet been sufficient survey of Circum Pacific orogenic zones, other than Japan, to assess the oxidation state of the igneous rocks they contain.

When the types of metal elements involved are considered, most of the asymmetrical changes seen in Circum Pacific orogenic zone may be the result of the change from the magnetite to the ilmenite series. However, an asymmetrical zonation may also be found in magnetite series igneous zones. For example, sulphur and iron sulphide ores in Quaternary deposits are abundant near the volcanic front in north-east (Tohoku) Japan, but decrease markedly towards the Japan Sea (Fig. 4.29). The same is true for Miocene-Pliocene Au, Ag, Cu, Pb and Zn. An arrangement of Cu→Pb–Zn→Au–Ag towards the Japan Sea can also be recognized in vein-type mineral deposits from slightly within the volcanic front (Ishihara, 1974a*).

These regional patterns mirror the zonation seen in ore deposits around a single pluton where the zonation is related to the temperature gradient of the mineralizing solution. When it is considered that large quantities of volcanic rocks are also erupted close to the volcanic front, it is clear that such regional patterns probably indicate that the temperature of ore solutions and intrusive magma decreased towards the Japan Sea.

These asymmetrical changes tend not to be apparent in ilmenite series igneous zones. In Malaysia porphyritic biotite granites occur to the west and equigranular biotite granites to the east, forming two parallel zones of differing rock type associated with remarkable tin deposits (Hutchison,

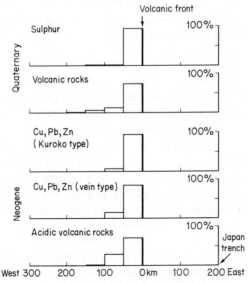

Fig. 4.29   Variations in quantities of ore deposits formed in Late Cenozoic across NE Japan. (After Ishihara, 1974b*.)

1977*). These are principally Triassic in age and both consist mainly of ilmenite series granites without magnetite (Ishihara *et al.*, 1979*). Magnetite series mafic igneous rocks lie along the western margin of the eastern zone of granites, which is thought to result from former island arc activity. The western zone possesses many cassiterite skarn-type deposits containing cassiterite pegmatites and malayaite, whereas these are not found in the eastern zone which instead contains Cornish-type cassiterite–quartz veins and magnetite–cassiterite skarns (Hosking, 1977*). East–west changes in Peninsular Malaysia are thus very difficult to define, and the slight asymmetry is attributed principally to differences in the conditions of formation of the deposits, in particular the depth (the east zone formed at a shallower depth than the west) (see Fig. 4.32D).

No obvious zonal arrangements or asymmetrical changes are discernible in ilmenite series granitoids. The reasons for this probably lie in the fact that this type of magma is less able than the magnetite series to generate sulphide deposits and hence it is unlikely that a variety of sulphide minerals could develop. Moreover, because ilmenite series granitoids contain a significant crustal component, the non-uniformity of crustal material is clearly reflected in the deposits. Ilmenite series magma may also be less differentiated than magnetite series magma, which may also be a pertinent factor.

(b) The role of oceanic plates

As it is believed that igneous activity in the Circum Pacific region has been caused by the relative movements of crustal and oceanic plates, an assessment of their individual roles is important to our understanding of mineral deposit formation. It has long been recognized that mineral deposits are often located where ocean transform faults cut across the continental crust intersecting orogenic structures (Schmidt, 1966). During the 1970s several theories concerning the speed and angle of subduction of oceanic plates, the potential of sea bed materials as source materials, etc., have been proposed, but no generally accepted criteria have emerged. However, if the distribution of Quaternary volcanoes is examined in relation to speed of subduction vigorous motion of the oceanic plates seems to produce large quantities of magnetite series magma. It is thought that the quantity of magmatic-hydrothermal ore deposits formed is primarily proportional to the amount of magma produced, and the above point is now considered in relation to the Japanese islands.

Figure 4.30 summarizes the chief constituents of ore deposits from the Late Cenozoic in north-east and south-west Japan. The concentration of Au is similar in the two regions because of the numerous gold vein deposits found in Kyushu, but the concentrations of other elements are clearly much lower in south-west Japan. (Gypsum is from Kuroko-type deposits and believed to have developed from sea water at the site of formation, and so is excluded from the

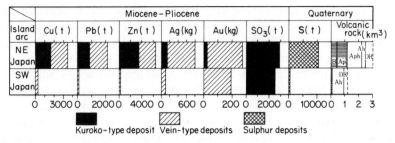

B Basalt, Ap Pyroxene Andesite, Aph Pyroxene-amphibole andesite, Ah Amphibole andesite, DR Dacite-rhyolite

Fig. 4.30 Comparison of quantities of ore deposits formed in Late Cenozoic in NE and SW Japan. Weight per 1 km length of island arc. (After Ishihara, 1978*.)

discussion.) Subduction of the westwards advancing Pacific plate under northeast Japan is believed to have been very active during the Miocene (9 cm/yr). In south-west Japan, however, subduction along the Nankai trough began only recently (5–10 Ma), and the Miocene ocean plate was thus inactive. In other words, the rate of subduction exerted a considerable influence on the quantity of sulphides formed in ore deposits.

Whether or not deep fissures in orogenic zones have played an important role in the development of ore deposits has been discussed at length (Spurr, 1923). Currently, although mineralizing magma source theories for the rift or hotspot types of non-orogenic zone deposits have been accepted, e.g. for the alkaline granites associated with tin deposits in Africa (Sillitoe, 1974*), the theory that calc-alkaline series magma is connected with the formation of igneous deposits in orogenic zones is thus related to the interaction of continental crust and oceanic lithosphere. In comparison to the traditional mineralizing magma theories, a consideration of the possible contribution of the oceanic plate and its abyssal sediments (whether directly or indirectly via the mantle wedge) to the generation of island arc magmas constitutes quite a new approach to the problem of ore genesis.

Hydrothermal alteration and processes of mineralization are not confined to the remarkable floor of the Red Sea, but also occur in the Pacific along the East Pacific Rise, Galapagos Ridge and other extensional areas. In fact the stratiform copper deposits in Cyprus are thought to have developed from just such mineralization. Such altered basalts on the ocean floor are thought to have been subducted together with overlying sulphide deposits and sediments. Subsequent fusion of this subducting plate could produce magma rich in S, Cu, Pb, Zn, etc., which was thus highly conductive to the formation of magnetite series igneous deposits. This theory was advocated enthusiastically in the first half of the 1970s (Sillitoe, 1972*) but was very difficult to substantiate.

Sasaki and Ishihara (1979*, 1980*) who examined $\delta^{34}S$ in plutonic rocks and ore deposits found that whereas this averaged about $+6‰$ for plutonic rocks and $+4‰$ for deposits in the green tuff zone of north-east Japan, which is associated with subduction, it was slightly less than $+2‰$ for plutonic rocks and about $0‰$ for ore deposits in the Kitakami area where igneous activity is not thought to have been the result of subduction. The latter value of $+2‰$ for plutonic rocks is close to the accepted 'mantle value', but the former value of $+6‰$ is clearly much heavier than this. Isotopic studies of mafic intrusive rocks have led to the general belief that the upper mantle possesses a sulphur isotope ratio of $\delta^{34}S = +1-+2‰$. Sulphur in igneous rocks is usually present as sulphides and its sulphur isotope ratio is probably determined by (1) the value in the source, (2) isotopic fractionation between types of dissolved sulphur in processes leading to consolidation, (3) the incorporation of extraneous sulphur from the continental crust. When magmatic sulphur with the mantle value fractionated isotopically between oxidizing and reducing sulphur species as it rose, the isotopic fractionation would only be slight because of the high temperature of the magma. The influence of extraneous continental crust is not generally discernible in plutonic rocks in the green tuff belt, and old sulphate mineral layers (e.g. evaporite) containing heavy sulphur are also unknown in the Japanese Archipelago. Sasaki and Ishihara thus believed that the heavy value of $+6‰$ showed that heavy sulphur of marine sulphate origin had been transported into the mantle together with the underthrusting oceanic plate, and became incorporated into the magma at the site of generation. Sulphate minerals of marine origin are known to be present in pelagic sediments overlying altered basalts on the ocean crust. In this instance, however, we are left with a problem of tectonic style, i.e. whether these sediments are subducted with the plate in the ocean trench or whether they are scraped off, forming part of an accretionary prism. Additionally, in places where ocean floor circulating hydrothermal systems are found, typified by a mid-oceanic ridge, one may expect the precipitation of large amounts of calcium sulphate resulting from the warming of the sea water, providing another source of heavy marine sulphate if these altered basalts are later subducted.

If it is accepted that both altered and unaltered basalts in the oceanic plate are important sources for magnetite series magma in island arcs, it is likely that magmas with high concentrations of S, Cu and Zn would be produced. As the Pb content of mafic igneous rocks is low, rocks with higher Pb contents such as pelagic sediments are necessary to form Cu–Pb–Zn metallogenic provinces. When the sulphur isotope data mentioned above are combined with the lead isotope ratios discussed in Sec. 1.4, there is a strong suggestion that pelagic sediments were incorporated into magma in the island arc trench systems of north-east Japan.

A discussion of extensional and compressional island arcs in the following section may throw further light on the problem of subduction of pelagic sediments.

(c) Porphyry copper deposits and Kuroko deposits

Both porphyry copper deposits and Kuroko deposits are associated with magnetite series acid igneous rocks, but in order to obtain more concrete information about their genesis, many geologists have tried to establish whether or not the two types of deposit ever do in fact coexist in one island arc. In the 1960s, many studies were undertaken in North and South America to establish the distribution of porphyry copper deposits and the fact that they were distributed on the continental side of orogenic zones, whereas Kuroko-type deposits were produced within the orogenic zones, led to the suggestion that continental crust was necessary for the formation of porphyry copper deposits while an oceanic environment was an indispensable prerequisite for Kuroko-type deposits (C. Mayer, 1975, personal communication). However, this does not account for the porphyry copper deposits which stretch from the Philippines to the Solomon Islands in the south-west Pacific. Ishihara (1974a*) tried to account for the fact that the two types of deposit do not coexist by considering that porphyry copper deposits produced at the base of sub-areal volcanoes and Kuroko deposits formed in association with sub-marine volcanoes reflected variations in the scale and form of hydrothermal circulation. Subsequently, however, it was also suggested that porphyry copper deposits in Highland Valley, Canada, had been produced in association with sub-marine volcanic activity during the Mesozoic (Osatenko and Jones 1976*).

Uyeda and Kanamori (1979*) divided island arc trench systems into two types depending on whether the back arc was enlarged or not, i.e. a Mariana arc type produced in an extensional regime associated with expansion of the back arc and a Chilean arc type formed in a field of compression without formation of the back arc basin. In the Miocene the green tuff region of Japan is generally believed to have been in an extensional regime with extreme movement of faulted blocks. It probably therefore belongs to the Mariana arc type. Chile, however, is endowed with numerous large prophyry copper deposits. This new classification of arc systems corresponds remarkably well with the textbook locations of porphyry copper and Kuroko-type deposits. Uyeda and Nishiwaki (1980*) then considered this correspondence not only for typical island arcs but also for island arcs in the south-west Pacific with highly complex structural histories where many porphyry copper deposits have recently been discovered (Fig. 4.31). The main porphyry copper deposits in the Philippines occur in the 'Philippine mobile belt' which lies between the westward sloping Philippine trench and eastward facing Manila trench. Many Miocene deposits occur in the igneous rocks produced by subduction from the

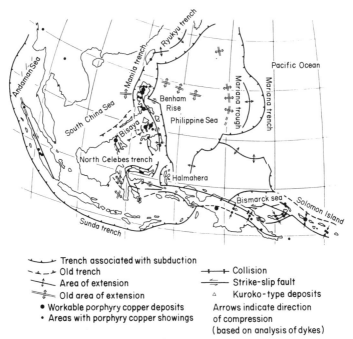

Fig. 4.31   Structure of SW Pacific and porphyry copper deposits. (After Uyeda and
Nishiwaki, 1980*.)

Manila trench when the subduction at the Philippine trench slowed down.
There was also a change in the direction of subduction in the Solomon Islands.
A compressional field was probably produced in such transitional periods
because of residual movement from the former subduction zone. In the Papua
New Guinea mobile belt where extremely young prophyry copper deposits are
found, an old island arc (currently New Britain Island) produced by
northwards subduction collided with the northwards advancing Australian
crust, and so the ore deposits probably belong to those of the Chilean type
which are formed in compressional regimes. It thus seems that all porphyry
copper deposits are formed in compressional-type island arcs.

     Sillitoe (1980*) considered the recent caldera hypothesis for the genesis of
the Kuroko deposits (Ohmoto, 1978*) and combined it with his own theory
concerning stratovolcanoes and porphyry copper deposits to propose that
differences in the forms of volcanic activity gave rise to the two types of
deposits. In caldera-type volcanic activity, magma at the top of the pool rich in
volatile components is completely dispersed during the ejection of pyroclastic
flows before caldera collapse. During the resurgence, even if there is an
intrusion of suitable size, there are little of the important volatile components

remaining so porphyry copper deposits do not develop. Loss of hot water from radiating cracks, etc., is also considerable. The magma probably remains at a shallow position for shorter time than is the case with stratovolcanoes.

Sillitoe proposed that vein or skarn-type deposits, not porphyry copper deposits, would form in volcanic zones containing many calderas, whereas Kuroko-type deposits would develop in areas of sub-marine volcanic activity such as the green tuff belt in Japan. However, if, as claimed by the authors (Ishihara and Sasaki, 1978*), the principal components of Kuroko deposits are magmatic from a deep source, the pyroclastic rocks underlying the deposits imply that the volatile components which had accumulated in the magma chamber, regarded by Sillitoe with such importance, predated the formation of the deposits and were erupted even in the case of Kuroko deposits. The author's opinion is that heavy 'sea water' (e.g. Sato, 1972*, type II) was produced by the ejection of mineralizing solutions into small crater-type calderas so that the principal ore components from the magma were not lost, and as a result large amounts of metals precipitated out as Kuroko deposits.

The hypotheses of Uyeda and Nishiwaki and Sillitoe provide plausible explanations for several problems relating to porphyry copper and Kuroko-type deposits. For example, there is a remarkably high Cu/Pb ratio in the Andes mineral zone as compared with the green tuff mineralized zone. The upper side of the oceanic plate is compressed in their Chilean type, so that pelagic sediments are not subducted. In the extensional type, however, there is a possibility that these sediments are subducted, bringing lead-rich material to the site of magma generation. Differences in the composition of source material may well bring about varying Cu/Pb ratios, even within one type of deposit. Enormous stratovolcanoes develop in Chilean-type island arcs (Uyeda and Kanamori, 1979*), and extensional arcs are probably prone to caldera collapse. For porphyry copper deposits to develop granitic magma incorporating hydrothermal fluids needs to be matured at pinpoint to a state at which it produces an explosion due to secondary boiling. The structural environment associated with caldera collapse is unsuitable for the formation of porphyry copper deposits. This can be applied to actual observations on the eastern margins of the Asian continent. In the Mesozoic igneous belt stretching from Sikhote Alin to the Gyengsang Basin and Fujian Province in China, shallow intrusive rocks of the magnetite series are found associated with remarkable collapsed structures, and no significant porphyry copper deposits have been found.

(d) The importance of the continental crust

Magma is believed to interact to varying degrees with the continental crust through which it rises and consolidates. In such cases ore-forming materials are believed to be more strongly affected than silicate melts because they migrate easily. Not all ore deposits derived from magnetite series magmas are of deep origin; Mn, Cu, etc., are perhaps increased to some extent by this contamination (Ishihara, 1978*). As most ilmenite series magmas are thought to derive from the continental crust, it is particularly important to establish the composition of this crust.

In south-west Japan ilmenite series granitoids are generally granodioritic containing mafic inclusions, but overall granite *sensu stricto* is most abundant in the tungsten zones of the Malay Peninsula or in southern China. In the latter case, there is no good correlation between the trace element concentration and differentation index (Ishihara *et al.*, 1980*), which probably means that this type of magma experienced only little differentiation. Therefore the initial concentration of trace elements is believed to have a significant influence on the formation of ore deposits.

The concentration of tin has been particularly well investigated in the characteristic deposits found in ilmenite series mineralized zones (Ishihara and Terashima, 1977). Magnetite series granitoids from orogenic belts generally have 2 ppm or less and tonalite (Tanzawa type) in oceanic island arcs has the lowest concentration with 1 ppm or less. On the other hand, the tin content of ilmenite series granitoids is generally about twice as high as the magnetite series (Table 4.2). In the magnetite series Sn is fixed in rock-forming minerals during the processes of magmatic consolidation (see Sec. 1.1) so its content reflects that of the original magma, whereas in the ilmenite series the original concentration was probably higher than the current content because Sn has been brought to the ore deposits by an aqueous solution phase.

Regional variations in Sn content are also found in sedimentary and metamorphic rocks intruded by granitoids and in much older metamorphic rocks and granitoids. In Japan rocks with a high tin content are found in the south-west of the country, which corresponds with the change in Sn content in

Table 4.2 Tin content in Japanese islands and Malay Peninsula (ppm). (After Ishihara *et al.*, 1976; Ishihara and Terashima, 1977; Ishihara *et al.*, 1980*.)

Area and rock type	Average value (no. of analyses)
Tanzawa (magnetite series)	0.6 (7)
Kitakami Mts. granite (magnetite series)	1.2 (75)
Hokkaido central granite (ilmenite series)	2.6 (22)
SW Japan Outer Zone granite (ilmenite series)	4.0 (169)
NE Japan metamorphic rock	0.9–1.7 (20)
SW Japan metamorphic rock	1.3–4.4 (53)
Malay Peninsula (S. Thailand) tin granite	17.7 (23)
Malay Peninsula (S. Thailand) tin-free granite	9.7 (21)
Thailand Precambrian metamorphic rocks and granite	8.7 (4)

granitoids and with the overall distribution of tin deposits. Remarkable tin anomaly is found in the Precambrian basement and all the Mesozoic granites throughout the Malay Peninsula (Table 4.2), the tin deposits produced there being on an extensive scale. This suggests that tin is an element which is recycled in the continental crust, and so-called 'tin granite' is thought to have developed due to recycling in the continental crust where amomalous amounts of tin were present initially. A similar idea is also commonly applied to ilmenite series granitoids in southern China (Tu, Wang and Yu, 1980*). For example, granites associated with rare-earth element deposits are thought to have formed from the partial melting of metamorphic rocks rich in the rare-earth elements (Wang *et al.*, 1980*).

A complete understanding is hampered by the complicated structural regime under which ilmenite series magmas are produced. Collision-type island arcs are a likely site for the generation of large amounts of magma due to the interaction of different types of continental crust. In such a situation, if a large amount of C was present in them all, an ilmenite series magma would probably form; further if it were rich in Sn, a tin granite would probably develop. Hutchison (1978*) suggested that small quantities of Late Palaeozoic granite (ilmenite series) in the Malay Peninsula was a result of subduction, but that the principal Late Triassic granites (ilmenite series; Ishihara *et al.*, 1979*) were produced under a collisional tectonic setting (Fig. 4.32). The abundance of magnetite series granites increased in this area during the Cretaceous (mainly in the Phuket-Tenasserim zone), and the Cenozoic Sumatra–Burma volcanic belt to the west is entirely a magnetite series igneous belt. Recent studies have led to the widespread belief that the massive ilmenite series granitoids associated with tungsten in southern China are of the island arc trench type (subduction type) (Wang *et al.*, 1980*) but the details are obscure.

Magnetite series are found on the coastal side and ilmenite series towards the interior of the Mesozoic igneous belt on the eastern margins of the Asian continent including southern China, the Korean Peninsula and Sikhote Alin. Furthermore, igneous activity is generally younger towards the coast, which differs totally from the asymmetrical changes found on the American continent. The author believes that the oceanic trench on the Asian side is regressing due to the development of marginal seas, and thus the igneous activity becomes younger towards the ocean. Observations that igneous rocks fronting marginal seas are usually magnetite series suggest that east–west change in the type of granitoid probably results from the thinning of continental crust around developing marginal seas.

Lateral variation and tectonic setting in the type of granitoid have been established in detail for the Miocene igneous zones on the Japanese Islands, and the ilmenite series has been produced on the oceanic side (Ishihara, 1979*). Because a Miocene whole rock Rb–Sr age has been determined for the granitoid along the central axis of Hokkaido (Shibata and Ishihara, 1979*) its

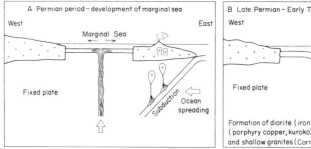
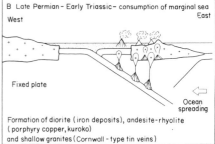

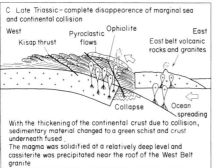
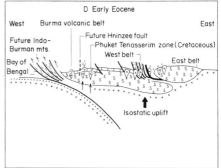

Fig. 4.32   History of tectonic development of Malay peninsula igneous rocks. (After Hutchison, 1978*.)

igneous activity forms a pair with that in the green tuff belt. The fact that the granitoids cut obliquely across the Kuril arc and their distribution is controlled by basement structures shows that this igneous activity was produced by movements in the continental crust related to the westwards-advancing Pacific plate, for example, as a result of a collision of an island arc from the Okhotsk Sea or fault movements in the north–south system. The petrochemistry of the granitoids and presence of graphite deposits in plutonic rocks shows that this part of the continental crust is rich in C but poor in Sn.

On the other hand, magnetite series, mafic igneous rocks are distributed along the Sanin area of south-west Japan, and moreover Outer Zone granitoids are cut by the Fossa Magma in the magnetite series igneous terrain of the Izu-Mariana arc. Therefore ilmenite series igneous activity in the Outer Zone could not have been produced directly by subduction. The fact that this igneous activity is closely bound up with the distribution of the Shimanto Supergroup implies an association in origin with so-called 'local' structural movements which took place after the supergroup was deposited. If one includes the Setouchi volcanic rocks, Miocene igneous activity was widespread across south-west Japan. This was probably the result of sluggish subduction of the warm Philippine plate accompanying the extension of the Shikoku

Basin. Judging by the characteristics of the granitoid and ore deposits in the Outer Zone of south-west Japan, continental crust rich in Sn, etc. could possibly still exist under the Shimanto Supergroup.

The pair of igneous zones seen in the Japanese Archipelago during the Miocene period is thought to have been brought about by an extensional field in the back arc and compressional field in the fore arc during the growth of the Japan Sea (Ishihara, 1979*). In some parts of continental regions, on the other hand, ilmenite series granites strike NNW, cutting across the magnetite series igneous zone of the prevailing north-east systems in East Asia, and in places are accompanied by tin deposits, as in the Kolyma-Indigirka tin area in eastern Russia. Ilmenite series igneous rocks seem to be produced in all sorts of tectonic fields and this fact conversely tells us that the source for this magma series was relatively less refractory than those for magnetite series.

(Shunso Ishihara)

References

Bird, J. M., and Dewey, J. F. (1970). Lithosphere plate–continental margin tectonics and the evolution of the Appalachian orogen, *Bull. Geol. Soc. Am.*, **81**, 1031–1060.

Briggs, G., and Roeder, D. (1975). Sedimentation and plate tectonics, Ouachita Mountains and Arkoma Basin, in *Sedimentology of Paleozoic Flysch and Associated Deposits, Ouachita Mountains-Arkoma Basin, Oklahoma*, pp. 1–22.

Bruns, T. R., and Plafker, G. (1975). *Preliminary Structural Map of Part of the Offshore Gulf of Alaska Tertiary Province*, USGS Open File Report 75-508.

Burgess, W. J. (1976). Geologic evolution of the Mid-Continent and Gulf Coast areas—a plate tectonics view, *Trans. Gulf Coast Assoc. Geol. Soc.*, **26**, 132–143.

Burke, K., and Dewey, J. F. (1973). Plume generated triple junctions; key indicators in applying plate tectonics to old rocks, *J. Geol.*, **81**, 406–433.

Cooper, A. K., Marlow, M. S., and Scholl, D. W. (1976a). Mesozoic magnetic lineations in the Bering Sea marginal basin, *J. Geophys. Research*, **81**, No. 11, 1916–1934.

Cooper A. K., Scholl, D. W., and Marlow, M. S. (1976b). Plate tectonic model for the evolution of the eastern Bering Sea basin, *Bull. Geol. Soc. Am.*, **87**, 1119–1126.

Craig, H. (1966). Isotopic composition and origin of the Red Sea and Salton Sea geothermal brines, *Science*, **154**, 1544–1547.

Dickinson, W. R. (1976). Plate tectonic evolution of sedimentary basins, in *Plate Tectonics and Hydrocarbon Accumulation*, Am. Assoc. Pet. Geol., Continuing Education Course Note Series No. 1, pp. 1–62.

Douglas, R. J. W. (1970). *Geology and Economic Minerals of Canada*, Geol. Surv. Canada.

Forbes, R. B., Carden, J. R., Turner, D. L. and Connelly, W. (1977). Tectonic implications of Alaskan blueschist terranes, in *Program and Abstracts of Alaska Geological Society Symposium*, April 1977, Anchorage, Alaska.

Goodwin, A. M. (1973). Archaean iron formations and tectonic basins of the Canadian Shield, *Econ. Geol.*, **68**, 915–993.

Heyl, A. V. (1969). Some aspects of genesis of zinc–lead–barite–flourite deposits in the Mississippi Valley, U.S.A., *Trans. Inst. Mining Metall.*, Sec. B, **78**, B148–B160.

Hoagland, A. D. (1976). Appalachian zinc-lead deposits, in *Handbook of Strata-bound and Stratiform Ore Deposits* (Ed. K. H. Wolf), Vol. 6, pp. 495-534, Elsevier, Amsterdam.

Hopkins, D. M., *et al.* (1969). Cretaceous, Tertiary, and early Pleistocene rocks from the continental margin in the Bering Sea, *Bull. Geol. Soc. Am.*, **80**, 1471-1480.

Hosking, K. F. G. (1977). Known relationships between the 'hard rock' tin deposits and the granites of Southeast Asia, *Geol. Soc. Malaysia, Bull.*, **9**, 141-157.

Hutchinson, R. W. (1973). Volcanogenic sulfide deposits and their metallogenic significance, *Econ. Geol.*, **68**, 1223-1247.

Hutchinson, R. W., Ridler, R. H., and Suffel, G. G. (1971). Metallogenic relationships in the Abitibi Belt, Canada: a model for Archean metallogeny, *Can. Inst. Mining Metall. Trans.*, **74**, 106-115.

Hutchison, C. S. (1977). Granite emplacement and tectonic subdivision of Peninsular Malaysia, *Geol. Soc. Malaysia, Bull.*, **9**, 187-207.

Hutchison, C. S. (1978). Southeast Asian tin granitoids of contrasting tectonic setting, *J. Physics Earth.*, **26**, Supplement, S221-S232.

Ishihara, S. (1974a). Magmatism of the Green Tuff tectonic belt, Northeast Japan, in *Geology of Kuroko Deposits* (Eds. S. Ishihara *et al.*), Mining Geol. Spec. Issue 6, pp. 235-249.

Ishihara, S. (1974b). The volcanic front, transverse seismic discontinuity and metal mineralization in the East Japan Arc, *Problems of Ore Deposition, 4th IAGOD Symp.*, **2**, 481-485.

Ishihara, S. (1977). The magnetite-series and ilmenite-series granitic rocks, *Mining Geol.*, **27**, 293-305.

Ishihara, S. (1978). Metallogenesis in the Japanese island arc system, *J. Geol. Soc. London*, **135**, 239-406.

Ishihara, S. (1979). Lateral variation of magnetic susceptibility of the Japanese granitoids, *J. Geol. Soc. Japan*, **85**, 509-523.

Ishihara, S., and Sasaki, A. (1978). Sulfur of Kuroko deposits—a deep-seated origin?, *Mining Geol.*, **28**, 361-367.

Ishihara, S., Sawata, H., Arpornsuwan, S., Busaracome, P., and Bungbrakearti, N. (1979). The magnetite-series and ilmenite-series granitoids and their bearing on tin mineralization, particularly of the Malay Peninsula region, *Geol. Soc. Malaysia, Bull.*, **11**, 103-110.

Ishihara, S., Sawata, H., Shibata, K., Terashima, S., Arrykul, S., and Sato, K. (1980). Granites and Sn-W deposits of Peninsular Thailand, *Mining Geol. Spec. Issue*, **8**, 223-241.

Kanasewich, E. R. (1968). Precambrian rift; genesis of strata-bound ore deposits, *Science*, **161**, 1002-1005.

Langford, F. F. (1977). Superficial origin of North American pitchblende and related uranium deposits, *Am. Assoc. Petroleum Geologists Bull.*, **61**, 28-42.

Lipman, P. W., Fischer, F. S., Mehnert, H. H., Naeser, C. W., Leudke, R. G., and Steven, T. S. (1976). Multiple ages of mid-Tertiary mineralization and alteration in the western San Juan Mountains, Colorado, *Econ. Geol.*, **71**, 571-588.

Lowell, J. D. (1974a). Plate tectonics and foreland basement deformation, *Geology*, **2**, 275-278.

Lowell, J. D. (1974b). Plate tectonics and foreland deformation. Reply, *Geology*, **2**, 571.

Lyle, W., **et al**. (1978). Tertiary Formations in the Kodiak Island Area, Alaska, and Their Petroleum Reservoir and Source Rock Potential, State of Alaska, Dept. of Natural Resources, Open File Report 114.

Marlow, M. S., Scholl, D. W., Cooper, A. K., and Buffington, E. C. (1976). Structure and evolution of Bering Sea Shelf south of St. Lawrence Island, *Bull. Am. Assoc. Pet. Geol.*, **60**, 161-183.

Newman, G. W., Mull, C. G., and Watkins, N. D. (1977). Northern Alaska paleomagnetism, plate rotation and tectonics, *Program and Abstracts of Alaska Geological Society Symposium*, April 1977, Anchorage, Alaska.

Ohmoto, H. (1978). Submarine calderas: a key to the formation of volcanogenic massive sulfide deposits?, *Mining Geol.*, **28**, 219-231.

Osatenko, M. J., and Jones, M. B. (1976). Valley copper, in *Porphyry Deposits of the Canadian Cordillera* (Ed. A. Sutherland Brown), CIM Spec. Vol. 15,pp. 130-143.

Packley, R. I. (1976). Origin of western-states type uranium mineralization, in *Handbook of Strata-bound and Stratiform Ore Deposits* (Ed. K. H. Wolf), Vol. 7, 89-156, Elsevier, Amsterdam.

Patton, W. W. Jr., Lamphere, M. A., Miller, T. P., and Scott, R. A. (1975). Age and tectonic significance of volcanic rocks on St. Matthew Island, Bering Sea, Alaska, *USGS Open File Report* 75-150.

Patton, W. W., Jr., and Tailleur, I. L. (1977). Evidence in the Bering Strait region for differential movement between North America and Eurasia, *Bull. Geol. Soc. Am.*, **88**, 1298-1304.

Plafker, G., Jones, D. L., and Pessagno, E. A., Jr. (1977). An upper Mesozoic accretionary flysch and melange terrain along the Gulf of Alaska margin, *Abstracts with Programs, 1977 Annual Meetings, Geol. Soc. Am.*

Ridge, J. D. (Ed.) (1968). *Ore Deposits of the United States, 1933-1967*, Vols. I, II, Am. Inst. Mining Metall. Engrs., New York.

Robertson, J. A. (1966). *The Relationship of Mineralization to Stratigraphy in the Blind River Area, Ontario*, Geol. Assoc. Can. Spec. Paper 3.

Sasaki, A., and Ishihara, S. (1979). Sulfur isotopic composition of the magnetite series and ilmenite series granitoids in Japan, *Contrib. Mineral. Petrol.*, **68**, 107-115.

Sasaki, A., and Ishihara, S. (1980). Sulfur isotope characteristics of granitoids and related mineral deposits in Japan, *Proc. 5th IAGOD Symp. E. Schweizerbart'sche Verlag. (Nägele u. Obermiller)*, Stuttgart, pp. 325-335.

Sato, T. (1972). Behaviours of ore-forming solutions in seawater, *Mining Geol.*, **22**, 31-42.

Sawkins, F. J. (1976). Metal deposits related to intracontinental hotspot and rifting environments, *J. Geol.*, **84**, 653-671.

Seyfert, C. K., and Sirkin, L. A. (1973). *Earth History and Plate Tectonics, An Introduction to Historical Geology*, Harper and Row, New York, 504 pp.

Shibata, K., and Ishihara, S. (1979). Rb-Sr whole rock and K-Ar mineral ages of granitic rocks in Japan, *Geochem. J.*, **13**, 113-119.

Sillitoe, R. H. (1972). A plate tectonic model for the origin of porphyry copper deposits, *Econ. Geol.*, **67**, 184-197.

Sillitoe, R. H. (1974). Tectonic segmentation of the Andes: implications for magmatism and metallogeny, *Nature*, **250**, 542-545.

Sillitoe, R.H. (1980). Cauldron subsidence as a possible inhibitor of porphyry copper formation, *Mining Geol. Spec. Issue*, **8**, 85-93.

Tailleur, I. L., and Blosge, W. P. (1970). Tectonic history of northern Alaska, *Proceedings of the Geological Seminar on the North Slope of Alaska, Pacific Section*, Am. Assoc. Pet. Geol.

Thompson, T. L. (1976). Plate tectonics in oil and gas exploration of continental margins, *Bull. Am. Assoc. Pet. Geol.*, **60**, 1463-1501.

Tu, K. C., Wang, Z. G., and Yu, X.Y. (1980). Genesis of granitic rocks in South China and related mineralization, *Mining Geol. Spec. Issue*, **8**, 189–196.

Uyeda, S., and Kanamori, H. (1979). Back-arc opening and the model of subduction, *J. Geophy. Res.*, **84**, 1049–1061.

Uyeda, S., and Nishiwaki, C. (1980). Stress field, metallogenesis and mode of subduction, in *The Continental Crust and its Mineral Deposits* (Ed. D. W. Strangway), Geol. Assoc. Canada, Spec. Paper, **20**, 323-339.

von Huene, R., *et al.* (1971). Deep sea drilling project Leg 18, *Geotimes, AGI Reprint Series*, October 1975.

von Huene, R., *et al.* (1976). A summary of petroleum potential, environmental geology and the technology, time frame and infrastructure for exploration and development of the western Gulf of Alaska, *USGS Open File Report* 76-325.

Walper, J. L. (1976). Geotectonic evolution of Wichita Aulacogen, Oklahoma, *Bull. Am. Assoc. Pet. Geol.*, **60**, 327–328.

Walper, J. L. (1977). Paleozoic tectonics of the southern margin of North America, *Trans. Gulf Coast Assoc. Geol. Soc.*, **27**, 230–241.

Wang, L. K., Zhao, B., Zhu, W. F., Cai, Y. J., and Li, T. J. (1980), Characteristics and melting experiments of granites in southern China, *Mining Geol. Spec. Issue*, **8**, 29–38.

White, D. E. (1974). Diverse origins of hydrothermal ore fluids, *Econ. Geol.*, **69**, 954–973.

Further reading

(1) The following are general treatises on metallogeny in North America:

Noble, J. A. (1970). Metal provinces of the western United States, *Geol. Soc. Am. Bull.*, **81**, 1607–1624.

Sutherland Brown, A., Cathro, R. J., Panteleyev, A., and Ney, C. S. (1971). Metallogeny of the Canadian Cordillera, *Trans. Can. Inst. Mining Metall.*, **74**, 121–145.

Guild, P. W. (1978). Metallogenesis in the western United States, *J. Geol. Soc. London*, **135**, 355–376.

Guild, P. W. (1966). Tectonic history and mineral deposits of the Western Cordillera, *Can. Inst. Mining Metall. Spec. Vol.*, **8**.

Strong, D. F. (1974). Plate tectonic setting of Appalachian–Caledonian mineral deposits as indicated by Newfoundland examples, *Trans. Soc. Min. Eng. AIME*, **256**, 121–128.

The following collection of papers from the 5th IAGOD Conference in August 1978 was published after the writing of this chapter was complete:

Ridge, J. D. (Ed.) (1979). Papers on mineral deposits of western North America, *Nevada Bur., Mines and Geology Rept.*, **33**, 213 pp.

(2) New ideas about igneous deposits in island arcs and orogenic zones can be found in the following three collections of papers:

The relations between granitoids and associated ore deposits of the Circum-Pacific region, *Geol. Soc. Malaysia, Bull.*, **9**, 276 pp., 1977.

This contains the Proceedings of the 5th Conference of the IGCP on 'Circum-Pacific plutonism' at Malaya University, 12–13 November 1975. Its content is not wholly consistent.

Metallogenesis in Mesozoic–Cenozoic orogenic belts, *J. Geol. Soc. London*, **135**, Part 4, 1978.

This collection of papers considers and describes the problems of ore formation in the following five areas, viz. Western United States, the Japanese Archipelago, South-east Asia, the Caribbean, Iran–Pakistan.

Granitic magmatism and related mineralization, *Mining Geol. Spec. Issue*, **8**, 1980, 247 pp.

This is the collected Proceedings of the Meeting of the Society of Mining Geologists of Japan held in Tokyo on 29–30 January 1979. It covers regional geology to experimental approaches with particular emphasis on porphyry-type deposits in the Circum-Pacific region. It also incorporates four papers from China.

(3) More information about the Kuroko deposits is collected in the special issues of *Mining Geology* detailed below.

Papers devoted to the Japan–U.S. Kuroko research project, *Mining Geol.*, **28**, No. 4, 1978.
An issue devoted to studies of Kuroko deposits, *Mining Geol.*, **28**, No. 5, 1978.

PART II

Development of the Earth's Surface

Introduction

A few years after the end of the Second World War the rapid economic recovery in Japan coupled with the introduction of new technology in Western countries, in particular the United States, enabled the development of numerous massive construction projects, typified by the Sakuma Dam. Engineering geology (or geological engineering) may be cited as one of the most important European and American technologies from which Japan has benefited.

Virtually all the concerns of civil engineering, such as tunnels and dams obviously, but also road construction, bridges or subway systems, are located on or in the soil or bedrock. An important problem for the earth sciences is thus to establish when and by what processes the soil and bedrock formed, and how they currently behave. Properties such as their age, developmental processes or behaviour are expressed as a range of engineering characteristics which a particular soil or bedrock possesses. At the same time, in order to be able to predict with any reliability what an individual soil or bedrock will be like in future, and in particular how it will behave in response to the excavation, moving and loading involved in construction projects, we must not only have an accurate understanding of the history through which the said soil or bedrock has passed but also be armed with a thorough comprehension of the basic laws of physics in relation to geological materials. This is essential for the engineering problems of the soil or bedrock and also applies to all the engineering problems of the earth's surface such as river and coast engineering.

We should indeed feel respect for the efforts of our engineering predecessors who undertook the construction of the Tanna Tunnel and the Kanmon Undersea Tunnel before and during the Second World War. Despite having an insufficient understanding of all the subjects mentioned above they nevertheless strove individually or together in groups to battle with all the problems.

After the War the concept of 'the role of geology in construction

211

engineering' spread rapidly throughout America and European countries such as Austria, Switzerland and France. The vast amounts of information related to the role of geology in construction projects in the United States Bureau of Reclamation or US Army were brought into Japan through the American Military General Headquarters. This information made a great impact on Japan's civil engineers and geologists. Japanese civil engineers learned the great significance of geology to construction processes such as design, survey, execution and maintenance, and Japanese geologists were made aware of a new aspect of the earth sciences which had previously been confined to 'interpretative' aspects only.

Construction of the Kurobe River No. 4 Dam involved various kinds of site test at great expense to obtain bedrock properties such as shear resistance or water permeability. On reading in the report that 'The strength of the bedrock is considerably less than that of individual rock pieces' a university geologist laughed 'Of course it must be, we can guess that easily without such expensive tests'. However, he did not really understand the meaning of the 'attempting to quantify bedrock strength on the basis of careful selection of the position and orientation of the site tests'. There is some doubt as to whether or not they could measure the true value of the shear strength of the bedrock, but it is no overstatement to say that the fact that they tried laid the foundations for engineering geology as we know it today.

The understanding of geology by civil engineers still appears to be quite inadequate. Unfortunately most civil engineering departments in Japanese Universities still have no, or very few, engineering geology courses for their students. However, the number of cases today where the vital advice given by geologists is ignored with greater emphasis placed on design and planning considerations are much fewer than before or during the War. The post-war changes have meant a remarkable improvement in the status of the geologist in the field of construction engineering which today includes projects for environmental preservation.

We now accept without question that for developments in construction engineering a basic understanding of the earth sciences and detailed analyses of geological data relating to individual sites are indispensable. The geological perspective will become more important as the scale of construction projects increases.

On the other side of the coin, construction projects, irrespective of their scale, provide the earth scientist with large quantities of dynamic and static information about various important problems relating to the earth's surface and just below. Geologists who have tried to study the geological structures of an area only from the results of surveys of weathered exposures along old roads and streams will be able to obtain huge amounts of high quality data on the area from examination of fresh outcrops over large distances exposed by the road construction or other cutting operations. The survey adits made in dam construction work—for a single dam there may be several tens of adits with a combined length of several kilometres—enable a three-dimensional analysis of the geological structures to be built up when information from them is combined with the actual excavation of the land surface. The vast walls of an underground power station excavated several hundred metres below the surface on a scale of hundreds × tens × tens of metres gives us a vivid picture of the sub-surface appearance of geologic structures in relation to surface features.

Measurements of 'latent pressure' and seismological surveys of the bedrock, conducted over a considerable period of time, when combined with data from large-scale underground excavation, provide important information about the structural evolution and geodynamics of an area.

The Japanese Society of Applied Geology, whose prime interest is engineering geology, was founded over twenty years ago. During this period there has been a rapid increase both in the number of engineering geologists and the level of research. We now increasingly have the ability to work at several hundreds or thousands of metres below the surface and in Japan a new term 'global engineering' or 'lithosphere engineering' has come into use. Recent advances in engineering geology are worthy of attention because they have enabled the collection of large amounts of data relating to the static and dynamic physical properties of rock masses and geological conditions both at the surface and to depths of several hundred metres. These data have then been used to establish the basic factors necessary for large-scale construction projects.

This series of books aims to describe the current situation and future prospects in various fields of the earth sciences, so we look here at the state of and the basic philosophy behind an earth scientist's approach to engineering and construction. Two specialists in the forefront of these activities in Japan have kindly agreed to write chapters for this part of the book, for which I am editor.

Part II of this book 'Development of the Earth's Surface' is divided into the following broad sections.

The activities of human society are bound up with the development and modification of the surface layers (including the sea bed) of the world on which we live. This sometimes involves utilizing the forces of nature but more often means going against them. In Chapter 5 we discuss how the earth sciences and geology, which study the history of natural global forces, apply to such developmental engineering.

The earth sciences relevant to engineering for the development of the earth's surface is called 'engineering geology'. In Chapter 6 we summarize the system and methodological analyses of engineering geology.

Japan is said to be one of the most problematical areas in the world in terms of engineering geology. The reason we have particularly chosen to discuss the engineering geological features of Japan in Chapter 7 is to make the reader realize what factors must be considered if we are to make the Japan of the future a more comfortable place in which to live.

In Europe, America and Japan, engineering geology has come to be recognized as an indispensable field of study for social development only after the earth sciences were successfully applied to the construction of giant dams more than 100 m high, such as the Hoover or Sakuma Dams. Such construction accelerated rapidly from the 1940s onwards. The current state of engineering geology is described in Chapter 8, citing the processes of planning, design, survey and execution involved in the construction of giant dams.

It is said that in developing the surface of the earth the environment is unavoidably altered to some degree. In Chapter 9 we cite changes in river beds such as silting upstream of dams and scouring downstream, land subsidence and regeneration of beaches by the provisions of offshore breakwaters, in an attempt to clarify some of the environmental problems related to engineering geology which result from the unleashing of the enormous forces of nature and the technology for Man's active development of the earth surface, i.e. the relationship between the natural earth sciences and engineering.

Many of the terms commonly used in civil engineering are likely to be unfamiliar to people concerned with the earth sciences. In view of this we have tried to avoid too much technical jargon, but where this is unavoidable brief explanations are included, although they are likely to be insufficient. The readers of this series may also include people involved with civil engineering who are unfamiliar with some of the terminology of the earth sciences. Comprehending the series may thus demand considerable efforts on their part. We similarly hope that our earth sciences readers will refer to a dictionary of civil engineering when necessary.

(Yotaro Seki)

Chapter 5

Development of the Earth's Surface and Engineering Geology

A cursory examination of one of the 1 : 25 000 maps published by the Japanese Geographical Institute often reveals sites such as that shown in Fig. 5.1.

If at first one looks for the location of towns and villages, the flat river terraces with easy access to water are an obvious choice for habitation. There indeed the village of Yaga has developed. The lower terraces or flood plains which run the risk of being flooded are used for rice fields whereas the well-drained loam plateau in the hills behind is used for growing tea. Small villages on the northern side of the river, such as Yufure, Tsuburano or Arashi are all located where the topography suddenly becomes more gentle at the extreme edge of the loam plateau. They are probably places where water is readily available and are convenient for cultivating the fields and tea plantations on the loam plateau. The old road which winds along the contours connecting the villages probably developed naturally by constant use. It is rather a roundabout route but it may be traversed with ease and in safety without disturbing the natural slopes and it has no steep inclines. As a road for

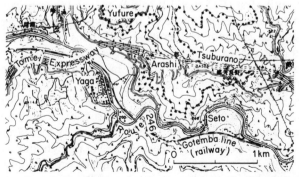

Fig. 5.1   An example of surface development (. . . margins of loam plateau). National Geographical Institute, 1:25000 series, *Yamakita*. An aerial photograph of the area is shown in Fig. 6.12.

215

transporting goods it took full advantage of the natural environment. Thus, the very first stage in the development of the earth's surface was when Man used his hands and then his tools to open up the mountains and plains to cultivation. Experience built up in the light of many errors and failures taught him to make the best use of nature as seen in this type of example. Looking again at the map, this time at the railway (the Gotemba line) and Route 246 between Seto and Yaga, it can be seen that in order to provide a route suitable for vehicular transportation, the railway required the building of tunnels where it met the mountains. Huge cuttings had to be made when building the new road so as to widen the old road and eliminate sharp bends. By making each short tunnel or cutting which conflicts with the stable gradients of natural slopes, nature is somewhat modified. At this stage, however, the location of both the road and railway are still basically determined by nature, and routes are selected which wind their way along the level ground between valleys in harmony with the topography.

However, when we look at the Tomei Expressway, which crosses the upper part of Fig. 5.1, the lack of usable space between the valleys combined with the desired line of the road and siting problems results in the selection of a route which appears oblivious to nature. Nature is adapted to the requirements of the road by building a huge tunnel through the mountains, because of the lack of flat ground, and by constructing enormous artificial slopes on both sides of the road, which deeply disect the mountains on the south bank of the river.

The pressures of population and civilization make it impossible for human activities to develop solely in areas which lend themselves to the use of nature, particularly in a country like Japan. Inevitably these pressures necessitate the development of the earth's surface in terms of the positive adaptation of nature. The bulldozer and the dumper truck, which have replaced the pick and the straw basket, have made the rapid advances achieved in such remodelling projects possible.

It was not until after the Second World War that Japan began to use heavy machinery in civil engineering projects, or more precisely, during the recovery after the disastrous Typhoon Catherine in 1947. This calamity brought serious flooding and damage to a wide area of the grain belt in Tokyo and its surroundings but heavy machinery brought in by the American military forces in Japan at that time was of enormous assistance in the recovery.

The earliest modern civil engineering projects, involving the widespread use of heavy machinery, may be traced to the construction of the concrete gravity-type Sakuma Dam with a height of 155 m and capacity of 327 million tons of water and the similar gravity-type Ikari Dam, 112 m high and with a capacity of 55 million tons. These dams were both completed in 1956 and construction techniques using heavy machinery were rapidly adopted throughout the country to accelerate projects modifying nature.

It was from about 1969 after the completion of the Tomei Expressway that visible alterations of the topography and landscape became obvious in areas such as that shown in Fig. 5.1. In 1978 the completion of the Miho Dam (rock fill, 100 m high), just upstream from Fig. 5.1, led to a striking transfiguration of the surrounding area. Route 246 which represents the stage of minor modification of nature has been used since the 1600s. Although it has been frequently improved during the 100 years or so since the Meiji era to make it suitable for automobile transport, and was considerably widened and paved in the 1960s, it still follows its original course. The Gotemba railway line was opened in 1889 but the only changes in the period of post-war recovery have been extensions to station facilities.

In large-scale remodelling projects, artificial cliffs up to 100 m high may appear in a matter of months in road cuttings. It may take natural erosion tens of thousands of years to make an underground cavern but tunnels are complete in a few years. Such rapid changes disturb the balance of geological processes which proceed slowly over vast tracts of time. These new slopes in road cuttings would soon deteriorate if left as they are, and much more damage would be caused after earthquakes or heavy rain. Tunnel construction is hampered by the pressure of the rock mass which tends to make the tunnel collapse as excavation proceeds, and by large amounts of ground water which seeps out into the tunnel during the construction workings. In 1972 during work on the Chuo Expressway a landslide caused by the cutting of massive slopes in connection with road construction occurred in the bedrock near Otsuki. Many cuttings were also damaged by the 1978 marine earthquake off the Izu Peninsula ($M = 7.0$), where damage was reported to be particularly severe on roads constructed relatively recently. One of the first considerations when developing the earth's surface must therefore be to prevent such accidents and to construct safe and economical structures which conserve their balance with nature. To achieve this, retaining walls are often built for the slopes of cuttings or concrete is sprayed over them. In tunnels steel frameworks or concrete are used to withstand the pressures. By 'safety' we mean the ability of the structure to withstand even torrential rain or earthquake without collapse both during and after construction and by 'economical' we mean as cheaply as possible but within the safety limits.

Furthermore, such engineering projects are often accompanied by changes in the landscape as in the case of cuttings, but tunnels frequently involve various changes in the geological environment such as the drying up of wells due to seepage of large amounts of ground water into the tunnel, subsidence or collapse of the surface or the contamination of rivers by excavated earth. Therefore a further prime concern when developing the earth's surface is to predict any secondary damage associated with such development and to take account of environmental preservation. Because exploiting the surface of the earth involves some destruction of nature we should strive as far as possble to avoid development in areas where nature needs to be protected, and we also need technology to enable us to restore artificially what has been damaged. America and Western Europe contain examples of mines in which nature, completely ruined by open cast working, has been artificially reconstructed and restored after completion of the excavation.

On the other hand, natural phenomena also produce changes in the topography or flow of ground water via the constant processes of erosion, transportation and deposition and may often occasion natural disasters such as landslides or floods. Floods during the rainy season in 1972 caused landslides and avalanches of earth and rocks said to have reached a million cubic metres in volume, even in the area shown in Fig. 5.1. In Hokizawa and Nakagawa Spa in Tanzawa, which were the most badly affected places in this area, damage to 'head family' communities built on old traditional sites of human activity was slight, but overwhelming damage was caused to communities of 'branch houses' built on the mountain slopes or places with a risk of landslips because suitable sites had been harder to find. A similar tendency was found in the landslides that occurred in the western part of Izu Peninsula following the 1974 earthquake off Izu Peninsula in that damage to the newer communities was far greater than that to the old. Anticipating natural disasters and choosing sites in harmony with nature are thus themselves also important considerations in the massive developments undertaken today.

Development of the earth's surface is thus closely bound up with the geology of the surface and geological phenomena such as erosion, landslides or floods. In a country like Japan, whose geology is said to be particularly 'bad', the importance of adequate survey work cannot be overestimated if projects are to be carried out both safely and economically. For example, a geological survey for a tunnel needs to contain the type of information shown in Fig. 5.2. Figure 5.2(a) is principally based on surface surveys. In surface or near surface developments which utilize nature, or make only minor modifications to it, one may assume that soft or argillaceous zones will occur along large faults, soft gravels or along dykes, and so a route should preferably be chosen which as far as possible avoids such zones. However, as we have mentioned already, in many of the large-scale projects undertaken today we often have no choice but to remodel nature even if the geology is unsuitable. In order to do this we must fully examine and interpret the underground geology along the proposed line of the tunnel, and so a detailed survey such as that in Fig. 5.2(b) is undertaken on the basis of (a), using a variety of techniques. The surveys shown in the diagram are obviously not all undertaken simultaneously, but are built up schematically at each stage from planning to construction. The results of these permit the drafting of a detailed geological profile such as that in Fig. 5.2(c), with the inclusion of new data relating to unconformities or intrusions which could not be assessed at stage (a). However, the geological information necessary for tunnel construction cannot be gleaned just by studying Fig.

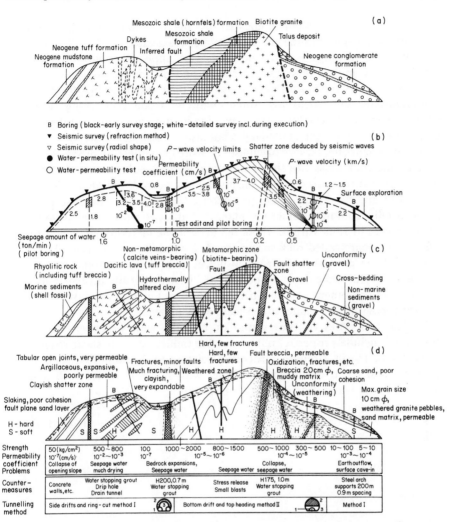

Fig. 5.2 Schematic geological profiles, geological engineering profile and observations (tunnel survey): (a) geological profile based mainly on surface survey, (b) contents of detailed geological survey, (c) cross-section derived from detailed survey, (d) engineering profile (*qu* single axial compressive strength. Numbers in column of tunneling method show sequence of excavation)

5.2(c). In order to overcome geological difficulties when constructing a tunnel, one also needs measurements of physical parameters and geological observations of the type shown in Fig. 5.2(d). Anticipation of the kinds of geological problems likely to be encountered in excavation work, in the light of previous experience, is also an indispensable consideration in the actual execution of the project. On the basis of such information, appropriate solutions for the problems indicated by the diagrams and the form of excavation best suited to the geology may be investigated.

Engineering geology is thus the science of applying geology to fields in which engineering surveys are undertaken and obtaining physical values for the properties of the soil or rock mass and their distribution. From these a comprehensive geological assessment may be made concerning proposed developments of the earth's surface, bearing in mind not only the safety of the structures and environmental changes but also the risk of disasters.

In subsequent chapters we often use the words 'engineering properties of the ground and rock mass'. In the field of engineering geology it is customary to use two terms: rock mass which means the mass composed of relatively hard rocks and ground which refers to unconsolidated layers. Because the rock mass usually contains numerous planes of discontinuity such as joints or faults, pieces of rock without these features or the material which constitutes the rock mass are called rock specimens. The word 'basement' is used to mean the underlying ground or bedrock in places where softer ground or bedrock overlies it. The scale and properties of 'basement' are diverse and may comprise the basement to a sedimentary basin or Quarternary layers forming ancient topographical planes underneath alluvial layers.

Typical properties of the ground or bedrock with which engineering is concerned include properties relating to the failure, such as shear strength or compressive–tensile strength, properties relating to deformation, such as the elasticity and creep coefficients, together with physical values such as their permeability to water, porosity or grain structure.

(Keiji Kojima)

Chapter 6

Engineering Geology Methods

6.1 Changes in engineering geology methods

Engineering geology seems to have been born when civil engineers and geologists came together to discuss the excavation of the large tunnels in the European Alps. As a result of bitter past experience with difficult projects and faced with the challenge of such a large project, some means of finding out where large faults were located and from where large volumes of ground water could seep into the tunnel was needed. For example, the Simplon No. 1 Tunnel (Switzerland), 19.8 km long and until recently the longest in the world, was completed in 1906. As excavation work progressed much structural and stratigraphical information was amassed which it had been impossible to obtain from surface surveys alone. This also gave a tremendous boost to academic geology, in the study of Alpine structures and the history of their development. At the same time it provided a good opportunity for geologists themselves to find out what engineers require from geology. It is not difficult to imagine how engineering geology developed from this situation.

The inauguration in 1918 of the complex Tanna Tunnel project in Japan educated our geologists. The Tanna Tunnel is 7804 m overall in length and, as is well known, was a difficult project which took 67 lives and 16 years to complete. It cut across several major faults and there was a succession of accidents in which large amounts of ground water, including hot spring water, caused the denatured clay to swell up, thus producing enormous pressures, causing collapse of the tunnel. The geological survey undertaken before the work began was of the type shown in Fig. 5.2(a) and was of virtually no help at all to the engineers. However, following these disasters, the importance of amassing the sort of geological information in Fig. 5.2(d) before work commenced was recognized and specialist engineering geologists began to be trained. It was also recognized that the failure of the St. Francis Dam (gravity dam) could be attributable to the geology of the site despite the topographical suitability of the site. Subsequently, detailed geological surveys were undertaken prior to dam projects. At exactly the same time, also in Japan, the Komoro Dam (height 16 m, buttress dam) gave way due to piping phenomena in the volcanic bedrock, causing an accident in which seven people were lost or died and nine houses were swept away. From this time on engineering geologists began to play a much more active role in dam construction.

However, because at that time surveys were still mainly undertaken at the surface using hammers and clinometers there were limits as to how much information could be deduced about the underground geological structures. Nevertheless, drilling instruments had already been used for the underground surveys undertaken immediately after the disastrous Kanto earthquake (1923). Work began on the Kanmon Tunnel, the first long undersea tunnel to be constructed in Japan, in 1936. For the first time elastic wave/seismic surveys were used with a considerable degree of success, in addition to preliminary drilling, to assess the geology beneath the sea bed. The first really systematic survey, including seismic and drill hole analysis, was carried out in connection with the Kamishiiba Dam (completed 1955, height 110 m), the first arch dam to be built in Japan. In 1959 the Malpasset Dam in France (height 60 m, arch dam) gave way when its gneiss bedrock foundations slipped, and five hundred people were killed or lost. Then in 1961 the Fraile Dam in Peru (height 74 m, arch dam) also collapsed when subjected to excessive pressures from fault movements in the foundation bedrock. These accidents led to a rapid increase world wide in demands for mechanical analysis of the bedrock forming the foundations to dams, and safety analyses using physical parameters relating to the strength and deformation of properties of the rocks came to be incorporated into dam design. In situ bedrock tests were first used in Japan in the construction of the Kurobe River No. 4 Dam. It thus became very important to understand how mechanical properties would change with variations in the geological situation such as fractures or weathering, and rapid progress was made in methods of rock classification, i.e. in ranking rocks by their relationship to mechanical properties. The basic current pattern of geological survey for dam construction was thus established in the approach to the construction of the Kurobe River No. 4 Dam.

From about 1965 mathematical analysis based on finite element methods (FEM) was adopted enthusiastically by the science of rock engineering and it became possible to analyse deformation and failure of rocks, taking account of non-uniformity. For this the geologist needed to know the precise distribution of mechanical properties within the bedrock, and developments in geological surveys turned to on-site bedrock tests and techniques of measurement down bore holes.

Progress was made in engineering methods also in the light of the increased content and precision of geological surveys. In the construction of tunnels, for example, huge tunnel-boring machines were introduced into Japan from about 1960. These did not depend on blasting but excavated the bedrock using revolving blades adjusted to the cross-section of the tunnel. Beginning with the Seikan tunnel connecting Hokkaido and the Mainland of Japan, they have recently come into use all over the country. A new demand on the geological survey is thus to establish bedrock properties such as hardness or fractures in terms of their relationship to the mechanical workability of the rock, and we are developing techniques to measure the ease of excavation whilst drilling survey bore holes.

In the 1960s NATM construction methods, which originated in the theories of the Austrian, L. V. Rabcevicz, began to attract attention. Unlike existing methods which involved supporting the bedrock around the tunnel loosened by the excavation with a framework and stabilizing it with a thick concrete covering, this method achieves stability and prevents the generation of loose material in the tunnel by driving lock bolts several metres long into the bedrock and spraying a thin layer of concrete onto the tunnel wall from alongside the excavation. This method is now very much favoured as a means of working effectively in relatively soft bedrocks which could expand into the tunnel. In Japan this method was used recently in parts of the Nakayama Tunnel and the Seikan Undersea Tunnel. In association with this, several new survey methods and measurement techniques have been incorporated into geological surveys to assess the rheological properties of rock masses, their residual strength and the distribution of these properties.

Geological engineering in Japan has thus benefited from the experience gained from difficult projects and major disasters, and developed new methods in response to the increasing scale of the projects undertaken.

According to a survey by the International Major Dam Conference, there have been about 500 accidents in dams across the world and of these about one third have been attributable to the foundation bedrock. Furthermore, most of the major dam collapses have been due to faults in the bedrock. The majority of major problems with tunnel projects have been caused by water pouring out of shatter zones in faults, or pressure on soft and weak rock masses. As may be seen in the example of the new Tanna Tunnel (7905 m) information gained from the excavation of the old tunnel coupled with developments in construction techniques, in particular the use of steel supports, meant that the project could be adapted far more successfully to the local geology. In comparison with the old Tanna Tunnel the new one was completed in only four years with no loss of life due to falling rock or flooding. This shows just how important the high-precision geological survey has become.

The appearance of Minamata disease in 1953 followed in 1955 by 'Itai-itai' disease (Auch-auch disease, a bone-breaking disease) of the Jinzu River area, and air pollution problems in the Yokkaichi industrial complex also began to appear at about this time. Environmental problems were thus suddenly brought into focus. During this period the expansion of areas of habitation due to the construction of enormous housing complexes and coastal reclamation threw the environmental changes associated with the remodelling of nature into stark relief—e.g. ground disasters such as landslides, rock avalanches caused by heavy rain and earthquakes, fluidization of soft ground during earthquakes and subsidence due to the pumping out of too much ground water, or accidents due to oxygen deficiency in urban civil engineering projects. To anticipate these and to consider a preservation of the environment are yet more vital problems.

A new direction for geological engineering to pursue is to observe and analyse the changes of various environmental features such as ground water and the deformation of the ground caused by construction projects—in other words, to determine the balance between nature and new geological forces created as a result of development.

6.2 The sequence of engineering geological surveys

The principal methods used in geological engineering surveys are illustrated in the example in Fig. 8.1, Chapter 8. However, returning to Fig. 5.2, we will briefly explain the order in which surveys containing such information are built up. Engineering surveys can broadly be divided into those undertaken at the design stage (pre-construction surveys) and those conducted during and after construction. Figure 5.2(a) shows the results of an outline survey at the design stage, and is mainly a geological reconnaissance compiled by collecting geological data and examining aerial photographs. If required, a few drill holes or a seismic survey may also be carried out at this stage. The form of Fig. 5.2(c) is obtained from a detailed survey at the planning stage. At this stage geologically important or remote locations identified on the basis of Fig. 5.2(a) are investigated by drilling, and seismic surveys, sometimes including radical shape seismic prospecting, are performed. Site tests using bore holes and survey tunnels are carried out to assess water permeability and deformational properties and a series of laboratory tests using a drill core, etc., are generally undertaken at this stage. On the basis of these results the sorts of geotechnological maps shown in Fig. 5.2(d) or Fig. 6.7 are obtained. At this stage pre-construction surveys are often undertaken in order to assess likely changes in the surrounding environments during and after completion of the work, such as subsidence or sinking of the water table. Particularly in the case of tunnel construction, surveys during the course of the work based on pilot drill holes or test adits are also very important to establish the work policy. As a result, errors in the estimates of the pre-construction survey are identified and Fig. 5.2(c) is revised, and the real values in Fig. 5.2(d) and in problematic areas can be established with greater accuracy. Post-construction surveys relate mainly to maintenance, administration and environmental protection. Long-term observation of changes in the bedrock or underground water level, etc., also come under this category.

The point of emphasis of geological surveys will vary, depending on the object of development. In surveys for the foundations to dams, one of the most important site tests on the bedrock is to obtain data necessary for designing the embankment, whereas little attention is paid to this in surveys for tunnels or cuttings. The risk to life if a dam were to give way after completion is one reason why very careful surveys are needed before commencing the work. With tunnels, however, it is very important to anticipate and plan for the generation of large pressures or accumulation of water during excavation. Greater emphasis is thus placed on surveys which establish the location and size of shatter zones and the amount of ground water rather than on the mechanical properties of the rocks themselves. The scale of the operation tends to be relatively small when making cuttings, so expensive tests cannot be undertaken. The items considered and the sequence of surveys will vary from site to site, but by and large they have the above points in common. From Sec. 6.3 on we outline the methods used in engineering geology, concentrating on the basic approaches to the compiling of surveys. We give details of a real geological survey in Chapter 8.

6.3 The geological viewpoint in engineering

The role of geology in engineering is primarily to assess the distribution of geological features and to represent the results as topographical, plan or profile maps. So-called 'surface geological maps' are widely used in engineering geology. These are full of engineering geological information about the surface layers not contained in general geological maps, including details such as the properties of alluvial layers, the thickness of talus deposit, the depth of weathering, the distribution of landslides and points where water emerges, all of which must be considered carefully in engineering projects. Such geological surface and profile maps are used in engineering projects to make an accurate geological assessment of the evolution of the current geology and topography or to show the distribution of strata and structures such as faults; to find geologically similar areas elsewhere and to collect and compare any geological data relating to development projects there; to put an engineering interpretation on the geological information for the area, e.g. by recognizing that the strength in a shatter zone is reduced, or to add a geological assessment when devising models of the ground and bedrock.

In preparing such maps to clarify the problems of engineering geology and the distribution of the physical properties of the ground and bedrock, it is vital to have an understanding of the processes involved in the following diverse geological phenomena. If one has a general appreciation of processes, for example, the knowledge that weathering proceeds continuously little by little from the surface towards deeper positions and that the tops of mountains are more susceptible to weathering and that rock strength decreases with weathering, it is then possible to make more precise estimates of the physical

properties throughout a weathered zone, such as shown in Fig. 5.2(d), from
the meagre data supplied from boreholes, etc.

In engineering geology as in other fields 'the present is the key to the past'.
A stratigraphical and historical approach beginning with the law of
superposition is vital as a basis for establishing the distribution of engineering
properties underground. As an example, the type of soil profile shown in Fig.
6.1(a) is widely used in the field of soil engineering. These are generally
prepared on the basis of N values, the grain size of samples derived from
geological data and the results of standard penetration tests: a standard iron
tube (63.5 kg weight, 75 cm drop), determined by the width of the bore hole, is
driven in to a depth of 30 cm, the number of strikes required being the N value;
samples are collected inside the tube. Figure 6.1(b) is a geological profile
obtained by applying a historical perspective to drill core data, analysis of
heavy minerals and fossils (pollen, diatoms, foraminifers) contained in the
core and ^{14}C dating. In particular, from a study of diatoms the history of
changes in sea level during the Ice Age can be elucidated. A study of the
profiles also shows erosion or deposition by rivers, and the presence of
continental layers and the buried topography beneath the river deposits are
thrown into relief. The difference between the two profiles (a) and (b) in terms
of engineering geology lies mainly in the presence of valley sediments or river
terraces, the continuity of gravel layers and the seismic characteristics of the
bedrock. Such differences mean major differences in terms of design and
execution, and in the case of (a), in which the geological map is inappropriate,
revisions would probably be necessary to the plans during execution of the
work depending on the structure involved. Figure 6.2 is a comparison of an
isothickness map (a) prepared using a computer with (b) and (c) which were

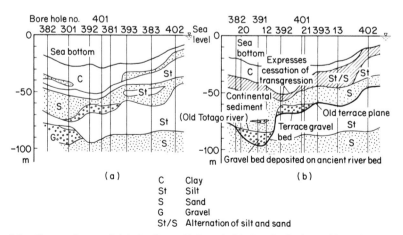

Fig. 6.1 Comparison of (a) 'soil profile' and (b) 'geological profile' of the same
foundation ground. (After Akutagawa, 1969*.)

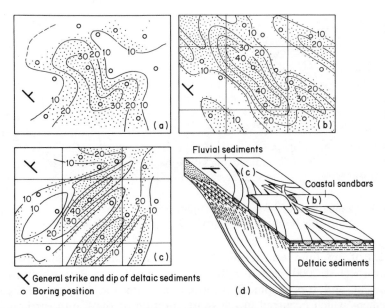

Fig. 6.2 Iso-thickness diagrams for sand layers and the geological interpretation: (a) mechanical drawing (computer), (b) case of coastal sandbar (b of d), (c) case of ancient river bed (c of d), (d) sedimentation phenomena seen in current delta. (After Dahlberg, 1977*; Hobson, 1978*.)

drawn by engineering geologists using the same data. The latter assessed the sedimentary environment from an examination of bore hole cores, etc., and are drawn with the knowledge of sedimentation seen today in river bed sediments or coastal sandbars such as Fig. 6.2(d). Figure 6.2(c) is the correct interpretation and reaffirms the importance of the geological interpretation when assessing the underground geological structure.

The meaning of 'geological time' measured in millions or hundreds of millions of years is also important. The results achieved by nature over long periods of time which can never be duplicated often differ considerably from the results of experiments performed during relatively short periods in the laboratory. We are therefore often unable to reproduce the former from the results of the latter. For example, if we model the compaction of sedimentary material in the laboratory and attempt to measure the porosity, this differs markedly from the 'experiment performed by nature' in an identical location (Kojima *et al.*, 1977*). Compaction is considerably more advanced in nature, where it may have taken 10 million years.

Data expressed in geological time are of particular importance in situations in which sudden small changes such as bedrock movements in an earthquake are superimposed over general long-term changes. Whether a trend measured now is merely a local phenomenon or not cannot be determined until one has

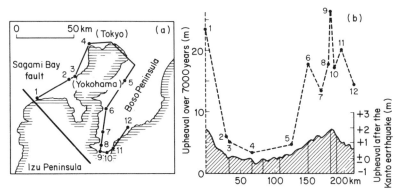

Fig. 6.3   Comparison of 7000 years of uplift around Tokyo Bay (- - - -) and uplift
after the Kanto earthquake (1923). (After Sugimura, 1973*.)

an idea of any long-term trends. Figure 6.3 compares the cumulative uplift during the last 7000 years for the area around Tokyo Bay, obtained from geological and topographical information, with the amount of bedrock movement which occurred in the short duration of the Kanto earthquake in 1923. These two sets of movements are of the same order of magnitude, so sudden movements during major earthquakes are obviously very significant.

Much common geological knowledge, such as limestone being readily soluble in ground or surface water, or granite being susceptible to weathering, are qualitative interpretations based on the results of nature's 'long-term experiments'. If these phenomena are considered in a real time scale, misconceptions could easily arise, such as thinking that water in dams built on limestone will seep into fissures in the rock and make holes, resulting in leakage or undermining of the dam wall, or that making a cutting through granite involves the risk of landslides with the rapid progress of weathering. The term 'active fault', if viewed in terms of our own time scale, gives the impression that movement is occurring even now, and invites excessive fears about any surface development. However, the fact that limestone is readily soluble poses no problems from the standpoint of engineering geology and the biggest problem it poses is the existence of subterranean caves which may have developed as a result of dissolution by ground water over aeons of geological time. The problem with granite weathering also is that weathering throughout geological time may produce softening and weakening to depths of some tens of metres. The changes in long-term geological features such as the development and migration of sandbars or coastal terraces, the shifting of river beds and changes in the type of deposits give us some idea of the way in which the geological environment changes and must be considered when engaged on projects developing the earth's surface. Thus, putting an engineering geology interpretation onto the results of nature's 'long-term experiments' and reflecting this in survey and design work is one important aspect of geological methods.

In the study of geology rocks are normally classified on the basis of their genesis. Therefore the name of the rock is the same even if it has been weathered or if it contains few or many fractures and it is simply not possible to assess the properties of the bedrock where the project is to take place just by discovering the rock names and looking at general geological maps. On the other hand, however, it is important to note that every rock does have its own characteristics chiefly based on its genesis. For example, andesite is a rock formed from solidification of lava, erupted fragments of which are very hard. However, cracks readily form in andesite flows due to shrinkage during rapid cooling and it thus has high permeability to water. Also as lava flows from continental volcanoes normally follow valleys, its distribution tends to be restricted to the valley topography at the time of the eruption.

Lava frequently occurs overlying fluvial sediments or terrace gravels and gives rise to reduced strength and increased water permeability in the bedrock. Andesite has often also softened hydrothermal alteration associated with fumarolic activity, and expandable clays such as solfataric clay may also be present. Similarly, depending on the rock type, there will be considerable variety in what a survey reveals, e.g. the deep layer weathering of granites, cooling joints in dyke-forming rocks, schistosity and minerals which slip easily such as graphite or talc in crystalline schists, or rapid weathering or expansion of Neogene mudstones due to repeated wetting and drying.

A method widely used in the early stages of a geological survey is to assess the geology from 'topography'. This is becoming a very familiar method with the developments in aerial photography techniques. Observation of lineaments due to faults and eroded topography such as water systems reflecting faults, fractures and other geological features have become the basis of geological assessments. Changes in geological processes and the environment caused by the development can be thought of as rapid changes in the topography and changes in vegetation due to the disturbance of nature.

An important theme in engineering geology is to establish the engineering properties of non-uniform ground and bedrock and their distribution. Most non-uniformity is connected with geological discontinuities such as faults, cracks, bedding, schistosity and planes of unconformity and with weathering or deformation.

With geological discontinuities it is particularly important to know the distribution of faults and shatter zones, the frequency and dominant orientation of fractures, the properties of the discontinuous plane (especially weathering feature clay infill, arrangement of slippery minerals and the width of the opening along the plane). The properties of geological discontinuities and methods of bedrock assessment taking account of these are discussed in more detail in another volume in this series 'Geological Structures', Chapter 7.

Table 6.1 Changes in geological elements in rock and bedrock associated with consolidation. (Additions to Kojima, 1967*.)

Comparative category	Soil	Soft rock	Hard rock
Geological age and rock facies	Alluvial–Diluvial sand–mud sediments	Late Diluvial–Neogene sedimentary rocks	Palaeocene, Mesozoic, Palaeozoic sedimentary rocks (plus volcanic and metamorphic rocks)
Geological continuity	Shallow marine–lake deposits nearly horizontal bedding planes. In spite of lateral variation of rock facies, relatively continuous in horizontal direction. Buried land-surface planes made in Ice Age from important discontinuous planes. Well correspondance between current upper loading and engineering properties	Bedding planes (generally inclined) is clearly observed. Mostly are marine-formed sediments. Because the strata are generally folded the engineering properties are governed not by the current upper loading but by their burial history.	Form stratiform structures but the engineering properties are governed by factors of deterioration such as faults or fractures rather than by its stratigraphic nature.

Properties of geological discontinuous planes

Bedding plane	No problems because skeletal structures incoprorating cementation of soil particles are not strong, best values based on tamped moulds of undisturbed samples, represent mechanical properties of these sediments having bedding planes.	Although showing anisotropy, the softer the rock, the weaker it becomes. The bedding planes which are the boundaries between layers of different mechanical characters of rock present some fixed problems in the case of thin alternation or steep dips.	Anistropy and non-uniformity in strength and deformation characteristics. Often treated as fractures.
Faults (shatter zones)	No degeneration of bedrock due to fault shattering	Stratigraphically lower layers pose the problems, but the scale of shattering is limited. Of more significance are the effects of rock facies changes due to slippage or strength and deformation	The emphasis of the survey is on location, deterioration due to shattering, argillization and increases in water permeability.
Fractures	No fractures. Wholly controlled by the rock (soil) quantity	Generally few fractures. Little effect to the mechanical properties of bedrock mass which can be expressed by the properties of the rock itself.	Strength and deformation of the bedrock are governed markedly by the number and condition of fractures, besides the rock type itself.
Effects of weathering and alteration	Virtually no deterioration affecting strength	Local deterioration associated with land slides or hydrothermal alteration is sometimes apparent but not remarkable. Weathering proceeds	Marked deterioration

Weathering and deformational processes have been the subject of intense study in the field of geology. In particular, X-ray and chemical rock analysis have been used to trace the progress of chemical weathering, and various weathering indices have been proposed. Porosity or seismic velocity are also widely used as physical indices of weathering. However, it is inevitable that no good correlation can be obtained between chemical indices and physical properties in assessments of decomposition due to weathering. The situation is further complicated by the fact that weathering has not progressed uniformly throughout a rock-mass. Weathering of bedrock is basically as described in Table 6.1. An attempt proposed by Dearman (1974*) to measure the degree of weathering is also shown by Fig. 6.4. Dearman's method is to find the degree of weathering by combining several types of weathering features in each block separated by geological discontinuities.

The lithification process (diagenesis) whereby sedimentary material is turned into rock (e.g. mud→mudstone→shale) is generally accompanied by a reduction in porosity and an increase in strength. The physical properties measured and the methods of surveying and testing necessary to produce the final design for a project will depend on the stage of lithification of the ground and bedrock. In the case of a completely consolidated hard rock mass, the physical character is generally controlled by geological discontinuities within the rock mass so that site and bedrock tests occupy a very important place in test and survey work. With soil or soft rocks more emphasis is placed on laboratory experiments, as the results of physical tests on small samples

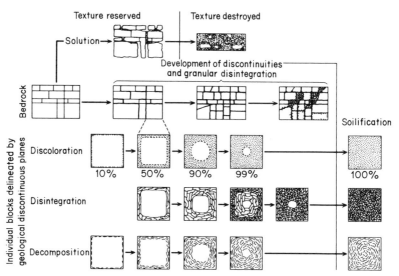

Fig. 6.4   Weathering classification of bedrock based on observations of the weathering of individual blocks delineated by discontinuous planes. (After Dearman, 1974*.)

correspond relatively well with the results of tests on the actual ground or bedrock.

6.4 Physical tests of the ground and bedrock and geological engineering maps

Assessing the engineering properties of the ground and bedrock and their distribution is one of the most important tasks of engineering geology. This is because the construction of any civil engineering structure needs to be planned and executed on the basis of quantified information regarding the geological properties of the ground and bedrock on or in which the structure may be designed. To do this direct or indirect methods are initially used to obtain the data needed for the design stage from representative positions within the proposed site. These include the strength, elasticity coefficient and water permeation coefficient of the ground and bedrock. These are then divided into ranges and plotted on a map to show the distribution of the various engineering properties. A geological perspective is important for the real understanding and three-dimensional distribution of the measured values at this stage (see Sec. 6.3).

In the case of soil or soft rocks (Table 6.1) reliance is often placed on laboratory tests using bore hole cores for the measurement of these parameters. With hard rocks, however, more emphasis is placed on site tests within survey shafts or using bore holes. The former includes tests for physical properties such as porosity and density, grain size, distribution and mechanical values such as uniaxial and triaxial compressive strength and the water permeability coefficient. In the latter case, mechanical tests and permeability tests such as lugeon tests using survey shafts or bore holes are usually performed (Fig. 6.5 a and b). (The lugeon test is a water-fill test carrried out inside the bore hole. The amount of water under 10 kg/cm² pressure to be poured per hour into a 1 m hole is measured—the lugeon value.)

In this case one has to contend not only with non-uniform distribution of the rocks but the distribution and properties of discontinuous planes such as faults or cracks, the degree of weathering alteration and the water content will also control the engineering properties of the ground and bedrock. Therefore no matter how good the precision of the instruments, there will often be a noticeable scatter in the measured results of the engineering properties for the bedrock as a whole and the actual values and their scatter may even vary depending on the size of the area of ground or bedrock under consideration. For example, in a jack test with a loading plate 30 cm in diameter, fractures spaced at intervals of a few to a few tens of centimetres will affect the elasticity coefficient and its variation throughout the rock mass. In the case of the rock foundations to a 100 m high dam, it is likely that this scatter due to minor fractures would average out, whereas the distribution of geological

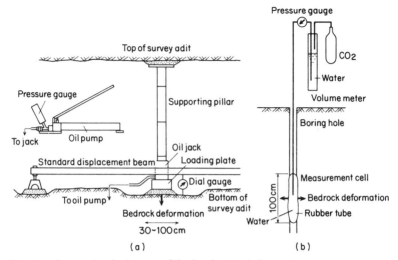

Fig. 6.5   In situ mechanical tests of bedrock: (a) deformation test in survey tunnel (jack test), (b) deformation test in bore hole (pressure meter test)

discontinuities on scales of a few to a few tens of metres would severely affect the engineering properties of the bedrock. Thus despite site tests one would often still be unable to determine mechanical properties of the bedrock as a whole from these alone. Measurement conditions must also be selected to be appropriate for the design conditions. For example, in determining the location and loading method for on-site jack tests for a proposed dam project, it is essential to bear in mind the load of the embankment after the dam is complete, together with variations in loading associated with changes in the water level once the dam has been filled.   Various relatively simple indirect methods have been devised with a view to assessing the engineering properties of bedrock and their distribution. Estimates based on the physical values obtained by geophysical prospecting and geographical logging methods are typical examples of these. However, these indirect measurements have their own disadvantages, and much care must be taken when dealing with such data. Generally speaking the range of variation of the physical properties of rocks is less than that of the mechanical properties. For example, although the density of Tertiary sedimentary rocks may range only between 1.4 and 2.7 g/cm^3 their uniaxial compressive strength varies in the range of 0.1–200 kg/cm^2. Therefore if one tries to assess mechanical values from physical data, there will inevitably be a greater scatter and the accuracy of any estimate will be poor. Measurements of physical properties are unlikely to show a one to one correspondence or correlation with the designed direct values. For example, factors affecting the seismic velocity V_p include the hardness of rock, the number of cracks, water content conditions and overlying load, etc. These

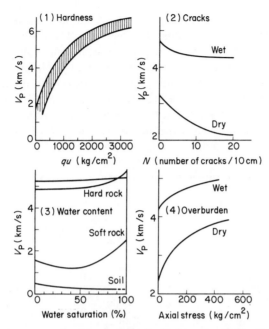

Fig. 6.6   Factors governing P-wave velocity V_P in rocks. (After Kojima, 1975*.)

each have the relationship to V_P shown in Fig. 6.6, but this does not invariably correspond to their relationship to the mechanical values of the bedrock. The differences between the amount of strain and strain rates under design conditions and those used in seismic prospecting is also a reason for the lack of correspondence between the two.

Various mechanical and physical properties obtained in this way are summarized, either individually or in combination, on geological engineering maps. The amount of data obtained from in situ tests, such as shear strength tests, is generally limited because of the great expense and the time taken to perform the tests. An understanding of the geology of the whole area together with a detailed examination of bore holes and survey shafts is necessary for a full understanding of the significance of these measured physical and mechanical properties. As shown in Fig. 6.7, this information is then comprehensively evaluated in terms of the distribution of rock types, rock quality, the distribution of discontinuities such as faults or any other relevant property, and used to make a comprehensive geological engineering map. This kind of map does not include detailed information such as the width of fault or shatter zones, which can be summarized in further detailed maps such as a fault map.

What in engineering geology is termed ordinary rock classification attempts to establish the ranking of rock mass by detailed observation of shaft walls or bore hole cores and expressing the geological situation in a standard fashion by ranking and classifying the ground and bedrock. The result of ranking can, roughly though, be correlated to the mechanical values obtained by several methods such as in situ tasks and can be used to infer the engineering properties of rock masss distributing between measuring points. Commonly used factors in rock classification include those listed in Table 6.2 in addition to seismic velocities. Rock classification shown in this table is qualitative and appears imprecise, but such a method of classification is widely used with fruitful results in engineering throughout the world. This means that if the amount of data is sufficient allowing for a certain amount of scatter, estimation of physical values by the human eye can be fairly precise. For

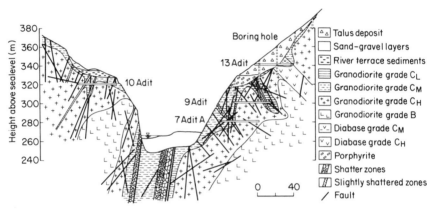

Fig. 6.7 An example of engineering geological profile or cross-section of a dam site. (After Japan. Soc. Civil. Engin., 1977*.)

example, in an area such as that in Fig. 6.8(a), despite the large scatter of values, the average does reveal a good correlation between the log of the bedrock's elasticity coefficient and the rock rank. Individual variation causes problems in human observation but given the same kind of rock and the same observation standards, as the comparison with area Fig. 6.8(b) demonstrates, no great variations in the measured values were produced despite different observers and different sites. In general, classification standards differ according to the objective of the survey and so variations such as the (c) and (d) ranges of Fig. 6.8 arise. With experience, however, this type of survey may be accomplished over a wide area in a short time, and bearing in mind that there is originally quite a scatter in measured values, the results of numerous observations on the basis of a uniform system of rock classification should be seen as a most useful tool in engineering geology. The reader is referred to Chapter 4, Tables 4.4 and 4.5, for a concrete example of rock classification.

Table 8.2 Schematic rock classification. A close relationship exists between the spacing of cracks and the development of faults and joints as the spacing does not invariably correspond with other factors associated with weathering classification. With the increase of argillization the permeability coefficient in the direction of the arrow generally increases

Classification symbol	Tunnel walls, outcrops	Hardness of fragments	Degree of weathering	Condition of fracture plane	Spacing of fractures	Core	Assessment
D		Can be crushed with finger	Soil with rock fragments	Cohesive strongly argillized Fractures indistinct	Less than 5 cm Shattered Sand or gravel-like cores		
C_L		Dull sound when struck with hammer Easily broken	Weathering to interior, most minerals were argillized	Obvious fractures but argillized cohesive	5–15 cm Gravel-like or rock fragment cores		Argillization
C_M		Dull sound. Easily broken	Browning throughout Marked alteration of rock-forming minerals	Many open fractures Clay infill	5–30 cm Fragments in short column cores		Permeability coefficient
C_H		Slight dull sound Easily broken	Slightly brown throughout Slight alteration of rock-forming minerals	Cohesive-slightly open Thin clay infill	15–30 cm Short column cores		
B		Metallic sound Difficult to break	Browning along fracture planes No alteration of minerals	Cohesive-slightly open fractures No clay infill	30–50 cm Short columns rock-like cores		Strength
A		Metallic sound Difficult to break	Fresh	Cohesive No clay infill	50 cm + Rock-like cores		Poor—Good

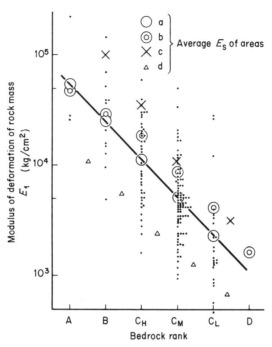

Fig. 6.8 Distribution of measured modulus of deformation for bedrocks of each rank (shown by dots for area a) and average of measurements in areas a to d with varying observers and sites

6.5 Geological interpretation of measured values, and models of the ground and bedrock—their relationship to design

The type of engineering geology map shown in Fig. 6.7 is important in establishing crucial features of the ground or bedrock to be borne in mind when planning or executing the project. Sometimes when undertaking preliminary calculations of the stability of the foundations to a dam wall or the pressure acting on the walls of a tunnel, detailed information concerning the distribution of faults or rock strength is not necessary. In such instances a more simplified engineering geological map is used.

An example of the type of simplified engineering geological maps used in real calculations is shown in Fig. 6.9. This diagram is a model of the physical properties of a Tertiary sandstone–mudstone sequence used to calculate (by finite element methods) the rock's deformation and fracture behaviour when a concrete structure is built on it. The detailed map shows this bedrock to be an alternating system of thin superimposed strata with extreme variations in strength, and mathematical calculations using the physical values for each layer would obviously be quite impossible. To simplify the calculation one must first look at the general features of the rock facies and divide the strata into thicknesses at which practical calculations are possible and then obtain average representative physical values for each division. Where there is a more complex bedrock, it is necessary to construct a rock classification and to determine representative values for each rank. In order to obtain average physical values for each division it is vital to thoroughly understand the geological features of the bedrock and the distribution of the physical properties. For example, in the rock mass shown in Fig. 6.9, the uniaxial compressive strength, measured to a depth of 100 m (Fig. 6.10a) in two bore holes A and B, shows that sandstone layers within this rock mass are found to exhibit extreme variations in strength, as shown in the histograms in Fig. 6.10(a). The average of test values obtained from tests of bore hole cores gives the 'simple average' shown in Fig. 6.10(c). This implies that there is a large difference in the average strength of the strata at the two points A and B. However, if the composition of these samples is examined closely it can be seen that bore hole B contains a far higher proportion of hard sandstone than is likely to be encountered by sampling. This difference in strength between bore holes A and B is thus due to disparity in sampling. If an average is taken, bearing in mind the probability with which each type of rock appears, then one may obtain the 'weighted average' shown in Fig. 6.10(c) and the values for the two bore holes become much more comparable.

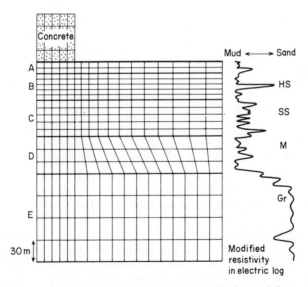

Fig. 6.9 Simplified engineering geological map (bedrock model) A to E strata identification. For HS, SS, M, see Fig. 6.10. Gr—granite. Specific resistivity curve—as in actual strata. Areas between thick lines calculated as having same physical properties

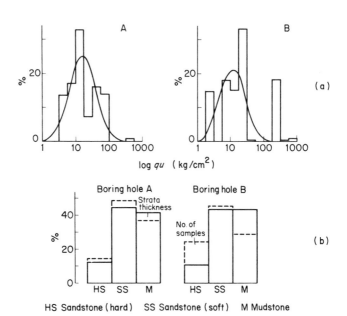

HS Sandstone (hard)   SS Sandstone (soft)   M Mudstone

(c)

	A bore hole				B bore hole			
	Total	HS	SS	M	Total	HS	SS	M
Thickness of strata	117.6 m	12.9%	45.4%	41.6%	100 m	12.1%	43.7%	44.1%
No. of test samples	41	14.6%	48.8%	36.6%	28	25.0%	46.4%	28.6%
qu (simple average)	34.4	141.0	17.7	13.9	135.3	425.2	20.2	17.9
qu (weighted average)	22.7	74.3	19.2	10.5	41.2	239.0	16.2	12.0
qu = less than 50	15.0				14.1			
qu = less than 100	22.1		qu: kg/cm²		14.1			

Fig. 6.10 Modelling of physical values of bedrock using two borehole samples and geological interpretation thereof. (a) Frequency distribution of compressive strength (qu) weighted by layer thickness (similar to lognormal distribution). (b) Appearance in strata of each rock type in 100 m bore hole and number of tests. (c) Average bedrock strength (qu) weighted with frequency of each rock type in the strata. (After Kojima, 1977*.)

However, as the probability of the appearance of the hard sandstone is at most about 10 per cent. of the total layer thickness it should not have a large effect in terms of the calculation of average values of strength, and the extent to which it can influence fracturing in the bedrock as a whole (as fracturing occurs in soft layers) would probably be very low. On the basis of this assessment, the average value excluding these layers produces almost equal average strengths at points A and B.

Thus representative physical values for use in a model may depend on how the geology and its properties are interpreted.

Another important problem encountered when developing models from engineering geology maps is how to simplify geological discontinuities, in particular faults. Commonly numerous faults can be identified, as shown in Fig. 6.7. It is impossible to calculate mathematically the behaviour of a rock mass if all these faults are considered in the calculations, so only the most important faults can be incorporated into a model which considers the relationship between the position of the designed structure and any faults and the width and length of any shear zones.

The examples above indicate just how difficult it is to simplify the structure of a rock mass and how important the proper geological interpretation is to derive meaningful models from geological engineering maps.

6.6 Assessing the workability of the ground and bedrock

In the previous section we discussed how to ascertain the distribution of the physical parameters of rocks forming the foundation to dams or bridges. Stability calculations, in which these data are used to construct models, were shown to be an important geological problem at the design stage. In the case of tunnel construction or cuttings, however, the approach is more commonly to relate the quality of the bedrock to its workability. For example, Table 6.3 illustrates the construction standards for supports and the thickness of

Table 6.3 Operational procedures according to bedrock rank (for JNR tunnels, rock I = rank D–C_L in Table 6.2, rock IV corresponds to B–A). (After Ikeda *et al.*, 1978*.)

Bedrock rank	I	II	III	IV
H-shaped steel supports	H 200 (0.7–0.9)	H 175 (1.0)	H 150 (1.2–1.5)	H 150 mm (1.5 m spacing)
Concrete lining thickness	60	60	45	45 cm

concrete coverings applied by Japan National Railways to its double track tunnels for various bedrock grades. A similar approach is adopted for the determination of slope gradients for cuttings or the selection of a suitable method of excavation. All are standards of assessment devised on the basis of broad experience gained from such undertakings. The particular problems of each position, such as shown in Fig. 5.2(d), must be added to such standard assessments of the bedrock, but by anticipating and devising countermeasures for these the project may be undertaken with relative ease.

6.7 Predicting changes in the geological environment and countermeasures

As the scale of modern development has risen so environmental changes such as landslides or changes in the outflow patterns of ground water attributable to human activities such as road and housing construction have become much more noticeable. We are ever more aware of the major impact we may have on our surroundings. Extreme examples are typified by the environmental changes that occurred around the Nile following construction of the Aswan Dam, or the global atmospheric and oceanic changes predicted if plans such as that to close off the Bering Sea were to be carried out. The so-called 'environmental assessment', i.e. the prediction and evaluation of environmental changes associated with large-scale developments, is fast becoming an aspect of the survey which cannot be omitted at the planning stage of any project.

If the natural environment is artificially changed or even if some countermeasure is adopted in an attempt to prevent the artificial changes, the balance of nature is disturbed and a sort of chain reaction may be set in motion bringing about other environmental changes. Any prediction is thus extremely difficult and one needs a very thorough and comprehensive understanding of the processes involved. Despite being a factor in an environmental change it is often far from certain just to what extent the relevant development is implicated, and so the greatest care must be exercised in any assessment of environmental alteration.

For example, the severe erosion along the coast of Toyama Bay is renowned (Fig. 6.11). Erosion of the pebble beaches along the eastern margins of the Toyama Plain has been particularly savage, the coastline near Kurobe having retreated some 100–150 m since 1868. On the other hand, the local rivers transport vast quantities of coarse earth and sand from the steep mountains in the hinterland and deposit it along the coast, forming several deltaic areas which encroach into the sea. The direct cause of the retreat of the coastline due to erosion undoubtedly lies in the winter storms caused by strong seasonal winds and the coastal currents associated with them. However, coastal regression is a phenomenon determined by the balance of erosion and deposition, and cannot occur if the supply of detritus from the interior is sufficiently great. One element in this example of coastline retreat is believed

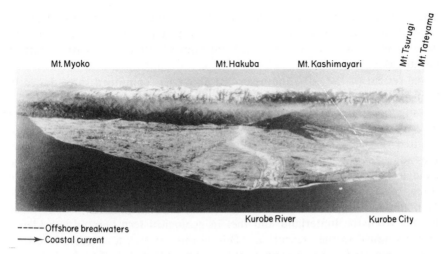

Mt. Myoko   Mt. Hakuba   Mt. Kashimayari   Mt. Tsurugi   Mt. Tateyama

Kurobe River   Kurobe City

----- Offshore breakwaters
⟶ Coastal current

Fig. 6.11   Looking from Toyama Bay towards the Kurobe River delta and coastline.
(Courtesy of Kurobe Works Office, Ministry of Construction.)

to be part of a chain reaction in which the river courses are consolidated by the
provision of flood dykes, thus restricting the outflow points for detritus and
preventing it from being supplied uniformly to the coast. As the consolidation
of the river banks easily results in a raised river bed and encourages seasonal
flooding, many check dams (erosion prevention dams) have been built
upstream, thus still further obstructing the outflow of detritus to the coast. A
further cause of the coastline retreat is thought to be an actual reduction in the
amount of sediment brought down by the rivers due to the construction of
dams near the top of the deltas and, more recently, due to the extraction of

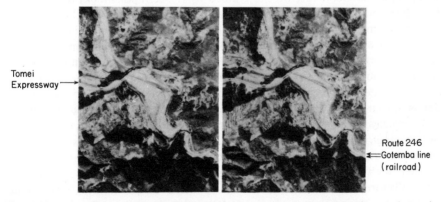

Tomei
Expressway

Route 246
⟵ Gotemba line
(railroad)

Fig. 6.12   An example of surface development. Aerial photograph of area shown in
topographical maps in Fig. 5.1

sand and gravel for the construction industry from the river beds. Another factor which has been suggested is the obstruction of sand drift by the construction of wave barrages in the fishing ports located at the eastern part of Toyama Bay.

The retreat of the coastline described above has continued since the early Meiji era (1868–1912) when there were few artificial causes of any significance. Investigations of ancient literature and the disappearance of historial sites have also revealed that such regression has been taking place for several hundred years and so the aforesaid artificial works on the river and coastline does not seem to be the only causes of the imbalance. Thus, if we look for the geological processes which have been the underlying cause of the coastline retreat, we find that subsidence of Toyama Bay and uplift of the mountains in the hinterland began during the Neogene, and the supply of large amounts of detritus from the hinterland and the, in geological terms, rapid subsidence have continued to the present day. During this process, a characteristic sub-marine topography with a narrow and steep continental shelf and sub-marine canyons together with a large-scale deltaic area composed of thick unconsolidated deluvial deposits have formed. The underlying cause of the coastline retreat is thus believed to be that these factors produced a geological environment which is readily eroded and where unconsolidated material does not remain on the coast but is taken out to sea. Recent surveys in the area where the Kurobe River delta comes into contact with the coastline have also suggested that most of the drift sand or sediments issuing from the rivers at times of flood easily flow out offshore down the steep sub-marine cliff or sub-marine canyons. If one considers the trend of erosion throughout the whole of Toyama Bay in terms of the geological background, the construction of the aforementioned barrages, dams or breakwaters no longer appears to be such a decisive influence on the coastline erosion phenomena. Breakwaters, wave-damping blocks (concrete blocks typified by the tetrapot block) and groynes have been built to minimize the encroachment of the sea onto the land, but winter storms often work away at their foundations destroying them or wearing down the blocks until after a few years their original form is completely lost. When breakwaters are constructed the deposition on the side facing the outflow may be restored, but commonly erosion is encouraged on the other side with the result that all that is achieved is a shift in the area of deposition and erosion. Thus the conflict between nature's work and Man's countermeasures continues. Here we are painfully aware of the difficulty of overcoming natural geological forces. However, recently some relatively successful attempts have been made to prevent, or at least postpone, such conflicts with nature; for instance piling up wave-damping blocks strategically into offshore breakwaters in eroded coastal areas so that drift sand accumulates behind them and a sandy beach develops again. This technique is fairly effective in preventing loss of material out to sea as a result of these underlying geological processes and is a potentially useful technique which does not meet nature head on but changes the direction of the geological action.

Changes in the natural environment often pose problems when assessing the geological environment. Individuals have varying opinions as to whether they consider bridges and dams harmonize with the environment and appear beautiful or whether they think there has been enough visual desecration of the landscape; it is very difficult to establish any basic policy in this matter. However, the one point on which there may be general agreement is that any damage to the natural landscape should be minimized and that the restructured landscape should, as far as is possible, resemble the natural one. For example, when constructing road cuttings, a naturally slipped slope may be visually more pleasing than an artificially slipped cliff, and untreated slopes, even if artificially made, are more attractive than those with concrete retaining walls or those sprayed with concrete. The problem, however, is that in giving priority to appearance one may be increasing the risk of disasters such as landslides and rockfalls; thus a pleasing appearance and safety may be incompatible. In recent years there has been an increasing tendency to destroy the natural landscape by spraying the slopes with concrete or building retaining walls. With time, untreated slipped cuttings begin to look natural, but if for safety reasons the cuttings are treated with concrete it takes a very long time for the natural landscape to be restored. Efforts must therefore be made to adopt economic and safe construction practices which preserve as far as possible the natural landscape. For example, one technique which has been tried is to leave a pipe of collapsed material between the road and the slope of the cutting. With time, weathering and minor collapse with the formation of natural-looking talus deposits can be expected although minor landslips after heavy rain may lead to temporary road blockages. The quantitative understanding of natural collapse, i.e. the progress of natural weathering or erosion, so as to predict the appearance of a site after ten or twenty years must be one of the important topics of engineering geology.

Methods which can predict and assess environmental changes due to geological processes have not, as yet, been established. It is clear, however, that studies of the geological environment must be based on a comprehensive understanding of the part played by geological processes together with a quantitative assessment of active geological forces. Case studies of the effect of successful and unsuccessful construction projects on the environment must be indispensible in establishing the basic policies regarding the development of the earth's surface.

(Keiji Kojima)

Chapter 7

Features of the Ground and Bedrock in Japan

'Because Japan is a part of the Circum Pacific Mobile Belt, crustal movements are dramatic and there is vigorous earthquake and volcanic activity. Thus geological structures are complex with many faults and cracks. There is an abundance of volcanic and pyroclastic rock and bedrock has frequently been weakened by the effects of hydrothermal alteration.' Accounts such as this are found in Japanese textbooks but when trying to judge just how 'bad' Japan's geology is, comparisons with similar bedrocks in other countries are rather difficult to realize. Any civil engineering project can be successfully completed when engineering geological problems have been solved and overcome. In this chapter some features particular to Japanese geology as related to surface development will be given.

7.1 Crust movements and complex geological structures

The most important feature for engineering geology related to the crustal movements is the presence of active faults or earthquake faults. Countless active faults are located in Japan, particularly in the Chubu and Kinki regions, on a scale unequalled anywhere else in the world. Despite their large numbers a particular characteristic is their relatively small scale, normally being less than 100 km long with total displacements of less than 10 km.

Another major feature has been the violent crustal movements during the Quaternary; the rate of movement in the Uetsu (Japan Seaside area of northeast Japan) folded zone in particular is quite remarkable. Old terrace gravel layers are often encountered even in the mountain areas and pose severe engineering problems when making cuttings or excavating tunnels. Furthermore, such large movements have resulted in high mountains being composed of poorly consolidated Neogene sediments which are highly susceptible to weathering and erosion. This is also thought to be the underlying cause of large-scale landslides.

Comparison of geological structures between countries are difficult for the relatively small areas of perhaps 100–1000 m considered in engineering

246

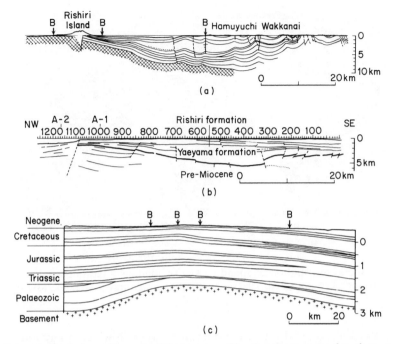

Fig. 7.1 Geological profiles of oilfield zones. The Japanese examples show many faults and short wavelength folds. (a) Hokkaido Tenpoku, Japan, (b) NE Miyakojima area, Japan, (c) oilfield area in Middle East. (After Jap. Assoc. Petroleum Tech., 1973*.), B—position of boring

geology, as local features predominate. Figure 7.1 shows three geological profiles of sedimentary basins in oilfield zones extending for 50–100 km each, with a different vertical scale but roughly equal horizontal scales. Figure 7.1(a) and (b) are Japanese examples consisting of pyroclastic rock ranging from Neogene to Cretaceous in age. Figure 7.1(c) shows an example from the oilfield zones of the Middle East chiefly composed of carbonate rocks of Neogene to Triassic age. The latter area has been disturbed by the intrusion of some salt domes, etc., but the basic forms of the profiles differ appreciably from the Japanese examples which are characterized by many faults and short wavelength folds. Figure 7.2, from an advertising brochure from the Swedish Skanska Company relating to underground oil reservoir caverns, ranks suitable sites for caverns throughout the world. Areas other than the top three ranks contain poor bedrock, are thickly covered in unconsolidated layers or ice, or are arid areas lacking ground water which effectively prevents petroleum from escaping through the bedrock. If these arid areas and the high latitude areas thickly covered in unconsolidated material or ice are excluded the remaining areas with poor bedrock are very limited. Japan obviously is one

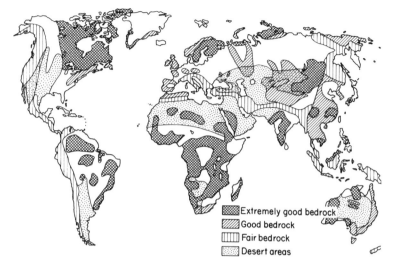

Fig. 7.2   World distribution of sound rock. Excluding high latitude areas, the white parts correspond to poor bedrock containing many fractures. (After Skanska-Sentab, 1975*.)

of the areas of the world with the poorest bedrock in which many faults and cracks are widely developed and weathered and hydrothermally altered soft rocks abound.

7.2 Fractures and fault shatter zones

In considering fractures and fault shatter zones, which reduce the strength of the bedrock facilitate seepage of water, we will compare the shield granites of northern Europe and other areas to those of Japan which belong to a mobile belt. Fine cracks predominate in Japanese bedrock whereas the spacing between fractures in granitic masses from shield areas tend to be greater and more regular.

The RQD values (rock quality designation, the proportion of the total length of rod-like cores 10 cm or more long in a 1 m bore hole core) for the Precambrian gneisses which form the petroleum reservoirs in Norway are generally over 90 (Bergh-Christensen, 1977*). In granite caverns in Wisconsin State, USA, bore holes at 180 m intervals show very good results with the RQD values of over 85 and water permeability coefficients generally less than 10^{-5} cm/s, as shown in Fig. 7.3(b). In contrast to this, a Japanese granitic mass, shown in Fig. 7.3(a) shows RQD values of about 60 even in highest grade bedrock and a fairly large proportion of the mass has an RQD value less than 50. In comparison with granites of cratonic areas of the world Japanese granites are in general much more fractured and weathered.

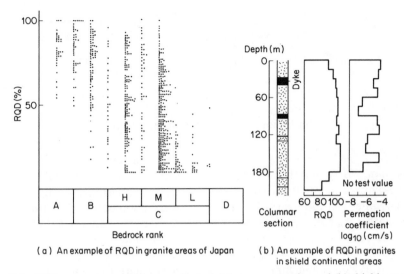

Fig. 7.3   Differences in crack frequencies in (a) Japanese granite and (b) shield granite. The smaller the RQD, the more numerous the cracks and the more developed the fragmentation. (After Takahashi *et al.*, 1973*; Haimson *et al.*, 1977*.)

7.3 Pyroclastic rocks and solfataric clay

Japan is renowned as a country of volcanoes, and volcanic and pyroclastic rocks cover its territory extensively. The most distinctive pyroclastic rocks are the so-called Green Tuff Formation consisting mainly of Neogene marine volcanogenic sediments, welded tuffs emitted from Quaternary volcanoes and volcanic rocks typified by the Kanto loam of the Tokyo area or the Shirasu (white ash) of Kyushu.

The so-called Green Tuff area is very extensive, accounting for more than half of the land area of Japan. The maximum thickness of the Green Tuff Formation is several thousands of metres. It is lethologically extremely diverse ranging from hard sandy tuffaceous layers to fine grained silty tuffs which rapidly become soft by absorbing water. In many places within the Green Tuff area, hydrothermally altered clay (the solfataric clay) has been produced in association with Tertiary sub-marine volcanism (see Fig. 7.8(c)). The solfataric clay, which contains large amounts of sodium montmorillonite, is also frequently found in Quarternary volcanic areas. The swelling of the solfataric clay due to absorption of water is quite remarkable. There were several major shatter zones containing solfataric clay in the old Tanna tunnel. An enormous flow of ground water, reaching 210 tons/minute, poured out from these shatter zones causing expansion of the solfataric clay and the generation of large overpressures, resulting in collapse of the excavated parts of the tunnel.

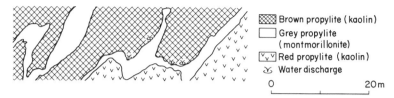

Fig. 7.4   Irregular distribution of hydrothermally altered propylitic andesite observed
in Jozankei Tunnel. (After Otani, 1970*.)

Because of such large flow rates and the enormous expansion of the clay it
took about forty months to excavate past each shatter zone. The distribution
of these hydrothermally altered clays is sometimes very irregular (Fig. 7.4) so it
is sometimes very difficult to predict their distribution before the onset of the
work. Most expandable clays in Japan result from hydrothermal alteration of
volcanic rocks or tuffaceous sediments, but in other countries expandable
clays have formed from weathered basic rocks in arid zones (e.g. Indian black
cotton clay) or sedimentary clays due to accumulations of montmorillonite
brought down by rivers (Fig. 7.5).

In the case of Quarternary pyroclastic rocks, highly permeable river bed
deposits or volcanic ash layers are frequently found underlying lava infilling in
ancient valleys as shown in Fig. 7.6. This mode of occurrence makes the
analysis of geological distribution or the assessment of permeability extremely
difficult. Because of the extensive development of joints formed by rapid
cooling at the time of eruption some welded tuffs have extremely high
permeability to water. The recent collapse of the Teaton Dam (an earth dam)
in the United States is believed to have been brought about when water

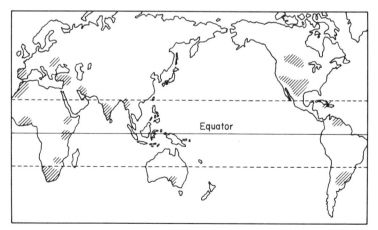

Fig. 7.5   Bedrock disaster areas associated with expandable clays. Oblique lines show
areas where incidents have been reported. (After Donaldson, 1969*.)

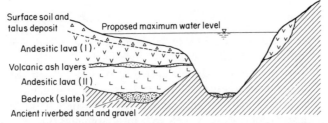

Fig. 7.6 An example of the occurrence of a pyroclastic layer between lavas of different periods and ancient river bed sediments buried by lava, whose distribution is difficult to predict. (After Jap. Soc. Civil Engineers, 1977*.)

surrounded the welded tuff bedrock and induced piping in the embankment. As shown in Fig. 7.7, volcanic ash deposits such as Kanto loam have a high plasticity index and show a wide variation of physical properties due to changes in humidity. Therefore, stable steep cliffs composed of volcanic ash are rapidly weakened if they contain more than small amounts of water, and often slip at the time of heavy rain. On the contrary, it must be noticed that volcanic ash formations sometimes form remarkable underground reservoirs as they absorb water far more readily than ordinary soil.

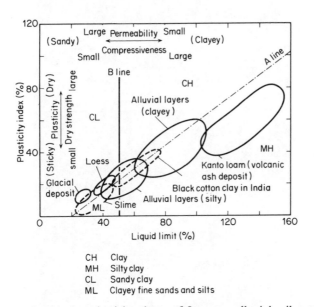

CH Clay
MH Silty clay
CL Sandy clay
ML Clayey fine sands and silts

Fig. 7.7 Comparison, using plasticity chart, of Japanese alluvial soils and specialized soils from other parts of the world. Lines A and B = boundaries of properties in the diagram based on experience. CH: Sticky clay, MH: Silty clay, CL: Sandy clay, ML: Clayish fine sand or fine silt

7.4 Non-calcareous rocks

About 40 per cent. of the world's oilfields are formed in sedimentary basins consisting mainly of carbonate rocks. As seen in the European Alps and the Jura Mountains, calcareous sediments seem to occupy a fairly major part of the world. It is probably reasonable to say that areas in which non-limestone rocks predominate, such as in Japan, are unusual. Considering only argillaceous clastic rocks, those which split into large and thin pieces suitable, for example, for roof tiles are rather the exception in Japan. In general, as has been mentioned above, most Japanese argillaceous rocks are strongly folded and fragmented and are highly weathered. The topography of areas with such geology tends to be undulating with wide valleys and flat mountain tops. On the other hand, despite being classified as clastic rocks, the relatively soft Neogene sediments are predominantly tuffaceous containing expandable montmorillonite formed from the hydrothermal alteration related to Tertiary-

Fig. 7.8

Quarternary volcanism. These Neogene sediments are easily weathered because of repeated expansion and contraction, correlating with wet and dry conditions as observed in the Teradomari formation in the Niigata area or the Kobe formation of the Kobe area. Landslides can mainly occur in areas composed of Neogene tuffaceous sediments (Fig. 7.8 d to f). Enormous excess pressures are commonly generated in these areas and in many cases H-shaped steel supports are bent as if they were aluminium bars and the tunnel collapses.

Carbonate rocks are apparently strong and seem to be a good bedrock but they are also readily soluble in ground water. Underground cavern systems develop through the long periods of geological time, resulting in remarkable water leakage in dam constructions. Geological processes proceed still more rapidly in evaporites such as gypsum, anhydrite or rock salt which often coexist with carbonate rocks. Rock salt is obviously extremely soluble, but hydration also proceeds rapidly in anhydrite ($CaSO_4$), turning it to gypsum ($CaSO_4 \cdot 2H_2O$). Because of the resulting volume increase fractures are formed

Fig. 7.8

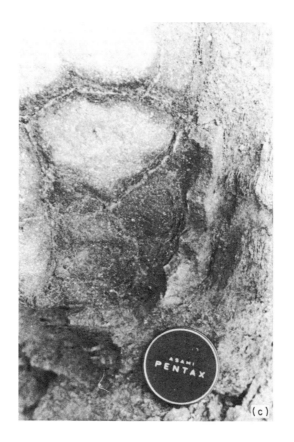

Fig. 7.8

Fig. 7.8   Characteristics of Japanese bedrock. (a) Highly cracked and faulted bedrock. Arrow shows fault shatter zone (oblique exposure in granite mass). (b) Clay infill (↑) burying cooling joints in andesite, associated with seepage of rainwater. This reduces the shear strength and effectiveness of cement injection (grouting). (c) Argillized andesite lava by hydrothermal alteration. Argillization develops from cracks which formed on cooling. ↑ indicates unaltered block. (d) Bore holes of Neogene expansible mudstone showing rapid weathering. They were hard when originally collected, but rapidly deteriorated with changes in their water content. Mudstone with much montmorillonite. Volume often increases several-fold upon water absorption. (e) Collapse of the same mudstone on a building site. The mudstone became clay-like following repeated wetting and drying associated with rainfall. (f) Example of landslide in which the same mudstone layers became the plane. Cracks appeared on the road traversing the landslide area (where asphalt has been removed for repairs)

in the bedrock. Such hydration is accelerated when dams built in these areas are filled with water, producing cracks in the bedrock around the fill zone and, in extreme cases, accidents where the bedrock actually collapses. For example, at Deep Creek 10 km north of Moran in Texas, USA, a river bed ruptured along 300 m in 1954 and the bedrock rose by 6-7 m. In Fork of Mustang Creek the bottom of a reservoir also rose 1.2 m over a distance of 150 m in 1960. This rise in the bedrock produced cracks so all the stored water leaked away. Moreover, because gypsum is markedly more soluble, weaker and softer than limestone, caverns are very prone to develop in it. At the McMillian Dam in New Mexico, USA, there was trouble due to the leakage of water out to the neighbouring valley through pre-existing caverns in the deep gypsum layer beneath the reservoir.

Most chalk formations, which are chiefly composed of fine grained carbonate granular crystals, are soft and permeable. By the circulation of ground water, however, the chalk formations become much stronger and mechanically much more stable because of the cementation of original carbonate grains by infilling of pore spaces by carbonate materials precipitating from circulating ground water. When a chalk sample from France and a mudstone sample from the Boso Peninsula (Kiwada formation) of Japan were subjected to artificial weathering by repeated wetting and drying, it was found that the mudstone was broken down much more easily and suffered a more remarkable loss of strength in response to the addition and withdrawal of water than the chalk. The results of observations in shafts also indicate the common presence of many cracks in mudstone, but virtually none in chalk (Kojima, 1976*). A cave to store 2 million m³ of oil was successfully made 150 m directly below the course of the River Seine in the Paris area without any change in the water table due to leakage.

7.5 Rain and geological actions

Komabayashi and Nakamura (1976*) stated that the Japanese climate varies unduly, ranging from arctic to tropical. Meteoric water (rain or snow) falls all year round and both the hourly and the daily rainfall is large. The only experience lacking is that of a dry season. Although the Japanese Islands are located in temperate latitudes Japanese bedrocks have suffered the strong effects of rainfall characteristic of tropical latitudes. In winter, deterioration of the bedrock in some areas is probably accelerated due to freeze/thaw processes. Repeated wetting and drying of rock surfaces associated with rainfall accelerates crumbling or fragmentation of the surface section and water seeping through cracks encourages chemical weathering inside the rock. Because of the large hourly and daily rates of rainfall, large amounts of rainwater seep into the weathered and permeable surface layers in a short time, causing an increase in the weight of the rock and loss of strength. As a result of this the surface erosion and landslides are induced in mountain areas and large amounts of detritus are rapidly removed and redeposited on the plains at times of flood. In Japan the loosening of the bedrock by the release of stress associated with crustal uplift and by earthquake must also be a factor which accelerates the erosion.

The rapid erosion and subsequent transportation and deposition of weathered material pose considerable problems for surface development and construction. For example, the countless natural disasters such as landslides which occur in Japan make it necessary for us to construct retaining walls, cuttings and erosion control dams on a scale unimaginable in dry countries. Moreover, many of the near surface cracks are infilled with clay brought in by percolating ground water (Fig. 7.8b). This lessens the strength of the bedrock and also makes bedrock improvement by liquid cement injection less effective. Most of Japan's cities are built on alluvial plains. With the marine transgression at the end of the Warm Ice Age clay layers were gradually deposited in these areas, creating in many places bedrocks composed of thick, soft and weak material, which is one factor complicating development in urban areas. When the ground is too soft, foundations have to be excavated after the ground has been frozen. The techniques of continuous underground walling, in which side walls are protected by making concrete palings and the interior is not excavated until protection against the upwelling of ground water has been made, are commonly used to successfully construct large-scale deep foundations in alluvial plain areas. Rapid and large-scale subsidence has occured in many alluvial areas due to the dewatering and contraction of these thick clay layers resulting from the pumping out of ground water.

In dry areas, however, bedrock weathers to fragments, mostly as a result of physical weathering processes, forming talus deposits. For example, the black cotton clay in India, which is a weathered surface earth formed from basalt as a result of the dry conditions, is capable of remarkable expansion. In India, subsidence due to contraction of this type of clay due to dehydration is an important problem for engineering geology. For example, after a building has been constructed, this dehydration is only prevented directly underneath the building, so that drying out of surrounding clay may lead to tilting of the building. This type of clay is also distributed fairly extensively in South Africa and Australia. In the semi-arid areas of Spain, however, a material known as dolomite clay, formed by weathering of the Dolomite Mountains, has infilled many basins. As described in the section on carbonate rocks, this clay-like material often cements clastic grains together. Any coarser horizons, which had not been cemented, can then be used as underground reservoirs for rainwater. Subsidence in this instance would be slight.

Another type of sedimentary material not found in Japan is that derived from glaciers. Boulder clay deposited around sorted glaciers is one example and consists of poorly sorted argillaceous gravels with mixed angular moraine and clay material. Both its areal distribution and grain size distribution are irregular. When piles for the construction of facilities connected with the North Sea oilfields were driven into this kind of glacial deposit, extreme variations in the force needed to drive them was found and the amount of support needed for the structures posed enormous problems of survey, design and execution. Loess, an aeolian clay, which has similar patterns of distribution to Japanese loam or Shirasu of volcanic origin, has the same problems related to erosion and landslides at times of heavy rain.

Figure 7.7 is a plasticity chart which attempts to summarize the characters of the various soils described above. It is obvious from Fig. 7.7 that there are many types of material which have quite different properties from those of the typical alluvial clays of Japan.

Finally, actual examples of the characteristics of Japanese bedrock are shown in Fig. 7.8.

(Keiji Kojima)

Chapter 8

Engineering Geology—A Case Study

8.1 The objectives of dams and dam construction in Japan

Since the dawning of Man's civilization as well as providing a water supply protection from flood damage has been one of the central tasks of a country's political economy. Building dams thus has two objectives, namely to control flood water and to make efficient use of the water.

When we try to utilize land more intensively by the use of water, some means of flood management becomes necessary. As flood management is developed so land utilization increases, thus raising the demand for water, until still safer levels of flood management become necessary. Flood control and water utilization are thus intimately correlated and are recognized as forming a harmonious unit.

In early societies which used natural rivers as water for agriculture, undoubtedly there were many occasions when drought prevented water from being applied to the fields and the rice plants died. In Japan it was not until the end of the Yayoi period (2200–1700 before present) that irrigation ponds were built, so water could be used in times of drought. There is a record showing the construction of a pond in Nara in 162 in the upper reaches of the Yamato River. This was the first reservoir recorded in Japan and the building of irrigation ponds subsequently flourished in western Japan. From then on until the founding of the modern Japanese state in the Meiji era (1868–1912) the history of dams was the history of irrigation ponds (Table 8.1).

Dams began to be constructed in the Meiji era for the purpose of electricity generation. The Kéagé Power Station, completed in 1892 using the waters of Lake Biwa, signalled the beginning of hydroelectric schemes in Japan. Projects were subsequently undertaken all over the country to build dams for hydroelectric power generation, starting with the Kurobe Dam (34 m high). Following major flooding in 1935 and 1938 a need was also recognized for dams whose primary objective was flood control, and work began on dams for this purpose in the upper reaches of some long rivers such as the Kitakami River. Many projects were interrupted during the Second World War, but after the War many large-scale dams such as Ikari Dam for flood control were

259

Table 8.1 Principal ancient irrigation ponds in Japan

Name of pond	River	Year	Height	Storage capacity (1,000 m³)
1. Kaerumata	Yamato	162	17	485
2. Ichiban	Ishite	460	15	140
3. Sumiyoshi	Bappu	708	20	2,230
4. Manno	Kanakura	750	32	15,400
5. Furotani	Kino	920	18	100
6. Kumamichi	Kino	920	18	9
7. Mimeno	Kino	920	16	15
8. Nagayuki	Ohashi	1,000	19.7	483

built in rapid succession as part of the recovery programme. Positive progress was also made concurrently in the construction of dams for hydroelectricity, typified by the Kurobe River No. 4 Dam. The increasing concentration in recent years of the population in urban areas has led to a rising demand for water, and numerous multi-purpose dams primarily to supply urban water are being planned as opposed to those for agriculture or power generation.

The current number of dams in Japan is as follows: gravity dams (dam height 70 m or more), 54; hollow gravity dams, 13; arch dams (dam height 70 m or more), 33; fill dams, 20.

8.2 Engineering geology in dam construction

Most dams, excluding very low types such as agricultural irrigation ponds, are constructed on foundations of bedrock. Early dam surveys thus concentrated on observing and assessing topographical conditions and the geology of surface outcrops. Sites where hard rocks were exposed forming cliffs along steep valleys were selected as dam sites. In fact, dams for water supply or hydroelectric power built before the Second World War were constructed at sites with excellent topographical and geological features and there are many examples of constructions by senior engineers, including foreign ones, for which we must still have great respect.

As the increasing demand for dams meant that there was no alternative but to construct them on less favourable topographical and geological sites, dams were built with an increasing awareness of geological problems. Bore hole and adit surveys were undertaken to prepare geological maps. From the early Showa era (1926–) to about the end of the Second World War nationwide explorations, surveys and tests were undertaken by Nippon Hassoden K.K. for the planning of dams, and our technical experience grew due to major dam construction projects throughout Asia, as typified by the Suiho Dam of Korea.

This experience was undoubtedly a factor in developing our subsequent ideas about dam technology and foundation bedrock.

New ideas and techniques from Europe and the United States which had been interrupted during the Second World War were introduced afterwards, and much effort was made to make up the lost ground. The scope and precision of bedrock surveys markedly increased with (1) the speeding up of excavation and increased recovery of cores due to rotary boring using diamond bits; (2) the acceleration of forward excavation of survey adits with compressed air drilling equipment; and (3) the increased precision of seismic surveys due to the improved performance of pick-up and recording instruments.

However, it was not until arch dams began to be built that full bedrock surveys and tests for dams were undertaken in earnest. The Kurobe River No. 4 Dam is the highest arch dam in Japan. Serious survey work began in 1956 and all the basic geological surveys and bedrock tests known today were undertaken during building of this dam (Table 8.2). In particular this was the first time that (1) the bedrock was classified using an engineering geology classification, (2) dyanamic elasticity coefficients were obtained from seismic survey and (3) in situ rock shear strength tests were performed. These experiences laid the foundations for future surveys and tests.

The role of engineering geology in dam construction is fundamentally the same as that for tunnels or bridges. It serves to provide the geological information needed to produce a structure (e.g. a dam) which will perform both satisfactorily and safely. This is founded on establishing the geological interpretation for the area where the dam is to be located, which means clarifying the sort of geological changes that have produced the current geology and topography. The results of this survey are generally illustrated on a series of geological maps or profiles which are of immense importance if mistakes in the interpretation of the geology and bedrock properties of the area around the dam site are to be avoided. When designing a dam various mechanical and physical properties of the bedrock which will support it must be expressed as engineering values. A current method of doing this is to rank the bedrock at the dam site in terms of its strength, tendency to deform and behaviour in response to water (so-called bedrock classification—often divided into several ranks). Site tests are then performed on the basis of this ranking and the correspondence between the two is used to give a numerical expression to the properties of the dam site bedrock. However, as we discussed in Chapter 6, the engineering properties of strata or bedrock generally not only show a lack of uniformity and anisotropy but also show a non-uniform distribution. This renders any numerical expression or modelling of the layers or bedrock extremely difficult. It is vital to use a proper geological perspective in this sort of process so that general errors can be avoided and to ensure that simplifications in the construction of dynamic models or for mathematical calculations are logical.

Table 8.2 Summary of a bedrock survey and tests for the Kurobe River No. 4 Dam

1.	Aerial photograph studies		
2.	Geological exploration	Preparation of geological maps. Regional maps. Detailed maps. Profile. Horizontal slice maps. Local maps. Foundation treatment plans. Geological map of excavation plane	
3.	Drilling		
4.	Adit survey		
5.	River bed tunnel survey		
6.	Seismic survey	Refraction method. Average velocity method	
7.	Electrical survey		
8.	Core tests	Physical tests. Uniaxial compression tests. Triaxial compression tests. Ultrasonic wave speed tests	
9.	In situ bedrock tests	Block shearing tests	6 places
		Rock shearing tests	2 places
		Fault shearing tests	2 places
		Bedrock triaxial compression tests	12 places
		Fault triaxial compression tests	3 places
		Jack tests	14 places
		Water chamber deformation tests	2 places
10.	Permeability tests	Preparation of lugeon map	

Geological surveys for dams are generally performed in the following order:

(1) Identification of the principal geological structures.
(2) Identification of the properties of the rocks.
(3) The survey is widened or contracted on the basis of a grid system to eliminate any bias in the data.
(4) The bedrock is ranked and site tests are performed on the basis of this ranking. The two are then compared.
(5) A comprehensive analysis on the basis of all the survey and test results is

performed and a classification incorporating all the data for the dam site bedrock needed for the design state is devised.

(6) The results of the comprehensive analysis is revised, considering data from supplementary surveys or the state of bedrock newly exposed by excavation.

Stages (1) and (2) are the most basic surveys and look merely for the dominant trends in the bedrock under consideration. This indicates the direction subsequent tests and surveys should take, and what their content should be. If there are problems left unsolved at this stage there is a risk of major disruption in the planning and design stages which come later. These surveys are based chiefly on indirect methods such as the study of aerial photographs, surface geological exploration or geophysical surveys, etc. (see Sec. 6.1), but may also involve some drilling and survey adit work. Using the method in (3) the network is then looked at more closely and 'blind points' in the survey are eliminated. At this stage direct methods of survey become more important. Stage (4) provides the most important information needed to assess the engineering properties of the bedrock. The greatest care must be given to the degree of correspondence between the bedrock rank and the test position/method. If a mistake is made in this process there is a risk of a considerable error in the results of the next stage (5). The supplementary information in (6) must obviously be gathered so that countermeasures can be easily devised, even if new information is found after the dam is complete. The basic test and survey processes form a system outlined in Fig. 8.1.

When a geological survey is undertaken during construction of the dam it looks at the following points: whether or not the geological conditions are really satisfactory for the scale and type of proposed dam, or whether some artificial means has to be employed to improve them. The most important factors under consideration are whether the supporting strength of the foundations, principally shear strength, is larger than the design value, whether these are water-permeable layers which could reduce the dam's performance and safety, and whether natural materials to be used for the dam are to hand. Various sorts of geological survey starting with exploration are undertaken, and the results relate to the following three points:

(1) Rock quality. This includes details of the rock type and its distribution, mechanical information about its strength, non-uniformity and anisotrophy. The water permeation, permeability and possibility of piping, etc., must also be investigated.

(2) Geological structures. We need to understand the major structures around the reservoir and its drainage area, and any minor structures around the dam site. The scale, length and characteristics of tectonic lines, faults, shatter zones and fold structures as well as their orientation and frequency

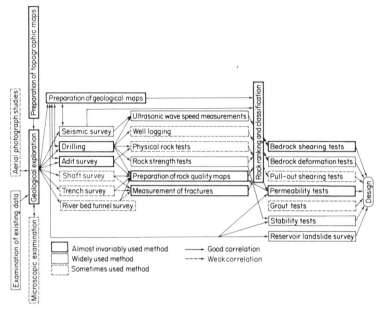

Fig. 8.1   General system of surveys and tests of bedrock for dam construction

must be noted in addition to contact relationships between rock types (fault, unconformity, volcanic contact, conformity, etc.).

(3) Weathering and alteration. Rocks formed before or during the Tertiary as well as some recent volcanics are generally hard but sometimes they have become weak due to a variety of geological processes. Special attention must be paid to the weathered part of the surface layers and hydrothermally altered rocks closely related to ore deposit formation or fumarolic activity.

Dams of various types are currently being built all over the country, and rather than selecting good dam sites, our efforts are being devoted to constructing dams which are safe and fulfil their required functions despite the many engineering geology characteristics making construction difficult, particularly in the areas composed of Tertiary strata. The geological problems we are currently facing in dam construction are of the following type:

(1) Insufficient strength throughout the bedrock as a whole. This may be related to the height of the dam, but is mainly caused by extremely weathered rocks or poorly consolidated Tertiary strata.

(2) Large shatter zones.

(3) Extensively cracked rocks. There is a risk of a drop in the shear strength of the dam site or widespread water leakage during or after full filling of the reservoir.

(4) Piping. There is a risk in unconsolidated pumiceous volcanic sediments.
(5) Large-scale rock slides. These may occur if layers containing shattered loose bedrock or potential slip planes such as a fault plane are present.
(6) Poor materials. There is sometimes insufficient good material available locally for fill-type dams.

8.3 Engineering geology in dam construction—Yahagi Dam

The Yahagi Dam is a concrete arch dam 105 m high built in the upper reaches of the Yahagi River by the Ministry of Construction in 1971.

The Yahagi River which is about 117 km in length rises in the southern extremities of the Central Alps of Japan and its upper reaches run through three prefectures, Aichi, Gifu and Nagano. In its central and lower sections it flows south-west through the western Mikawa Plain in central Aichi Prefecture and enters the Mikawa Bay. It drains an area of 1830 km² and is one of the first class rivers in the country.

The geology of the drainage area of the Yahagi River is mainly composed of granitic rocks and the river bed of its lower reaches is occupied by weathered sand and gravel.

The Yahagi Dam lies in the middle river section of the Yahagi River which runs from north-east to south-west through mountains of heights of 400–800 m above sealevel making, steep V-shaped valleys.

The geology of the Yahagi Dam area is characterized by an extensive distribution of granitic rocks together with biotite schists and banded gneisses. The dam site is occupied by good quality bedrock consisting of two mica granites. Rocks situated at low levels, particularly lower than 240 m above sealevel, are hard and fresh and with few fractures. Rock on the right bank tends to be better than that on the left. Relatively large faults such as the F-3 fault with a 5–10 m wide shatter zone upstream of the dam, EL and HL faults on the left bank and the ER fault on the right bank are observed.

Granitic rocks around the river bed are subjected to hydrothermal alteration and the so-called 'green zone' formed by chloritization of granitic rocks is distributed as irregular en echelon blocks nearly following the course of the river. The SE–NW trend of the river near the dam site is thought to have resulted from the erosion of this weak green zone. A large-scale shatter zone called the '100 metre fault' also runs from north-east to south-west through the Yahagi Valley.

(a) Summary of the geological survey

In 1959 a preliminary geological survey started with a surface field investigation followed after 1962 by an execution and planning survey. As the years passed so the accuracy of the survey increased and by 1966 had involved

43 bore holes (2400 m in total length), 23 survey adits (1830 m in total length), 5 sets of seismic surveys (4830 in total length), elasticity measurements at 7 sites, bedrock shear tests in 21 sites, and water permeation tests. These permitted a highly detailed geological classification and a comprehensive assessment of the bedrock to be made.

A 1 : 5000 surface geological reconnaisance was used to compare seven possible sites for the dam in the middle reaches of the Yahagi River and the present dam site was assessed to be the best choice. As a result of a precise 1 : 500 surface survey it was concluded that the foundation bedrock was not deeply weathered and that despite the problem of fault F-3, the construction of a 100 m class of arch dam should be feasible. On the basis of this result the geological survey plans shown in Figs. 8.5 to 8.8 were drawn up.

Because the river flows almost north–south, the grid was arranged in a north–south and east–west direction and all positions throughout the duration of the survey were identified with reference to this. When the main construction work was undertaken a new set of construction coordinates was devised.

Both adit and seismic investigations based on the grid system were used in determining the plane of excavation for the foundations. T and L shaped adits were not excavated through faults but particular importance was attached to confirming the scale and geological features of the fault F-3.

Before 1963 survey work was mostly undertaken for an early plan to build the dam upstream from the present site. As the characteristics of the F-3 fault became clear, however, geologists concluded that building an arch dam in the 100 m class over this fault would be virtually impossible with our current technical level. A position about 100 m downstream was judged as being suitable for the dam site, and so the focus of the survey including adit excavations and bore holes was moved to this position after 1964.

(b) Survey of geological structures around the dam site

The following information about the principal faults and weaknesses at the dam site relevant to the dam's design was established (fault positions are shown in Figs. 8.9 and 8.10).

(1) Faults EL and HL (left bank) The EL and HL faults run almost parallel to each other with a strike and dip of N 35–40 °E, 85–65 °N. They belong to the group I faults (Table 8.3). The distance between these two faults is about 4 and 10 m at 270 and 240 m above sealevel respectively. As seen in an adit, the DL fault runs between them. It was very difficult to clearly identify and trace these three faults, which were regarded as belonging to a single fault zone.

(2) Green zones (highly chloritized area) The green zones occur as irregular blocks, and the one which has the greatest effect on the dam structure appears

Table 8.3 Principal groups of planar discontinuities developed at the Yahagi Dam site

Group	Strike	Dip
I	N 40-45°E	65-90°N
II	N 85°W	60°N
III	N 45-55°W	80-85°N

almost in the middle of excavated bedrock of 200 m above sealevel. It has ovoidal shape with the long axis corresponding almost exactly with the centre axis of the dam. It is inclined at about 70 ° to the east. The maximum width of the green area reaches 20 m. The green zones, composed of relatively soft and highly chloritized granite having a width of 5-15 m, are found at about 180 m above sealevel upstream of the dam and 165 m above sealevel downstream of the dam.

As observed in adits in the river bed, the green zones have an extremely low permeability with lugeon values 1.0-2.5 (at heights of about 190 m) and 0.5-1.0 (at heights less than 190 m). Adit surveys revealed one problem area within the green zone where fracture planes, trending N 40-60 °E dipping 45-70 °N, almost parallel to fault F-3, are developed.

(3) Fault ER (right bank) The fault ER was identified in both the R-14 and R-12 adits. It trends N 60-62 °W and dips 80-86 °N and belongs to group III of Table 8.3. It is also found in the excavated portion at the 257 m level and has a fracture zone 50-70 cm wide composed of a well-packed mixture of brecciated material.

(4) Fault TL (left bank) The fault TL, observed in the L-12 adit, strikes N 10 °E-N 5 °W dipping 85-90 °N and is 4-15 cm wide with a thin 1 cm thick clay layer. When traced downstream it divides into two faults, TL and TL′, the former having a throw of about 25 cm. Both these faults have a limited horizontal extension and could not be found in an adit at the 230 m level. These faults are thus much smaller than initially supposed.

(5) Fault F-3 The fault F-3 was first identified in adits on both banks as a fault accompanied by an extremely wide shatter zone (10-15 m) (Fig. 8.9). The results of bore holes in the river bed, however, showed that in certain areas the shatter zone is much thinner and is divided into several minor faults, the individual components of which easily converge, disperse and disappear.

The strike and dip of this fault varies from place to place but is generally N 40-70 °E, 50-68 °N.

In a by-pass tunnel, the fault was found 280–287 m from the downstream exit with a shatter zone of up to 6–7 m wide. Several clay layers of 30–50 cm thickness were contained within it but were extremely dessicated.

The fault F-3 lies about 30 and 55 m distance away from and beneath the dam respectively. Permeability tests gave an average value of 0.01–0.14 lugeon.

(6) Others The results of seismic and bore hole tests during the six month survey led to the conclusion that a large fault ran parallel to the river almost at right angles to the fault F-3. Detailed geological investigation of adits at the level of the river bed indicated that the presence of several small-scale faults rather than the presumed major fault.

The strikes and dips of the faults, joints and clay seams were projected into a Schmidt net as in Fig. 8.2. It is clear that they were three groups of planar discontinuities with remarkably different orientations on the left as well as the right bank.

The density of each group decreases in the order II→III→I and III→II→I on the left and right bank respectively. Most of the large-scale faults are included in group I. In other words, the faults in group I are the most important for the engineering geology although the number of group I faults is much less than group II and group III.

These findings were deduced mainly from the geological investigation of the surface and from adits with a total length of about 1000 m in the area around the dam site, but seismic surveys undertaken five times during the surface survey period in the area were also useful. Figure 8.3 shows the survey results

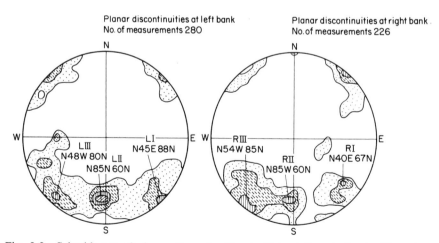

Fig. 8.2   Schmidt net of planar discontinuities in Yahagi Dam bedrock. There is a marked development of three groups of cracks with the direction indicated in Table 8.3.

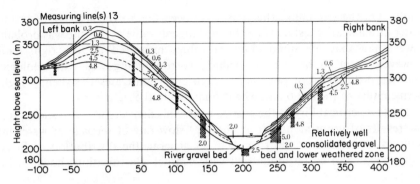

Fig. 8.3   Profile showing seismic survey measurements

Seismic wave speeds (km /s)

0.3	Surface soil
0.6	Talus and sand-like weathered granite
1.3	Upper weathered zone
2.5	Lower weathered zone
4.5	Transition zone
4.8~5.0	Hard bedrock (granite)
2.0~2.5	River gravel bed and shatterzone (XXX)

for a typical fault plane near the dam's axis. The seismic velocity (V_p) of fresh granite forming the bedrock of the dam site ranged from 4.8 to 5.0 km/s, although a lower velocity zone was detected along the river bed.

So as to assess the permeability of the dam bedrock, permeability tests were performed concentrating on the river bed to prepare a lugeon map (Fig. 8.4). Very near the surface the lugeon value was 5 or less, but decreases to below 1 at only shallow depths. The permeability of the bedrock under the dam site under consideration is thus lower than that for other possible dam sites. Some slightly higher lugeon values were obtained from test holes drilled on both

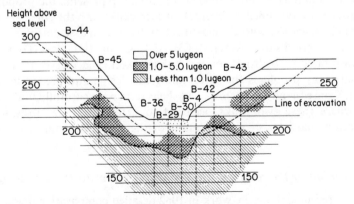

Fig. 8.4   Lugeon map of Yahagi Dam. B—position of bore holes

banks. On the left bank, this may have been due to the seepage of ground water into a nearby test adit, i.e. the real lugeon value at this site was probably lower than that measured. Lugeon values measured on the right bank, however, seem to be the real values, corresponding well with geological features deduced from bore holes. Figure 8.4 illustrates the slightly higher permeability of the left bank, when compared to the right bank.

The low permeability of the granite below this dam site was also shown from the results of grouting and from the very slow rate of seepage of water into adits excavated below the river bed. In general, the distribution of lugeon values (Fig. 8.4) corresponds well with bedrock classification shown in Fig. 8.10.

(c) Rock classification at the dam site

Engineering geological surveys of bedrock, carried out to determine a rational design and to enable successful completion of the large-scale dam construction project, now emphasize a thorough understanding of the mechanical properties of the bedrock as well as the ordinary geological investigation. In the case of the Yahagi Dam, the bedrock classification was carried out as objectively as possible and various types of in situ test were carried out on the basis of this classification. By combining the results of the in situ tests with the bedrock classification, the engineering properties of the bedrock over the whole dam site area could be expressed numerically. Table 8.4 shows the standard classification of a rock mass and Table 8.5 shows the bedrock classification of the Yahagi Dam site chiefly based on an overall assessment in the light of experience.

Actually the distribution of these ranks of bedrock was complex and there were also many showing intermediate rank. Figure 8.5 shows an example of an adit survey based on the rock classification. This type of survey was conducted in adits of total length about 1000 m. Figure 8.6 represents the proportion of the length of adit occupied by bedrock of each rank, with the correlation of the standard classification with the classification by overall assessment.

Amongst the rocks of classes (A), (B), (C_1), (C) and (D), class (D) was found to be unsuitable as bedrock for the Yahagi Dam, and classes (C_1), and (C) presented many problems for determining the design and precise location of the dam. Consequently, jack tests and shear tests were carefully undertaken at places where these two ranks occurred to determine shear resistance and deformation characteristics. The results of these tests are shown in Figs. 8.7 and 8.8.

(d) Application of the results of the geological survey to the dam design

After the preliminary survey work in 1962 detailed comparative investigations were made to determine the type of dam: gravity, hollow gravity or arch type.

Engineering Geology—A Case Study

Table 8.4 Standard bedrock classification

	Adit observations		Bore hole core observation	
Hardness and weathering	A	Fresh, hard	A	Fresh, hard
	B	Slightly weathered, slightly soft	B	Slightly weathered, slightly soft
	C	Visibly weathered, easily broken with hand or hammer	C	Very soft
Spacing of cracks	I	Over 50 cm	I	Columnar
	II	50–15 cm	II	Semi columnar, rock fragments
	III	Less than 15 cm	III	Brecciated to gravel-like
Shape of cores	a	Cohesive, no indication of weathering along cracks	IV	Sandy or clayey
	b	Cohesive, but some weathering along cracks, thin clay material adhering to plane of cracks		
	c	Slightly opened fractures about 2 mm width or fairly marked weathering along cracks, clay material in cracks		
	d	Open		

Table 8.5 Rock classification based on overall assessment (Yahagi Dam)

Rank based overall assessment	(a) Adit observations Details (general summary)	Rank based overall assessment	(b) Bore hole core observations Details (general summary)
[A]	Large spacing of cracks, which are cohesive. Hard. Provides suitable condition as bedrock to dam	[A]	Hard, good quality rock. Cores are columnar in shapes and hold their shape. Long cores (5–6 cores or less per metre) is general.
[B]	Spacing of cracks slightly less than [A]. Condition of cracks slightly inferior to [A], but still hard and suitable as dam foundation	[B]	As above, but short cores (more than 5–6 cores per metre)
[C₁]	Spacing of cracks slightly less than [B]. Weathered and altered along plane of cracks, more advanced than [B], but rock is hard and generally can be used as dam foundation	[C$_H$]	Cracks more numerous than in [B]. As cores do not hold their shape, they consist of relatively large fragments. If reassembled, can generally be restored to their original shape
[C]	Spacing of cracks similar to [B] and [C₁], but weathered and altered along crack planes, more advanced than [C₁]. Rock generally slightly weathered. If evenly distributed near abutment of dam, then undesirable as foundations	[C][a]	As above, but fragments are small so that core cannot be reconstructed to its original form
		[C$_L$][a]	As above, but still fine. Core consists of fine fragments
[D]	Fractured, extensively weathered and altered. If evenly distributed near abutment of dam, quite unsuitable as foundations	[D]	Faults, etc., sandy or clayey. In the case of no core, this is regarded as [D]

[a] With rocks weakened by weathering or hydrothermal alteration, the overall assessment was made according to their degree of weathering and alteration, despite the shape of cores.

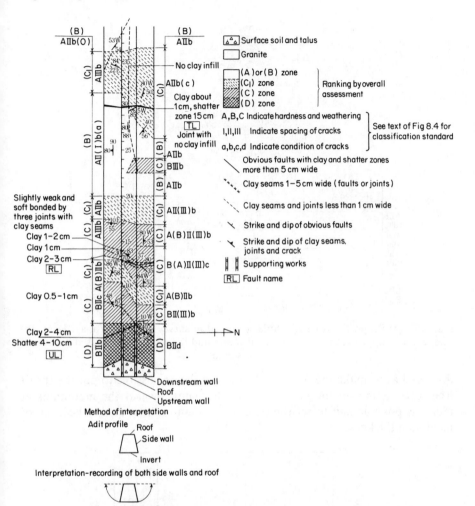

Fig. 8.5   An example of adit survey results based on rock classification (Yahagi Dam, adit L-12)

In 1964 when we obtained the overall conclusion that an arch-type concrete dam would be the most suitable, preliminary designing started. The locality of the dam site was still not finally determined but was known to within 500 m from the discussion of benefits related to the topography, geology and planned water storage capacity. The large fault, F-3, cut across the upstream part of the river and the topography and geology of the downstream area are generally unsuitable. Therefore besides conducting a precise survey using adits, etc., to obtain detailed information about geological structures such as faults and the mechanical properties of bedrock, the design of the dam was severely

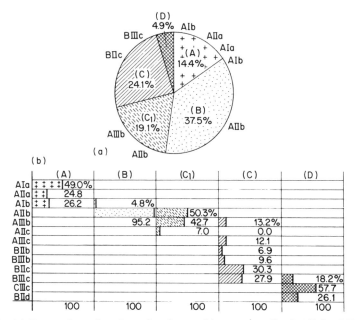

Fig. 8.6   (a) Proportion of rock ranks observed in survey adits for Yahagi Dam. (b) The relationship between standard classification and the classification based on overall assessment

discussed as to make the form of the dam as flat as possible to put the thrust (the force acting on the bedrock from the dam) towards the mountains as much as possible and to set the base of the dam on high quality bedrock of maximum thickness.

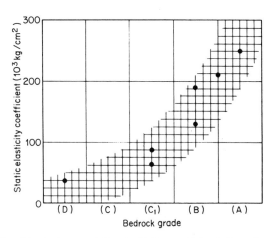

Fig. 8.7   Relationship between static elasticity coefficient (based on jack tests) and rock classification (see Table 8.5) (Yahagi Dam)

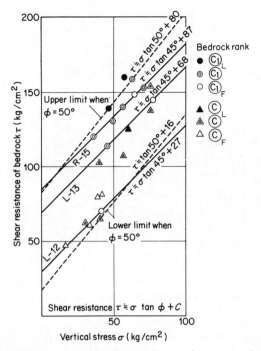

Fig. 8.8 Relationship of rock classification to shear resistance–vertical stress (Yahagi Dam). R-13, L-12, L-15 the numbers of adits; $\emptyset$ angle of internal friction

In the course of designing, we had to give special attention to the existence of the fault F-3 with its 10 m wide shatter zone cutting across the river dipping downstream. Because the dam could not be built too close to this fault photoelastic tests were used to ascertain the minimum allowable distance between the two. The granitic rock forming the bedrock near the base crown of the dam had been weakened by hydrothermal activity producing soft weak areas, 'green zones', of chloritized rock.

Special attention was given to the faults EL, HL and TL, located at intermediate heights in the left bank abuttment (fixing position). Each of the two faults EL and HL was thought likely to cause serious problems such as deformation of the dam, and the combined movement along both faults could deform a slip plane which might damage the dam site.

—The topography and geology at the higher level of the left bank were not so desirable as an abuttment for the dam, but if the dam were set further downstream a need for the concentration of large-scale thrust blocks, etc., could be anticipated. As the geological survey proceeded, the shape, extension and characteristics of the fault F-3 became clearer. Investigations to ascertain whether this fairly large-scale fault should be treated or avoided suggested that

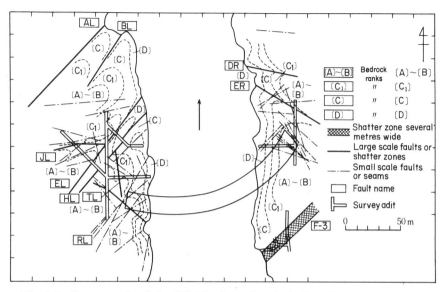

Fig. 8.9   One example of simplified horizontal geological profile of Yahagi Dam

treatment was inadvisable and it was recommended to move the dam site slightly downstream.

Following such investigations at the final design stage, the position of the dam was arranged to be about 30 m away from the fault F-3. This fault which dipped downstream would penetrate the basement of the dam (see Fig. 8.12). The fault in the river bed had been inferred to extend to deeper levels as it had a large-scale shatter zone, as observed in adits on the left and right banks. However, detailed geological and bore hole surveys, after the completion of the preliminary designs, showed that although it gently approaches the base of the dam the fault extending to the river bed is composed only of several thin shatter zones on a much smaller scale than had previously been imagined. When the detailed design of the dam was drafted on the basis of a more

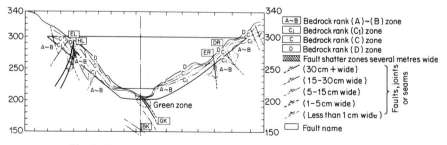

Fig. 8.10   Rock classification along centreline of Yahagi Dam

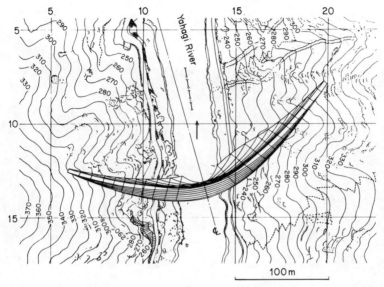

Fig. 8.11   Plane feature of Yahagi Dam

detailed geological map it was decided to move the final position of the dam 3–5 m downstream again.

With the results from the geological investigation and bedrock tests, the final position and shape of the dam were determined using model tests and numerical investigation. At this point the figures expressing the strength and

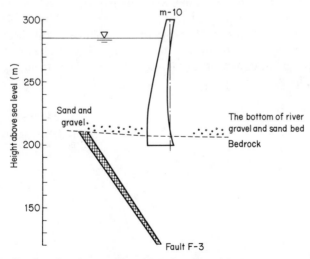

Fig. 8.12   Section showing positional relationship of Yahagi Dam and fault F-3

Fig. 8.13   The Yahagi Dam nearing completion (June 1969)

deformative characteristics of the bedrock had been determined by the aforementioned rock classification and associated bedrock tests. Figures 8.9 and 8.10 indicate a vivid demonstration of the cooperation of geologists and civil engineers to ensure the greatest stability and best management of the bedrock by positioning the dam as far downstream as possible from a principal fault F-3 and by setting the thrust due to the dam at right angles to fairly large-scale and moving faults such as EL, HL and RL developed on the downstream side of the left bank. Figure 8.11 shows the final shape of this beautiful arch shape dam, its positional relationship to the fault F-3 being shown in Fig. 8.12. A photograph of the dam nearing completion taken from upstream is presented in Fig. 8.13.

(Tomomitsu Yasue)

Chapter 9

Geology and the Environment—Case Studies

The role of geology or engineering geology in environmental problems is to predict and assess changes in geological conditions or geological environment. Such changes may be divided into artificial ones, such as the construction of civil engineering structures, and those due simply to natural causes. The former include weathering or loosening of the bedrock associated with cuttings for roads or the excavation of tunnels, changes in underground water courses associated with tunnel construction, subsidence due to pumping out ground water, silting up of dams, the lowering of river beds due to housing construction, changes in sea bottom topography due to offshore breakwaters, changes of groundwater temperature by geothermal electricity generation, etc. Examples of changes in the geological environment occasioned by nature include earthquake disasters, associated movement along active faults and volcanic explosions. In this chapter we consider examples of the former type of change brought about by Man's development of the environment.

9.1 Silting up in reservoirs

The quantities of silt built up in Japanese reservoirs is far greater than in other countries. For example, according to data from the Rivers Section of the Ministry of Construction, the amount of silt deposited up to 1971 in 352 reservoirs was 650 m³ against 9996 m³ of stored water, i.e. reaching 6.5 per cent. of total capacity. Moreover, the yearly rate of deposition (average amount deposited per year/storage capacity × 100) is nearly 2 per cent. which clearly illustrates the rapid progress of silting up. In Japan where it is only 50 years since the beginning of large-scale dam construction, there has already been 5 per cent. of dams which have already silted up to 80 per cent. or more of their capacity and virtually lost their original function.

There will obviously be considerable variations in the degree of silting up at a dam depending on the backwater area and river system involved. Table 9.1 shows that the amount of silting is greater in the Chubu region (central part of Japan) reaching 290 m³ in 1971 and accounting for 44.6 per cent. of the

Table 9.1 Amount of silt deposited and silting ratio by regions in Japan

Region	No. of storage reservoirs	Total capacity (10^8 m^3)	Volume of sediments (10^8 m^3)	Silting ratio (%)
Hokkaido	16	7.26	0.28	3.9
Tohoku	37	9.87	0.38	3.9
Hokuriku	78	28.95	1.57	5.5
Kanto	52	10.29	0.33	3.2
Chubu	52	14.34	2.90	20.0
Kinki	27	12.56	0.23	1.8
Chugoku	36	5.78	0.11	1.9
Shikoku	20	4.17	0.41	9.8
Kyushu	34	6.74	0.29	4.3
Nationwide	352	99.96	6.50	6.5

national total, followed by the Hokuriku region (Japan Sea side area of central Japan) with 157×10^6 m^3 or 24.2 per cent. of the national total. These two areas combined thus account for about 70 per cent. of all silt deposition in Japan.

The amount of silt classified by river systems is shown in Table 9.2. Again the rivers of the Chubu and Hokuriku regions such as Tenryu, Kiso, Oi, Sho and Agano Rivers carry down much greater amounts of silt than those in other regions. However, because this information is related to the number of dams built on a river system and to their storage capacity, a ranking based on the

Table 9.2 Total amount of silt deposited in principal river systems

Name of river	Volume of sediment / No. of dams (10^8 m^3)	Volume of sediments (10^8 m^3)	Name of river	Volume of sediment / No. of dams	Volume of sediments
Tenyu	0.150	1.35	Ishikari	0.014	0.14
Kiso	0.035	0.92	Yoshino	0.015	0.14
Oi	0.055	0.55	Tokachi	0.022	0.13
Sho	0.055	0.55	Oyodo	0.032	0.13
Agano	0.022	0.52	Kitakani	0.011	0.12
Kurobe	0.100	0.20	Naka	0.018	0.09
Yodo	0.033	0.23	Shinano	0.004	0.08
Shingu	0.017	0.17			

amount of silt/number of dams leaves the Tenryu River in first place, but it is followed by the Kurobe, Oi, Sho and Kiso Rivers. The Tenryu River which runs through the Median Tectonic Line area composed of highly sheared rocks accounts for about 20 per cent. of the amount of silt deposited nationally.

The Miwa Dam completed in 1958 on the Mibu River, a tributary of the Tenryu River is a typical example of how reservoirs become silted up. This is a concrete gravity dam of 69.1 m height built on gneiss bedrock with a water storage capacity of 20 745 000 m³. The degree of silting up over the years is shown in Fig. 9.1. It must be noted that an astounding amount, 6 million m³, of silt was recorded just after the dam was built in the wake of Typhoon 7 in 1959 and by inundations during the 1961 rainy season. Thus 6 590 000 m³ of silt allowed for in the design was nearly reached in one event. Subsequently the rate fell off to a level of about 300 000 m³ per year until 1972. After 1972, as a result of positive efforts to remove the silt as an aggregate for concrete on a scale which would not damage the river bed or the bridges of upstream area, the amount of silt deposited tended to decline. In 1978, the average yearly rate of deposition since completion of the dam was found to be 570 000 m³.

9.2 River bed changes due to silt-saving dams (check dams)

The purpose of erosion control is to prevent damage to the ground due to heavy rain, etc. Erosion control dams, work on hillsides or water courses, and banks and water control work are all for the control of erosion. Collapse of hillsides and landslides are not only the direct cause of major disasters, but also affect the flow and deposition of earth and sand in rivers and reservoirs.

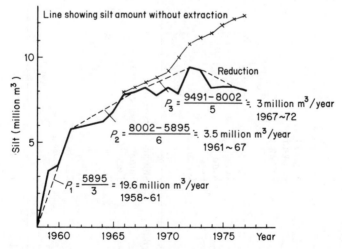

Fig. 9.1   Time chart showing the amount of silt deposited in the Mibu River after the completion of the Miwa Dam in 1958

Table 9.3 Ratios of degraded areas to drainage areas of principal Japanese rivers (km^2)

Regional construction office	River	Drainage area (km^2)	Degraded area (km^2)	Proportion of degraded areas (%)	Geology
Tohoku	Mogami	810	7.07	0.9	G, P
	Abukuma	246	7.36	3.0	P
	Kitakami	154	7.20	4.7	P
	Total	1210	21.63	1.8	
Kanto	Tone	1634	7.40	0.5	P, SS
	Kinu	453	6.83	1.5	P
	Fuji	794	40.30	5.1	G, P
	Watarase	505	3.36	0.7	HS
	Total	3386	57.89	1.7	
Hokuriku	Shinano (upstream)	811	14.47	1.8	C, Sl, G
	Shinano (downstream)	1688	2.81	0.2	P, G
	Joganji	354	5.00	1.4	P, G
	Tetori	444	13.37	3.0	P
	Jinzu	761	10.71	1.4	G
	Hime	284	6.08	2.1	G, P
	Kurobe	484	3.43	0.7	G
	Arakawa	1072	10.10	0.9	G
	Total	5898	65.97	1.1	
Chubu	Tenryu	1285	50.40	3.9	G, M, SS
	Abe	146	6.04	4.1	HS
	Kiso	158	3.66	2.3	G, R
	Shonai	118	0.39	0.3	G
	Kano	270	9.44	3.5	P

	Ibi	730	19.09	2.6	HS
	Fuji	13	0.97	7.5	B
	Total	2720	89.99	3.3	
Kinki	Rokko area	127	0.86	0.7	G
	Seta	94	0.76	0.8	G
	Kizu	347	2.00	0.6	G
	Total	568	3.62	0.6	
Chugoku	Oyama area	232	1.37	0.6	P
	Total	232	1.37	0.6	
Shikoku	Shigenobu	137	0.26	0.2	HS (Izumi sandstone)
	Yoshino	464	2.95	0.6	M
	Total	601	3.21	0.5	
Kyushu	Kuma	446	2.30	0.5	Sa, Mu, C
	Oyodo	215	1.30	0.6	P
	Sakurajima	22	4.13	18.8	P, Volcanic ash
	Total	683	7.73	1.1	
Hokkaido	Ishikari	1386	61.40	4.4	P
	Tokachi	565	21.48	3.9	Gneiss
	Total	1951	82.88	4.2	
Total excluding Hokkaido region		15 298	251.41	1.6	
Grand total		17 249	334.29	1.9	

Mu—Mudstone   B—Basalt   Sl—Slate   P—Pyroclastic rocks   HS—Hard sedimentary rocks
M—Metamorphic rock   Sa—Sandstone   G—Granite   SS—Soft sedimentary rocks
C—Chert   R—Rhyolite

They also markedly reduce the performance of flood control facilities thus causing major disasters. Crumbling mountainous areas which produce such huge amounts of silt are distributed widely all over Japan, reflecting the country's natural conditions. Table 9.3 shows the rivers on whose hinterlands the Ministry of Construction is actively involved in erosion control works. Erosion control dams are the most important form of erosion control facility and have been arranged throughout the country with the objective of preventing new collapse of earth following rainfall, limiting the amount of silt produced by erosion through mountain streams and controlling the migration of the drifting silt.

From the Meiji era (1868–1912) until the 1920s when there were few erosion control installations, the beds of almost all the rivers which carried large amounts of silt were observed to rise, forming so-called 'raised bed rivers'. 'Flood control' in such cases meant raising the dykes. The Joganji River flowing out into Toyama Bay is a typical example of a river along which

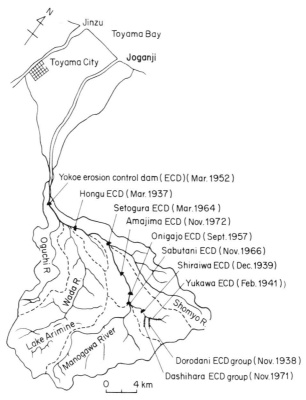

Fig. 9.2   Distribution of principal erosion control dams along mainstream of Joganji River

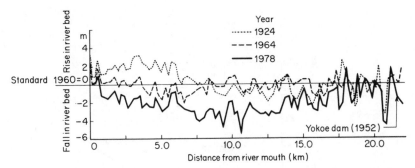

Fig. 9.3 River bed changes (1924 to 1978) in the mainstream of Joganji River

erosion control work was undertaken at an early stage. Major flooding in the 1890s was thought to have been caused as a result of its raised bed and erosion control works was thus begun in earnest in the early Showa era (1926–) with the aim of suppressing and controlling the harmful silt (see Fig. 9.2). Figure 9.3 shows the average changes in the river bed and clearly demonstrates a trend where the downstream river bed becomes lower as more erosion control structures were built to suppress and control the silt. Figure 9.4 is a record of

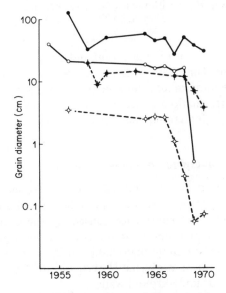

o 3.1 km from river mouth. Max. grain size
✧ 3.1 km from river mouth. Average grain size
• 18.0 km from river mouth. Max. grain size
+ 18.0 km from river mouth. Average grain size

Fig. 9.4 Changes in maximum and average grain diameter of fluvial sediments in the delta of Joganji River (from 1954 to 1970). (After Ikeya and Noda, 1976*.)

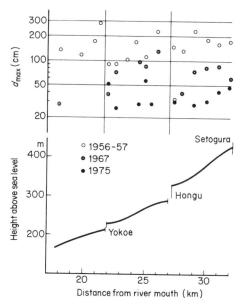

Fig. 9.5   Relationship of changes in maximum grain size (d_{max}) of fluvial sediments in the mainstream of Joganji River with the average river bed gradient. (After Ikeya and Noda, 1976*.)

the changes over the years in the maximum and average grain sizes found in the river's alluvial fan. One may see from this diagram that as more erosion control projects were undertaken, the average grain size was reduced. Figure 9.5 combines the information concerning changes over the years in the maximum grain sizes with sectional diagrams of the average river bed.

9.3 Subsidence due to pumping out underground water

Bedrock may be uplifted or may sink as a result of crustal movements or earthquakes, but subsidence may sometimes be a consequence of Man's activities. For example, the subsidence caused by the excavation of mine shafts, the construction of tunnels for roads or railways and the increased loading resulting from building high banks over soft and wet bedrock. Socially, however, the most problematic type of subsidence is that due to excessive pumping out of underground water.

The principal cause of land subsidence in densely populated areas such as Tokyo, Osaka, Nagoya and Niigata is believed to be compaction and contraction of the bedrock due to the removal of excessive amounts of underground water. In coal mining areas where underground caverns were excavated, however, many elements may combine to produce the land subsidence. Damage and injury attributable to the subsidence may be either direct or indirect. Direct damage due to the sinking bedrock is easily observed in surface structures and underground installations. Indirect damage caused by land subsidence means that when coupled with natural disasters such as high tides, floods or earthquakes, the disasters will be greater than they would otherwise have been. For example, when the typhoon of Autumn 1958 in Ise Bay destroyed the shore defences of reclaimed land in the wide coastal area of Aichi Prefecture, the paddy field areas were flooded by sea water causing unbelievable damage. It took about two months to close off the broken coastal embankments and to eliminate the flood waters. During the two months the local population suffered a lot of hardship including shortage of drinking water and disease. Before the typhoon many people noticed the subsidence of this area from the presence of salt in the paddy fields and from the worsened performance of drainage installations, but no one had imagined that such a wide area from the coast up to Tsushima had sunk so much (Fig. 9.6). Twenty years later, the area which was afflicted by this major disaster has completely recovered and now virtually no traces of past events remain. Nevertheless, the subsidence has been increasing at an accelerating rate and by 1973 the area below sealevel (the so-called 0 metre area) has become 1.5 times as great as it was at the time of the Ise Bay typhoon. Although the rate of subsidence is decreasing very slowly since this peak in 1973, this area is still subsiding at a maximum annual rate of about 10 cm.

Because of subsidence which began in 1950 the southern Nobi Plain (Fig. 9.6) has subsided 1.8 m from its average level of +0.2 m above sealevel and the 0 metre area has spread to about 240 km². The natural drainage of rainwater to sea has become impossible and the flooding due to land waters has become a serious social problem (Fig. 9.6). Figure 9.7 shows the geological profile of the Nobi Plain.

There are three types of countermeasures to stop this subsidence, i.e. restricting the pumping up of ground water, artificial recharge of ground water and restoration of the functional capacity of damaged flood control installations.

The pumping out of ground water has been effectively controlled by the Industrial Water Act, the Aichi Prefecture Anti Pollution Regulations, The Nagoya City Anti Pollution Regulations and voluntary controls of the Gifu Prefecture.

It is clear that subsidence has slowed down since 1974, and that the maximum amount of subsidence in the major centres of subsidence was reduced in 1975 to 30–50 per cent. of the previous years' amount, and for towns like Nagoya, located at the edge of a subsidence area, subsidence was eliminated. This trend illustrates the very close relationship between the cessation or decrease in the rate of subsidence and the restoration of ground water levels (see Fig. 9.8).

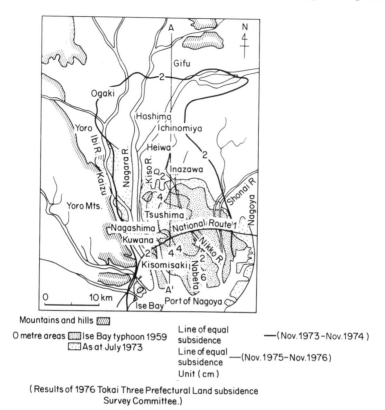

Mountains and hills ▨

O metre areas ▤ Ise Bay typhoon 1959
            ▥ As at July 1973

Line of equal
subsidence   ——(Nov.1973–Nov.1974)
Line of equal
subsidence   ——(Nov.1975–Nov.1976)
Unit (cm)

(Results of 1976 Tokai Three Prefectural Land subsidence
Survey Committee.)

Fig. 9.6   Expansion of area below sealevel in the southern Nobi Plain

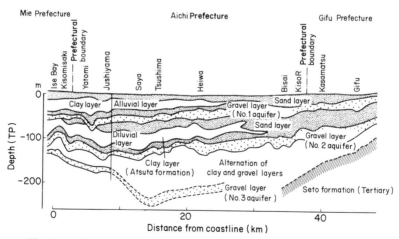

Fig. 9.7   Geological profile of Nobi Plain (section A–A in Fig. 9.6)

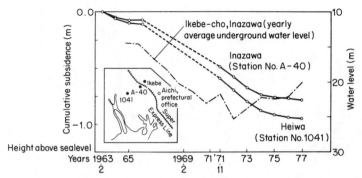

Fig. 9.8 Diagram to illustrate the relationship between restoration of the water table (chain) in Nagoya after 1972 and alleviations of subsidence (solid lines)

9.4 Changes in coastal topography due to offshore breakwaters

Coastal erosion has been known to occur in Japan since ancient times. With the increase of social value and in demand for flat land along the coast, coastal erosion has caused immense problems for people living along the coast. In recent years there have been many attempts to prevent coastal erosion by constructing breakwaters just off the shoreline, with some successful results. In this section we consider how the coastal topography has changed as a result of offshore breakwaters in the case of the shoreline at Kochi, western Japan.

The sandy beach about 30 km long which extends from Cape Teyui to Cape Ogi in the centre of Tosa Bay is called Kochi Beach. The Monobe River and Niyodo River flow down to it on the east and west respectively and in the centre the Ureto-Kagami and Kokubu Rivers are flowing down (Fig. 9.9). The cities of Kochi, Nangoku and Tosa are located along Kochi Beach.

Originally Kochi Beach was the epitome of picture-postcard beauty with its white sands and green pine trees. Dragnet fishing pulleys turned slowly round, and two or three racehorses would be being exercised along the shore in the spray. The people who live there have fond memories of this tranquil coast.

In recent years, however, erosion of the coast has become severe. For example, in Hisaeda in Nangoku near the mouth of the Monobe River the foreshore has retreated as much as 100 m during the last 30 years, so that only about 30 m of the foreshore remains between the embankment and the shoreline. The average rate of erosion was 4 m per year. The destructive power of the waves became ever greater with the consequent increase in the depth of the water and if left in such a state the breakwaters of the whole area of the bay would be in paramount danger. Therefore offshore breakwaters were constructed in order to expand the width of sandy foreshore from 40–50 m to 80 m and reduce the power of waves against the present coastal defence structures.

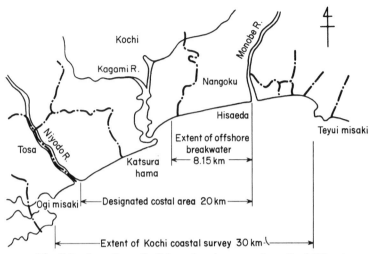

Fig. 9.9   Location of offshore breakwaters along Kochi Beach

Because of deep water and steep slopes, it would have been ideal if the offshore breakwaters could have been positioned on an offshore sandbar (i.e. sand 1–2 m high, sub-marine forming a belt parallel to the shoreline, tens of metres offshore, where the waves just begin to break). However, the construction of offshore breakwaters at such a place was found to be too expensive and there would have also been many problems related to its execution. It was therefore decided to locate it closer to the shoreline.

A profile of an offshore breakwater is shown in Fig. 9.10. Its original height was designed to be high tide $(TP + 0.7\,m) + 1.0\,m + $ subsidence after

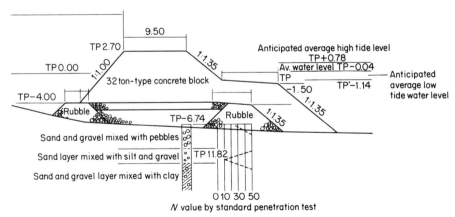

Fig. 9.10   Profile of offshore breakwater built along Kochi Beach. (After Tsukamoto, 1978*.)

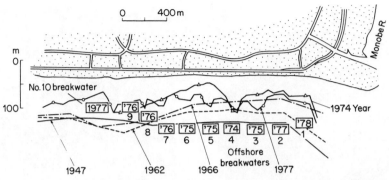

Fig. 9.11 Changes in Kochi Beach coastline 1947 to 1977 in area provided with offshore breakwaters. ☐ shows position and year of emplacement of each breakwater. (After Tsukamoto, 1978*.)

construction (1.0 m) = 2.7 m and a length of 100 m with a 50 m gap. This design was determined from the results of indoor experiments using models.

Work on the offshore breakwaters commenced in November 1973 in front of Hisaeda where the foreshore had severely reduced; the first breakwater No. 4 was set and by August 1978 these were 11 breakwaters successfully completed.

Changes during and after the construction of this series of breakwaters are shown in Fig. 9.11. After the construction of breakwater No. 4 in 1974 and while the work for breakwater No. 3 was in progress during 1975, Tomboro was beautifully developed. By comparison with the pictures taken in 1975 and those taken in 1977 when the construction of No. 10 breakwater was

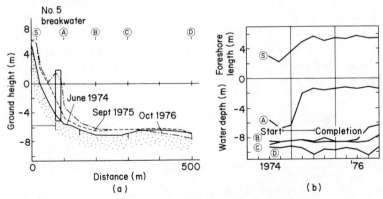

Fig. 9.12 (a) Sea bed topographical profile of the area of Kochi Beach to be provided with offshore breakwaters, together with measuring positions. (b) Changes of the width of beach and water depth at each measuring position after completion of breakwaters. (After Tsukamoto, 1978*.)

Fig. 9.13   View of offshore breakwaters along Kochi Beach. The eroded coastline is gradually returning. (a) Breakwaters Nos. 4–5, 1975. (b) Breakwaters 2–10, 1977. White breakwater is the most recently completed

completed, it is clear that this construction project has been highly successful and the shoreline has been restored to its 1962 condition.

Furthermore, changes with time in the coastal topography due to the construction of the breakwaters are shown in Fig. 9.12.

A number of years have now passed since the offshore breakwaters were built. The breakwaters are protecting the coast from the fierce Pacific waves and the beautiful sandy shoreline is growing again (Fig. 9.13). In trying to gain a rather better understanding of natural phenomena which include so many unknown and imprecise elements, we do hope we may forever preserve our coastlines in the form we remembered when we were young.

(Tomomitsu Yasue)

References

Akutgawa, M. (1969). Civil engineering and Quaternary studies (in Japanese), *Civil Eng. Journ.*, **4**, No. 10, 1–2.
Attewell, P. B., and Farmer, I. W. (1976). *Principles of Engineering Geology*, Chapman and Hall, London, 1045 pp.
Bergh-Christensen, Jan. (1977). Geo-planning of unlined compressed-air surge chamber for 24 atmospheres working pressure, *Storage in Excavated Rock Caverns*, Proc. 1st Inst. Sympo., Stockholm, **2**, 431–432.

Blyth, F. G. H. (1966). *A Geology for Engineers*, Edward Arnold, 351 pp.

Civil Engineer of Japan Association (Ed.) (1977). *Geological Surveys for Dams* (in Japanese), Civil Engin. Jap. Assoc., 188 pp.

Civil Engineer of Japan Association (Ed.) (1970). *Rock Mechanics for Civil Engineers* (in Japanese), Civil Engin. Jap. Assoc., 676 pp.

Dahlberg, E. C. (1977). Relative effectiveness of geologists and computers in mapping potential hydrocarbon exploration targets, *J. Int. Assoc. for Mathematical Geology*, 7, No. 5-6, 373-394.

Dearman, W. R. (1974). Weathering classification in the characterization of rock for engineering purposes in British practice, *Bull. Int. Assoc. of Engineering Geology*, 9, pp. 32-42.

Disaster Prevention Centre (1972). *Studies of Coastal Erosion in Toyama Bay* (Part 2) (in Japanese), Bulletin for Disaster Prevention Technology, No. 28, 119 pp.

Flawn, P. T. (1970). *Environmental Geology*, Harper and Row, 313 pp.

Haimson, B. C., Doe, T. W., and Fuh, G. W. (1977). Geotechnical investigation and design of annual tunnels for energy storage, *Storage in Excavated Rock Caverns*, Proc. 1st Int. Sympo., Stockholm, 2, 275-282.

Hobson, G. P., (Ed.) (1978). *Developments in Petroleum Geology-1*, Applied Science Publishers Ltd., London, 335 pp.

Iida, R., Okamoto, R., and Yasue, T. (1970). Geological rock classification of dam foundations (in Japanese), *Rock Mechanics in Japan*, I, 161-163.

Ikeya, H., *et al.* (1974). The effects of silt on rivers (in Japanese), *30th Meeting of Ministry of Construction (Japan) Technical Research Association*, pp. 787-793.

Kojima, K. (1967). Continuity of strength distributions in soft bedrocks (in Japanese), *Civil Eng. Journ.*, 9, No. 10, 20-28.

Kojima, K. (1975). Seismic velocity in bedrock (in Japanese), *Constr. Techn.*, 8, No. 9, 82-84.

Kojima, K. (1976). Chalk and mudstone (in Japanese), *Constr. Techn.*, 9, No. 4, 60-63.

Kojima, K. (1977). Ground assessments from bore holes (in Japanese), *Constr. Techn.*, 10, No. 4, 76-78.

Kojima, K. *et al.* (1977). Thoughts on equations for the compaction of mudrock and compacted water flow (in Japanese), *Journ. Jap. Assoc. Petr. Tech.*, 42, 110-116.

Komabayashi, M., and Nakamura, K. (1976). The climate of Japan (in Japanese), *Science*, 46, 211-222.

Obert, L., and Duvall, W. I. (1967). *Rock Mechanics and the Design for Structures in Rock*, John Wiley and Sons, 650 pp.

Otani, M. (1970). Swelling geology and tunnel construction (in Japanese), *Constr. Techn.*, 3, No. 7, 50-55.

Seki, Y. (1976). *Petrology for Construction Engineers* (in Japanese), Kashima Publ. Company, 149 pp.

Skanska-Sentab (1975). *This is a modern storage plant for 1/2 million m³ of oil*, Skanska-Sentab, Stockholm, Sweden, 19 pp.

Takahashi, H. (1974). *Geology for Civil Engineers* (in Japanese), Kashima Publ. Company, 268 pp.

Tokyo Bedrock Survey Committee (1959). *Bedrock Map of Tokyo* (in Japanese), Gihodo Publ. Company, 114 pp.

Tsukamoto, Y. (1978). Erosion control projects along Kochi Beach (in Japanese), *Coastal Engineering*, 18, 93-107.

Zaruba, Q., and Mencle, V. (1976). *Engineering Geology*, Elsevier, Amsterdam, 504 pp.

Index

Acadian orogeny, 148, 168, 173
Active fault, 228, 246
Adit, 262
Aerial photograph, 262, 263
Aleutian trench, 189
Algoma-type banded iron formation,
    106–108, 161
Alpine-type deposits (Pb–Zn), 124–127
    ultrabasic rocks, 21
Anhydrite, 253
Anorthosite, 23–24
Appalachian belt, 168, 171–174
Aqueous solution
    see Ore solutions, and Mineralizing
        solution
Aqueous solution–sea water mixture,
    115–118
Argillaceous rock, 252
Argillic alteration zone, 132
Argillization, 231, 237
Asymmetrical zonation of metallogenic
    provinces, 194–196
Aulacogen, 151, 172, 184

Back arc basin, 147–149
Bacterial sulphur, 125
    see also Biogenic sulphur
Banded iron formation (BIF), 106–109
    Algoma-type, 106, 108
    Superior-type, 106
Barberton (Mountains), South Africa,
    55, 110, 112
Basalt–sea water interaction, 30
Basement, 220
Basic–ultrabasic intrusions, 17
Bedding, 229, 231
Bedrock, 211, 225, 229, 230, 233, 261,
    262
Besshi-type deposits, 54, 118
Bingham, Utah, 43
Biogenic sulphur, 123, 125
    see also Bacterial sulphur
Blind River, Canada, 109, 164
Boring, 219
Broken Hill, Australia, 52, 53, 111,
    118
Bushveld complex, 18–23

Calc-alkaline rocks, 24, 132, 197
Caldera, 200
Canadian shield, 160–167, 174
Carbonate-hosted Pb–Zn deposits, 124
Carbonatite, 23–24, 171, 174
Carbon preference index (CPI), 82
Cellulose, 65, 66
Chalcophile elements, 14
Chalk, 256
Check dam, 281
Chilean-arc type subduction, 199–201
Chloride complexes, 28
Chlorine, 26, 28, 33–38, 134
Chromite, 15, 18, 21
    deposits, 21–23
Circum Pacific igneous belt, 193
Clarain, 68
Coal basins, 136
Coal deposits
    ages of, 135–139, 140
    cratogen type, 135
    intermediate type, 137
    Japanese, 139, 141–144
    North American, 137–139
    orogen type, 139
    source materials of, 64
    · types of, 135–139, 140
Coal petrology, 67
Coal rank, 71
Coal reserves, 140
Coalification, 70–79, 143
Coastal topography, 289
Coastline retreat, 242
Collision-type plate boundary, 149
Colorado plateau uranium deposits,
    127–129, 170, 175
Compaction, 227, 286
Compressional island arcs, 198
Compressive strength, 220, 240
Condensed fossil organic matter, 62
Conglomerate-type uranium–gold
    deposits
    see Witwatersrand-type deposits
Consolidation, 230
Continental crust, 201
Convection of hydrothermal water, 40
Convergent-type plate boundary, 147

Copper belt, 119–123
Copper–lead–zinc vein, deposits
    epithermal, 36, 38
Cordilleran belt, 174–180
Cratogen type coal deposits, 135
Creep coefficients, 220
Crustal movement, 246
Cyprus, 54, 197
Cyprus-type deposits, 101, 103, 173

Dam, 259, 260, 265
Dispersed (non-reservoir)-type
    hydrocarbons, 80
Divergent (aulacogen)-type plate
    boundary, 151
Drilling, 262
Duluth complex, 18, 166
Durain, 69
Dynamic elasticity coefficient, 261

Earthquake fault, 246
East Pacific Rise, 30, 36, 197
Elasticity, 220, 233, 274
Electrical survey, 262
Engineering geological map, 238, 239
Engineering geology, 211, 214, 220,
    221, 225, 229, 236, 261, 264, 265,
    279
Erosion, 242, 257, 281, 289
Erosion control dam, 284
Evaporites, 48, 118, 122, 129, 168
Extensional island arcs, 198
Extensional tectonic regime, 178

Failure, 220
Fault, 219, 220, 229, 231, 237, 241,
    248, 255, 263, 265, 267, 268, 273,
    277
FeS–FeO–SiO$_2$ system, 12–14
FeS–Fe$_3$O$_4$–SiO$_2$ system, 12–13
Fe–S–O–H system, 37
Finite element method, 222
Flood, 218, 287
Fluid inclusions, 31–32
    Cl concentration in, 36
    oil in, 125
Fluorine, 27
Fluvial sediment, 285, 286
Fore arc basin, 147–149
Fossil fuel deposits, 61
Fracture, 231, 237, 248

Fumarolic activity, 229, 264
Fusain, 69

Geological discontinuity, 229, 232, 241
Geological engineering, 211, 224, 235
Geological map, 225, 238, 261, 262,
    277
Geological profile, 218, 219, 226, 236,
    288
Geological structure, 227, 262, 263,
    266, 273
Geological survey, 218, 229, 265
Geological time, 227
Geophysical survey, 263
Geotechnical map, 224
Geothermal areas, 30, 39
Ghawar oilfield, 150
Glacial deposit, 258
Global evolution of ore deposits, 99
Gold deposits
    associated with banded iron
        formations, 108–109, 162
    in greenstone belt, 162
Gold–silver vein deposits
    epithermal, 36, 38, 179
Gold–uranium deposits
    see Witwatersrand-type deposits
Granite, 249, 265
Granitoid magmas, 24
Greenstone belts, 55, 104, 106, 109, 162
Green tuff, 142, 199, 201, 249
Grenville orogeny, 172
Ground, 220, 233
Ground water, 217, 279
Gulf of Alaska, 188–191
Gulf of Mexico, 152, 186
Gypsum, 48, 196, 253

Humification, 66
Hydrogen isotopes of ore solutions,
    43–47
Hydrogen shift, 45, 46
Hydrothermal alteration, 229, 250,
    252, 255, 265, 272
Hydrothermal ore deposits, 28
Hydrothermal ore solutions, 27–42
Hydrothermal systems, 30
Hydrothermal processes, 27

Ilmenite deposits, 23
Ilmenite series (granitoids), 25–27, 50,
    196, 202, 203, 204

Immiscible sulphide melt, 7, 8, 11–16,
   18, 105
Inertinite, 69
Inorganic origin theory of petroleum,
   80
In situ test, 222, 234, 261, 262
Interior lowland, North America, 167–
   171
Island arcs, 175, 192
   collision-type, 203
   compressional, 198–201
   continental-type, 193
   extensional, 198–201
Isoprenoid hydrocarbons, 81

Jack test, 233, 234, 274
Joint, 220, 237, 255

Kenoran orogeny, 163
Kerogens, 82, 146
   diagenesis of, 87
   maturity of, 90
   metamorphism of, 88
   pyrolysis of, 84
Kieslager, 118
K-metasomatism, 42
Komatiite, 15, 18, 20, 103–106, 109
Kupferschiefer, 48, 119, 121–123
Kuroko deposits
   lead isotopes of, 54
   ore fluid* (solution) of, 43, 45–46
   ore-forming environment of, 38
   porphyry copper deposits and, 199–
      201
   sulphur isotopes of, 49–50
Kuroko-type deposits, 101–103

Labrador trough, 165
Landslide, 218, 255, 257
Land subsidence, 279, 286, 288
Laramide orogeny, 169, 175, 182
Latent pressure, 213
Lead isotopes, 51–56
Lignin, 65–67
Liptinite, 69
Lithophile elements, 14
Lithotypes of coal, 68
Loam, 215, 251
Loess, 258
Lugeon map, 269
   test, 233
   value, 267, 269

Macerals, 67, 69, 72
Magmatic deposits, 5
Magmatic water, 24, 33, 34
   isotopic study of, 43
Magnetite/ilmenite series, 131, 193, 195
   granitoids ratio, 131
   granitoids distribution, 193
Magnetite series (granitoids), 25–26,
   50, 196, 199, 202–204
Major lead orebodies, 53–55
Malay peninsular, 196, 202–204
Mariana-arc type subduction, 199
Massive sulphide deposits, 174
   see also Volcanogenic massive
      sulphide deposits
McArthur deposits, 114–115, 118, 174
McArthur-type (lead–zinc) deposits,
   111, 114–119, 123
Merensky Reef, 11, 18–20
Metal ratio, 100
Metallogenic provinces, 194
   asymmetrical zonation of, 194–195
   in Andean orogenic zone, 194
   in Japanese islands, 194
Meteoric water, 24, 43, 134, 179
Meteorite impact, 16, 19
Microlithotypes of coal, 69
Middle East oilfields, 149
Mineralizing solution
   of Mississippi Valley-type deposits,
      124
   –sea water mixture, 115–118
Mississippi Valley-type deposits, 36,
   124–127, 168–169, 172
Modified sea water, 29
Modulus of deformation, 238
Montmorillonite, 125, 252, 255
Mount Isa, Australia, 52–53, 111, 114,
   118

$Na_2O-K_2O-SiO_2-Al_2O_3-HCl-H_2O$
   system, 33
NATM construction method, 223
Nevadan orogeny, 169, 175, 182
Nickel/copper ratio, 104–105
Nickel–copper sulphide deposits, 11,
   16–18
Nickel deposits, 103–106
Noranda type deposits, 101, 161
Noril'sk, USSR, 18, 21
N-value, 226

Oceanic plate as source of ore metals, 197
Offshore breakwater, 289, 290
Oilfield brine, 125
Ore solutions, 28
  boiling of, 134
  chemical composition of, 28–39
  Cl⁻ concentration of, 33
  migration of, 39
  oxygen fugacity of, 38
  pH of, 33
  sources of, 41
Organic carbon, 63
Organic metamorphism, 77–79, 142
Organic origin theory of petroleum, 80
Orogen type coal deposits, 139
Orthomagmatic deposits
  see Magmatic deposits
Oxydizing magma, 194
Oxygen in atmosphere, 106, 111, 124
Oxygen isotopes of ore solutions, 43–47
Oxygen shift, 44, 45

Palisade diabase, 174
Partial fusion of mantle materials, 23, 105
Partition coefficients, 9, 11, 14
Partitioning of elements, 23, 29, 33
Peat, 66
Pelagic sediments, 53, 201
Penetration test, 226, 269
Permeability, 40, 237, 262
Petroleum
  accumulation of, 90
  evolution (maturation) of, 74, 93
  exploration, 180
  in aulacogen, 151
  in back-arc basin, 147
  in fore-arc basin, 149
  inorganic origin theory of, 80
  migration of, 90, 125
  organic origin theory of, 80
  source rocks, 89
Petroleum basins
  Alaska, 186
  Bering Sea, 190
  Cordillera, 180
  Mid-continent, 184
  North America, 180
  Rocky Mountains, 181
Petroleum deposits
  disappearance of, 93

formation of, 145, 147
  in the Middle East, 149
  world distribution of, 144
Philippine mobile belt, 199
Phyllic alteration zone, 132
Piping, 251
Placer, 110
Plasticity index, 251
Plate boundaries and petroleum deposits
  collision-type, 149–151
  complete separation-type, 152
  convergent-type, 147–149, 184
  divergent aulacogen-type, 151
  interrupted divergent-type, 151–152
  transform-type, 152
Platinum deposits, 18
Porosity, 220
Porphyry copper deposits, 24, 130–134, 173, 176, 193, 199–201
  age variation, 130–131
  distribution, 130–131
  genesis, 133–134
  types of deposits, 132–133
Porphyry molybdenum deposits, 130
Porphyry-type deposits, 129–134
Potassic alteration zone, 132
Principal zone of oil formation, 88
Propylite alteration zone, 132
Proto-Atlantic Ocean, 171, 173

Rare-earth elements, 9, 11, 23
Red Bed-type copper deposits, 122
Red sandstone, 122
Red Sea, 36, 150, 197
Red Sea-type deposits, 118, 172, 174
Reducing magma, 194
Retaining wall, 217
Road cutting, 217
Rock classification, 222, 236, 237, 239, 261, 270–276
Rock engineering, 222
Rock mass, 213, 220
Rock quality, 263
Rock quality designation (RQD), 248, 249
Rock specimen, 220
Rock-water interaction, 29, 42, 44–46
Roll-type uranium deposits, 127–129
Ruhr coalfield, 77

Salton Sea, 30, 179
Sandstone-shale type copper deposits, 119–124, 127, 129, 169

Sandstone-type uranium deposit
  see Colorado plateau uranium
    deposits
Schistosity, 229
Sea water, 29, 33, 34, 36, 42, 45–48,
  50–51, 116–117
Seismic survey, 219, 222, 235, 262
Seismic velocity, 234, 236, 269
Sevier orogeny, 182
Shatter zone, 225, 229, 231, 248, 263
Shear resistance, 212, 275
Shear strength, 212, 220, 235, 263
Siderophile elements, 14
Silicate melts, 12, 14, 23
Silting, 279
Silt-saving dam, 281
Single axial compressive strength, 219
Single stage model, 54
Site test, 212, 233
Skaergaard intrusion, 6–11, 18, 105
Slope, 217
Soil, 211, 251
Soil engineering, 226
Soil profile, 226
Solfataric clay, 249
Solubility of sulphides, 28
Stillwater complex, 12, 20, 21
Strain, 235
Stratabound type deposits, 49, 101, 108
Stratiform copper (zinc) deposits, 171
Stratiform lead–zinc deposits, 111–119,
  174
Subduction
  Chilean-arc type, 199
  Mariana-arc type, 199
Submarine exhalative sedimentary
    deposits, 101
Subsidence, 286
Subterranean cave, 228
Sudbury deposits, 15, 16–18, 48, 58,
  167
Sullivan deposits, 111, 118, 167
Sulphate-reducing bacteria, 48
Sulphide droplets, 12, 14
Sulphide melt
  see Immiscible sulphide melt
Sulphur in magma, 7, 10, 26
Sulphur isotopes, 47–51, 114, 125, 198
  of granitoids, 50–51
  of terrestrial materials, 48
  of stratabound-type deposits, 49–50

Sulphur species in aqueous solutions,
  28
Superior Province, 161
Superior-type banded iron formation,
  106–108, 163
Surface survey, 218, 219

Taconic orogeny, 148, 168, 173
Tar sands, 94
Tectonic line, 263
Tensile strength, 220
Thio-complexes, 28
Tin deposits, 27, 195, 203
Tin granite, 203
Tin in rocks, 27, 202
Tomboro, 291
Traps, 146
Triaxial compressive strength, 233, 262
Troodos ophiolite, 54
Tunnel-boring machine, 222

Ultrasonic wave-speed test, 262
Unconformity, 229
Unconsolidated layer, 220
Under-clay, 66
Underground cavern, 253
Underground water, 286
Uniaxial compressive strength, 229
Uranium deposits, 127, 163–165, 170

Vanadiferous magnetite, 19, 23
Vitrain, 68
Vitrinite, 69
  carbon content of, 143
  Japanese, 73–74
  reflectance of, 72, 77, 85, 139, 141
Volcanic front, 195
Volcanogenic massive sulphide
    deposits, 49, 101–103, 117, 161,
    172

Wairakei, New Zealand, 39–40
Water permeability, 212, 219, 224, 233
Water table, 289
Weathering, 228, 229, 231, 232, 237,
  255, 264, 272
Witwatersand-type deposits, 109–111
Workability, 241

Zambian copper belt, 120–121
Zero (o) meter area, 287

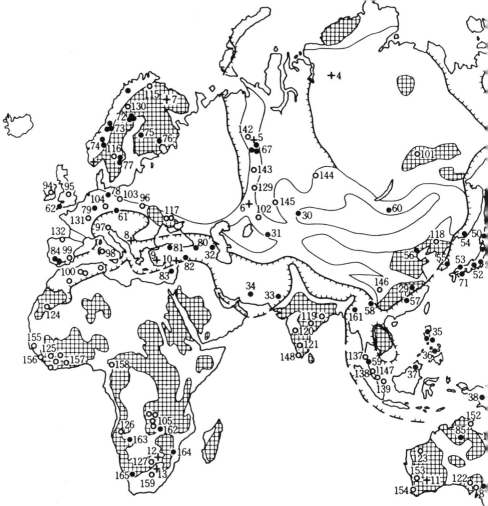

[Orthomagmatic deposits in basic igneous rock (+)] **1** Thompson (Ni, Cu) **2** Allard Lake (Ti) **3** Sudbury (Cu, Ni) **4** Noril'sk (Ni, Cu, Pt) **5** Saranovo (Cr, Pt) **6** Kempirsay (Cr, Ti) **7** Monchegorsk (Ni) **8** Kukës (Cr) **9** Muǧla (Cr) **10** Iskenderun (Cr) **11** Kambalda (Ni, Cu) **12** Great Dyke (Cr) **13** Bushveld (Cr, Pt, Ti) [Porphyry-type and related deposits (●)] **14** Gaspé Copper (Cu, Mo) **15** Endako (Mo) **16** Highland Valley (Cu, Mo, Au) **17** Butte (Cu, Zn, Au, Ag) **18** Bingham (Cu, Mo, Pb, Zn, Au, Ag) **19** Climax (Mo) **20** Arizona, Cananea (Cu, Mo) **21** La Luz (Cu, Mo) **22** Cerro Colorado (Cu, Mo) **23** Michiquillay (Cu, Mo) **24** Morococha (Cu, Mo, Pb, Zn, Au, Ag) **25** Toguepala (Cu, Mo) **26** Chuquicamata (Cu, Mo) **27** El Salvador (Cu, Mo) **28** El Teniente (Cu, Mo) **29** Dexing (Cu), Yangchuling (W, Mo) **30** Kounrad (Cu, Mo) **31** Almalyk (Cu) **32** Kafan (Cu, Mo) **33** Saindak (Cu, Mo) **34** Sar Chesmeh (Cu, Mo) **35** Mar Coper (Cu, Au) **36** Atlas (Cu) **37** Mamut (Cu, Au) **38** Ertsberg (Fe, Cu, Au) **39** Ok Tedi (Cu, Au) **40** Panguna (Cu, Au) **41** Mt. Morgan (Cu, Au) [Hydrothermal deposits such as vein or skarn types (●)] **42** Coeur d'Alen (Pb, Zn, Ag) **43** Mother Lode (Au) **44** Pine Creek (W) **45** Tintic (Pb, Zn, Au, Ag) **46** Leadville (Pb, Zn) **47** Santa Eulalia et. (Pb, Zn, Ag) **48** Pachuca etc. (Ag) **49** Potosi (Sn, Ag) **50** Toyoha (Pb, Zn, Ag) **51** Ashio (Cu) **52** Kamioka (Pb, Zn, Ag) **53** Akenobe, Ikuno (Cu, Pb, Zn, Sn, W, An, Ag) **54** Primorye (Sn) **55** Sangdong (W) **56** Yangchia Zhangzhi (Mo) **57** Nanling Range (W, Nb-Ta) **58** Yunnan (Sn, W) **59** Yod Nam (W) **60** Transbaikalia (Sn, W) **61** Erzgebirge (Sn, Ag) **62** Cornwall (Sn) [Volcanogenic massive sulphide deposits (incl. McArthur-type deposits (●)] **63** Anvil (Pb, Zn) **64** Lynn Lake-Snow Lake (Cu, Zn) **65** Sullivan (Pb, Zn) **66** Noranda (Cu, Zn) **67** Buchans (Cu, Pb, Zn) **68** Bathurst (Pb, Zn) **69** Boleo (Cu) **70** Hokuroku (Cu, Pb, Zn) **71** Besshi-Sazare (Cu) **72** Skellefte (Cu) **73** Skorovas etc. (Cu) **74** Lokken etc. (Cu) **75** Vihanti (Pb, Zn) **76** Outokumpu (Cu, Pb, Zn, Co) **77** Khalilovo (Cu) **78** Rammelsberg (Pb, Zn) **79** Meggen (Pb, Zn) **80** Murgul (Cu) **81** Kure (Cu) **82** Ergani (Cu) **83** Cyprus (Cu) **84** Rio Tinto (Cu) **85** McArthur River (Pb, Zn) **86** Mt. Isa (Pb, Zn, Cu) **87** Broken Hill (Pb, Zn) **88** Cobar (Cu, Zn) **89** Mt. Lyell (Cu, Pb, Zn) [Mississippi Valley-, Alpine-type deposits (○)]